Deterrence without the Bomb

The Politics of Israeli Strategy

Avner Yaniv
University of Haifa

Lexington Books
D.C. Heath and Company/Lexington, Massachusetts/Toronto

Library of Congress Cataloging-in-Publication Data

Yaniv, A. (Avner)
    Deterrence without the bomb.

    Bibliography: p.
    Includes index.
    1. Israel—Military policy. 2. Israel—History, Military. 3. Deterrence (Strategy). I. Title.
UA853.I8Y27   1987   355'.0335'5694   85-45018
ISBN 0-669-11104-X

Published simultaneously in Canada
Printed in the United States of America
Casebound International Standard Book Number: 0-669-11104-X
Library of Congress Catalog Card Number: 85-45018

The paper used in this publication meets the minimum requirements of American National Standard for Information Sciences—Permanence of Paper for Printed Library Materials, ANSI Z39.48-1984.
∞™

87 88 89 90 8 7 6 5 4 3 2 1

Contents

Figures

Preface

I n the early 1980s I was asked to attend an academic discussion at the Israel Defense Forces' National Defense College. The participants were experienced colonels and brigadier-generals who had become students at this prestigious academy either at the end of a distinguished career or on their way to further promotion. Their discussion was lively and stimulating. It projected tremendous sensitivity to the complexities and constraints of real life. Hence it was truly educational and rewarding for an academic like me. Yet, for all these virtues, the discussion also reflected a certain lack of clarity concerning the overall landscape of Israel's national security policy. The participants were at their best in analyzing the specifics of tactical and technical problems. But their ability to rise above the commonplace platitudes of a social evening seemed limited whenever it came to a macro evaluation of trends.

Such an impression led me to make some inquiries into the college's syllabus and required reading. To my astonishment, I discovered that there was no authoritative text on Israel's single most important problem. To be sure, the wealth of literature on specific aspects of Israeli national security policy was stunning—and has become even more so. But the students in what constitutes Israel's advanced school of national security studies—not to mention ordinary students at Israeli or other universities—had no text on which to rely for an up-to-date evaluation of the single most important problem in their life.

Before long, this increased awareness of a major lacuna steered me toward a search for an organizing concept in which to encase a university course and, subsequently, a written study. The concept of *national security* is perceived in Israel in almost all-encompassing terms. Hence a study of the Israeli experience that attempted to rely on this concept as a guide could last for a decade and result in a volume so large that almost no publisher would print it and few potential readers would be able to afford it. Clearly there was a need for a narrower concept emphasizing that part of Israel's national security policy wherein military tactics, strategic doctrines, and political processes meet. As I proceeded with the preliminary research, it increasingly dawned on me that such a focus could be found in an application to the materials of the Israeli experience of the essentially universal concept of deterrence.

While I was still wondering about the pros and cons of such a project, I was confronted by another important stimulus for pursuing this study. In January 1982 I was invited by Professor Michael Brecher of McGill University to prepare a paper on the topic of international crises for presentation at the twelfth annual conference of the International Political Science Association (IPSA), which took place in August of that year. Entitled "Deterrence and Crisis in a Protracted Conflict: The Case of Israel," the paper was my first written attempt to collect my thoughts on the topic.[1]

Fortunately the discussants of the presentations at the panel were two leading authorities on international relations and strategic studies: Professor Dina Zinnes of the University of Illinois and Professor Alexander L. George of Stanford University. In her comments Professor Zinnes drew my attention to the need for a broader theoretical and comparative framework for my specific research on Israel. Professor George seemed to have broadly endorsed my expanded interpretation of the meaning of conventional deterrence as well as my application of this notion to the minutiae of the Israeli experience. This encouraging response converged with friendly and supportive advice from Professor Brecher—probably the single most important contributor to the study of Israel's experience as an international actor. In a word, by the autumn of 1982 I had ample evidence that I was onto a very promising project.

At this stage I engaged in a more sustained attempt to appraise the state of the art of the study of conventional deterrence. It did not take long to discover that as a result of the outstanding contribution of Alexander L. George and Richard Smoke in their 1974 study of *Deterrence in American Foreign Policy*[2] and the important integration and reappraisal of deterrence theory by Patrick Morgan three years later,[3] the sensitivity of scholars to the complexities of conventional deterrence was growing. It also seemed clear, however, that the field was dominated by U.S. scholars, who could not help being overwhelmingly influenced by their nation's concerns, cultural heritage, and recent international experience.

More specifically, the culture-bound nature of the study of deterrence up to that time was reflected in four debatable underlying assumptions:

1. That deterrence is primarily a test of nerve and intelligence in the course of brief and spasmodic crises

2. That deterrence is not a complex political process involving whole nations but essentially a confrontation between two relatively small-decision-making units

3. That deterrence typically requires a rough symmetry in power between the parties

4. That deterrence is an absolute phenomenon: either it completely succeeds or it completely fails.

Somewhat uncomfortable with all four assumptions, I found myself shifting the emphasis in my own emerging study to the *problématique* of pursuing deterrence in the long haul; to the impact of power asymmetry on the dynamics of deterrence; to the complexities of pursuing deterrence against the background of a lively domestic political debate; and, above all, to the relative, sequential, and fragile nature of deterrence. By following this path, I may have overemphasized the peculiarities of the Israeli experience. Nevertheless, along with a growing community of armchair strategists who rely extensively on data from Arab–Israeli wars, I remain convinced that at least some of the lessons of the Israeli experience have a far wider application than is apparent at first glance.

Having gone through such an attempt at adapting elements of the general theory of deterrence to the specific study of Israeli strategy, I then evolved my own research design and proceeded to address the case of Israel in detail. At this stage I had to make two important methodological decisions. The first related to the choice between the intensive case study approach and the extensive bird's-eye view. Since Michael Brecher had done wonders in studying Israel through case studies,[4] and since I wanted to emphasize the less familiar *problématique* of general, long-term deterrence, my choice was the bird's eye view plus one illustrative case study. The main cost that this entailed was that I had to cut many historical corners, so to speak. But as I do not see this study as a definitive history, I am inclined to think that the bird's-eye view paid off. It shifted the emphasis to continuities and changes over time and, in doing so, also provided a comprehensive survey that students and less well informed readers could use.

My second decision related to the manner of presenting the key concepts. There were two alternatives, one "vertical" and one "horizontal." The first was to take each set of key questions—for instance, the question of capabilities—and study it vertically—that is, longitudinally from 1949 to the present. I tried this method in the first draft of this study and in a brief article that was published in Hebrew.[5] Having gone through these experiments, however, I came to the conclusion that it would be preferable to maintain the wholeness of distinct historical periods. Hence the core of the present study falls into four "horizontal" or chronological parts (1949–56, 1957–67, 1967–73, and 1974–84), each of these parts being subdivided "vertically" or conceptually. Looking back at my decision, I feel confident that this method saved the study from the misfortune of excessive fragmentation—from becoming an obscure theory that only specialists would be able to comprehend.

This phase of trial and error yielded three additional journal and book articles[6] and one sizable monograph,[7] in which I tested a variety of ideas and a number of alternative methods of presentation. It also resulted in—and greatly benefited from—university courses on the topic at four different institutions: the University of Haifa and Tel Aviv University in Israel and Georgetown University and the University of Maryland, College Park, in the United States. The encounter with Israeli students was important because it forced me to find ways of dealing in a detached and scholarly manner with a topic that for them was provocative and charged. The encounter with U.S. students, on the other hand, sensitized me to the needs and preferences of an uninvolved audience with little (and often no) real background knowledge.

Indirectly I also derived an immeasurable benefit from fifteen years of service as a regular and later a reserve staff officer with an Israel Defense Forces (IDF) paratroop battalion, as well as from a stint as a civilian consultant with the Planning Division of the IDF General Staff. More directly, I was greatly assisted by the critical and perceptive comments on various drafts of the project by Alan Dowty of Notre Dame and Haifa Universities; by Ze'ev Ma'oz of the University of Haifa; and by Steve Gibert, Robert J. Lieber, and William V. O'Brien of Georgetown University.

The sustained effort without which a study like this is unthinkable requires a variety of less intellectual forms of support as well. In this respect I am greatly indebted to the chairman and directors of the Jaffe Foundation, which provided generous and timely financial assistance; to the friendly hospitality of the chairman and members of the Government Department of Georgetown University, who hosted me as a visiting professor during 1982–83; to the equally friendly hospitality of the chairman and members of the Department of Government and Politics of the University of Maryland at College Park, where I was a visiting professor in 1985; to David Bukai of the Research Authority of the University of Haifa, who went out of his way to provide all the necessary technical services; and, last but not least, to my wife, Michal, who showed more forbearance during the various stages of this project than anyone would be entitled to expect.

Mount Carmel
June 1986

1
Deterrence Theory and Israeli Strategy

The Problem

Deterrence is the be all and end all of Israeli strategy. It is celebrated as a central concept in numerous statements on national security affairs by Israeli politicians, officials, intellectuals, and professional officers alike. It is mentioned ad nauseam in manuals, brochures, and orders of the day of the Israel Defense Forces (IDF). It is, in the words of one observer, "the most commonly used" term "of the jargon of strategic studies," an "integral part of the vocabulary of the public debate"[1]; an article of faith; an ultimate, undisputed yardstick by which performance is evaluated; the single most important rationale for launching military operations; *the* organizing concept inspiring definitions of situations, of goals, of achievements, and of failures. To prevent its perceived depreciation, Israel went to war in 1956; launched endless "reprisals" during the 1950s and 1960s; went to war again in 1967; escalated the war of attrition on the banks of the Suez Canal during 1968–70; seized additional parts of the Syrian Golan plateau and of Egyptian territory in the latter stages of the 1973 war; raided Entebbe airport in faraway Uganda; bombed the nuclear reactor Osiraq near Baghdad, the capital of Iraq; escalated the struggle with the Palestinian Liberation Organization (PLO) in Lebanon during the 1970s; went into Lebanon in 1982 and withdrew from Lebanese territory in the course of 1983–85.

Yet, for all the fervor with which Israelis speak about deterrence and act in its name, many apparently have only a dim appreciation of what deterrence is all about. What does it entail in the specific context in which Israel pursues it? How does a strategy of deterrence and, most particularly, of conventional deterrence differ from an ordinary defensive posture in terms of force structure, deployment, and military hardware? What does such a strategy entail in terms of threat articulation? How does it affect the Jewish state's relations with third parties, in particular with those—both in the Middle East and beyond—whose interests converge with Israel's? What does a strategy of deterrence boil down to in terms of the employment of force? Does every resort to force signal a failure of deterrence (as it no doubt would in any instance of a resort to nuclear force), or should a strategy of conventional deterrence assume a more flexible definition of failure and success? How does a small power such as Israel maximize the efficacy of its general, long-term deterrence without perilously compromising its ability to cope with the problem of specific deterrence in the course of brief but highly dangerous crises? How does Israel's domestic political setup affect its ability to project a viable deterrence? Above all, is Israel really capable of resisting the abiding attraction of a nuclear panacea?

Questions like these are difficult to answer because of the thicket of secrecy that has shrouded the making of Israel's national security policy. However, Israel is an open society in which national security issues are openly, and often hotly, aired in public. Consequently, a great deal of valuable information is available, at least to observers with a good command of the Hebrew language. Nonetheless, it ought to be assumed as a matter of course that whereas the bulk of the less important data has already become public property, a significant portion of the most important information has not become available— and most probably will not. Hence any study of Israel's national security policy remains, at least to some extent, a tentative exercise—a matter of deduction and perhaps even conjecture.

A second, and perhaps far more significant, difficulty that faces anyone attempting to investigate Israel's national security policy is a conceptual one. The questions regarding the Jewish state that have been posed here subsume, in their ensemble, a wider unifying query: *What is conventional deterrence?* Although the subject has been addressed in recent years by a growing number of distinguished scholars[2]—although, indeed, the notion itself is, as the late Raymond Aron once pointed out, "as old as humanity"[3]—it nevertheless remains one of the least developed areas of contemporary strategic theory. The scope and nature of this lacuna were identified with characteristic perceptiveness by Alexander L. George:

> Though the practice of deterrence in interstate relations goes back to ancient times, theorizing about deterrence is a relatively recent phenomenon. The problem of deterrence took on new urgency in modern times with the advent of thermonuclear weapons and long-range delivery systems. Yet, it is surprising how slowly deterrence theory, and even clarity about the concept, developed after World War II. At first, deterrence was understood and conveyed in relatively simple terms. The doctrine of "massive retaliation" was invented by the Eisenhower administration in an effort to use the threat of strategic nuclear air power to deter not only a Soviet strategy attack but a variety of lesser encroachments on the Free World. Massive Retaliation, however, was subjected to increasing criticism as Soviet capabilities grew and as its lack of relevance to low-level conflicts was demonstrated. Accordingly, the Kennedy administration and its successors moved to refine deterrence strategy and to differentiate

its requirements for different types and levels of conflict. By the late 1960s, deterrence theory and practice were proceeding on several levels.

It is now necessary to reconceptualize the problem of deterrence somewhat differently for different levels of conflict. These are (1) the deterrent relationship of the two superpowers' strategic forces to each other; (2) the deterrence of local and limited conflicts; and (3) the deterrence of "sublimited" conflict at the lower end of the spectrum of violence.

The first of these three levels has received the greatest attention in deterrence theory at the strategic level. . . . The quantity and quality of deterrence theory falls off sharply and steadily for the second and third levels. Deterrence theory at these levels remains relatively underdeveloped and is ridden with difficult problems both of conceptualization and methodology. Largely because deterrence theory at the strategic level, dealing as it does with a relatively simple structural situation was so much better developed, theorists were tempted to employ the logic of strategic deterrence as the paradigm case for thinking about deterrence in general. This has proven to be quite unsatisfactory, however, for there are major differences in the problem of applying deterrence effectively at the second and third levels of conflict. Deterrence at those levels is much more context-dependent than at the strategic level, i.e. it is subject to the play of many more variables that change from one situation to another and, moreover, that are likely to be unstable over time for a particular situation.

As a result, not only are the requirements for deterrence often more complicated for the second and third levels of conflict, they are also more difficult to identify reliably and more difficult to meet. As historical experience amply demonstrates, conflicts at the second and third levels of violence are less easily deterred than the initiation of a strategic nuclear strike. And yet, by far the largest volume of conflict-related developments in other parts of the world with which U.S. foreign policy has attempted to deal lie at the lower end of the spectrum. Many of these low-level conflicts are essentially nondeterrable, at least by threats of military intervention, for such threats either lack credibility or arc irrclevant to thcsc conflict situations.

What this brief review of the intellectual history of deterrence theory highlights, therefore, is that theorists have not had much success in extending the logic of deterrence from the simplest strategic case to the more complex cases at the second and third levels. The problems of deterrence at these levels cannot be squeezed into the analytical and policy framework of the logic of strategic deterrence.[4]

Chronologically, deterrence theory is just about as old as the Jewish state. Its real coming of age, so to speak, occurred in the late 1950s and early 1960s, when Israel already had behind it a long history of ferocious conflict. Differently stated, even if the emerging body of deterrence theory were more developed, the fruits of such an intellectual endeavor would still have been of little immediate value to the Israelis during the crucial formative years of Israeli strategy. This is all the more so because Western thinking on conventional deterrence really has been as underdeveloped as George argues, whereas the Israelis have meanwhile accumulated nearly four decades of experience.

Indeed, one of the principal theses of this study is that, broadly speaking, the Israelis have not been unsuccessful in finding answers to the questions raised earlier. Their success, however, has been more practical than intellectual. Lacking any mature body of theory to draw on, skeptical of the utility of clearly spelled-out doctrines, and faced in quick succession with formidable challenges requiring immediate responses, Israeli policymakers groped for answers and ideas incrementally, haphazardly, and often inconsistently. Gradually a set of assumptions and operational reflexes evolved, which taken together added up to a discernible theory of deterrence based on conventional weapons.

Impressive as this achievement may have been, however, it was not accompanied by a similar success in articulating and in critically evaluating the Israelis' own actions. They may have been acting on an implicit theory, but so far they have been slow in spelling it out. The result is not only a glaring absence of any direct Israeli contribution to the development of a general theory of conventional deterrence, but also, arguably, some damage to Israel itself. The eminently practical inclination of the authors and architects of Israel's implicit concept of deterrence has been its principal source of strength. Over the years, however, it has also become an important source of weakness, leading to intellectual inertia and, inevitably, to serious fallacies, costly blunders, and entrenched misperceptions.

The purpose of this discussion is not, however, to investigate Israeli failures or, indeed, to hail Israel's successes. Rather, the objective is to state explicitly the main elements of Israel's implicit theory of conventional deterrence, to trace principal trends in the emergence of this strategic concept, to identify the main factors leading to both continuity and change, and to search for clues to this strategy's future thrust.

With such a diachronic emphasis, this study differs somewhat from previous investigations of similar themes, which often sought deliberately to play down the evolutionary, historical dimension. Nevertheless, in the final analysis, the purpose here is not so much to exhaust the historical record as it is to underline, illuminate, and explain through a detailed survey of the particular Israeli experience the rich complexity of a strategy of conventional deterrence in general. The history of the Israeli quest for conventional deterrence, then, is treated as a case study from which broader generalizations may perhaps be subsequently deduced. Given the paucity of advanced theoretical work on the topic of conventional deterrence, however, and given the fact that—to put it bluntly— important parts of the theoretical groundwork of the topic have yet to be laid, it is necessary to preface the discussion of the specifics of the Israeli experience with a brief statement of some guiding hypotheses.

The Essence of Deterrence

Deterrence has been variously defined. To one scholar it is "a calculated attempt to induce an adversary to do something, or refrain from doing something, by threatening a penalty for non-compliance." To another writer it appears to be a situation in which "State A seeks to prevent State B from doing Z by threatening B with unacceptable costs if it does Z." A third definition presents deterrence as an "inducement of another party . . . to refrain from a certain action by means of a threat that this action will lead the threatener . . . to inflict retaliation of punishment. . . . In other words, deterrence is persuading the deterred that his own interest compels him to desist from committing a certain act."[5]

The differences between these three definitions are evidently more a matter of style and semantics than of substance. In this sense they are not unique. Almost all definitions of the term in legions of books and articles on the topic say more or less the same thing: to deter is to dissuade an adversary from doing harm or, more broadly, to alter the adversary's strategic calculus so as to make it more compatible with the deterrer's own interests. This alteration is normally sought by threatenting to administer a penalty. Occasionally, however, deterrence is pursued in a more sophisticated manner that brandishes not only a big stick, but also a sweet carrot: the attempt to shape the adversary's calculus relies not only on the threat of punishment, but also on an offer of rewards.

It follows, then, that the conventional variety of deterrence means the combination of four necessary conditions:

1. It is a state policy.
2. It is designed to dissuade adversaries from committing acts deemed harmful by the defender.
3. It seeks to achieve its purpose either through the threat of retribution or through a combination of threatened retributions and promised rewards.
4. Such retribution as is threatened *would be carried out by a variety of diplomatic, economic, and psychological measures but also, above all, by armed forces relying exclusively on conventional weapons.*

To the extent that one can speak of a "common wisdom" concerning conventional deterrence, it is the acceptance of the logic of the foregoing definition but the restriction of its application to the all-important yet somewhat narrow military aspects. Thus a recent study identified three alternative approaches to the topic. The first postulates that a conventional deterrent is effective when defensive weapons predominate in the arsenals of the adversaries. Conversely, this approach suggests, deterrence is likely to fail if both adversaries emphasize offensive weaponry. Offensive weapons, in this view, combine firepower and mobility in roughly equal proportions. Defensive weapons, on the other hand, stress firepower at the expense of mobility. A tank is thus an offensive weapon par excellence, whereas a field gun is a typical defensive weapon. If the parties to a conflict rely on stationary weapons, deterrence is likely to succeed. Conversely, if the adversaries emphasize their offensive capabilities, deterrence is likely to fail.

The second approach to conventional deterrence questions the contention that weapons can be classified as either inherently offensive or defensive. Instead, this approach draws attention to the balance of forces between adversaries as the critical variable determining whether or not a conventional deterrent will work. Analyses falling into this category consider indicators such as the number of tanks, soldiers, pieces of artillery, and aricraft in the possession of the adversaries and proceed to add them up to composite, and presumably comparable, force ratios. More sophisticated analyses of this type take the quality of weapons into account by weighing the relative value of different categories of weapons as well as differences within a given category. The main proposition on which this second approach is predicated is that "deterrence fails when the attacker has superiority in men and arms. Conversely, deterrence is expected to obtain when there is a rough equality in the size of the opposing forces."

If the type-of-strategy school (the first approach) is taken to task because of the difficulty of classifying weapons, the balance-of-forces school (the second approach) has been criticized for its inability to account for cases—like Israel's preemption of Egypt in 1967—in which a country possessing a far smaller military force was not deterred by its adversary's seeming superiority. The key to a stable conventional deterrence, a more recent third school argues, must be sought in the strategic concept by which the adversaries are informed. Broadly speaking, this argument continues, there are three distinct types of conventional strategic postures: blitzkrieg, attrition, and limited gains. A strategy of *blitzkrieg* emphasizes *moving* (or *striking*) power. A strategy of *attrition* emphasizes *staying* power. A *limited-gains* strategy rests on the assumption that the optimal solution lies in the *combination of staying and moving power.*

When adversaries are informed by the same strategic concept, this third approach to the topic further contends, deterrence is likely to succeed. Thus, if the parties to a conflict base their military posture on the anticipation of a blitzkrieg or a war of attrition or a sequence of assaults for limited gains, they do not entertain a high expectation of making a worthwhile gain in the event of war. The parties will therefore be mutually deterred. If, however, the adversaries adopt contrasting strategic concepts, then deterrence is very likely to fail.[6]

Each of these contending views of conventional deterrence addresses at least one important dimension of the problem. If adversaries spend most of their resources on constructing shelters and trenches rather than on tanks, mobile artillery, and air power, they are not very likely to initiate a war. Conversely, if adversaries have no strategic depth and no defenses worthy of the name, and emphasize instead their war-winning capabilities, then it makes no sense for either to permit its opponent the privilege of launching a preemptive strike. The parties to such a conflict are in fact locked into what game theorists call a prisoners' dilemma: they would avoid preemption if only they could be certain that the other party would avoid it too. Assuming that a heavy premium is paid on preemption, however, they are inclined to suspect that their opponent would not be able to resist the temptation to preempt. The only logical operative conclusion to which this kind of calculus could lead is that the sooner one preempts, the safer it will be (from its point of view).

The type-of-strategy approach illuminates this deadly logic when it touches on an important aspect of deterrence at the medium, nonnuclear, level of violence. Moreover, it seems equally plausible to contend, as the balance-of-forces school does, that the perceived balance of forces has a critical impact on the calculi of countries in conflict. If the adversary appears weaker and the existence of a real bone of contention is taken for granted, then it makes ample sense to launch a war.

Paradoxically, it also makes sense to launch a preemptive strike when the adversary appears more powerful. Under such circumstances, a successful surprise attack adds a critical increment of power, so to speak, to the weaker party. Given the fact that conflicts breed arms races and that arms races are dynamic, the prospects for a simultaneous and mutual acknowledgment of the existence of a stable equilibrium are therefore dim, as are the prospects for a stable mutual deterrence.

Finally, the choice-of-strategy argument raises at least two important points: first, that the real test of a conventional deterrence posture lies in its ability to dissuade an opponent from resorting to less than all-out wars of the attrition and limited-gains varieties, and, second, that the choice of the same strategy by both parties to the conflict lessens the prospects of deterrence failures. At the same time, however, this third approach, like the other two schools of thought it criticizes, appears to oversimplify the problem of conventional deterrence. Deriving their hypotheses from a paradigm of deterrence that emerged from studies of nuclear conflicts, assuming as they do that conventional deterrence "is directly linked to battlefield outcomes," they lead inadvertently to an excessive fascination with the minutae of battlefield strategems and, more broadly, to the naked display of military force.

Such "micro" military concepts of conventional deterrence rob the topic of some of its most essential festures. It becomes virtually indistinguishable from that posture which, since time immemorial, has been known as defense. Unaware as it is of the fact that deterrence, "the negative aspect of political power," is "a function of the *total* cost-gain expectation of the party to be deterred,"[7] the choice-of-strategy approach—no less than the two earlier approaches, which it criticizes—pays only lip services to the political and psychological dynamics whose interplay ultimately determines whether or not deterrence will obtain. It does not address the basic question of why states should choose to base their national security on deterrence rather than on alternative types of national strategy. It has little to say about the role of alliances in the pursuit of deterrence; about the intricate *problématique* of manipulating the adversary's behavior through the studied dissemination of threats; about the impact of domestic politics on the style and outcome of a deterrence strategy; about the importance of accommodative political gestures in changing the adversary's strategic calculus; or, for that matter, about the complexities of deterring guerrillas and managing deterrence in episodes dominated by naval and air warfare. In a word, though formulated after George's critique, just quoted, of the state of the art, the choice-of-strategy approach pays only scant attention to the former's wise and perceptive advice and leaves the problem of conventional deterrence almost as unattended as it had been previously. What, then, is the essence of conventional deterrence?

The beginning of wisdom in any attempt to comprehend conventional deterrence is the recognition that it is not just another word for what, since time immemorial, has been called defense. Rather, it is a mode of behavior unto itself—a distinct, perhaps even *generic,* type of macrostrategic posture. It may involve a great deal of strategic-military maneuvering, but it is not merely a question of battlefield stratagems. It entails a complex array of decision-making processes at a great variety of levels, but it is not merely an exercise in rational decision making. It is inseparably linked to the construction, training, equipping, and displaying of military capabilities, but it is far more than the balancing of naked military forces. It is, rather, a complex combination of all these factors and far more. It is a state of mind, an image both of oneself and of the adversary, a disposition, an organizing concept, a conceptual beacon in the light of which governments organize their efforts in the field of national security. In a word, deterrence is very nearly a special form of what Sir Basil Liddell Hart called a "grand strategy."[8]

Defining the scope of deterrence in such wide-ranging and inclusive terms, however, is not the same as identifying it with national security policy as a whole. Critical as it may be in the final analysis, deterrence is no more than one part of the total field of national security. Although this caveat should not be forgotten, it still remains plausible to contend that the very choice of a deterrence posture has a significant bearing on a whole range of other national choices. It impinges on the allocation of resources; on the structure and deployment of military force; on the specifics of military doctrine; on the choice of allies; on the articulation, dissemination, and signaling to the adversary of both accommodating inducements and assertive threats; on the preferences of when and how force should be employed; and even on the style, texture, and pace of the domestic political process.

In all these respects, *deterrence* is related to, but should not be confused with, two equally distinct alternative types of international disposition—*defense* and *offense*. The heart of the distinction between these three mutually exclusive types lies in their fundamentally different alignment of *political ends* with *military means*. An offensive posture should by no means be confused with the operational doctrine of the armed forces. Rather, it too, like deterrence and defense, constitutes a grand strategy, an all-embracing outlook emphasizing an attitude toward the world at large *as well as* a specific military doctrine. As the case of Nazi Germany suggests, an offensive posture starts from a fundamental, deep-seated dissatisfaction (whose origins may be ideological, irredentist, or both) with the prevailing international status quo, at least in the nation's immediate international vicinity.[9] It therefore advocates an international reshuffle. In turn it leads to an emphasis on a military capability with which to carry out such a program. The ends of such a program are pervasively offensive, as are its choice of military means. Such an international actor, to use the language of the choice-of-strategy approach, invests the bulk of its resources in the construction of the largest possible blitzkrieg capability.

A defensive national posture—for instance, that of Czechoslovakia during the interwar period—means precisely the opposite. It, too, constitutes a grand strategy. Its ultima ratio, however, is preservative in the most fundamental sense. Based on satisfaction with the international order as it is, it would not lead to the investment of any resources—least of all military resources—in an endeavor to change this order.[10] Therefore, it leads to a defensive military doctrine with an emphasis on staying power, and not—as in the case of an offensive posture—on moving (or striking) power. In the battlefield conditions of the twentieth century, this means an emphasis on fortifications, civil defense, antiaircraft capability, and coastal defenses, and a marked preference for antitank capability and stationary artillery over mobile armored "fists" combining movement and fire.

A national defensive posture as defined here is not readily distinguishable from what Glenn H. Snyder once described (with reference to nuclear conflicts) as "deterrence by denial."[11] The main reason that the two terms are not mutually exclusive is that the best form of deterrence is, arguably, a good defense.[12] A nation that is capable of generating sufficient military force to envelop itself permanently within a robust defensive wall, as the Chinese apparently assumed millennia ago, deters effectively by its evident ability to thwart almost any type of conventional attack. This is, of course, an ideal type, which does not exist in the real world of today and may have seldom existed in the past. But it seems to underline the basic conceptual difference between real or generic deterrence, on the one hand, and a dissuading image derived from alternative strategies (such as defense), on the other hand.

Deterrence in its purest form, then, is fundamentally distinct from both defense and offense. While combining elements of both these classical postures, it constitutes a category unto itself. Informed by a basic satisfaction with the prevailing international order, it is defensive in its overriding political ends. At the same time, it is offensive in its choice of military means.[13] This somewhat incongruous strategic-political posture is intrinsically complex, if not in the longer term counterproductive. Entailing as it does the simultaneous pursuit of both an aggressive and a peace-loving international image, it inevitably leads to charges of duplicity. It is escalatory by its very nature. It leads to tensions with one's allies abroad and friction with one's political constituency at home. In short, it is an imperfect posture, one that a nation adopts reluctantly only if and when all other alternatives appear even less attractive.

In more concrete terms, deterrence is typically the strategic posture of weaker parties. The logic of this hypothesis runs as follows. If nation A (Gnomeland) faces an adversary, B (Giantland), whose war potential is perceived to be significantly superior, then the defending power, A, has no viable defensive option. If Gnomeland deploys its forces in fortified positions along its entire frontier, it is bound to be outnumbered, outgunned, and easily overwhelmed at almost any point along the boundary with Giantland. Confronted with such a predicament, Gnomeland has no logical alternative but to fall back on an inherently offensive military doctrine that stresses, and by its very nature facilitates, preemption; at the very least, it calls for the allocation of offensive force to specific theaters of operation only after the detection of Giantland's main effort. Given the imbalance between the weaker Gnomeland and the more powerful Giantland, even an offensive military doctrine may well constitute an inadequate deterrent. Knowing this, however, does not alter the fact that for Gnomeland, the weaker party in the conflict, an offensive military doctrine is more logical than a defensive one.

The contention that deterrence in its offensive form is a posture of necessity and not of choice suggests two more important postulates. First, it is never a question of having a deterrent or not having one but, rather, a matter of relative efficacy. The realistic purpose of a strategy of conventional deterrence is not to prevent hostilities altogether but, rather, *to maximize a nation's projection of power in order to minimize its need to resort to force.* The relation of a nation's deterrent to its objective capabilities is in this sense analogous to the relation of the productive capacity of a firm to the value of its shares on the stock market. A ceaseless, long-term process of influence, deterrence is inherently given to failures. It is a relative, contextual, flimsy, nimble, and elusive quality—a stock in a tumultuous threat exchange rather than a palpable commodity in a stable market.

Notwithstanding this inherently enigmatic nature of deterrence, it is plausible to posit the existence of four basic degrees of deterrent efficacy: *firm, stable, vulnerable,* and *fragile.* When the adversaries in a dyad—say, the United States and the Soviet Union—are of roughly equal strength and both possess nuclear weapons, deterrence is most (though by no means entirely) effective. As Robert Jervis has pointed out, this is not a matter of policy but a fact: "No amount of flexiblity, no degree of military superiority at levels less than all-out war, can change the fundamental attribute of the nuclear age. Not only can each side destroy the other if it chooses, but that outcome can grow out of conflict even if no one wants it to. Most dilemmas of U.S. policy," argues Jervis, "stem from the vulnerability of its cities, not from policies which might permit the Soviets marginal military advantage in unlikely and terribly risky contingencies. Once each side can destroy the other, any crisis brings up the possibility of this disastrous outcome."[14]

The awesome and overbearing influence of nuclear capabilities also operates quite effectively (though possibly less so than in the previous case) when one of the parties is substantially weaker (say, France versus the Soviet Union). This is an instance of so-called limited deterrence, which (along with other factors) has inspired the French to develop their *force de dissuasion*. A nuclear capability in such a case acts as an equalizer or at least as a power multiplier. It assists the minor adversary in narrowing the gap in power potentials through the deployment of a massive, albeit partial, capability to punish.[15]

A third and still lesser degree of stability obtains in conflicts in which neither party has a nuclear capability but both are roughly of the same strength (say, India versus China before either had acquired nuclear weapons). The absence of a nuclear capacity makes for a substantial depreciation in the stability of mutual deterrence. Losing a war becomes an acceptable proposition, and no move is likely to lead to irreversible consequences (except, perhaps, for the individuals who make the decision to launch the war and, certainly, for the soldiers who lose their lives on the battlefield). In such a context, it should be emphasized, the impact and the weight of the political, nontechnological, and nonmilitary intangibles such as morale and domestic cohesion on the credibility of the nation's deterrent increases immeasurably. Whereas in nuclear balances the mainstay of mutual deterrence is the blind and, in itself, non-political destructive potential of weapons systems, in conventional conflicts no amount of hardware can utterly insulate the efficacy of a deterrent from the impact of a whole gamut of "soft" political intangibles.

To argue in this vein is not, however, to say that numbers, technology, strategic concepts, and the like do not count. When neither party possesses nuclear weapons, and when the parties are significantly unequal in their overall war-making potentials, the deterrent of Gnomeland, the weaker party, is more likely to be less effective. It is then that reliance on an offensive posture even though the overriding purpose is the preservation of the status quo becomes an inescapable necessity. It is also then that an effective deterrent is difficult to obtain. This most vulnerable fourth category is what was described earlier as the generic or prototypical deterrence.

Moreover, the inferiority or weakness that renders deterrence, fragile as it may be, an existential imperative, a nation's only realistic strategic and political posture, stems not only from *objective* liabilities like size and strength, but at least as much from somewhat more *idiosyncratic* sources of weakness, such as the type of regime. Open, pluralistic societies tend to subordinate foreign policy to domestic needs. Closed, totalitarian or authoritarian regimes, on the other hand, often have their priorities in the opposite order.[16] The difference, however, may not be so conspicuous in the course of a war or even in the course of a crisis when war appears imminent. Judging by the British and Soviet experiences during World War II, both open and closed societies tend to pull themselves together in the face of adversity. Conversely, the difference between open and closed societies in terms of their order of priorities is underlined over the long-run "normal" conduct of their external affairs. Closed societies are prone to exhibit a high degree of mobilization, regimentation, and consequently military outlays. By contrast, open societies have a built-in preference for keeping military expenditures to the bare minimum. They suffer from a problem of power convertibility. They are the underachievers of the international system with respect to their ability to play the system's game of power. In all but the most extreme situations of adversity, in other words, their potential military power tends to be greater than their actual projection of power.[17]

The logical corollary of this hypothesis is as follows: when an open, pluralistic society faces a closed, authoritarian or totalitarian opponent in a protracted conflict, a certain imbalance in actual capabilities is bound to occur, even if the ultimate war potentials of the two parties are the same. The result may be an intriguing paradox: the "open" party, though more likely by its very nature to be satisfied with the status quo, is impelled to emphasize an offensive military doctrine (namely, deterrence); its closed, totalitarian or authoritarian adversary, on the other hand, feels free to adopt a defensive posture. To be sure, it may well be an overstatement to argue that deterrence— as defined here—is *only* the choice of democracies. But it seems a plausible hypothesis that democracies are more prone than nondemocratic societies to adopt deterrence as the guiding principle of their national security policy. The North Atlantic Treaty Organization (NATO) countries, as well as neutralist democracies such as Sweden and Switzerland, offer telling examples—as does Israel.[18]

The Premises of Israeli Strategy

The extent to which the Israeli experience fits into the foregoing concept of conventional deterrence hinges on two principal factors. First, it must be established that the Jewish state has persistently acted on the assumption of an unbridgeable gap in overall war-making potentials between itself and its Arab adversaries. Second, it must be established that Israel is, and has always been, a status quo power, whose overriding purpose is to preserve a given regional order.

That Israel has been acting (rightly or wrongly) on the assumption of an unbridgeable inferiority (in terms of power rather than culture or intellect) is virtually a banality. The state's founder and first prime minister, David Ben Gurion, articulated the essence of this permanent Israeli theme shortly after the establishment of the state. Addressing the Knesset—Israel's unicameral legislature—he reminded the 120 members that the Jewish state was

> in fact a small island surrounded by a great Arab ocean extending over two continents—in Asia and in North Africa, from the Taurus Mountains in south Turkey to the Atlas Mountains on the Atlantic coast. This ocean is spread over a contiguous area of 4 million square miles, an area larger than that of the United States, in which 70 million people . . . most of them Arab-speaking Moslems, live. Only four of these countries have a common border with Israel—Egypt, Jordan, Syria, and Lebanon. These cover an area of 460,000 square miles and have a population of 29 million people, approximately fifty-eight times the size of Israel.

Hence, he said on another occasion, "Israel has to observe with cruel clarity the fatal difference" between itself and its "adversaries" . . .[the latter] think that they are capable of solving the problem of Israel once and for all by total destruction . . . [Israel, for its part] cannot and does not wish to achieve security through a military victory . . . [Israel] is incapable of eliminating millions of Arabs in the Middle East."[19]

The same fundamental assumption has also been just as much of a center-piece in the thinking of Ben Gurion's successors and disciples. Note, for instance, the following passage from Yigal Allon's survey of Israel's strategic thinking:

> From a demographic point of view, Israel's two and a half million Jews [in the 1950s] had to contend with more than a hundred million Arabs from the Atlantic to the Persian Gulf. Geostrategically speaking, Israel was a narrow strip of land, had its back to the sea, and was surrounded; the lands of the enemy, by contrast, formed a sub-continent. Israel was a country desperately poor in natural resources pitting itself against countries possessing almost inexhaustible natural wealth: oil, big rivers, vast areas of arable land, about half of the world's hydrocarbon reserves. Both in its own region and in the larger world Israel was uniquely isolated. Apart from its bonds with world Jewry, it had no ethnic or religious links with any other nation.[20]

Statements such as this were made in the context of the 1950s, Israel's first decade of statehood, when the perception of isolation and vulnerability was most acute. Later, however, in the heady atmosphere of excessive self-confidence that prevailed in the Jewish state in the wake of the 1967 victory over the armies of Egypt, Jordan, and Syria, this theme of insurmountable inferiority lost much of its salience. But the 1973 Yom Kippur War revived the somber mood. Even retired Major-General Moshe Dayan, the hero of Israel's victories in the 1956 Sinai campaign and the 1967 Six-Day War and a person who would normally underemphasize Israel's weakness, hastened in the course of the Yom Kippur War to stress Israel's instrinsic inability to sustain the rigors of a protracted war. "If we do not achieve a decision" in the battlefields of Sinai and the Golan, Dayan told his cabinet colleagues as well as the IDF General Staff,

> our strength will be whittled away and we shall be left without sufficient military force in the middle of the campaign. The Arabs possess great staying power. There are 70–80 million Arabs and we are fewer than three million. In their armies there are about one million soldiers, the USSR supplies them with all the arms they need. They dispose of vast financial resources. Aside from the Arab states currently fighting, the others, too—Iraq, Saudi Arabia, etc.—are ready to join. We have turned to the United States and urgently requested additional arms. But, in any case, no one will fight for us.[21]

The first Likud government (1977–81) seems to have also acted on the assumption of an innate military inferiority. The Arabs, speculated retired Major-General Ezer Weizman—commanding officer of the Israeli Air Force until shortly before the 1967 war, nephew of Israel's first president, and the minister of defense in Menachem Begin's first cabinet—view Israel's victories "as a passing episode, a temporary imperative of history. . . . We, the Israelis," Weizman continued,

> embraced the notion that the Arabs are mystics and that our power stems from our rationality. But an objective examination of the circumstances and of the numerical aspects turns us into mystics and the Arabs into realists and rationalists. We argue that three million Jews can hold their own against one hundred million Arabs. They argue that in the long run their overwhelming quantity and fantastic wealth will give them an edge. In order to win, say the Arabs, they don't have to be as efficient on the battlefields as we are. It is enough for them to be far less efficient [since] quantity will ultimately turn into quality. The Jews have already flexed their muscles to the limit. . . . Soviet weapons, European and some U.S. support have built Arab power; frequent wars and an Arab belief that ultimately the wheel of fortune will turn in their favor even if they have to go through fourth, fifth, sixth, endless new wars constitute a powerful motivation.[22]

During Menachem Begin's second Likud administration (1981–84), Israel's national security policy under the influence of retired Major-General Ariel ("Arik") Sharon initially reverted to something resembling the confidence and assumption of regional preponderance of the immediate aftermath of the Six-Day War. Sharon's successors, however, returned to the old state of mind, assuming as a matter of course that Israel is inherently the weaker party in the Arab–Israeli conflict. "In the 1967 Six-Day War," said Moshe Arens, a leading "hawk" who succeeded Sharon as minister of defense in February 1983,

> we thought that we obtained peace, or at least that we created the basis for peace. Despite our tremendous desire to concentrate all our efforts, to make

a superordinate endeavor, come what may, and terminate the problem once and for all, make peace, disarm, reduce the defense budget, we do not have the ability to do so. The objective situation is such that it is not in our capacity to achieve what the Allies achieved in World War II: subdue the Germans. . . . The balance of forces in the area is different. We can defend ourselves. We can cause the Arabs pain. We can destroy their armies for a while. But solving the problem once and for all is beyond our capacity.[23]

If this assortment of statements over a period of four decades demonstrates the basic continuity of the Israeli perception of an unbridgeable inferiority, it does not in itself support the hypothesis that the Jewish state has also been a status quo power. Indeed, establishing this proposition appears to be a far more demanding task, since even a cursory glance at Isarel's map underlines the glaring gap between the United Nations' 1947 Partition boundaries and Israel's borders in the 1980s. But to deduce from Israel's variable political geography a fundamental and determined intent to reshuffle the status quo is to confuse afterthought with premeditation.

The initial blueprint, so to speak, of the Zionist movement that begot the state of Israel, the thoughts and dreams of its leaders, included a Jewish state in the territory of what in the 1980s is Israel proper within the 1949 armistice demarcation ("green") lines, as well as the West Bank, the Gaza Strip, the Gilad region in northern Jordan, the Howran in the Syrian Golan, and that part of southern Lebanon lying south of the Awali River. Moreover, both the Achdut Haavodah movement on the left of the Israeli political spectrum and Herut on the right have continued to espouse this cause with very minor changes to date.

Yet such grandiloquent dreams notwithstanding, the prestatehood Zionist record and the record of Israel as a state reflect a persistent inclination of the mainstream of political opinion to settle for far less than the boundaries of the biblical Promised Land. In 1937—following a near fratricidal debate—the Zionist movement accepted the notion of a truncated Jewish state in a marginal part of historic Palestine. In 1947 the leadership of the Yishuv—the prestatehood Jewish political community in Palestine—accepted the very limited and not entirely logical boundaries offered by the U.N. Partition Resolution. In 1949 Israel's government accepted the armistice demarcation lines (ADL) that resulted from negotiations with all its neighbors. Indeed, in the course of these negotiations, Israel demanded that the agreements have a political content and suggested that the provisional demarcation lines, corresponding as they did to the cease-fire lines at the end of the 1948 war, should be affixed by mutual agreement as the final borders of the Jewish state.

In 1956, furthermore, Ben Gurion initially expressed a desire to maintain Israel's hold over some parts of the Egyptian territory that had been captured in the Sinai campaign, but withdrew this claim a few days later. A decade later, on June 19, 1967, a week after the Six-Day War, the National Unity cabinet of Prime Minister Levi Eshkol (which included both Begin's Herut and the Achdut Haavodah) endorsed the principle that the recently occupied territories of the Golan and the Sinai be returned to their Arab owners if and when peace agreements were signed with them. The decision was ambiguous about the future of the West Bank, but it left the door ajar for negotiations concerning this part of historic Palestine as well. Contrary to the claims of most apologists for the Arab cause, then, the 1967 war was not launched for the purpose of acquiring territories but, rather, in response to a challenge that was perceived by the Israelis themselves in strategic and even existential terms.[24]

Nevertheless, the fact that the 1967 war was followed not by negotiations but instead by further wars, because the Arabs presented as a precondition to negotiations the return of their lost territories, gradually caused a hardening of Israeli attitudes. The long-suppressed territorial dreams of some elements of Israeli society returned to the fore and ultimately were officially legitimized as concrete political objectives under the Likud governments of Menachem Begin and Yitzhak Shamir (1977–84). The latter, to be sure, returned the Sinai peninsula—three times the size of Israel and the West Bank combined—to Egyptian hands within the framework of the Camp David Peace Accords of September 1978. However, they also extended Israeli law to the Golan and vowed not to allow any "foreign" rule over the West Bank ("Judea and Samaria" in official Israeli utterances ever since the Likud's advent to power).[25]

Israel, then, would never launch a war for the purpose of changing the status quo, although important elements on the Israeli domestic scene would not agree to the return of some territories occupied in the course of one war or another. Seen in these terms, the Jewish state clearly qualifies as being inherently a status quo power. This fundamental disposition runs deeper, however. In its simplest form, it is directly related to the deep-seated Israeli suspicion that the Arabs want nothing less than the liquidation of the Jewish state. Assuming this, most Israeli Jews (17 percent of the citizens of Israel within the 1967 armistice lines are Arabs) have always been united in viewing the state's ultimate purpose as the preservation of its existence. The status quo, then, means *a regional order in which a sovereign Jewish state continues to exist side by side with all existing Arab states.* The precise location of specific boundaries is a secondary issue that can be settled in direct negotiations. What matters, in this Israeli perception, is, first, that Israel's existence be accepted by its neighbors, and, second, that no new entities—for example, a Palestinian state on the West Bank or a Greater Syria consisting of present-day Syria, Lebanon, and Jordan—be superimposed on the existing regional structure.[26]

The overriding strategic problem facing Israeli policymakers from the outset was how to preserve this status quo under conditions of abject inferiority. Ben Gurion, again, set the tone in this regard for decades to come. Asked in April 1949, during the Knesset debate on the Security Service Act, why the armed forces of the Jewish state should be called the Israel Defense Forces when its emerging strategic doctrine was offensive, the prime minister had this to say:

The person who asked the question does not distinguish between a title which refers to foreign policy [on the one hand] and methods of warfare [on the other hand]. The title *Israel Defense Force* [emphasis added] is intended to indicate that the State of Israel has no offensive intentions against its neighbors and that it is peace loving. But if we are attacked, we will defend ourselves in the most efficient way, which is a blasting and dramatic offensive [carried out] to the extent possible on enemy territory and vital centers in order to thwart its offensive and [minimize] its ability to harm. Therefore, we shall maintain the peace-connoting title [Israel Defense Force] and the war-winning strategy.[27]

A decade later, Yigal Allon's analysis of the same fundamental problem would lead him to very similar conclusions. "No modern country can surround itself with a wall," Allon wrote—certainly not a country with such a small population, facing such overwhelmingly superior forces, and locked within "unmanageably long" boundaries. A defensive posture, then, is not feasible. It follows that

if the enemy did not intend war, it was his business not to make movements which would justify a preemptive counterattack. If [on the other hand] he did intend war he could not justifiably protest if his intentions are thwarted. It could be argued, moreover, that the recognition of the right of preemptive counterattack [would] increase the persuasive power of the defender's deterrent and thereby diminish the possibility of a hostile action. For the mere possession of armaments . . . could not necessarily deter the enemy. It is the knowledge that the defender was ready to use them, promptly and effectively—namely his credibility—that might prevent their having to be used at all.[28]

Such statements by Israeli decision makers reflect their intuitive understanding, distilled by rich practical experience, of the nature of conventional deterrence. Moreover, fully alive to the relative precariousness of the Israeli deterrent, on the one hand, and assuming intuitively that conventional deterrence is a sequential, aggregative, and long-term value, on the other hand, Israeli policymakers have tended to emphasize the *cumulative* nature of their own version of deterrence. "Israel's conflict with the Arabs," said a former commanding officer of the IDF's Officers Training Academy, "can be compared to a match between a heavyweight and a lightweight boxer. The former has a good chance, though not a certitude, of winning by a knockout. His lightweight opponent knows that he has no such capability. He can only hope to win the match if he attempts to deny a knockout to his superior rival and strives ultimately to win by points."[29]

Explicating the Israeli doctrine that this metaphor suggests is exceedingly difficult because, unlike most pluralistic democracies, the Jewish state has never had a comprehensive, integrated, and fully coherent doctrine in the form of either a defense white paper or a comprehensive annual statement by the minister of defense to the Knesset.[30] Nevertheless, a rich assortment of press reports, memoirs, interviews, and analytical writings by Israeli practitioners has already become available to the general public. From such sources it is quite possible to reconstruct a reasonably accurate profile of this doctrine.

It starts from a hidden assumption that Arab intentions are not static but are a product of opportunity. They change according to the vicissitudes of inter-Arab politics; the global context in which they take place; the dynamics of the regional (not only Arab–Israeli but also Arab–Arab and, for instance, Arab–Iranian) arms race; and, above all, the perceived likelihood of either pain or gain. If Israeli policy in all its aspects succeeds in impressing on the Arabs the diminishing likelihood of realistic opportunities to defeat the Jewish state, then the Arabs will ultimately resign themselves to Israel's existence.

Ostensibly the Arab world is so overwhelmingly superior that Israel does not stand a chance. In reality, however, the Arabs are so divided that, given a judicious manipulation by Israel, their theoretical potential will never be successfully converted into a corresponding power of decision on the battlefield. Indeed, pan-Arabism, the ideology of Arab unity that, if half successful, could confront Israel with a formidable threat, has increasingly revealed itself to be an empty word, a charade, a delusion—a cover-up for intense competition, rivalry, and mistrust among the Arabs themselves. Arab nation-states are emerging, and these develop their own *raison d'état*. Inevitably this brings them into conflicts of interest with one another and increasingly creates tacit strands of limited but real convergence of interest between some of them and their Jewish adversary.

Against such a background, Israel's survival is perceived as a realistic proposition if only the Israelis play it right. They should assume that years, decades, perhaps even centuries will have to pass before "real" peace (as among the Benelux countries, between Canada and the United States, or among the Scandinavians) will become the rule. Meanwhile Israel should do anything it can to limit the damage. Divisions in the Arab world ought to be encouraged, induced, and exploited. Allies in the Middle East and beyond who have their own disputes with Israel's principal adversaries should be cultivated. The Arabs should be denied opportunities for surprise attacks, wars of attrition, guerrilla warfare, terrorism, economic boycotts, psychological pressures, and hostile propaganda.

To succeed in this struggle Israel may have to resort occasionally to preventive wars, preemptive strikes, retaliations of various types and scales. The overriding purpose should be to project maximum power through a minimal resort to force; the governing principle should be to accumulate strength, militarily, economically, and psychologically; to use force sparingly, but with devastating effect. The ultimate objective of the use of force should be not only to achieve military results but also, above all, to erode Arab self-confidence. Gradually, with the passage of time, the Arabs—according to this thesis—would simply despair of their intention to undo the Jewish state. A string of brief but decisive encounters will simply wear down the Arab determination to persist with the conflict. Their campaign will lose momentum. Their coalition will disintegrate, and their war against Israel will eventually grind to a halt—not out of any love for their Jewish neighbors, but from sheer loss of appetite for costly and unsuccessful wars. As Yigal Allon once put it, "In the long term deterrence leads to resignation and resignation—to peace."[31]

Restated as a theory of deterrence, this thesis essentially posits that the combination of adroit political maneuvering and an unknown but manageable number of Israeli battlefield victories over an unspecified but reasonable period of time will gradually modify the Arab strategic calculus. From the expectation of a swift, cheap, and decisive victory (such as the Arabs entertained on the eve of the 1948 and 1967 wars), the Arabs will gradually move to tacit acceptance of the permanence of the Jewish state in their midst. Tacit acceptance will be following by normalization of relations (that is, free movement of people, commodities, and ideas across boundaries), which will ultimately lead to peace. The empirical validity of this thesis remains to be proved even after close to four decades of Israeli independence. There is no doubt, however, that it is predicated on a rather compelling logic.[32]

Theses and Organization of the Book

Israeli policymakers, then, have acted on explicable and shared common premises and, for the most part, have been informed by a good intuitive understanding of the essence of conventional deterrence. This general proposition, however, should not be confused either with unanimity or with efficacy. In fact, Israeli strategy has often been inconsistent, erratic, even illogical. Deterrence has been more persistently advocated than systematically applied. Though elevated to the status of a virtual creed, it has frequently been misapplied, with costly repercussions for all concerned—above all for the Israelis themselves. Nonetheless, in many respects Israel's deterrence strategy has added up to a spectacular success story, even if the same success could often have been achieved at a lower price or, alternatively, if a greater success could have been obtained for a similar investment in blood, money, and human energy.

This, in a nutshell, is the overall thesis that emerges from an evaluation of four strategic "packages" evolved by successive Israeli governments in the course of the periods 1949–56, 1957–67, 1967–73, and 1974–84, respectively.[33] Each such package offered its own solutions to five key policy problems:

1. What military capabilities should be constructed, and how should they be organized in relation to space?
2. Could alliances strengthen Israel's deterrence and, if so, with what powers and under what terms?

3. What are Israel's essential security margins, and to what extent this should be reflected in the enunciation of casi belli and specified "red lines"?

4. Should Israel's force employment doctrines deliberately emphasize preemption, retaliation, and escalation (both vertically—in weapon systems—and horizontally—in space), and to what extent should they be publicly enunciated in advance?

5. How should the preferred strategic package be related to constraints imposed by domestic politics, and what should be done to ensure that the domestic political process strengthens the nation's deterrent?

Although in principle all Israeli governments to date have addressed themselves to more or less the same agenda, each government has evolved its own peculiar mix of strategic preferences. The emphasis in the first package, during the 1949–56 period, was primarily defensive—namely, on deterrence by denial. The second package, which evolved between the Sinai campaign and the Six-Day War, shifted the emphasis markedly to deterrence by punishment. The third package, adopted beween the 1967 and the 1973 wars, sought unsuccessfully to adapt the previous package to the geostrategic configuration that resulted from the victory of 1967. Finally, the fourth package, which is still in force at the time of writing, reverted again to deterrence by punishment, though attenuated by the bitter experience in Lebanon and by the spectacular rise of Syria's power.

The most important stimulus for change in each of these strategic packages was the occurrence of a major war. This is reflected, for example, in the seesaw movement from denial to punishment, back to denial, and then halfway back to punishment again. Revisions, however, were never carried out as systematically as might be suggested by this analytically convenient packaging of prevailing concepts. An almost equally important source of transition from one package to another was the fragmented, unstructured, incremental, occasionally almost chaotic nature of the decision-making process. There were, however, important differences in this respect between governments. As long as David Ben Gurion was still at the helm, Israeli strategy evolved within the parameters of his own comprehensive and more or less coherent strategic-political concept. To be sure, even under this grand old man, cardinal decisions were often made incrementally. But the breadth of his strategic-political vision, his overbearing stature, his subordinates' utter personal loyalty to him, his firm insulation of the defense establishment from any competing political advocacies (for which he would be subsequently accused of "politicization" of the military)[34]—all these ensured an overall consistency in action and, in particular, a prudent balance between political ends and strategic-military means.

Under Ben Gurion's successors, some of them his own devout disciples, the defense establishment became more democratic (that is, more permeable to a variety of contending advocacies), but this was achieved at the cost of the disruption of internal balance and conceptual cohesion. A foretaste of things to come could be observed during 1954, when Ben Gurion retired to a kibbutz in the Negev Desert and his powers were divided incoherently between Moshe Sharett (as prime minister and minister of foreign affairs); Pinchas Lavon (as minister of defense); and, in effect, Moshe Dayan (as chief of staff of the IDF). The damage done during this brief interlude, though substantial, was at last controlled by Ben Gurion himself upon his return to power in February 1955.

Not so, however, after Ben Gurion's final retirement from politics in 1963. Levi Eshkol, Golda Meir, Moshe Dayan, Yitzhak Rabin, Menachem Begin, Ezer Weizman, Moshe Arens, Ariel Sharon, and Shimon Peres could each for the most part draw on an exceedingly rich practical experience, including for some of them a long and distinguished career in the armed forces or in the civilian management of national security. Although some of them tended to articulate their opinions in the grandiloquent style of Ben Gurion, most of them proved far less capable than Ben Gurion of striking an optimal balance among the five main items on the nation's deterrence agenda.

Levi Eshkol, on the one hand, and Menachem Begin and Ariel Sharon, on the other, failed to manage the domestic political dimension. Whereas the former inspired loss of confidence in his government, the latter two had such a divisive impact that at moments they seemed to be driving the Israeli polity to the verge of civil war. Golda Meir was not a great success in this sense, either; but her worst mistake was the failure to notice in time an ever-widening gap between the government's overall political disposition and the IDF's operational doctrines.

By contrast, Yitzhak Rabin and Shimon Peres, as prime minister and minister of defense, respectively, cannot be blamed for any dramatic calamity. But they can be faulted for having permitted the IDF to grow quantitatively above and beyond what the Israeli economy could conceivably bear. This was partly due to sheer panic in the aftermath of the Yom Kippur War. But it may also have reflected a certain failure of perception of the optimal manner in which the IDF should be organized, deployed, and employed.

Moreover, the decline in Israeli strategic thinking was paradoxically accelerated, perhaps even created, by the rise in influence over policymaking of professional soldiers and national security bureaucrats. Under Ben Gurion the influence of so-called micro military thinking over macro, grand strategic policies was relatively limited. Ben Gurion's immediate successor, Levi Eshkol, however, was far less capable of acting as a political devil's advocate against technical and essentially tactical military advice. The result was that professional, technical, micro military definitions of situations and choices of responses had a disproportionate influence over the policies of his government.

Golda Meir, Eshkol's successor as prime minister, fell into the same trap. Her own minister of defense, Moshe Dayan, was, to be sure, a far more sophisticated political-strategic thinker than were Eshkol's aides. Contrary to his image as an unruly and brusque warrior, however, Dayan proved strangely passive, almost fatalistic, whenever his better strategic-political judgment was incompatible with the views of the domineering, but unimaginative, Mrs. Meir. Consequently, Meir's views, which were greatly influenced by the advocacies of such military technocrats as Generals Bar-Lev and Elazar, ultimately prevailed.

With Rabin's advent to the prime ministership, this process, whereby able military and civilian experts were promoted to their level of declining competence, reached its peak. For the next three years (1974–77), Israel's national security was entrusted to a leading ministerial team whose apprenticeship had been overwhelmingly within the military and civilian bureaucracies. Yesterday's outstanding technocrats of national security thus became today's somewhat less impressive policymakers.

Menachem Begin seemed, during his first two years in office, to have pushed the pendulum back to the Ben Gurion model. Here at last, or so it seemed, was a prime minister with a broader vision, who would be able to strike a more promising balance between the political-strategic macro and the military-tactical micro approaches. Such hopes, however, were dashed even before the end of Begin's first term. In his fourth year in office, national security was virtually the monopoly of the chief of staff, Rafael Eitan, one of the bravest, yet also one of the most simpleminded soldiers in Israel's history. Then, in 1982, Eitan was subordinated to Sharon, a person whose pretense as a grand strategist had proved far in excess of his actual competence in this sphere.

Sharon's ouster in disgrace from the Ministry of Defense in February 1983 brought about the nomination of Arens, the very epitome of the national security technocrat. After the elections of 1984, Arens was replaced by Yitzhak Rabin, this time as minister of defense in a government headed by Shimon Peres. The continuity of this pattern, whereby military and managerial experts were placed at the apex of national security decision making, was thus maintained.

In retrospect it appears that the cumulative consequences of this decline in strategic vision, political wisdom, and leadership since the departure of Ben Gurion were dismal. Deterrence became identified exclusively with the denial to the adversary of any territorial gains and with a tactical war-winning capability (*ko'ach hakhra'a* in Hebrew). The subtler *political* dimensions of deterrence—and, in particular, the impact of Israeli action on Arab motivation and the role which power multipliers such as alliances, casi belli, and domestic consensus play in the cultivation and maintenance of deterrence was—increasingly overlooked. The problem at hand was perceived as primarily one of keeping abreast of the arms race with the Arabs and holding on with dogged determination to the bulk of the territory that the IDF had captured in the 1967 war.

What added impetus to this process, above and beyond the decline in the intellectual quality of strategic-political leadership, was the ever-deepening domestic schism. The Israeli national security machinery, at all its levels, is a

:tion of Israeli society. When the latter enjoyed a high degree
performance of the IDF reflected that consensus accurately.
came increasingly divided by a schism between territorial max-
nalists, between messianic dreamers who overlooked the needs
d cynical pragmatists who neglected the longer-term implications of their actions altogether, between supporters of the war in Lebanon and
opponents of this war, the IDF could not be insulated. The result was an inci-
pient and diffuse, yet nevertheless significant, perversion of strategic-political
thinking by ideological, bureaucratic, and even sheer personal preferences.

The growing poverty of Israeli strategy led some observers to the conclusion that Israel's conventional deterrence had become a chimera. "Can one really
talk about Israeli deterrence?" One prominent Israeli scholar asked shortly after
the Yom Kippur War.

> After all, the term [deterrence] is borrowed from the world of nuclear powers,
> which have the capacity for mutual destruction, which, owing to the glaring
> asymmetry between Israel and the Arabs, does not pertain to the Arab–Israeli
> conflict. Moreover, one should not overlook the fact that Israel's deterence
> has never survived longer than was required for the Arabs to build capabilities
> which would be adequate to overcome their fears born out of their latest defeat.
> In this sense, Arab defeats proved to be more of a stimulus for further wars.
> Thus [it may be argued] under the psychological conditions generated by the
> asymmetry in resources in which the Arabs have such a clear edge (above all
> in their own eyes), it seems that conceptualizing Israeli strategy in terms of
> conventional deterrence is more misleading than helpful.[35]

It did not take very long for such views to be extended to their seemingly
logical conclusion: Israel has no alternative but to disclose a nuclear option
and, in fact, to turn nuclear devices from weapons of last resort to an integral
part of the "normal" order of battle. Moshe Dayan muttered something to this
effect in the immediate aftermath of the Yom Kippur War, when he and most
Israelis were still recovering from the shockwaves of this "earthquake."[36] Nor
was it long before Dayan's cryptic comments were echoed in academe.[37] By
1982 the thesis that Israel should "go public with the bomb" had given rise
to a well-documented and elegantly argued book-length study. Unperturbed
by the fact that throughout the West a massive movement for a nuclear freeze
was fast gaining respectability, this study advocated openly and unreservedly
that Israel should introduce an explicit nuclear strategy to buttress its
presumably failing conventional deterrence.[38]

Whether or not Israel's disclosure of a nuclear strategy has already become
pertinent depends, in the final anlaysis, on an evaluation of its conventional
deterrence. If a detailed reappraisal, such as in the present study, were to lead
to the conclusion that Israel's conventional deterrence has already outlived its
usefulness, the inescapable implication would be that a nuclear deterrent has

become the only alternative. But this is not the main finding of this st
Although the discussion that follows is critical of many aspects of Israel's
strategic conduct, it also leads to an unequivocal rejection of the notion that
the Jewish state should introduce nuclear weapons into its regular strategic
arsenal. Israel's conventional deterrence has not always been optimal, and often
it was substantially weakened by ill-advised Israeli policies. It still remains viable,
however, and it can be reinforced further by steps that are within Israel's capacity.

These theses emerge from a discussion of the four observed strategic
packages. Chapter 2 of this book focuses on the 1949–56 period, the formative
years in which the ground rules of Israeli strategic-military doctrine took shape.
Chapter 3 pursues the topic further against the background of the 1957–67
decade, the era in which Israel's concept of conventional deterrence was first
consciously articulated. Chapter 4 traces the conceptual, strategic, and political
dynamics that caused the pendulum to swing back to an essentially defen-
sive/denial posture during the 1967–73 period. Chapter 5 discusses the partial
shift back to something resembling deterrence by punishment. Finally, chapter
6 reassembles the various strands of the analysis and addresses the question of
whether or not an Israeli nuclear strategy is inevitable in the foreseeable future.

Period — Strategic Package / Issue Area	1949 – 1956	1957 – 1967	1967 – 1973	1974 – 1984
Capabilities and Force Structure				
Threats				
Alliances				
Force Employment Predispositions				
The Domestic Political Backdrop				
Outcome: The Prevailing Strategic Package				

Figure 1–1. The Organization of the Study

Even though some of the titles may suggest otherwise, the agenda remains the same throughout the discussion: every part begins—as figure 1–1 illustrates—with the topic of capabilities and force structure and then moves on to the topics of alliances, threats, force-employment dispositions, and the relevant domestic political backdrop. Hence, whereas in its ensemble the study tells the history of Israeli strategy, separately its component parts constitute comparable case studies. This methodology facilitates a modest attempt in chapter 7, the final chapter of the book, to draw from the examination of the Israeli experience some broader theoretical thoughts about the nature of conventional deterrence.

2
The Formative Years: 1949–1956

At about 4:00 P.M. on Friday, May 14, 1948, Israel proclaimed its independence. During its first twenty-four hours, the Jewish state was recognized by the United States and the Soviet Union and invaded by the armies of five Arab states. For the next eight months the focus of Israeli attention was the Arab invasion. The strategic concepts that emerged were designed to deal with the immediate situation at hand. The armed forces, which hastily came into existence, were tailored to immediate needs. Weapons were purchased haphazardly by stealth and deceit, from government depots and from private merchants of death according to availability rather than to any coherent concept of requirements. The question was not how to win the war but, at least during the first three months, how not to lose it.

The war ended early in 1949, with mixed results. A decisive victory was obtained over Lebanon. The Lebanese lost all appetite for further fighting while the Israelis held a small portion of southern Lebanon. The war also ended with a virtual rout of the Egyptian army. A small contingent of Egyptians still held on tenaciously to an enclave in the middle of the Israeli-controlled Negev Desert. But the IDF had captured portions of the Egyptian Sinai and were stopped from advancing deeper into Egyptian territory only by British and U.S. threats underlined by actual British involvement in the fighting on the side of Egypt.

The situation on the Syrian and Jordanian fronts, however, was different. The Syrian army succeeded in capturing three minuscule parts of the Galilee, Israel's northern region, and all Israeli attempts to dislodge the Syrians were unsuccessful. Ultimately Israel could perhaps win this contest, but it would mean prolonging the war and risking friction with great powers such as France and the United States. So Israel turned to diplomacy, involving both inducements and some veiled threats, as the chief means of attempting to force the Syrians out.

The situation on the Jordanian front was to a certain extent similar. Jordan, like Syria, did not lose the war. In fact the Arab Legion—as the British-commanded army of the Kingdom of Transjordan was then called—denied the IDF victory wherever the two armies clashed. Thus by the end of the war, Jordanian forces controlled most of the areas west of the Jordan River that the

U.N. Partition Resolution of November 1947 had allotted for a Palestinian Arab state. Although some Israelis viewed this situation as both a calamity of historic proportions and an unmitigated strategic disaster, the unchallenged leader of the Jewish state in the course of the war, head of the provisional government David Ben Gurion, was basically inclined to accept this outcome. Insisting that Israel should retain control at least over parts of Jerusalem, he was inclined to believe that Jordanian control over what otherwise would be a Palestinian state would save Israel from both domestic and international pressures that it would find virtually impossible to withstand. Informed by such a definition of the situation at hand, Ben Gurion warded off the pressures of some of his lieutenants and of some of his political opponents and gradually inched Israel toward acceptance of Jordanian control over Judea and Samaria. For the next nineteen years (1949–67), these areas would be referred to as the West Bank of the Kingdom of Jordan.[1]

As far as can be judged, Ben Gurion's ultimate design was to forge a peace treaty with Jordan on the basis of the cease-fire lines at the end of the 1948 war. This would break up irreparably the already-tattering Arab coalition while stifling the clamor of the Palestinian Arabs for independence under the (then) seemingly imposing structure of a British-supported Jordanian-Palestinian state.[2] Logical as it may have seemed at the time, the Ben Gurion–Abdullah design was ultimately thwarted by the latter's Palestinian Arab opponents. King Abdullah was assassinated by a Palestinian sent by the king's arch enemy, the grand mufti of Jerusalem. The armistice agreements negotiated between Israel, on the one hand, and Lebanon, Syria, Jordan, and Egypt, on the other hand, during the spring and summer of 1949, which were supposed to be a major step toward peace, became instead a means by which the Arabs could gain time while engaging Israel in a military, economic, and political war of attrition. Simultaneously the Arabs were preparing for what they called a second round (the 1948 war being the first round in this match). In fact, the agreements merely obliged Israel to accept the authority of a U.N. Truce Supervision Organization (UNTSO), without imparting to this body a corresponding ability to restrain Israel's adversaries.[3]

The unraveling of the armistice and the dashing of Israel's anticipation of a quick transition from a state of war to a state of peace caused both chagrin and alarm—all the more so since it took place against the background of adverse international developments from the Israeli point of view. Specifically, the most important change taking place during the 1949–56 period was the decline of British and French status in the Middle East and the gradual replacement of their historic rivalry by the global East–West conflict.[4]

Initially this epochal process worked in Israel's favor, as was dramatically illustrated by the instant recognition of the new state by both superpowers at the very moment in which they were heading to the brink of war in what came to be known as the Berlin crisis. Before long, however, the evolving cold war interjected into the Middle East a superpower race for Arab favor. From this point of view it was no accident that the polarizing global conflict coincided with the gradual collapse of the Israeli–Arab armistice regime. After all, Israel's adversaries were clearly unwilling to make peace even when military defeat seemed to have conclusively proved their inability to stand up to the Jewish state. The evidence of U.S.–Soviet rivalry over Arab friendship must have therefore reinforced the Arabs' conviction that denying Israel peace, and even accelerating the preparations for another war, did not carry with it any intolerable international penalty.

If mounting Arab hostility on the one hand and international isolation on the other were two critical determinants of Israeli strategy during its formative years, the Jewish state's domestic weakness was a third important factor. At independence Israel had a population of 600,000 Jews, but within the period under discussion this number more than doubled. The balance of nearly a million new citizens was made up of immigrants from eastern and central Europe, from the Middle East, and from North Africa.[5]

Broadly speaking, the existing political and social structure that the Jewish state inherited from the Yishuv—the organized Jewish community in Palestine under the British Mandate—was extraordinarily flexible and proved eminently capable of absorbing the newcomers. But although the spectacular increase in the state's population was a boon in the long run, it inescapably weakened the new nation in the short run. The postindependence new immigrants, unlike a significant portion of those who had come before World War II, had not arrived out of choice and ideological motivation. Rather, they were for the most part immigrants of necessity, uprooted refugees who came because they had nowhere else to go. Their professional and occupational preparation for life in the new country had been minimal. Most of them had come from urban centers, whereas Israel's first national priority in the early 1950s was, to use the slogan of that time, "From Town to Country." These immigrants came to a country that was just emerging from a war that had taken a toll of nearly one percent of the population and had cost more than the budget of a whole fiscal year. They were housed in tents and tin shacks within poverty-stricken compounds run by impatient and often insensitive and condescending government officials. They were transferred from place to place, humiliated, bossed around, and then settled in locations that might have seemed logical in the overall planning scheme but could not possibly have made much sense to the bewildered immigrants themselves. For them, the concept of an independent Jewish state may well have become associated with unemployment, austerity, bureaucracy, an inordinate degree of government intervention in daily life, black marketeering—and with consequent alienation, deprivation, disorientation, and demoralization: in fact, with all the ingredients of both personal and collective insecurity.[6]

Such were, broadly speaking, the background conditions, the psychological and operational environments, in which Israeli strategic-political thinking began to take shape. It was with such perceptions of the dangers at home and abroad that all decisions were made relating to military capabilities, threats and commitments, external alignments, and the use of force. These conditions led initially to a strategic concept emphasizing defense rather than deterrence. Then, as the external noose seemed to be tightening, as the arms race took its course, as technology on the one hand and fear of a domestic crisis on the other forced Israeli decision makers to take stock of their policies, the emphasis increasingly tilted toward deterrence. The details of this learning process shed light not only on the evolution of Israeli strategic thinking but, arguably, also on some of the most intricate problems, choices, and strategic dilemmas that any nation in adversity is forced to face.

Capabilities: Manpower, Firepower, and Deployment

In a broad sense the term *capabilities,* like the term *power,* connotes an infinitesimal number of factors. Weapons are capabilities; likewise, the quality and quantity of manpower are dimensions of a state's military capabilities; so are its size, geography, climate, population distribution, road system, level of industrialization, level of education, quality of leadership, and of course morale. Most of this list, however, is as trite as it is impossible to pin down to policy-relevant specifics.

This is not the case with the three dimensions of military capabilities that every government must address—namely, manpower, weapons, and the deployment of manpower and weapons over space. *Manpower* relates to the problem of making the most effective use of the available human resources for the nation's security. *Weapons,* the second of these critical dimensions, relates to the optimal choice of arms or, in a sense, to the maximization of overall national firepower at the lowest possible outlay. *Deployment,* the third critical issue, relates to the method of dispersing manpower and firepower over space with a view to maximizing deterrence or, at least, the ability to defend national territory from likely external threats.

In the Israeli experience the most important decisions relating to manpower allocation were made even before the end of the 1948 war. The gigantic war effort in the face of the invasion manifested itself first and foremost in the fact that by September 1948, 112,000 recruits, or close to 15 percent of the population, had been called to the flag. This staggering degree of mobilization enabled the IDF to assemble in the latter stages of the war an armed force of nearly 100,000 soldiers.[7] Thus although the total population of the Jewish state was no more than roughly 700,000, whereas the total population of its adversaries numbered close to 30 million, the new state's fighting force at its peak was larger in absolute terms than those of its five Arab adversaries combined.[8] The long-term implication of this state of affairs was starkly clear. If

Israel wished to maintain a capacity to defend itself in the future, it would have to reduce the army of 1948 to a far smaller size. Recognizing this fact earlier than did most of his colleagues, the minister of defense of the provisional government, David Ben Gurion, pressed his subordinates as early as the summer of 1948—in other words, six months before the termination of hostilities—to take steps to reduce the size of the army. A special task force was set up for the purpose of studying the problem, and an agreed-on solution was already thrashed out before the end of the year.

The task force drew inspiration from two sources: the experience of the Jewish defense organization under the British Mandate and the structure of the Swiss army. During the years 1938–48, the Jewish defense organization in Palestine rested on a system that combined a small kernel of a strategic reserve, the PALMACH (Hebrew acronym for "strike companies"); a larger network of territorially based field forces, the HISH (Hebrew acronym for "field forces"); and an even larger network of a home guard, the HIM (Hebrew acronym for "guard force"). All three organizations were based on a voluntary service and, for long periods, on the clandestine affiliation of an otherwise civilian population. The PALMACH, however, was based on a small number (roughly six companies) of younger, better-trained, and more intensely motivated volunteers, who lived on kibbutzim (collective farms) and spent at least part of their time working on these farms in order to pay their upkeep. The HISH drew a far larger number of volunteers of a lower combat quality. They were for the most part ordinary citizens who, along with their private occupations and trades, also devoted some time to training and to the implementation of various operational orders. The HIM was similar, but it was incapable of carrying out any duties other than the protection of its members' own communities.

The Swiss system, which a number of senior Israeli officers studied in some detail during 1949–50, offered a thoroughly tested method whereby the voluntary prestatehood structure could be adapted to the long-term needs of an independent state. In this system a small nucleus of regular and conscripted personnel trains, maintains depots and command structures, and carries out routine security duties. This nucleus is also available in the event of an emergency and should be able to hold its ground for several days against a surprise attack. The bulk of the armed strength consists, however, of reserves—namely, civilians who were previously trained as conscripts and who are permanently assigned to operational units. Every reserve soldier takes home his personal military equipment, including weapons. In the event of an emergency, they are called back to active duty while the small kernel of regulars holds the line. As soon as the call-up of reserves is completed, the main burden of military operations until the end of hostilities falls on them. They are, in the final analysis, the backbone of the state's fighting force. This system appeared ideally suited to Israeli needs. It could facilitate the maintenance of a large army with high professional standards without imposing an unacceptable burden on the national economy. Since the experience of the Yishuv before statehood was not dissimilar to the proposed new system, it was realistic to hope, as Israeli planners did, that the IDF could revert to such a structure swiftly, cheaply, and effectively.

During the deliberations leading to the final blueprint, the following aspects were especially emphasized. The permanent nucleus of regulars and conscripts would have to be limited to roughly 30 percent of the total available manpower. Regular service for conscripts would have to be compulsory, universal, and at least two years long. The proportion of combat-ready "teeth" to logistical "tail" would have to be exceedingly rigorous, so that very few potential combatants would be wasted in noncombat duties. Women should serve, too, in order to reduce the need for able-bodied men in the logistical "tail." Reserve units would participate fully in both routine security duties and all-out war situations. The reserves would not be an auxiliary militia but part and parcel of a unified command structure that draws no lines between professional regulars and part-time amateurs. The entire system would have to rely on a first-rate intelligence operation capable of providing an alert of at least seventy-two hours in which the reserves could be called up. Finally, the performance standards of the reservists would be maintained through intensive training periods every year that would not, however, last longer than thirty to forty days per individual reservist, irrespective of rank.

It took less than two years for a system based on these guiding principles to be worked out and put into effect. It was not fully universal because ultra-orthodox Jews, non-Jewish citizens, and women with fewer than ten years of formal education were exempted from the very beginning. All the other guidelines, however, were more or less observed. The upshot was that the forces in being of the IDF were reduced from some 90,000 to about 35,000, but its total strength on call soon exceeded the wartime peak. The system was tested several times during 1950–53, and the call-up methods were further improved. In the future they would include a choice not only between total and partial mobilization, but also between a publicly announced and a secret call-up.[9]

In retrospect, it seems that one important reason that the transition from full mobilization to a reserve-based army proved so relatively smooth was that the IDF of 1948 was, in terms of its weapons, an infantry army. To be sure, at the end of the war the IDF already had two partly mechanized brigades (out of a total of about twelve brigades), each containing one fully armored battalion. In addition, the IDF also had an air arm, the Israeli Air Force (IAF), consisting of a few dozen planes of various piston-engine types, as well as a tiny naval command, the Israel Navy (IN), consisting of a handful of corvettes, frigates, PT boats, and the like.[10] Such an army, with its heavy emphasis on only partly mobile units of riflemen, had neither extensive training requirements nor a significant problem of maintenance and logistics. Two and a half years of service could easily produce well-trained soldiers, a great number of petty officers, and an adequate number of qualified noncommissioned officers.

These could be reassigned into reserve units and keep up their basic professional standards on the basis of thirty or forty days of service per year.

This state of affairs persisted with only minor changes until the fall of 1955. During this period, arms supplies to the Middle East were under the tight control of the three leading Western powers, which were more or less successful in maintaining a stable arms control regime as had been envisaged by the Tripartite Declaration of May 25, 1950. There was, to be sure, a steady growth in the military expenditures of both Israel and its adversaries. Indeed, Ben Gurion reportedly boasted on one occasion that the IDF had succeeded in trebling its strength in terms of manpower and equipment.[11] But this did not result in a revolutionary change in the IDF's order of battle: infantry remained the backbone. No new mechanized units were added to the two original post-1948 brigades. The IAF began to move into the jet age with the acquisition in 1953 of small quantities of British Meteor (subsonic) jet fighters and subsequently of the slightly more advanced French-built Ouragans and Mystères. But the main force of the IAF remained piston-engine fighters and interceptors such as the Messerschmidt, the Mosquito, the Mustang P-51, and the Spitfire.[12]

The Egyptian–Czech arms deal announced on September 27, 1955, however, heralded an entirely new era, in which the IDF's infantry-based force was no longer adequate. According to IDF intelligence sources, in 1955 Egypt was due to receive within a few months 120 MIG-15 jet fighters, 50 Ilyushin-28 twin-engine bombers, 14 Ilyushin-14 transport planes, 60 half-tracks with 122-mm guns, 200 armored troop carriers, 275 T-34 and Stalin III tanks, 56 130-mm multiple rocket launchers, 100 self-propelled SU-100 tank destroyers, a few hundred field guns of various calibers, 2 destroyers, 15 minesweepers, 2 submarines, 150 heavy vehicles, as well as radar systems and recoilless guns.[13]

The Egyptian army at that time consisted of sixteen brigades, of which anywhere from nine to eleven were deployed along the Israeli border. The IDF estimated that by the spring of 1956 this Egyptian force would complete the absorption of the new Soviet weapons and would thus be ready to launch a full-scale war. In the face of this prospect, the immediate response in Israel was to try to expand the total size of the IDF (reserve and regular together) from eleven to fourteen brigades, thereby exhausting the reservoir of qualified manpower. Simultaneously Israel stepped up its efforts to obtain arms from France. Because of the growing French preoccupation with Egypt's support for the Algerian rebels, the French responded favorably to Israel's requests. Consequently, by the early summer of 1956 the IDF already had 60 additional Mystère A-4 jets, 6 more Ouragans, half a dozen more Meteors, 5 S-55 helicopters, 120 French-built light AMX-13 tanks, 80 U.S.-built M-1 (Sherman) tanks, 75 Hyspano-Swiza 30-mm antiaircraft guns, large quantities of Belgian FN semiautomatic rifles and light machine guns, front-wheel-drive vehicles, bazookas, and radar systems.[14]

The acquisition of these new weapons soon generated pressures for a reappraisal of the IDF's deployment doctrine. One of the lessons of the 1948 war was that the regular armed forces were not Israel's only shield against an Arab attack. During the first phase of the Arab invasion (May 15–June 11, 1948), the advance of the Arab armies was largely checked by a chain of isolated and seemingly weak settlements. Many of these "points" (as they were called at the time) had been established during the decade prior to the outbreak of the 1948 war explicitly with a view to augmenting the defensive capacity of the Yishuv. Each one of them separately did not amount to much as a military unit. Kibbutzim such as Deganya near the Sea of Galilee, or Ramat Rachel in the southern approaches of Jerusalem, or Yad Mordechai and Negba in the south, had no more than a hundred to two hundred members (including children and women); no more than a few scores of combatants (often including reinforcements); and only a small quantity of light firearms. But they were organized from the start as paramilitary units in disguise; they were surrounded by trenches, fences, and mine fields; and, most important, they were very successful in exacting a high price from the invading Arab armies, in causing the latter's morale to falter, and in substantially deflating the Arabs' overall zeal to fight and confidence in their ability to do so.

During roughly 1949–54 the Israelis remained persuaded that the Arabs had not yet recovered from their defeat. The Jewish state, on the other hand—despite some morale problems of its own—was still caught up in a mood of self-confidence.[15] From such a perspective it is understandable that segments of the Israeli military and political leadership assumed (until the Egyptian–Czech arms deal) that settlements could be employed as an important instrument of national security. The advocates of this method contended that a more or less contiguous chain of settlements should be established along all the boundaries as a means of underscoring the legitimacy of these lines as well as a substitute for a lack of strategic depth. Such a chain of paramilitary "hedgehogs," together with the small kernel of regulars, would be able to deny any significant territorial gains to any combination of Arab forces during the first seventy-two hours after an Arab assault. This in turn would buy time in which the reserves could be called up and brought to the front.[16]

In order to put this system into effect without delay, the Israeli government initiated two parallel operations. The first of these was to establish as quickly as resources permitted a line of settlements along all armistice boundaries. This was achieved by settling civilians, including a great number of bewildered new immigrants who had almost no inkling of the overall strategic purpose that their presence there was supposed to serve. The second operation was to set up NAHAL (Hebrew acronym for "pioneering fighting youth") settlements.

The NAHAL program was an extension into the IDF of an element that greatly resembled the prestatehood PALMACH. But although NAHAL volunteers came from political-ideological organizations, all traces of such affiliations were suppressed for the duration of their service. The NAHAL boys (the units also included girls) received advanced infantry training, normally within the paratroop corps. They also participated extensively in small-scale military operations. But at least half their tour of duty was spent on a kibbutz, and, toward the conclusion of their service, they were expected to settle somewhere and thus establish a new frontier *nekudah* ("point"). The NAHAL settlement, it was hoped, would ultimately mature into a self-supporting civilian community capable of being incorporated effectively into the state's Spatial Defense system.[17]

The NAHAL proved extremely effective. It led to the creation of a great number of new frontier settlements, which added an important element of security: they acted as a kind of a substitute for strategic depth and for large border garrisons. At the same time, however, NAHAL, drawing as it did on the prime of Israel's youth, soon became the cause of a perennial dispute concerning IDF manpower allocation. Whereas David Ben Gurion, the prime minister and minister of defense during this period, was unreservedly committed to the idea, Chief of Staff Moshe Dayan argued that NAHAL drained a critical ferment from the rest of the IDF. If the best and the brightest, argued the chief of staff, were dispersed throughout the army, they would bring about an upgrading of standards of performance throughout the IDF. If, on the other hand, they were all concentrated in a small elite unit and spent half their service working as farmers, then the impact of their talents and superb motivation would be somewhat lost. Ben Gurion would not accept Dayan's arguments, however, and NAHAL was not disbanded.[18]

The second method of incorporating the Spatial Defense system into the country's military structure was through its organization *qua* military units. The individual frontier settlement, whether a kubbutz (fully collective community), a *moshav* (partly collective farming community), a *moshava* (an old, established small town) or a so-called Development Town (a more recent type of frontier small town) was in one sense an ordinary social unit. Its population was mixed and included as many women, children, and senior citizens as able-bodied men. Its inhabitants did not wear uniforms, and the atmosphere was always casual and perfectly civilian in character. All locales that were incorporated into the Spatial Defense system, however, also had a parallel identity as military units in almost the full sense of the term. Each locale was designated a "region" (*ezor*). The region would normally have a *MA'AZ* (Hebrew acronym for "regional commanding officer")—namely, an experienced person, normally a former junior officer or noncommissioned officer, who would be entrusted officially with the authority of a commanding officer in the event of an emergency. At his disposal would be both men and arms, organized as a military unit with a clear division of labor and a chain of command. The equipment, including rifles, machine guns, bazookas, mines, grenades, torchlights, first-aid gear, and the like, would be kept in good order in a special place allotted to it by the government.

A cluster of such regions would fall into a bloc (*goush*—namely, a proper, full-time, military headquarters with a complete staff headed by a lieutenant-colonel or a major). The *goush* headquarters would be in charge of all military operations in that area during war and also be in charge of local intelligence operations, equipment maintenance, and training of personnel in peacetime. In addition to the manpower in the various locales, a *goush* would also have at its disposal preassigned reinforcements, a kind of strategic reserve for operations within the area under its command as well as in its immediate vicinity. Finally, a *goush* would also have elements of heavier weaponry, including field guns, as well as a certain engineering capacity.

All the *goushim* (plural of *goush*) would be coordinated by a special corps at General Staff level termed HAGMAR (acronym for "Spatial Defense"). Thus a structure embracing the entire country was set up with a view to augmenting the IDF's ability to cope with the country's defense in the event of a surprise attack or, as was expected in the early 1950s, of a replay of the 1948 invasion. Yet, logical and neat as it may have seemed in the aftermath of the 1948 war, the Spatial Defense system was challenged as soon as the Arab–Israeli arms race began to pick up momentum.

To be effective, the Spatial Defense system had to be reasonably well endowed with resources. These, however, had to be drained from other operations. Hence as the arms race was confronting the IDF with urgent, new, and increasingly expensive requirements, the temptation grew to reduce the budget allotted for Spatial Defense. Before the Egyptian–Syrian–Czech arms deliveries of September–December 1955, the pressures to cut back appropriations for Spatial Defense could still be somehow contained. But the influx of vast quantities of sophisticated Soviet weapons to Egypt and Syria called for an abrupt reappraisal of all previously held concepts, including that of Spatial Defense. (See figure 2–1.)

The strategic rationale for phasing out the Spatial Defense system can be summed up as follows. The urgent need for a major effort to match the Egyptian and Syrian buildup called for a staggering rise in both financial and manpower requirements. As a result, Israel was in fact losing its previous ability to maintain both an offensive and an extensive Spatial Defense system. Previously, when the IDF's offensive capability rested primarily on lightly equipped infantry, the two elements could be sustained simultaneously and even perceived as complementary. The new dimension that was introduced into the arms race implied that Israel would have to shift its emphasis to a mechanized, jet-age, war-winning capability. This would conceivably enable it to deter its adversaries by a putative ability to destroy any attacking force, whether on the adversary's side of the border or on the Israeli side, within days of the outbreak of hostilities. But this strategy had to forego any attempt to defend settlements. If the adversary succeeded in penetrating Israeli territory, settlements might have to be abandoned in the interest of force concentration and in pursuit of a decisive

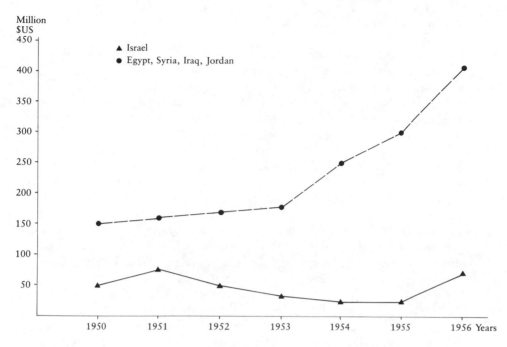

Source: Based on data in Evron, "Two Periods in Arab–Israeli Strategic Relations," p. 115.
In constant $U.S.

Figure 2–1. The Arab–Israeli Arms Race, 1950–1956

battle. Israel's main effort, therefore, should be invested in the construction of large, mechanized "fists" combining speed and firepower and capable of throwing any enemy column off balance.

Theoretically, of course, there was another alternative: shifting the emphasis entirely to a defensive posture while foregoing any offensive option. This alternative, however, made no sense at all. For one thing, the emphasis in the Egyptian and Syrian buildup was markedly on offensive capabilities. Given Israel's elongated shape, its physically exposed boundaries, and its uneven population dispersal (with two-thirds of the population crowded into a small rectangular strip of land along the Mediterranean and the rest of the country only very thinly populated by Jews), the construction of a defensive capability that could match the emerging Arab force would be far more expensive, and ultimately less effective, than shifting the emphasis almost exclusively to the construction of a war-winning offensive capacity. In turn there was no escaping the conclusion that the Spatial Defense system might have to be gradually phased out. The shift from defense (deterrence by denial) to deterrence (by punishment) had begun.[19]

Threats and Commitments

In the wake of the 1948 war, Israel had no clear perception of external threats other than a replay of the Arab invasion. The Arabs, it was assumed, would launch a second invasion if only an opportunity to do so presented itself; but, having been beaten, the Arabs were likely to take a long while to do so. Diplomacy, meanwhile, might be able to transform the armistice agreements into peace treaties, thereby terminating the conflict. That this image of the future was simplistic became crystal clear within less than a year after the cessation of hostilities. According to U.N. resolution 194 passed on December 11, 1948, the world organization set up the Conciliation Commission for Palestine (CCP), whose task was to establish an Arab–Israeli peace. The CCP began its work with a visit to the capitals of all parties to the conflict and then proceeded to convene a conference in Lausanne, Switzerland. By the time this conference opened, in April 1949, bilateral talks between Israel on the one hand and Jordan, Egypt, Syria, and Lebanon on the other were already making significant headway toward the conclusion of bilateral armistice agreements. It was, therefore, not entirely unrealistic to assume that the Lausanne Conference could ultimately lead to peace.[20]

This hope was not to be realized. Although the bilateral armistice negotiations were businesslike and ultimately successful, the multilateral conference degenerated into acrimony as Arab delegates declined to enter into face-to-face negotiations and attempted to outbid one another in a show of militancy toward the Israelis. Faced with this impasse, the CCP ultimately gave up and, on September 19, 1949, called off the conference. This failure had no immediate impact on the situation in the Middle East. For the rest of 1949 and even through 1950, Arab–Israeli relations seemed reasonably stable. Yet gradually, at first almost imperceptibly, the impasse in the political-diplomatic process began to yield serious repercussions. Having lost the war, and propelled by frustration, domestic instability, and rivalry among themselves, the Arabs began to brace for a war against the Jewish state by other means. This took the form of economic boycott, naval blockade, diplomatic quarantine—all on a large scale—a vociferous war of words, as well as small-scale skirmishes along the armistice demarcation lines (as the Israeli borders were officially termed) and various threats to prevent Israel form carrying out a variety of important development projects. Though extensively discussed in Arab official councils, in the Arab League, and in the Arab media, this building up of a sustained campaign against Israel was not the fruit of a coherent master plan. It emerged gradually, slowly giving rise to administrative structures, to policy directives, to military moves and preparations. In Israeli eyes, however, it all added up to an image of a rapidly tightening noose. The upshot was, at first, an incremental chain of political and military reactions and, subsequently, the official and authoritative delineation by Israel of some of these threatening actions as casi

belli—provocations that, if not stopped, would ultimately lead Israel to resort
to force. The details of this process, in which Israel gradually evolved a posture
of deterrence, are worth studying at some length.

Freedom of Navigation as a Casus Belli

Chronologically, the first event that could be connected to what later became
a casus belli was the Egyptian decision, after the conclusion of the armistice,
not to lift the ban on Israeli shipping through the Suez Canal that Egypt had
imposed in December 1947, relaxed in January 1950, and reintroduced on
February 6, 1950, with the publication of a royal decree closing the canal to
Israeli "war contraband" and setting penalties for violations of this decree, including a blacklist. Subsequently the scope of the ban was gradually expanded
to include ships of so-called neutrals (vis-à-vis the Arab–Israeli conflict). With
the publication of further Egyptian restrictions in November and December
1953 which banned the shipping to Israel even of foodstuffs, the Suez Canal
became completely sealed to any shipping, under any flag, to or from Israel.

The Egyptian ban violated the terms of the armistice agreements and
significantly compromised Israel's ability to develop commercial links with Asia
and East Africa. Nevertheless, Israel never declared this Egyptian policy a casus
belli. In fact, Israel confined itself to diplomatic action in the United Nations
and to a number of prodding operations designed to test Egypt's resolve. The
first Israeli reaction was to appeal to the Israel–Egypt Mixed Armistice Commission (MAC). MAC discussed the issue at some length, but its ruling that
the Egyptian act was in violation of the terms of the armistice was ignored.
Israel proceeded to lodge a complaint in the U.N. Security Council. On
September 1, 1950, the council ruled against Egypt. The latter at first responded
in a conciliatory spirit, and a number of ships carrying cargo to Israel were
allowed to pass through the canal in the course of the following two years.
But when Egypt imposed the restrictions of November 1953, Israel lodged
another complaint in the Security Council. On March 29, 1954, the council
once again ruled against Egypt, but the decision was vetoed by the Soviet
Union.[21]

The Soviet veto foreshadowed what became a routine in the ensuing
decades. From the Israeli point of view, this act not only raised the menacing
specter of Soviet support for an Arab war effort but also underscored the futility
of turning to the United Nations. In turn, Israel faced the question of what
to do about Egypt's conduct. Was the ban on shipping to Israel through the
Suez Canal worth the use of force? If so, Israel would have to declare it officially a casus belli. If not, Egypt might be encouraged to think that it could
perhaps push Israel further—as would other Arab states. The latter view was
shared by the IDF and elements in the Ministry of Defense. The prime minister
and minister of foreign affairs of the day, Moshe Sharett, balked at the thought

of committing Israel by declaring the ban a casus belli. He was also apprehensive about the reactions of the Western powers to such an Israeli posture. Consequently, the March 29, 1954, U.N. vote was followed by a prolonged period of infighting within the Israeli government concerning the correct response. Ultimately a compromise was worked out. The *Bat Galim,* a small ship waving an Israeli flag, was sent to sail through the canal in order to test the Egyptians. The latter apprehended the vessel without much ado, and Sharett's government was confronted again by the same dilemma: Was this a casus belli or was it not? Unwilling to go to war over such a dispute, Sharett's cabinet persisted in its reluctance to declare shipping through the canal a casus belli.[22]

Not so, however, in the case of shipping to the port of Eilat, Israel's Red Sea outlet. An Egyptian intention to impose a ban on shipping to and from Eilat could be discerned during the armistice negotiations early in 1949, when, with Saudi permission, Egypt constructed military installations in Sharm el Sheik and on the islands of Tiran and Senafir at the tip of the Sinai peninsula, where the Gulf of Suez and the Gulf of Aqaba meet. Immediately after the signing of the armistice agreements, the Egyptians relaxed their control over passage through these straits. Nevertheless, traffic through these waters was still very limited. The town of Eilat had not yet been established by the Israelis, and Um Rashrash, where Eilat would subsequently be built, had no port facilities capable of servicing commercial shipping. Conversely, as soon as there were signs of an Israeli intention to develop Eilat, the Egyptians moved to block passage through the Sharm el Sheik straits. Early in 1953 they detained a Danish cargo ship en route to Eilat. In September 1953 they treated a Greek vessel in the same way, and on January 1, 1954, they opened fire on a small Italian cargo vessel.[23]

Initially Israel tended to treat the questions of shipping through the Suez Canal and through the straits of Tiran as inseparable. The main reason for this tactic was a lingering hope that the great powers, especially Britain and the United States, which had a vested interest in preserving the freedom of navigation through the Suez Canal, might be able to force the Egyptians to relax their hold on the straits as well. Differently stated, the future of shipping to Eilat was indirectly added as a rider to the question of shipping through the Suez Canal.

This tactical predisposition, however, gave way to a different approach as it became clear that if Israel desisted from using force concerning the Suez Canal, it was powerless to change the Egyptian position.[24] Furthermore, the Israelis became increasingly haunted by fears that made the question of Eilat more burning. Specifically, there were apprehensions that the West, in its anxiety to lure Egypt into a pro-Western alliance structure, would attempt to force Israel to cede the Negev to Egypt and Jordan and thus facilitate territorial contiguity between Egypt and the Fertile Crescent. The evidence that such ideas were seriously being mooted in Britain and the United States was overwhelming.

Consequently, Ben Gurion, who had always regarded the Negev as Israel's only uninhabited reservoir of land, became eager to take every possible step to thwart this design of the Western powers. He decided to settle in the Negev himself in order to set an example that other Israelis might emulate. He upgraded the development of Eilat as a port, as a city, and as a military base to the top of the nation's priorities. In this context there was no escape from sooner or later declaring the Egyptian blockade a casus belli, and Ben Gurion in fact did so for the first time in a public speech on May 6, 1955. Three months later, on August 8, he repeated the same threat in a speech at his party center in which he clearly drew the line between shipping to and from Eilat through the Gulf of Aqaba and shipping through the Suez Canal. Then, on September 29, 1955, he went one step further. In an interview given to the *New York Times,* Ben Gurion explicitly threatened that if Egypt did not lift the blockade within one year, Israel would resort to force. The die was thus cast: Israel's freedom of navigation to and from its southern port and perhaps, by implication, to and from any port, was authoritatively declared a casus belli.[25]

Border Violence as a Casus Belli

While pondering whether or not to declare the Egyptian blockade a casus belli, the Israeli government was faced increasingly by another, equally formidable challenge along its borders. At first this was the result not of any premeditated, coherent plan but, rather, of the fact that Palestinian Arab refugees simply did not recognize—and perhaps did not even fully comprehend—the armistice demarcation lines. For the Israelis, these were borders not only in the legal but also in the cognitive sense. For the bewildered, destitute Palestinian refugees in the Gaza Strip and the West Bank, however, these lines, which were not even very clearly drawn on the ground, simply did not make much sense. The Palestinians could see the sites of their former homes from their present camps. They had been accustomed to walk from, say, Hebron to Gaza, and they could not fully understand why now, because of political negotiations between some remote, faceless Arab and Jewish officials, they could no longer move freely in these parts.

The result was a great deal of what the Israelis saw as illegal infiltration and consequently, insecurity, in border areas, coupled with a growing anxiety on the Israeli side concerning the status of the borders. Still not entirely adjusted to political independence, faced by ample signs that the international community had not yet fully accepted the notion of sovereign Jewish state in Palestine, the Israelis tended to fear that if the tidal wave of infiltration were allowed to continue, it would ultimately serve to delegitimize the Jewish state's boundaries. Moreover, since much of the Jewish population along the frontiers consisted of new immigrants, whose motivation for holding on was low, the Israeli government was haunted by fears of a collapse of the system of border settlements that they had been at pains to consolidate.

As in the case of freedom of navigation, the initial Israeli inclination was to turn to the various MACs (Mixed Armistice Commissions under the aegis of UNTSO), and through them to the U.N. Security Council. But this led nowhere. The main reason was that the only way to stop the infiltration was through disciplinary action by the governments of Lebanon, Syria, Jordan, and Egypt, from whose sovereign territory the infiltrators were coming. These governments had no reason at all to help the Israelis in this (or, in fact, in any) regard. Having lost the 1948 war, they were on the whole delighted to see the Israelis in such a plight; in any case, in terms of both their standing at home and their position in the Arab world as a whole, the governments of Israel's neighbors had no incentive whatsoever to discipline the infiltrators. On the contrary, some even had a positive incentive for boosting this phenomenon.

Perceiving the situation in these terms, the Israelis began to resort to reprisal raids.[26] The term itself was, of course, misleading. It created the impression of a primitive "eye for an eye." To say that the Israelis were entirely beyond such primordial sentiments would be implausible. At the same time, however, their ultimate purpose was political utility rather than psychological satisfaction: Israel could not afford to clash with any one of the Western powers as it might have to if it were to launch a major military operation against its neighbors. This consideration dictated a cautious policy of limited actions, which would serve warning to those governments permitting infiltration from their territory and force them to take measures to stop their own population from crossing the border into Israel. Differently stated, this was a limited form of coercive diplomacy presented publicly as retribution in order to counteract international criticism.[27]

Although in the short run this policy did buy Israel some respite, especially in the case of Jordan, where the British-commanded Arab Legion had no problem understanding the Israeli message,[28] in the long run this policy had a singularly escalatory effect. Infiltration of Palestinian Arab civilians was, in fact, brought to a complete stop. But instead of countering mainly unarmed civilians, the Israelis now began to confront trained commandos and, ultimately, large army units. Thus through a process of runaway escalation, Israel was brought to a point at which it had to decide whether to back down or, alternatively, to continue to escalate until this led to a general war. Backing down might encourage its adversaries to believe that the Jewish state was losing its resolve and that, accordingly, they should step up their pressure in order to exploit their success. Continuing to escalate would, in fact, signal that border insecurity, though emanating from a rather limited form of violence, had become, from the Israeli point of view, a casus belli in the full sense of the term. Given this basic choice, it is not at all surprising that Israel, especially under Ben Gurion as premier but also under Sharett (during 1954–55), preferred to escalate the retributions rather than to back down.

Even Ben Gurion, however, did not go as far as actually threatening to resort to a full-scale war. He stated repeatedly that there would be no tranquility on the Arab side of the border if there was none on the Israeli side. He thundered at Arab governments for perpetrating violence. He delivered strident speeches defying the judgment of the United Nations and challenging the evenhandedness and fairness not only of the Soviet Union but indeed of the Western powers, too. He clearly regarded the insecurity of the border areas as an intolerable situation and attempted, as will be seen, to persuade his cabinet colleagues to initiate a large-scale military operation. But he would not attempt to deter the Arabs from further border violence through the enunciation, openly and unambiguously, that it constituted a casus belli.[29]

Foreign Military Intervention in Neighboring Countries as a Casus Belli

Both the question of free navigation and the problem of border insecurity suggest a simple, almost trite feature of the Israeli approach: the Jewish state was attempting to obtain only the preservation of the status quo that prevailed in the immediate aftermath of the 1948 war. This common denominator of the first two issues in the present discussion was also the hallmark of Israel's third type of casus belli—namely, adverse changes in the political and/or military situation within Jordan, Syria, and Lebanon. Broadly speaking, Israel had no specific ideological preferences insofar as these regimes were concerned. Socialists and liberal democrats for the most part, Israeli leaders were not particularly enamored of the patriarchal and (in Israeli eyes, at least) often thoroughly corrupt regimes in the Arab world. Because of this outlook Israel was initially favorably disposed toward the 1952 Egyptian revolution that ousted King Farouq and brought Nasser to power.[30] This episode notwithstanding, however, Israeli leaders in the final analysis never regarded the ideological complexion of Arab regimes as an issue of any intrinsic consequence. On the other hand, they were very particular about the domestic affairs of Israel's neighbors when these could conceivably lead to a military and political balance not consonant with the security and well-being of the Jewish state.

This attitude focused initially on the Hashemite Kingdom of Jordan and its neighbor to the east, Iraq (until July 1958, the Hashemite Kingdom of Iraq). The Iraqis took part in the 1948 war but, not having a common border with Israel, refused to enter into armistice negotiations after the cessation of hostilities; thus at least technically they remained at war with the Jewish state. The Israelis, for their part, insisted in their bilateral negotiations with Jordan that the Iraqi forces should be withdrawn completely, at least from the West Bank of the Jordanian kingdom. The Jordanians, who in the spring of 1949 realized that Israel had become sufficiently strong to capture the West Bank and who knew that some influential Israelis were, in fact, advocating this step, hastened to comply with the Israeli demand.[31]

During the 1950–56 period, the possibility of Iraqi involvement in Jordan as well as in Syria seemed imminent on a number of occasions. This was particularly true after the Egyptian revolution, when Iraqi–Egyptian rivalry reached a new peak while Jordan became one of the main battlegrounds of this rivalry. Indeed, whenever the regime in Jordan seemed in danger, there would be almost instantly a distinct possibility of Iraqi involvement for the purpose of propping up the Jordanian monarchy.[32]

Although Syria was a republic and was not ruled by relatives of the Iraqi royal family, its internal circumstances at that time were not dissimilar to those of Iraq. For one thing, a succession of coup d'états demonstrated the extreme fragility of the Syrian regime. As in Jordan, moreover, Syria was divided down the middle between pro- and anti-Nasserists, with the latter being almost automatically pro-Iraqi and ipso facto pro-Western, and the former taking a pro-Soviet line. To make matters even more confusing, the Hashemite regime of Iraq nurtured an aspiration for the creation of a Fertile Crescent Union under Iraqi suzerainty.

The Soviets were actively and single-mindedly wooing the pro-Egyptian elements in Syria, whereas the Western powers were divided. France objected to the Anglo-American idea of a Baghdad pact and, therefore, made little effort to encourage Syria, where it still had a measure of influence, to join the proposed treaty organization. Britain and the United States both favored Syrian participation in the pact because they sought to expand the regional alliance framework as a bulwark against further Soviet penetration and, incidentally, to legitimize in Arab eyes the continued presence of British troops on the Arabs' sovereign territories. Iraqi influence and, under certain circumstances, intervention in both Jordan and Syria was thus tacitly supported by Britain and the United States but actively opposed by France, Egypt, the Soviet Union, and to a certain extent Israel as well.[33]

Israel, to be sure, would not object to changes in the Fertile Crescent if these were consonant with its own interests. An Iraqi takeover of Jordan and/or Syria, which would lead to the deployment of Iraqi forces in close proximity to the Israeli border, would be strenuously opposed. On the other hand, if Jordan, Syria, or Lebanon for that matter were to be subsumed within a larger anti-Nasserist and pro-Western framework that would make peace with the Jewish state, there would be no objection. The trouble was that the Israelis could not really make up their minds about Iraq's real objectives. Faced with the rising tide of militant Nasserism, the Hashemite regime in Iraq could not afford to be accused of being "soft on Zionism" or of entertaining territorial ambitions at the expense of fellow Arab states. The Iraqis, therefore, had to justify every introduction of troops into either Syria or Jordan by claiming to be standing up to an Israeli threat. From Israel's viewpoint it was therefore impossible to tell whether an Iraqi contingent on Jordanian territory was a boon or a menace.

Under these perplexing circumstances, the Israelis searched for a compromise. They would not be adamant about any entry of Iraqi forces into Jordan itself, but they would not agree to the stationing of an Iraqi expeditionary force west of the Jordanian capital, Amman, and certainly not west of the Jordan River. Anxious to avoid friction with Britain, which was bound by treaty to defend Jordan, Israeli governments during the period under discussion would not even state their position on this issue in public. Thus when Foreign Minister Golda Meir announced publicly on October 13, 1956, that Israel would not tolerate an Iraqi deployment inside Jordan, she was instantly subject to a great deal of criticism not only from her cautious subordinates in the Foreign Ministry but, indeed, from none other than the formidable David Ben Gurion. Neither the prime minister nor any member of his cabinet thought that Israel should become publicly committed to a clearly stated definition of a casus belli in this regard. Contingency planning for military moves in the event of an Iraqi intervention beyond an ambiguously defined "red line" was one thing. A public commitment to act was quite another proposition.[34]

Changes in the Deployment of Arab Forces

Though successfully repelled, the Arab invasion of May 1948 left an indelible imprint on the Israeli psyche. With Israel's elongated shape, multiplicity of adversaries, lack of territorial depth, and heavy reliance on a reserve army, its policymakers could not but be virtually obsessed with the nighmare of a replay by the Arabs of the coordinated 1948 invasion. Such an invasion could begin simultaneously from four or five directions. Since Jordan's West Bank created a narrow Israeli "waisteline" of 15 to 17 kilometers, it could lead to the split of the country into two separate parts, one in the north and one in the south, within a few hours of the beginning of an invasion. The most important ingredient in such a scenario was undoubtedly the Arabs' ability to mass forces on Israel's border prior to the beginning of the invasion. If they succeeded in doing so, Israel could be subsequently taken by surprise, and there would not be enough time to call up the reserves. The results could be catastrophic. Arab armies could roll into Israel without encountering any serious resistance. They could, under such circumstances, completely disrupt the mobilization of the reserves. If such a scenario ever materialized, Israel would lose the war and possibly its independence within a matter of a few days, if not hours.[35]

Whether or not the Arabs actually developed detailed operational plans for carrying out such an invasion is essentially immaterial. The Israelis acted on the assumption that the Arabs had such plans and that, given an opportunity, they would not hesitate to carry them out. Accordingly, from the Israeli point of view it was imperative to acquire an extensive strategic depth, a kind of demilitarization of all Arab territories that could be used as launching pads for an invasion. The obvious means to achieving this were deterrent threats declaring the concentration of Arab forces on *their* side of the border a casus belli from the Israeli point of view. Nevertheless, prior to the 1956 war Israel never took such a step, at least not explicitly, primarily for two reasons.

First, until late in 1954, the bulk of the Egyptian army was concentrated in the Suez Canal area. Egyptian attention was almost exclusively focused on the struggle against the British, and the British forces acted, from the Israeli point of view, as a decoy, a barrier separating Egyptians and Israelis. Under these circumstances the Sinai peninsula was not a launching pad for another Egyptian invasion, but rather a de facto demilitarized zone. The Israeli government was fully alive to this and so apprehensive about the consequence of a British departure that at least one cabinet member contemplated the possibility of disrupting Egyptian–British negotiations concerning the evacuation of the British.

Having failed disastrously in this misguided move—the infamous Lavon affair—Israel soon faced precisely the situation it had dreaded most. The Israeli–Egyptian confrontation in the Gaza Strip rapidly escalated as Egyptian *fedayeen* (guerrillas, martyrs), were deployed in the strip and sent on sabotage operations inside the Jewish state. The IDF stepped up the scale of its own reprisals against Egyptian army installations in the Gaza Strip and in northern Sinai. Egypt's status as the emerging leader of an awakening Arab world was challenged, and the revolutionary regime of Gamal Abdul Nasser was impelled to pour reinforcements into those parts of the Sinai and the Gaza Strip adjacent to Israel. He was also prompted to seek Soviet aid.

The result was an even more extensive series of attacks and counterattacks involving already sizable formations of regular Israeli and Egyptian troops. In the short run Israel had the upper hand in this escalating encounter. Egypt, however, did not yield. Instead it augmented substantially the forces deployed on Israel's border; in a matter of a year these were increased from one to eleven brigades. Israel, which had not previously defined such an Egyptian deployment as a casus belli, thought it made little sense to do so once the heavy concentration of Egyptian forces had become a formidable reality. An insecure, proud, and ambitious regime such as Nasser's could not be expected to withdraw its forces from their positions along Israel's border simply because the Israelis so demanded. Not having previously succeeded in playing deterrence, the Israelis could not realistically hope to succeed in a (far more intricate) game of compellence.[36] The Jewish state was thus faced with a choice between two courses of action: waiting for an Egyptian attack or launching a preventive attack themselves. In a word, the opportunity to play deterrence through the designation of a casus belli had been missed.

Second, Israel could not declare the concentration of Jordanian forces in the West Bank a casus belli because of the British involvement in Jordan; indeed, it may not even have been all that interested in preventing the presence of Jordanian troops in the area. As long as the bulk of the Egyptian army was committed to the Canal Zone and as long as the Arab Legion was still under the command of professional British officers, headed by Sir John Glubb (Glubb Pasha), the presence of the Jordanian forces in the West Bank was not a threat; to some extent, indeed, it was a source of confidence. Controlled by Britain, a weak and intimidated Jordan would not launch a war against Israel. At the same time, British control over the Arab Legion turned this force, in effect, into an instrument of Israeli policy, almost into a tacit Israeli surrogate.

Israeli reprisals, as has been argued, were designed to impress upon the government at the receiving end—be it Jordan, Egypt, Syria, or Lebanon— that unless it was prepared to countenance the prospect of a large-scale showdown with the Jewish state, that nation's own best interests were to go to any length to discipline infiltrators. This message was not lost on the Jordanians, at least as long as the British cohort was still in charge. In fact, after a number of reprisals the Arab Legion hastened to deploy no fewer than six battalions astride the armistice demarcation lines. Their orders, however, were not to pose a threat to Israel but quite the opposite: to shoot on sight anyone who tried to cross the lines from east (the Jordanian side) to west (the Israeli side).

This effective, but tacit, collaboration between the IDF and the Arab Legion collapsed, however, following the ouster of General Glubb and the rest of the British officers early in March 1956. To a certain extent, the extremity of the about-face in the Jordanian position could be accounted for by the intemperate conduct of the new chief of staff, General Ali Abu Nawar, a fiercely nationalist, anti-British and pro-Egyptian officer. In addition, the change could be attributed to the decline of discipline in the ranks of the Arab Legion and to extensive subversion by Moslem Brotherhood surrogates, inspired and assisted by the Egyptian consul general in Amman. All these factors together led to a sharp increase in terrorist activities in Israel by Arabs crossing from the West Bank. Israel's reply was to step up reprisals against Jordanian army (hitherto referred to as the Arab Legion) installations on the West Bank. Since the expulsion of the British officers had not been accompanied by the abrogation of the 1948 mutual defense pact between Jordan and Britain, Israel had to be careful not to issue broader casus belli threats that called for the Jordanians, in the form of an ultimatum, to remove their troops from the West Bank or even only from the vicinity of the Israeli border.[37]

Thus during the 1949–56 period, Israel's only clearly declared casus belli was Ben Gurion's ultimatum to Egypt to remove the naval blockade of Eilat within one year. Israeli leaders issued profuse warnings to their adversaries through third parties and in public speeches. They attempted to impress the general message on the Arabs through ever-escalating reprisals. In the final analysis, however, they balked during this period at the thought of undertaking irrevocable commitments to resort to force. To a certain extent, this hesitation may have resulted from the Israeli government's total preoccupation with a frantic search for alliances as a means of buttressing the Jewish state's deterrence. A bellicose posture enunciating a number of casi belli vis-à-vis all the Jewish state's neighbors may have been perceived instinctively as an impediment to obtaining such alliances.

In Search of Allies

In a sense Israel's alliance experience dates back to the very origins of the Zionist movement. The leadership of what came to be known as *political* (as distinct from *practical*) Zionism assumed from the outset that the patronage of a leading world power was indispensable to Jewish national revival. Theodor Herzl, the founding father of political Zionism, sought Ottoman and imperial German support but obtained neither. Chaim Weizmann and Nahum Sokolov, who led the movement from the middle of World War I, sought and obtained the open and formal support of Britain and the tacit support of France. Within less than two decades, however, Britain was visibly reversing its alliances and heading toward a vigorous bid for the patronage of an awakening Arab world. The Zionist response was to turn to the United States. The shift in Zionist orientation became inseparably intertwined with the struggle for the leadership of the movement. The aging Weizmann's faith in Britain remained unshaken, whereas David Ben Gurion, formerly a trade unionist in Palestine and by World War II the chairman of the Zionist executive, forcefully advocated a shift to the United States. The latter won both the leadership of the Zionist movement and the shift in the movement's alliance orientation. After the end of World War II, this was reflected in the intensification of the struggle against the British Mandate in Palestine, with its severe restrictions on Jewish immigration and land purchases, and in a vigorous campaign for U.S. support in the final stages of the struggle for independence.[38]

This preindependence alliance policy was, however, predominantly diplomatic-political rather than strategic. A patron was sought primarily for purposes of international recognition, not effective participation in a balance-of-power game of nations. As the United Nations organization, during the spring and summer of 1947, was moving toward its momentous decision to partition Palestine, Ben Gurion and some of his associates became convinced that a major war, in which the Arab world as a whole would assault the Jewish state as soon as it came into existence, was virtually a foregone conclusion. Moved by such a grim perception of the main trends of events, Ben Gurion focused his entire attention, as of the spring of 1947, on preparing the Yishuv for such a war. The result was also a shift in the perception of international patronage. Political-diplomatic support remained crucial. But strategic backing, or at least the supply of arms, became the first priority.[39]

From this perspective, Israel's options were very limited. The Truman administration was split. The State and Defense Departments were adamantly opposed even to the idea of an independent Jewish state, let alone the proposition that the United States should offer it an alliance. President Truman himself was favorably disposed and felt, apparently, that by helping the Zionist struggle he could also improve his seemingly poor prospects in the approaching presidential elections. The result of this split in the administration was an inconsistent policy. The United States moved reluctantly toward support for the partitioning of Palestine and, subsequently, toward the de facto recognition of the fledgling Jewish state. Although by doing so it aroused a great deal of resentment in the Arab world, the United States nevertheless proceeded to impose a virtual embargo on arms to the Middle East, where the only state without any assured sources of arms was Israel. The dispute inside the administration thus produced a policy that left both Arabs and Jews almost equally frustrated.[40]

Britain openly supported the Arabs. This support included arms supplies, political backing in the United Nations, and large-scale involvement of British personnel in the armies of Israel's three leading adversaries: Egypt, Jordan, and Iraq. France acted in much the same way toward Israel's remaining two adversaries, Lebanon and Syria.[41] By contrast, the Soviet Union was supportive of Zionist demands at the United Nations, hastened to recognize Israel de jure, and authorized Czechoslovakia to supply the beleaguered Jewish state with arms.

Against the background of a polarizing international system, this constellation presented Israel with a major foreign policy dilemma. Going along with the Soviet bloc would cause colossal damage to Israel's relations with the United States. Inside Israel itself, moreover, only a small fraction on the left of the political spectrum was prepared to countenance affiliation with the East and distant relations with the United States. Ben Gurion and his political party, MAPAI—the precursor of the Israeli Labor Party (ILP)—were as critical of the Soviets and their conduct in eastern Europe as anyone in the West. Along with the majority of Israelis they were also apprehensive lest a breach with the United States owing to Israel's dependence on the Soviets place the five million strong U.S. Jewish community in an awkward situation.

Since Soviet support in the United Nations and, beyond that, Soviet support of Czech military supplies were crucial, Israel had to find a way of obtaining this support without causing irreparable damage to its relations with the United States. The solution was a careful balancing act whose purpose was to keep up the flow of arms from the Eastern bloc without antagonizing the United States, and to maintain close relations with the United States without arousing the suspicions of the already paranoid Soviets. This perception of the problem led Israel during its first two years of independence to a policy of nonidentification. Such a policy served the requirements of domestic coalition building and coalition maintenance as well. At least as far as Ben Gurion was concerned, however, this was a stop gap, an interim policy rather than the expression of a long-term policy preference. Whatever his public statements on this matter, he was unquestionably convinced that an alliance with the United States was indispensable for Israel's long-term security and well-being.[42]

The policy of nonidentification served Israel well during its first two years. Without Soviet assistance, the Jewish state might never have succeeded in holding its own in the 1948 war. Given the acute polarization between East and West during the same period, however, the balancing act that nonidentification entailed became increasingly untenable. By 1949 there were signs that the Soviets were not content to bail Israel out of trouble with the Arabs without a quid pro quo in the form of a more positive identification with the East in its struggle with the West. Arms supplies from the Eastern bloc dwindled to a trickle and then stopped altogether. There was a great deal of consternation in Moscow following the enthusiastic reception that Soviet Jewry gave Golda Meir, Israel's first ambassador to the Soviet Union. Trials of Soviet Jewish doctors accused of subversion were stage-managed by the Soviet government. The Soviet press indulged in a wave of anti-Semitic propaganda. Above all, there were the first signs of Soviet interest in the Arab world.[43]

The break came with the Korean War. Israel could not afford to dodge the U.N. vote on the Uniting for Peace resolution nor could it oppose the U.S. request that the U.N. force in Korea pursue the North Koreans beyond the 38° parallel. The Soviets drew the inevitable conclusion. Although Israeli relations with the Soviets were not immediately severed, they became chilly and tense. This, however, was not paralleled by a simultaneous improvement in Israel's relations with the West. In May 1950, a month before the outbreak of hostilities in Korea, the United States, Britain, and France had issued a communiqué—dubbed ever since the Tripartite Declaration—committing themselves to a virtual embargo on all arms shipments to the Middle East. Given that the flow of arms from the Soviet bloc had already been terminated earlier, Israel was left not only without a reliable patron but, indeed, with no major source of arms.[44]

Thus began a period of about five years that has gone down as one of the darkest in Israel's history. Earlier hopes that the great victory in the 1948 war and the subsequent armistice agreements would lead to peace had been shattered. The Arab world was visibly preparing for another war. The British and the French were (in Israeli eyes) playing a kind of appeasement toward the Arabs in order to salvage their declining influence in the region and, beyond that, their status as world powers. The United States and the Soviet Union were vying for Arab favor in order to consolidate their newly acquired positions as the world's superpowers. Israel was perceived as a burden, an irritating factor, an unwelcome fruit of a bizarre and almost unnatural twist in world history, an embarrassment, a liability to be ignored rather than an asset to be cultivated.

The question, to be sure, was not merely one of status, although to the hypersensitive Israelis this too was important. If the Arabs were preparing for war, Israel needed an alliance with a great power in order to improve its ability to deter, to have a dissuasive impact on the Arabs' strategic calculus, to offset the Arabs' fundamental military superiority. If the Arabs were faced by an Israel in alliance with a major power, they would have to take into account the possibility that starting a war might bring them face to face not only with the tiny Jewish state but also with the might of a major outside power. In the early 1950s, when the United States, the Soviet Union, and even Britain and France were still widely regarded as invincible superpowers and not (as in the post-Vietnam era) as Gullivers in chains, an alliance with one of them would matter. It could not guarantee that no war would break out between Arabs and Israelis. But Ben Gurion and some of his colleagues believed that by ensuring the flow of arms to Israel and by committing in advance a major power to Israel's defense, an Israeli alliance with a major power would substantially reduce the likelihood of such a war.

The first instance in which it appeared for a brief moment that such a security guarantee might be within Israel's reach occurred in December 1950, when Richard Crossman, a visiting British Labor member of Parliament with a strong pro-Israel record, made unofficial inquiries about whether or not Israel would consider some link with Britain. Eager to obtain an alliance, the Israelis were prepared to overlook their resentment toward Britain on account of its policy in the previous decade and apparently responded favorably. Crossman reported the talk in Whitehall, and several weeks later the Israeli ambassador to the Court of St. James was asked in an official manner whether his government would consider a military liaison with Great Britain. When the Israeli response was again favorable, the British government sent the commanding officer of British forces in the Near East, General Sir Brian Robertson, on a visit to Israel.

The talks with Robertson revealed, however, that what Britain was prepared to offer was a far cry from what the Israelis were hoping for. The main concentration of British forces in the Near East was in the Suez Canal area. The threat on which the British were focusing was that of a Soviet incursion into the Arab heartland of the area. Implicitly the British were also interested in exaggerating the Soviet threat as a means of justifying their own request to maintain a presence along the Suez Canal. In their talks with the Israelis, however, this aspect was not apparently discussed. What was discussed extensively was a British request for a right of passage for their forces in Egypt across Israeli territory to the Fertile Crescent.

Robertson's ideas infuriated Ben Gurion, who found them condescending, patronizing, and exploitative. He told the British general that Israel would accept the British proposals only if they were made part of a larger package with a clear strategic-political, and not just logistic, significance. Israel, Ben Gurion demanded, should be admitted to the British Commonwealth as a full member. Britain should offer Israel military supplies and economic assistance. It should also proffer its good offices as a go-between seeking to launch peace talks between the Jewish state and its Arab neighbors, especially those—like Jordan, Iraq, and Egypt—that were still within the British sphere of influence. Robertson's reaction was that, as a soldier, he had no authority to go into such broad political matters. The general took the matter to the new foreign secretary, Herbert Morrison, who subsequently wrote to Ben Gurion. Morrison responded ambiguously to the Israeli conditions for accepting Robertson's ideas, and the Israelis decided that there was no point in pursuing the matter further.

In October 1951, Churchill, widely regarded a lifelong pro-Zionist, became Britain's prime minister again. Hoping that the formation of the new Conservative government might pave the way to some strategic understanding with Britain, Ben Gurion at last replied to Morrison's letter. He addressed it, of course, to the new foreign secretary, Sir Anthony Eden. The Israeli prime minister did not return to the Commonwealth idea, but proposed instead a more modest degree of military-strategic cooperation. Eden, the godfather of the Arab League, was not at all impressed by Ben Gurion's arguments. He looked forward to the formation of a Supreme Allied Command for the Middle East (SACME) that could be established on the basis of British–American –Turkish–Arab cooperation. This would take care of both the Soviet threat (which in the Middle East concerned the United States more than it did the British) and the threat to the British position in the Middle East from Arab nationalism. Within such a framework, as within the framework of the Middle East Defense Organization (MEDO) proposed by the British later, when it became clear that Egypt would not participate in SACME, Eden saw no role for Israel—certainly not before the establishment of a firm Arab–Israeli peace.

From the Israeli point of view this attitude was at once an insult and an injury—insulting insofar as it rejected the outstretched Israeli hand, and injurious insofar as it proposed to strengthen the Arabs rather than help deter them from what the Israelis saw as aggression. Be that as it may, the Israelis, by their own perception of their vital interests, could not afford to be choosy or indignant. Thus when it transpired that the British had decided to vacate the Suez Canal Zone, the Israelis made another approach. This time it was made by the new prime minister, Moshe Sharett, who proposed that British bases be transferred from Egypt to Israeli territory. Specifically Sharett had in mind the establishment of British bases in the Negev Desert in the south of the country. Again, however, the British were not impressed. They did not even consider this new Israeli idea seriously but proceeded instead to move their bases to Cyprus.[45]

The utter frustration of these contacts with the British reinforced the Israeli tendency to turn to the United States. As long as the Truman administration was in power, there was little of use that could be achieved. But the advent of the

Eisenhower administration in January 1953 aroused new hopes. The firey an-
ticommunist rhetoric of Secretary of State Dulles, in particular, caused some
Israelis to hope that perhaps there could be a basis for closer cooperation. Indeed, at one point even Ben Gurion was led to believe that the United States
under the new administration would be interested in establishing military bases
on Israeli territory.[46]

This, however, was not to be. There was an on-again, off-again dialogue
between the two governments concerning the possibility of U.S. security
guarantees to the Jewish state. Primarily as a result of American rather than
Israeli reservations, however, it never really approached a point of decision,
for three apparent reasons. First, the United States insisted that a "security commitment" to Israel could only be offered once the United States' strategic relations with Israel's neighbors were fully consolidated. Secretary of State Dulles
contemplated a treaty between the Western powers and the Arab world that
would be linked to a Central Treaty Organization based on Turkey, Iran, and
Pakistan—the so-called Northern Tier. He hoped that Egypt would ultimately
agree to participate in this framework. Because of the intensity of Egyptian
hostility toward Israel at the time, he would not jeopardize prospects for obtaining Egyptian participation by undertaking any far-reaching commitment
to Israel.

Whether or not they really intended to substitute U.S. for the British
hegemony they were determined to abolish, the Egyptians demanded, as a
precondition, that the United States force Israel to cede parts of the Negev.
This was to facilitate territorial contiguity between Egypt and the Hashemite
regimes of the Fertile Crescent. Both Secretary of State Dulles and the British
foreign secretary, Eden, who rarely saw eye to eye on any topic, concurred that
the demand was worth exploring. Thus not only was the Israeli request for
a security guarantee turned down, but Israel was also made to understand that
it might have to pay with its own territory for the consolidation of a
U.S.–British–led strategic alliance from which Israel would be excluded.

Second, the United States repeatedly demanded an Israeli commitment to
endorse the armistice demarcation lines as final boundaries as a precondition
to any commitment on the part of the United States itself to offer a security
guarantee. This was, of course, perplexing to the Israelis: while making such
a demand, the United States was at the same time discussing with Egypt and
Great Britain the possibility of Israel's ceding parts of this same territory in
order to establish contiguity between Egypt and the Fertile Crescent.

Third, the United States also requested Israeli assurances that reprisals
would be stopped forthwith. The U.S. government did not offer ironclad promises that the cause of the reprisals—namely, Arab infiltration and guerrilla warfare against the Israelis—would be stopped. All they could do was to urge the
Israelis to stop the reprisal attacks while promising to request that the Arabs
stop the harassment of their Israeli neighbors. Such an attitude not only annoyed

the Israelis but also made them aware of the prohibitive price they might have to pay in order to obtain a security guarantee. They had hoped for a U.S. guarantee as a means of bolstering their ability to deter the Arabs from launching a general war. In the terminology of Israeli strategic discussion, a U.S. guarantee would ameliorate the problem of "basic" security. It would also oblige Israel to consult with the United States before resorting to force on any scale, including small acts of retribution for small-scale harassment. Differently stated, although Israel would gain a major increment of improvement in terms of "basic" security, it might have to pay dearly in terms of its freedom to attend to problems of "current"—that is, subwar, low-level—security.[47]

The growing awareness on the part of most leading Israeli policymakers of this aspect of the issue of a security guarantee somewhat reduced their interest in and enthusiasm for a full-fledged alliance with a major power. At any rate, the negotiations with the United States and Britain on this issue led nowhere and merely created in Israel a growing sense of resentment, isolation, and anxiety. Thus when on April 3, 1955, the government of Israel received yet another evasive U.S. reply to queries about a security guarantee, the minister of defense, David Ben Gurion (Sharett was still prime minister at that time) suggested that all appeals to the United States should be stopped. Israeli emissaries should concentrate instead on attempts to obtain arms—with no political arrangements attached—from wherever they could be obtained.

What prompted Ben Gurion to suggest such an approach was not only the continued U.S. evasion of serious discussion, but also the fact that by the spring of 1955 it was increasingly apparent that Israel could turn to France for those arms that the United States would not supply. The French, to be sure, did not offer any security guarantees. But Israel's frustration with the other Western powers and doubts about the value of such a guarantee if it was tied to restrictions on Israel's freedom to deal with current security caused the Israelis, especially Ben Gurion, Chief of Staff Dayan, and Shimon Peres (then director general of the Ministry of Defense), to shift their attention in another direction. The idea that Israel needed a comprehensive great power patron to reinforce its deterrent capacity was not abandoned. Assuming that the likelihood of a major round of hostilities was rapidly increasing, these policymakers now focused their attention on the problem of military readiness. In this context, the window of opportunity that seemed to be slowly opening for purchasing arms in significant quantities from the French shifted emphasis from the negotiation of a political guarantee to the acquisition and absorption of badly needed arms.[48]

The roots of the change in the previously almost hostile French attitude lay in the French struggle to retain control in North Africa. Increasingly it became clear that in order to advance his position in the Arab world, Colonel Nasser, Chairman of the Free Officers' Committee ruling Egypt since the coup of July 1952, was eager to play a role in supporting national liberation movements in Tunisia, Morocco, and above all Algeria. Under Premier Pierre Mendès-France, the French granted independence to Morocco and Tunis in the hope that this would help them consolidate their hold over Algeria. Nasser, riding the crest of his success in ejecting the British from the Canal Zone, was determined to assist the Algerian National Liberation Front (better known by its French acronym, FLN) in its struggle against the French. In December 1954 the FLN declared an all-out rebellion. Since the FLN's main sanctuary outside Algeria was Egypt, France—which until the previous year had supplied Egypt with arms—suddenly found itself in the same boat with Israel—namely, with Nasser as its main adversary. This was recognized by the Ministries of Defense in Israel and France before it was acknowledged by the respective Foreign Ministries. Consequently, a tacit alliance quickly emerged in which the main channels of communication were not embassies but the military attachés within them.[49]

All this gathered momentum from the autumn of 1955 after the signing of the Czech–Egyptian arms deal. Nasser's morale and self-confidence were boosted, and he stepped up his assistance to the Algerian rebels. From the Israeli perspective it seemed that within six months—by the spring of 1956—the Egyptians would be ready for war. The objective of Israeli policy thus ceased to be deterrence—if, indeed, during this period it ever was. Assuming that war was imminent, the Israeli government focused on preparations. Should they initiate hostilities or should they allow Egypt to determine whether or not there would be hostilities, on what scale, with what participants, and when?

The Use of Force

In the wake of the 1948 war, Israel had no clear doctrine laying down rules concerning the employment of force. There was, to be sure, a rich legacy of previous experience from which a doctrine could draw valuable insights. Thus during the prestatehood period it was taken for granted, almost without dispute, that Israel would not be the "aggressor"—that it would never initiate hostilities. On the other hand, the Hagana (the largest underground Jewish defense organization under the British Mandate) and even more so the PALMACH and the militant fringe underground organizations, the Irgun (IZL) and the Stern Group (LEHI), had tended during the last decade of the struggle for independence to prefer massive punitive retaliation over a limited tit-for-tat (flexible response).

Although the latter two groups were involved in a fierce dispute with the former organization, the difference among them on this basic question of when and how to use force was one of degree and not of principle. The Hagana was the instrument of moderate, mainstream resistance to both the British and the Arabs. The PALMACH was a special operations unit affiliated with the same body.

The Irgun and the Stern Group, on the other hand, represented militants who challenged the authority of the mainstream Yishuv leadership. Accordingly, Hagana units were the least involved in military operations, whereas Irgun and Stern Group units deliberately sought to shake opinion in Palestine and beyond by carrying out spectacular acts of sabotage. All four instruments of resistance tended, however, to carry out operations that were far out of proportion to the British or Arab actions preceding them. They acted on the assumption that military and sabotage operations should be designed to attract attention and on the related presupposition that a limited game of tit-for-tat would emphasize Arab, and even British, comparative advantages. Even in the 1930s, in fact, these assumptions were already at the heart of a stormy and divisive debate in the Yishuv. But by 1948 the proponents of restraint (*havlaga*) had already become a small minority, whereas the advocates of retaliation (*tguva*)—in fact, of massive retaliation—had won the day.[50]

During the same period there was, however, an important difference between the Hagana and PALMACH, on the one hand, and the Irgun and the Stern Group, on the other hand, concerning the choice of targets. The former espoused the doctrine of *tohar haneshek* ("purity of arms"), which objected to the deliberate (as distinct from accidental) use of force against civilians. The latter tended to be far less particular about the loss of life of civilians; they argued, with a certain degree of justice, that the distinction between combatants and noncombatants in what was essentially a state of civil war was untenable and that, in any case, their adversaries did not observe it.[51]

With the establishment of the state of Israel, all these political militias were incorporated into the IDF. The latter essentially adopted the approach of the hagana and PALMACH—namely, that military operations against civilians (the tactical-conventional implementation of strategic countercity warfare) should be avoided. In practice the IDF, too, found it very difficult to implement this high ethical principle. After all, during the first six months of the 1948 war (December 1947–May 1948), the main battles raged in mixed (Arab–Jewish) cities like Tel Aviv–Jaffa, Jerusalem, and Haifa; it was therefore almost impossible to avoid civilian casualties in great numbers. Indeed, the fighting units themselves still occupied an unclear status and could be regarded as armed bands of civilians.

Later, after the invasion of Israel by its neighbors, the war became more regular. At this stage Israel at last had a clear opportunity to put into practice the distinction between front and rear (or military and civilian, for that matter). Under pressure, however, and impressed by the fact that their Arab adversaries did not hesitate to engage in aerial bombardment of cities, the Israelis were sometimes tempted to engage in similar practices. The IAF, to put it bluntly, bombed Damascus, Cairo, and Amman—and it did so under orders from the highest authority.[52]

Many of the makers of these chapters in Israel's history were also the people who subsequently laid down the ground rules of the national security doctrine of the Jewish state after independence. Nevertheless, they did not proceed to set out a detailed doctrine as soon as the 1948 war was over. Having emerged as leading policymakers in a system that placed much store on the fine points of ideology but also, paradoxically, on a pragmatic attitude of trial and error, hypersensitive to the domestic political implications of a clearly enunciated doctrine, and concerned above all with avoiding friction with the great powers, they proceeded to evolve an implicit doctrine, a set of discernible rules of conduct and operational reflexes. This did not happen abruptly. It was a protracted process in which the Israeli political-military elite essentially reacted to Arab initiatives and then, retroactively, analyzed and articulated its own actions. If there was a doctrine, then, it often followed rather than preceded its own implementation.

The starting point was essentially an extension of previously held notions. Israel's self-image was that of a peace-loving nation. It accepted the armistice demarcation lines as final boundaries. It demanded that the armistice regime be regarded as a state of nonbelligerency, a temporary halfway house between war and peace. It repeatedly emphasized its desire to sign peace agreements with all its neighbors. Hence it did not envision itself initiating a war but, rather, the reverse: it saw itself encircled by hostile neighbors who themselves contemplated war against it.[53]

Since Israeli policymakers looked forward, somewhat wistfully, to a period of reasonable stability, if not to peace in the full sense of the term, they paid little or no attention to the question of retaliation if and when the Arabs initiated hostilities. The Israeli posture in these early days of statehood was thus patently defensive. Deterrence may have been instinctively assumed to be the ultimate goal. The term itself may even have been used occasionally. But no Israeli leader was aware of any need to enunciate clearly, as a proper strategy of deterrence requires, how Israel would respond to Arab provocations.

There were, however, two repeatedly announced ground rules. The first was that of reciprocity: peace would prevail on both sides of the border or on neither. The Arabs would be misleading themselves if they believed that they could indulge in hostile acts without expecting any Israeli response. They had the option of living in peace, but if they chose to reject it they should expect an Israeli response in kind. Second, if a war ever broke out, the Arabs should expect a vigorous and deliberate Israeli attempt to carry the fighting over to the Arab side of the border. Israel was small and vulnerable. It had neither the space nor the demographic size nor, indeed, the psychological capacity to sustain the effects of warfare on its own territory. Hence every war would be fought, if the Israelis were capable of having it their way, on the back of the Arabs.

In specific and concrete terms, then, the Israelis were telling their neighbors that the next war would be, from the outset, similar to the last stages of the 1948 war, in which the IDF was inside Lebanon and Egypt. It would not resemble the early stages of that war, in which the Egyptian army was close to Tel Aviv and Jerusalem, the Arab Legion besieged Jerusalem, the Iraqi army threatened Natanya and Hadera, the Syrian army was inside the Galilee, and even the Lebanese held small chunks of Israeli territory.

What was not clearly specified initially was whether these principles applied to hostilities on any scale or only to large-scale wars of the 1948 type. It was not long, however, before it transpired that the Israelis intended to adhere to these principles as pedantically in the case of small-scale harassment as in the case of major wars. In 1950 19 Israelis were killed and 31 were injured by Arab marauders. In 1951 the figures were 48 and 49, respectively. In 1952 there were 42 fatalities and 56 injuries; in 1953, the figures were 44 and 66, respectively. This steady rise in casualty figures continued uninterrupted until the 1956 Operation Kadesh. All told, Israel suffered during the 1949–56 period a loss of 486 lives (of whom 264 were civilians) and injuries to 1,057 of its citizens (of whom 477 were civilians).[54] In absolute terms this was not a heavy toll for a country whose population was rapidly expanding beyond the 1.5 million mark. The damage, however, was perceived as extensive, not only in material terms but above all in terms of people's state of mind. Incidents leading to death and injury of Israelis by Arabs who had crossed over from the neighboring countries created a pervasive sense of insecurity. People became afraid to travel at night—even, in certain areas, in broad daylight.

In turn, the government rapidly became exceedingly apprehensive about the potential cumulative results of this escalating attrition. Much of the border population consisted of new immigrants who had been placed there against their will and who remained there merely because they had nowhere else to go. Their motivation to sustain the effects of terrorism was therefore as low as it could be. If Arab harassment were not stopped forthwith, it could lead to a collapse of the entire border settlement policy—ultimately even to a kind of social domino effect, with people running away from the periphery into the small and already overcrowded urban centers.

Initially the official Israeli response was restraint. Incidents would be reported to the U.N. Mixed Armistice Commissions, and the Israeli government would issue solemn pleas urging the neighboring countries to prevent such incidents from recurring. Meanwhile, in order to prevent the collapse of the morale of the victims of Arab harassment, the government paid special attention to them both materially and symbolically. Money was invested in a variety of ways: shelters were built; volunteers from the well-established populations of the kibbutz and moshav movements were sent to weak areas; and the prime minister, the chief of staff, members of the cabinet, the leadership of the Histadrut (the Israeli trade union movement), and others visited especially hard-hit areas almost every time an incident occurred involving the loss of life.[55]

When this combination of external restraint and internal fortitude led nowhere, the Israelis moved again, from *havlaga* ("restraint") to *tguva* ("retaliation").

At first retaliation was carried out clandestinely, in a tit-for-tat fashion. If insecurity was wrought by small bands of Arabs on the Israeli side of the border, then insecurity could be created on the Arab side of the border as well, using similar methods. At this stage, whereas the Arabs crossing the lines were for the most part acting on their own volition rather than in the service of governments, Israeli retaliation was carried out strictly by IDF personnel. Small parties of soldiers would cross the border, lay an ambush somewhere, cause a number of casualties, and then retreat. If Arabs burned an Israeli barn, Israelis would burn an Arab equivalent. If Arabs stole an Israeli herd, the Israelis would retaliate in kind. And if Arab governments denied responsibility for these activities from their territory, so did the Israeli government. The latter's retaliation was deliberatley calibrated to the scale and linked to the timing and location of the Arab act directly preceding it.[56]

This type of response, though flexible in principle, did little to solve the problem. In fact, the number of incidents and the numbers of casualties increased. Consequently, the IDF under Chief of Staff Makleff was tempted to institutionalize and strengthen the instruments of retaliation. The result was the formation in the summer of 1953 of Unit 101, a commando formation of forty to fifty nonuniformed men headed by (then) Major Ariel Sharon. Its sole purpose was to carry out intense sabotage and harassment operations on the Arab side of the border as a means of deterring Arabs from doing the same thing on the Israeli side.[57]

On October 14, 1953, the new unit overplayed its hand. In an attack on the West Bank village of Qibyeh, two days after the murder of a mother and her two children in the Israeli village of Yahud, Unit 101 left behind roughly fifty homes in ruin and sixty-nine civilian casualties. This was no longer "an eye for an eye" (flexible response); it had become "twenty-three eyes for one eye" (massive retaliation). Moreover, by deliberately seeking to terrorize civilians as a means of compelling governments to change their policies, this method entailed a variant of countercity strategy.[58]

The Qibyeh operation was carried out shortly before the appointment of Major-General Moshe Dayan to the position of IDF chief of staff. Dayan had been skeptical of the deterrent utility of the strategy embodied in the employment of Unit 101. He applauded the technical military aspects of the Qibyeh operation, but he became convinced that the rationale that had led to it was questionable. The result was a significant change of policy. From then on the IDF would openly engage in operations across the armistice demarcation lines and would attack only military objectives. The disproportion between provocation (by Arabs) and response (by Israelis)—that is, the emphasis on massive retaliation—would be maintained. But the emphasis on terrorizing civilians (a countercity strategy) would, in a sense, be replaced by a new emphasis on attacking strictly military targets—that is, on a micro variant of counterforce.[59]

The logic of this coercive diplomacy, whose effectiveness has been forcefully questioned,[60] is worth a more detailed explanation. In the first place, Dayan explicitly perceived these actions as part of a strategy of deterrence, not as reprisals in the primitive sense of the term. Israel, he argued, was simply too poor in manpower and too exposed in terms of its physical features to be able to rely on a defensive strategy. It could not possibly guard every house, tree, or irrigation system. Hence, although it had no territorial ambitions and was simply seeking to defend its sovereign territory from attacks, it had to maintain an active form of defense. Differently stated, the only way for Israel to defend its citizens was deterrence based on exacting a high price for every Israeli casualty.

Furthermore, although the so-called reprisals were small operations, they constituted instruments of a larger policy. The Arab governments had no incentive for stopping their citizens from carrying out attacks against Israelis. In fact, harassing Israel was a popular cause in the Arab world, and any government that tried to stop it would face certain domestic and inter-Arab risks. Against this background, if the IDF carried out a military operation causing the death of Arab soldiers and/or damage to Arab military installations, the Arab armies' ability to carry out their main duty was thrown into sharp relief. If the army in question did not counterattack, it would appear weak. If it did counterattack, it would run the risk of a larger-scale showdown with the Israelis. Given the Arabs' explicit and oft-repeated commitment to the cause of undoing Israel as a political reality, an Arab government capable of standing up to Israel would not be waiting for an Israeli attack. If it did, Dayan argued, it meant that in its own estimate it was incapable of standing up to Israel. If other Arab governments, equally committed to the struggle against Israel, did not come to the aid of the most recent victim of an Israeli reprisal, their lack of resolve was indirectly exposed as well. Reprisals, then, constituted an index of mutual deterrence, a method of evaluating the shares of the adversaries in the "threat exchange," of measuring the overall balance of forces and resolve in the Arab–Israeli conflict. In other words, reprisals were not merely instruments of primitive psychological satisfaction.[61]

The logic of Dayan's argument was seemingly flawless. As he soon discovered himself, however, it overlooked the escalatory impact of this policy on Arab conduct. Could a proud country like Egypt, with its aspirations for leading both the Arab world and the nonaligned bloc—could a proud Egyptian like Gamal Abdul Nasser, who was just discovering the joys of world leadership on a par with venerable leaders such as Tito and Nehru—really afford to concede weakness? Clearly not. Nasser, therefore, intensified the economic, diplomatic, and ultimately military campaign against the Jewish state. And he succeeded in exacting from the Israelis an ever-higher price. Indeed, at one stage in 1955, Egyptian *fedayeen* reached the outskirts of Israel's main city, Tel Aviv, and made travel in Israel so hazardous that all nighttime traffic between Tel

Aviv and Jerusalem, the capital, was restricted to army-escorted convoys. This situation was so alarming that Ben Gurion, for one, began to contemplate the seizure of the Gaza Strip. Meanwhile, the very least that could be done to dissuade the Egyptians from continuing the *fedayeen* raids was, by the same logic, to escalate against the Egyptian army. This was manifested by a series of attacks on Egyptian military positions in the northern Sinai, in and around an area that, according to the 1949 armistice agreements, was supposed to have been a demilitarized zone (DMZ).[62] Nasser was intimidated, all right. Rather than withdrawing from this dangerous test of nerve, however, he turned to the Soviets for military aid. By September 1955, consequently, Israel was facing an entirely new situation: a distinct possibility that Egypt would be powerful enough within six months to initiate large-scale hostilities.

The result was an Israeli drift away from the second-strike posture it had adopted in 1949 and toward what amounted to a first-strike strategy. The change was not announced as a means of deterring Egypt. By this stage, it may well have been too late for the Israelis to play deterrence. They could conceivably attempt this by arming themselves to the teeth. But the French, who had begun to supply them with arms, would continue doing so only under conditions of strict secrecy. Nevertheless, even if the Israelis could have advertised their new armaments program, it is doubtful that that would have been enough to dissuade the Egyptians from carrying out their own program.

In the absence of an effective defensive option, Israel could either attempt compellence—that is, issue ultimata demanding an Egyptian withdrawal of forces away from the Israeli border—or prepare for a preventive war. The first alternative was hardly likely to succeed, given Nasser's euphoric and hypersensitive state of mind. There had been several intense Israeli attempts to seek a change in Nasser's position through negotiated political solutions. But all these attempts had demonstrated conclusively—at least to the Israelis—that the Egyptian leader was unwilling to meet Israel halfway or unable to do so or both.[63]

Against this background it seemed unlikely that the Egyptians would withdraw their forces from the Israeli border—within an area that was Egyptian sovereign territory—simply because Israel threatened to eject them from there by force. Egypt appeared willing to consider a partial disengagement, provided Israel agreed to withdraw the IDF a similar distance from the international border. Because of Israel's minuscule size, however, this either would be too limited to be effective as a means of conflict reduction or, if it were extensive enough to be effective, would entail a unilateral Israeli demilitarization of the bulk of the country's territory. Israel could in no way agree to the Egyptian counterproposal of mutual and balanced disengagement, and Egypt alone would not volunteer for or agree to be bullied (that is, compelled) into a unilateral withdrawal.

Nor was the second alternative—namely, waiting for the Egyptians to initiate hostilities—any more acceptable from the Israeli point of view. It would expose Israel to the hazards of a war initiated by the adversaries—the very nightmare that had haunted them since 1948. It could mean a heavy toll (in 1948 Israel had lost some seven thousand dead, then about 8.9 percent of its population). Moreover, it could mean a protracted war fought, at least initially, on the backs of the Israeli population. Determined, once the 1948 war was over, not to allow another war to be fought on their side of the border, the Israelis had inadvertently chosen a strategy that would not permit an Arab initiation of war. Bluntly, when push came to shove, the only thing this principle could imply was what Israeli governments had attempted to avoid from the very beginning: a decision to launch a preventive war themselves.

One Israeli strategist who was out of power in those days, Yigal Allon, was brought by this realization to advocate a strategy of a "preemptive counterattack"—a non sequitur that stood, in fact, for an interceptive first-strike strategy.[64] Neither Ben Gurion nor Dayan nor anyone else in power in these fateful months of the spring and summer of 1956 ever used Allon's tortuous term. In practice, however, their own policy during the previous years had rendered Allon's ideas the most logical operational conclusion. Having adopted a strategy of escalation for dealing with low-level hostilities ("current security"), having caused the conflict to escalate, they could not continue to adhere much longer to a second-strike strategy concerning all-out war ("basic security"). Dayan, the chief of staff, realized this quite early in the process. Other, probably less perceptive members of Israel's military-political elite at the time were slower to draw the necessary conclusions or, it seems, reluctant to accept them. Consequently, the entire policy analyzed so far, complete with its force structure, threats, alliances, and—of course—force employment dimensions, became the source of one of the most divisive disputes in Israel's political history.

The Politics of Strategic Choice

A cursory overview of four decades of Israeli national security policy could easily lead to the impression that until 1967 that policy commanded complete and unshaken consensus among the Israelis themselves. It could be argued that only later, with the acquisition of the occupied territories in the course of the Six-Day War, did Israeli society begin to develop deep rifts. These showed with growing intensity during the war of attrition, even more so after the Yom Kippur War, and above all in the Israeli experience in Lebanon.

The evidence in support of such an interpretation seems compelling. Israel was highly successful in its first three wars (1948, 1956 and 1967), but less so in its later wars. This could be attributed to poor generalship, to a lack of motivation, or to both. On the face of it, however, the possibility of poor Israeli generalship appears unconvincing. After all, even in the 1973 war the problem was not poor performance in the course of the war but an intellectual failure before the outbreak of hostilities. After this war the IDF performed exceptionally well on a number of occasions except, of course, for the war in Lebanon, in which the blame again could be placed on Sharon's deception.

The most plausible explanation for the overall decline in Israel's wartime performance, therefore, seems to rest somehow on an apparent correlation between domestic consensus and the ability to win wars. The argument is enticing in its elegant simplicity, in its emphasis on high democratic principles, and in its hidden opposition to wars. It is also not entirely without basis in the case of Israel insofar as the general public is concerned. There is little doubt, in fact, that the Israeli public began to show signs of fatigue and division only after the third successful war (in June 1967).

This, however, is not the same as saying that Israel had not experienced deep divisions concerning national security policy before 1967. In fact, both in the course of the 1949–56 period discussed in this chapter and in the course of the 1957–67 period, to be discussed in the next chapter, Israeli foreign policy in general and national security policy in particular made up the single most potent source of elite division. The general public, to be sure, gained only occasional glimpses into the raging debate at the national "high table." But the secrecy surrounding the making of national security policy was not thick enough to conceal the fact that the course, pace, style, and tenor of Israel's national strategy were critically affected by these divisions.

The common interpretation of the main axes of dispute in the 1949–56 period—namely, the policy of reprisal—is infatuated with the personal relations among the decision makers. Ben Gurion, Sharett, Lavon, Dayan—and (in the background) Golda Meir, Zalman Aran, Shimon Peres, and then Major-General Chaim Laskov—added up to a colorful gallery of personalities. Understandably, this reinforced the all-too-common tendency to relegate the substantive issues to the background and focus on rivalries, friction, whims, and peculiarities of individual decision makers. But although the role of personalities here, as in any political interaction, is of great importance, the temptation to overstate its importance should be strenuously resisted. During the seven-year interval between the 1948 and the 1956 wars, Israel faced an acute problem of national security. The Jewish state had just come into existence; it was still reverberating with the consequences of the extensive bloodshed of the war; it was struggling to absorb a vast population of bewildered new immigrants; yet almost without respite it had to deal with a growing problem of insecurity as a result of infiltration and sabotage.

Such a situation inevitably meant high stakes, and playing for high stakes is likely to be divisive. Should Israel accept border instability and Arab threats of a second round as a "normal" state of affairs in the same way that people resign themselves to the frequency of traffic accidents, floods, and typhoons? Or should the Jewish state rebel against this state of affairs and look for ways and means of stopping it? If the consensus was—as it would be in any state—that this was an abnormal situation, should Israel turn to outside support or fall back on its own resources, on self-help, in order to stop it?

A tradition of thought dating back to Jean Jacques Rousseau predicts that in the face of a problem like this, most nations would ultimately turn to self-help. This means precipitative, preemptive, assertive behavior and, ultimately, a greater degree of insecurity for those who follow this logic. But despite the evidence suggesting that in the long run cooperative behavior is more beneficial, this school argues, it is logical for most nations to take care of their interests in the short run through assertive behavior. If they do not, they may appear weak; thus, rather than deterring their adversaries, they may well encourage them to take advantage of this putative weakness.[65]

The logic of this argument seems compelling, but that does not mean that every individual decision maker responds to every particular policy problem in the same way. In the Israeli context during the 1949–56 period, most decision makers ultimately could not challenge the logic of falling back on self-help. But whereas some leading decision makers came to such a conclusion quite early on, others were slower to grasp this logic or resisted its grim implications a while longer.

The quickest to draw the conclusion that self-help and assertion were Israel's best guarantee of obtaining a reasonable degree of security was General Moshe Dayan. During 1949–50 he was Officer Commanding (OC) of the Jerusalem District. Then, in quick succession he became OC Southern Command; OC Northern Command; head of G3 Division at IDF General Staff (and thus in effect deputy chief of staff); and finally chief of staff for nearly five years beginning in December 1953. Given this series of important positions, Dayan was second only to Ben Gurion in his impact on Israeli policy during the 1949–56 period.

Dayan was not a systematic planner. He virtually epitomized the Israeli preference for quick fixes, trial and error, and improvisation. He did not enter office as chief of staff convinced that war was inevitable, but he did proceed in fairly discernible stages as he developed his concepts of what the national policy should be. In the first stage he tended to believe that reprisals would be an adequate answer to the problem of infiltration, especially if they were on a large scale, directed against military objectives, and thus exceedingly painful from the viewpoint of the adversaries. The escalation in the reprisals and the Egyptian arms deal with the Soviets convinced him, however, that the reprisal policy as such had outlived its usefulness. The specific method he had proposed worked as long as it was novel. Once it had been repeated several times, however, the adversaries learned it and found effective ways of dealing with it. The result was a significant escalation, not only in Arab–Israeli hostilities but also in the cost incurred by Israel itself. When the ratio of Israeli to Arab casualties was 10:1 or better from the Israeli point of view, Dayan considered the reprisals policy to be effective. When, however, the ratio was steadily declining until it plummeted closer to 2:1, as in the last few reprisals before Operation Kadesh, Dayan became skeptical of the efficacy of this drill as a method of fixing a high rate for Jewish blood—as he saw it. The question was how to deal with what the Israelis saw as the root cause of the reprisals—the harassment of Jews by Arab marauders. Dayan never believed that Israel could afford to yield—that is, to stop the reprisals and accept constant attacks as a normal situation. He was thus logically led to the conclusion that only something bigger—a large operation coming close to the scale of an all-out war—could solve the problem.

To be sure, Dayan virtually took it for granted that there was no miraculous way of forcing the Arabs to make peace. He assumed that the depth of Arab hostility was such that the IDF might have to go to war once each decade. Even though he started from this grim outlook, Dayan did believe that a substantial reduction in the frequency of small-scale, subwar hostilities could be obtained through Israeli action. Having failed to achieve this through "reprisals" (which he originally perceived as a cheap, ingenious substitute for all-out war), Israel's way to a solution might lie in a larger showdown. But since Israel's international position was weak and since there may not have been a domestic consensus on such a drastic step, further "reprisals" might be needed as a catalyst leading to war. Israel should escalate, the Arabs would respond with escalatory acts of their own, and within a short while a large-scale war would result anyway. In the event it could not be blamed solely on Israel, but since Israel would win it hands down—as Dayan believed—it would buy the Jewish state a respite, a few years in which the impact of a decisive victory would suffice as a deterrent against both small- and large-scale forms of harassment.

Assuming that sooner or later a major war would become inevitable and that it would have to be decided quickly in Israel's favor, Dayan was the first leading Israeli to challenge the utility of the Spatial Defense concept. The next war, he thought, would involve large, mobile, imaginatively maneuvering armies; it would not be a mere replay of the slow and poorly focused war of 1948. Israel did not have the resources to build both a mighty defensive capability and an adequate offensive power. In the event of a general war it should not preoccupy itself with the protection of settlements, since this would dissipate its military power. Instead, force should be concentrated and then employed in daring and focused maneuvers for the purpose of encircling and destroying enemy forces as quickly as possible.

Finally, Dayan thought, an Israeli show of force would constitute a more effective deterrent than would a docile reliance on a great power guarantee. The notion that an Israel that looked weak could obtain a security guarantee from a great power was incomprehensible to him. If Israel appeared weak, no great power would have any interest in propping it up and defending it. A weak and dependent image, in Dayan's view, added up to an invitation for international pressures on Israel to cede the Negev to Egypt or to avoid reprisals as means of defending itself. On the other hand, if the Jewish state appeared strong and determined—an image that could be projected only through demonstrative acts like the reprisals—its appeal as a partner for outside powers would grow accordingly.[66]

Standing almost opposite to Dayan on most of these issues was Moshe Sharett, foreign minister since independence as well as prime minister during the period December 1953–June 1955. Like Dayan, Sharett had grown up in Palestine, spoke Arabic very well, had many contacts with Arabs, and felt that he knew how to deal with them. That, however, was more or less the extent of the similarity between the two men. Whereas Dayan had shaped his world view in the harsh, squalid conditions of a miserably poor Jewish village, in the Hagana, and in the IDF, where his contacts with the outside world were minimal, Sharett had shaped his view of the world in an Arab village where he lived as a child and through a constant exposure to the outside world—as a diplomat for the Zionist movement and as head of the Political Division of the Jewish Agency. Whether Sharett became a diplomat because of his personal attributes or acquired many of his habits in the course of this career is a moot point. What seems important, however, is the fact that he tended to be obsessed with form and appearance and to view Israel's needs through a singularly diplomatic perspective. Dayan, by contrast, was impatient with anything but real substance and tended to observe reality through a markedly strategic prism.

The most fundamental assumption guiding Sharett, it seems, was that Israel was weak and excruciatingly dependent on the good will of world opinion, especially that of the great powers. Without their support, the Jewish state would never have become a reality. It followed, Sharett argued, that Israel had to act in a restrained manner so as to avoid antagonizing these international actors. He had little doubt in his mind concerning Arab intentions. No less than Dayan, he was convinced that given half a chance, the Arabs would attempt again what they had failed to achieve in the 1948 war. But whereas Dayan was confident that Israel could stand up to the Arabs, even in almost total isolation, Sharett was full of forebodings. Without international support, he felt, Israel would be unable to hold its own.

Dayan, on the other hand, felt that demonstrations of Israel's military prowess would strengthen its international standing and weaken the Arabs' resolve. Sharett advocated "empathy" for the grievances of the Arabs and warned that a policy of force would only intensify Arab enmity and undermine Israel's international standing. It was important, he insisted, for Israel to play by the rules, to observe the rule of law not only internally but also in the international arena, to avoid steps that might give the great powers—either directly or through the United Nations—unnecessary excuses for punitive action. Assuming too readily that the world surrounding Israel was a jungle would,

Sharett warned, act as a self-fulfilling prophecy. Escalation and the threat of a showdown were not in Israel's interests, since, given Arab superiority in manpower, space, natural resources, and international standing, the Arabs could not be beaten. Ultimately they would prevail, and Israel should therefore avoid escalation to the best of its ability. It should never tire of signaling to its adversaries a willingness to seek accommodation and to pay for it with significant concessions.

Occasionally Sharett, too, would concede that the Arabs should be taught a lesson, since otherwise Israel would look weak and the Arabs' appetite for further harassment would merely grow. More often than not, however, he instinctively preferred to avoid military action or at least to postpone it, or—if that too was impossible—to limit it to the best of the IDF's ability. Suspecting the IDF in general and Dayan in particular of reckless adventurism, and rejecting almost out of hand Dayan's strategic logic, Sharett found himself time and again authorizing military action for the wrong reasons—that is, not because he was convinced that it was in the national interest, but because he feared damage to his domestic position if he dared reject the IDF's or his cabinet colleagues' urgings to resort to force.

Sometimes, indeed, the matter would become a subject of horse trading between Sharett, the prime minister, and his colleagues and subordinates. He would decline one or two successive requests for permission to launch a reprisal and then reckon that from the point of view of preserving his personal and political standing he could not do so for a third time. In the event, however, the bargaining would focus on the scale. Sharett would invariably argue for a smaller operation. Dayan or Lavon (who was minister of defense under Sharett for a short while) or indeed Ben Gurion (who became Sharett's minister of defense in February 1955) would attempt to convince him of the logic of massive retaliation. Sharett, without truly understanding the strategic calculus, would press for a more limited tit-for-tat.

The result was tragic. Convinced that he was wrong, his subordinates and colleagues would interpret his instructions in whatever way they saw fit, leave him in the dark about some of their actions or take advantage of his absence abroad in order to launch an operation which they thought was long overdue but to which Sharett had constantly objected. It was in such circumstances that, under Pinchas Lavon as minister of defense, Israeli Military Intelligence carried out the sabotage operations that led to the infamous Lavon affair. It was under Sharett as acting prime minister that Unit 101 carried out the Qibyeh operation. It was, finally, under Sharett (though in his absence on a visit to the United States) that Ben Gurion ordered Dayan to launch a massive raid on Syrian forces in December 1955.

Sharett was so adamantly opposed to any thought of using force that after the announcement of the Egyptian–Czech arms deal he found himself arguing even with some of his closest advisers in the Foreign Ministry. Avowed "doves" (to use a term that was not yet in vogue) who fully shared Sharett's fundamental world view, these advisers saw no escape from a preventive war against Egypt. Sharett resisted this argument and proposed instead that Israel should threaten Nasser as a form of a bluff. When the topic began to be discussed by the cabinet, Sharett found few allies among ministers from his own party, MAPAI. He had a formidable ally in Minister of Education Aran. But members of the cabinet from MAPAI such as Minister of Labor Golda Meir and Minister of Finance Levi Eshkol, both already of acknowledged prime ministerial caliber, were prepared to consider the possibility of a preventive war. At the same time, Sharett drew important support from ministers from other parties. Thus, beyond the personal dimension of the problem, there was increasingly a complex political situation, whereby the prime minister and leader of the party that was the mainstay of the cabinet was at odds with his own party's emerging policy preference. This aspect became critical with the return to power, after a year's retirement, of the formidable David Ben Gurion.[67]

Ben Gurion's position was somewhere between Dayan's and Sharett's concerning the national security agenda. On the issue of great power patronage and a security guarantee, he had no quarrel with Sharett. He, too, was convinced that obtaining a great power security guarantee was one of the most important objectives of Israeli foreign policy. Both in private and in public Ben Gurion was occasionally scathing and denigrating toward the role of the United Nations, which he referred to, derogatorily, as "UM-shmum" (*UM* is the Hebrew acronym for "United Nations"; *shmum* is merely gibberish). He was also widely quoted as saying that it did not matter what the Gentiles said—only what the Jews did. In practice, however, not even Sharett was more careful than Ben Gurion to avoid clashes with major powers on issues that could seriously antagonize the latter. Indeed, one ground rule of Israel's national security policy that outlived Ben Gurion was exclusively his: under no circumstances should Israel ever engage a great power in war; and, when Israel went to war, it should do its utmost to ensure the backing of at least one leading power before the outbreak of hostilities.

If on this issue Ben Gurion was closer to Sharett than to Dayan, he was also in disagreement with the latter on the issue of Spatial Defense. The roots of the difference can be traced to variance in their respective definitions of the scope of national security. The establishment of a Jewish state, Ben Gurion insisted (thereby often finding himself at loggerheads with Sharett), was not due to a consensus in the United Nations but attributable to the fact that the Zionist movement had succeeded in establishing itself as a formidable reality in Palestine. Given this presence, Ben Gurion argued, a Jewish state could be created even against the wishes of the world organization. From this point of view, the U.N. Partition Resolution sanctioning the establishment of a Jewish state (as well as an Arab Palestinian one) was little more than an acknowledgment of reality, an ex post facto blessing.

It followed, Ben Gurion argued, that Israeli settlements, the building of the economy, the absorption of new immigrants, the strengthening of the IDF, and the consolidation of higher education and scientific research were the only ways to ensure Israel's existence. Whether or not the United Nations passed resolutions condemming Israel was of little consequence as long as Israel itself was continuing to grow and develop. Within this frame of reference, which put Ben Gurion poles apart from Sharett, the establishment of new agricultural settlements along the country's boundaries was a crucial dimension of national security. If these settlements were prosperous, they would endow the borders and, ipso facto, the society and state structure within them, with a quality of an enduring reality. Without such settlements, however, Israel would remain a temporary, dubious, questionable, illegitimate, insecure, and transient entity.

Thus Dayan's argument that more combat units in the IDF with more sophisticated weapons would be a better shield of the nation's security than a defensive "shield" based on armed agricultural settlements came up against Ben Gurion's broader definition of national security. To state their positions in a somewhat oversimplified manner, for Ben Gurion an additional Kibbutz or moshav on the border added a greater increment of security than another company of infantry. For Dayan, at least as long as he was chief of the IDF General Staff, the calculus appeared (not very surprisingly) precisely the opposite. Hence Ben Gurion would not permit Dayan to phase out Spatial Defense altogether. Despite the chief of staff's repeated pleas for permission to undo the NAHAL elite corps, Ben Gurion insisted that this unit should continue to absorb some of the IDF's prime recruits, hastily train them as paratroopers, and then assign them the task of setting up new frontier settlements.

If Ben Gurion was close to Sharett on the topic of alliances and at variance with Dayan on some aspects of the nation's force structure and deployment agenda, he was closer to the chief of staff than to the foreign minister on the thorny issue of reprisals. A long life in Palestine as a farm hand, a political activist, and subsequently a leader; an intense observance of Arab conduct stretching over decades; and numerous exchanges with Arab leaders had convinced him that only a forceful policy could persuade the Arabs to accept the fact of a Jewish state. In his view, if he were an Arab he would never accept an independent Jewish state unless and until he became convinced that this could not be prevented by force. The Jewish state, in Ben Gurion's concept, would have virtually to impose itself by force on an unwilling Arab world.

This did not imply an unwise reliance on force alone. Israel should be careful to spare its energies and accumulate force rather than squander it in a vain attempt to obtain a final victory over its adversaries. At the same time, to impress upon the Arabs that the Jewish state would not flinch and had the capacity to inflict untold punishments, to force them to reconsider their positions, to dissuade them from resorting to force themselves, Israel had no alternative. Its only course lay with a policy seeking to demonstrate military prowess and striving simultaneously to keep the Arabs divided and incapable of converting their vast potential into actual power.

In moments of weakness Ben Gurion would wonder how many rounds of hostilities Israel could sustain before it would be subdued by the overwhelmingly superior Arabs. In the shorter term, however, he tended to share Dayan's confidence that reprisals and a general posture of determination, resolve, and military skill would ultimately change the Arabs' calculus. Hostile to the memory of Jewish humiliation and submission throughout two millennia of dispersal, Ben Gurion harked back to the days of Jewish statehood in biblical and Hellenistic times. From this perspective, he was enormously impressed with the youthful courage, skill, and esprit de corps of the IDF, as these qualities were emerging in the course of the reprisal era.

Yet, for all this, Ben Gurion was constantly torn between two opposing impulses. On the one hand, the policy of force that Dayan carried out with his blessing and under his guidance increasingly escalated the conflict; as a result, it was leading to the conclusion that a major showdown could not be deferred much longer. On the other hand, Ben Gurion was reluctant to drag Israel into a war that would tarnish its image and could easily lead to an open rift with the world's great powers. To solve the problem of infiltration and sabotage, he realized, Israel would have to capture the Gaza Strip or seize, as he proposed at one stage, the Hebron province of the West Bank. It would have to declare that it would not leave it without a clear Jordanian commitment to stop infiltration across the armistice demarcation lines. To save Eilat and the Negev, Israel might have no alternative but to seize the Straits of Tiran and hold onto them until an ironclad Egyptian guarantee to allow free navigation was obtained. To deal more effectively with Syrian harassment, the IDF might have to seize the DMZs and perhaps more Syrian-held territory. To thwart the Nasserist attempt to unite the Arab world and throw a noose around Israel's neck, there might be no alternative to subversive activity in Lebanon leading to the creation of a smaller, Christian-dominated Lebanon in alliance with Israel, as well as to the seizure of Lebanese territory between the Litani River and the Israeli border. All these actions, he also realized, were bound to have their adverse repercussions as well.

In a sense, then, Ben Gurion was torn between the world of Dayan and the world of Sharett; the greater the pressure of events to launch a preventive war, the greater was his agony. What made things worse was the fact that Sharett led a group of ministers who not only shared his views but also constituted a substantial enough bloc to prevent a cabinet decision to launch a military operation. Thus, while struggling with his own doubts, Ben Gurion also had a major political battle on his hands. He evidently assumed that before a military operation could be launched, at least two critical conditions would have to be met: there should be a solid domestic consensus for a military operation, and Israel should have exhausted all possibilities for obtaining significant great power support. Meeting both conditions was an immensely complicated and time-consuming task. Hence Ben Gurion seems to have launched a campaign for both even before he fully resolved actually to launch the planned military operation. His final decision on whether or not to go to war, then, depended on what he could achieve on the domestic and international fronts.

Nasser's nationalization of the Suez Canal consolidated Israel's tacit alliance with France. By bringing the British into the picture as well, it seemed to have guaranteed that Israel's Jordanian flank would be reasonably covered, too. The search for a secretary-general of his party, MAPAI, gave Ben Gurion an opportunity to solve his domestic problem. Having tried in vain several times to win Sharett's support for the proposition of a military campaign initiated by Israel, he apparently saw no alternative to the removal of Sharett from office. In a ruthless maneuver that sent Sharett into fits of anguish, Ben Gurion forced him out of the Foreign Ministry and appointed Golda Meir, who shared Ben Gurion's views, in Sharett's place. The latter never recovered from the shock and humiliation. But Ben Gurion, whose attitude toward most of his colleagues was more instrumental than personal, could be satisfied that he had eliminated the oppositon to a military campaign and ensured that a unified cabinet would follow him through thick and thin if and when he resolved to lead the country to war. All this took more than a year. The vicissitudes of domestic politics thus had a critical bearing over the manner in which national strategy evolved.[68]

The First Strategic Package

Israel's national security was initially intended by its leading architects to be based on what could be described, retrospectively, as a posture of deterrence by denial. The IDF would be based on a small kernel of regulars and a large reserve force. It would be mainly an infantry army, with elements of navy, air force, armor, and artillery in supporting roles. It would include a tightly knit network of border settlements, organized as Spatial Defense, to endow the country with a substitute for strategic depth. Such a system was expected to be politically buttressed by an alliance with one or another of the leading Western powers. Since in the immediate aftermath of the 1948 victory all this appeared adequate, there was no clear concept of casi belli. It was taken for granted that Israel would never initiate a war. If the Arabs were not deterred and if they were to launch a war—envisaged by Israeli planners as an improved version of the invasion of 1948—Israel would quickly mobilize and seek to shift the fighting to the adversary's territory as soon as possible. In the event of such a war, Israel would not limit itself to the repulsion of the invader. It would retaliate massively, seeking to inflict on the adversary the most severe punishment in its power.

This initial image of the preferred national security doctrine did not persist for very long. Technology and the arms race made the concept of an infantry-based army appear outdated. Gradually the pressure to increase the weight of armor, artillery, mobile infantry, and air force increased. Infantry remained the queen of the battle, but defense outlays constantly climbed, and the pressure to phase out Spatial Defense mounted accordingly. Simultaneously the Israelis discovered that an alliance with a great power was a pipe dream. The Soviet Union was quick to lose interest in Israel, whereas the West was slow to embrace it and presented unacceptable preconditions. By an ironic twist of international politics, France drew tentatively closer to the Jewish state in the wake of the Egyptian arms deal with the Soviets. But the French were divided in their attitude and would not go as far as the Israelis wished them to. Supplying the Israelis with arms secretly, and for their full market price, was one thing. An openly declared deterrent alliance that would make an attack on Israel similar to an attack on France itself was quite another proposition.

The inability to obtain a meaningful deterrent alliance gradually shifted the Israeli strategic posture to something resembling deterrence by punishment, a shift in emphasis nurtured at least as much by the repercussions of border insecurity. Having failed to stop Arab infiltration and sabotage through diplomatic means, Israel increasingly relied on punishments that were deliberately based on a disproportion between provocation and response (massive retaliation) and that for the most part were consciously directed at the adversary's military (counterforce). The decoupling roughly during 1953–55 of stratregy for low-level hostilities ("current security") from strategic preferences concerning full-scale war ("basic security") could not be maintained for very long. Ultimately the change in the force structure of both Israel and its adversaries, and the habits of thought and action acquired as a result of the experience with reprisals, caused a reappraisal of the strategy for all-out war. It led, specifically, to a shift from a defensive/denial second-strike posture to an offensive/punishment first-strike one.

Yet because of the lingering concern over avoiding friction with the great powers as well as of the fierce internal dispute in the Israeli political-military elite, the shift to a first-strike posture was not announced as boldly as a genuine and systematic strategy of deterrence requires. Israel increasingly acted on the assumption that it would initiate war if need be. Afraid to publicize this posture, however, or even to designate clear-cut casi belli, the Jewish state in fact shrank from tying its own hands through an irrevocable commitment. This streak of hesitancy undercut the efficacy of Israel's deterrence and thus, arguably, made an actual resort to force more likely.

3

Deterrence Comes of Age: 1957–1967

O peration Kadesh, the Israeli code name for the October 1956 Sinai campaign, was launched because of the Israeli perception of an unacceptable decline in the efficacy of the nation's deterrent. It was part of a larger maneuver involving the armies of Great Britain and France that, under the title Operation Muskateer, sought to recapture control of the Suez Canal for the West and, perhaps, to bring about the deposition of Nasser. Britain and France moved slowly, were not particularly successful on the battlefield, and succumbed quickly to U.S. pressure for an immediate halt to hostilities and an immediate withdrawal of all foreign forces from Egyptian territory. Israel, the junior partner in this trilateral action, brought about the collapse of the Egyptian army in the Sinai and in the Gaza Strip. In a matter of five days the Israeli army was in control of vast expanses of desert, three times the size of the Jewish state itself.[1]

The capitulation of the British and French to U.S. pressure turned the whole affair into an Egyptian victory. Nasser, whose army did not fight well, could claim that Egypt had single-handedly repelled the forces of two world empires. He could not hide the poor showing of his army in the Sinai peninsula. But he could lead himself, his people, the Arab world, and the emerging bloc of nonaligned nations to believe that the defeat in the battle for the Sinai was not due to Israel's superior battlefield performance, but had occurred only because of the undeniable fact that Egypt was primarily preoccupied with the (then) pending British and French landing.

The British–French decision to yield to U.S. pressure also undercut Israel's position. If these two leading Western powers could hold their own against the United States (the Soviet Union's threatening noises did not unduly trouble anyone, since the Soviets were then preoccupied with a rebellion in Hungary and Poland and had not yet deployed missiles capable of reaching London, Paris, or Tel Aviv), Israel's ability to stand up to U.S. pressures would be substantially strengthened, too. Conversely, having utterly given up the political struggle with the United States, Britain and France had placed Israel in the focus of U.S. attention, the main target for the frustration and fury of the Eisenhower administration.

Consequently, Israel was ultimately forced to withdraw from the Sinai and the Gaza Strip in exchange for little more than a tacit understanding that Egypt would agree to a unilateral demilitarization of their Sinai possessions. This agreement would be buttressed by the presence, on the Egyptian side of the border only, of a United Nations Emergency Force (UNEF) as well as by a letter from the president of the United States to the prime minister of Israel. This note suggested, somewhat vaguely, that Israel would be free to take care of its interests and security if and when the Egyptians were to revert to the pre-Sinai campaign status quo ante.[2]

With grave forebodings Israel gave way, and by the beginning of 1957 the IDF was out of the Sinai and the Gaza Strip again, whereas Egyptian personnel had returned—contrary to all promises made to Israel—to the Gaza Strip. Nevertheless, in the final analysis the Sinai campaign gave Israel a great deal. It was followed by a decade of stability on the Egyptian–Israeli border. It created conditions in which the Negev, in particular Eilat, could develop. It reassured the Israelis about their ability to take care of their own security. Though the Jewish state was noisily branded as an aggressor and a party to an unsavory conspiracy, Israel's international standing improved spectacularly. Relations with the Western powers became far closer. Israel's efforts to establish its presence as an actor on the continent of Africa, in Asia, and in Latin America were highly successful. Immigration to the country ground to a half, but this created an opportunity for consolidation.[3]

Meanwhile, the Arab world, which prior to Operation Kadesh had appeared to be on the march toward union under Egyptian hegemony, was increasingly torn asunder by a "cold war" between the radical allies of the Soviets and the conservative, pro-Western monarchies. Egypt became bogged down in a hopeless war in the Yemen. Iraq had a Kurdish uprising on its hands and was at loggerheads with Kuwait, with the Saudis, with Syria, and with Jordan. The energies of both Syria and Iraq seemed to be sapped by successive coups and countercoups. As a result, not only Israel's Egyptian border but also its Jordanian and Lebanese borders became placid, at least in comparison to the Israeli experience during the 1949–56 period.[4]

Divided and preoccupied with their own internecine quarrels, the Arabs seemed (from the Israeli point of view) adequately impressed by the Jewish state's military prowess. There were, to be sure, two lingering reasons for concern— the quickened pace of the arms race and the continuous trouble on the Israeli–Syrian border. But even these potential sources of danger did not convince the Israelis that war was imminent or even likely, at least in the course of the 1960s. The rhetoric of political leaders continued to emphasize the ubiquitous external threat. But in terms of people's perceptions and of the government's own policies, the urgency and anxiety of the pre-1956 era had been replaced by a sense of routine.

Cast in strategic-political terms, this perception of Israel's situation during the 1957–67 decade implied that the nation's endeavor to cultivate effective deterrence had become an established success story. Generally speaking, deterrence seemed to have been proved a reliable foundation for national security. Specifically, it had been explicated, consolidated, explained, researched, exercised. The IDF, in this strategic package, was pictured as a gigantic harpoon, a powerful and pointed instrument of massive punishment. If called on to retaliate, it would exact from the Arabs an intolerable price. Its effectiveness as the mainstay of the deterrent, therefore, appeared to be beyond doubt. Meanwhile, it was becoming amply clear that the idea of a deterrent alliance was unworkable. Israel could forge beneficial relations with many states both in the Middle East and among the world's leading powers. But it could not—and many contended it should not—obtain a deterrent patronage.

To compensate for the absence of a reliable alliance and as a means of buttressing the retaliatory capabilities of the IDF, with its deliberate emphasis on decision in battle rather than on defense, Israel would have to fall back on a number of specified red lines, the crossing of which by the Arabs would be regarded as a deliberate act of hostility and would, therefore, lead to an instantaneous Israeli riposte. The Arabs should know, it was assumed, that if it ever came to that, Israel would not hesitate to act. But to preserve the element of surprise and to avoid friction with friendly powers and an acrimonious domestic debate, Israel should preserve an element of ambiguity in its force employment preferences. This, in brief, was the strategic package that evolved in the course of the 1957–67 decade. The processes and lessons that shaped it and the crisis in which it was subject to the test of reality form the topic of this chapter.

The New Order of Battle

Neither Operation Kadesh nor the political and strategic developments that followed it had a significant bearing on the Israeli solution to the problem of manpower allocation. The reserve system seemed to have conclusively proved its efficacy. The scores of thousands of civilians who in the years preceding the war had trained within the stringent conditions that a reserve system permitted—in particular, the limiting of training time to thirty days or so per calendar year—did not seem to have affected adversely the IDF's performance in battle. The logistical system, too, had withstood the demanding conditions of a short war. An army of civilians, whose only previous battle experience had been in a slow-moving, defensive war, revealed itself capable of fighting a brief, intensive war based on a decisive-victory concept.

Starting from this assumption, IDF planners had no reason to change the overall regular/reserve ratio, the call-up system, the depot system, or their approach to the long-term peacetime training philosophy. Although the introduction of complex weapons systems made it imperative to enlarge the regular, professional core, especially in the IAF and in the armored corps (*Gyasot Hashiryon* or, for short, *HaGayis*), it is still true that between the 1956 and the 1967 wars the IDF remained, by and large, a reserve-based army along the lines of its organization in the immediate aftermath of the 1948 war. Indeed, if anything, the system seemed to be rapidly improving. The bulk of the reserves in the 1949–56 period had had very little systematic training. They were recruited hastily, trained briefly, and put into action. By contrast, the post–1956 IDF, especially the regulars but also increasingly the reserves, were recruited by the IDF and trained within an orderly training system. No longer a ragtag militia, it became a professional fighting force with good, standardized training; a solid, experienced officer corps; a rich folklore of interservice and interunit competition; reasonably standardized and professionally maintained equipment; a common set of clearly established procedures; and, despite its young age (as an institution), high morale nurtured by two successive victories.[5]

As a result of the impact of an accelerating arms race and of the battle experience of the previous years, this army rapidly changed its face in terms of its priorities, emphases, equipment, and doctrine. Wars in the Middle East, as probably elsewhere, too, tend to boost the arms race and carry it into new (and generally more dangerous and more complex) phases. After—or even in the course of—every round of hostilities, the adversaries hasten to replenish their depleted armories, both in the fear that otherwise the adversary will take advantage of their weakness and in the hope that procuring greater quantities of more sophisticated weapons will give them an advantage.

In this sense the 1956 Israeli–Egyptian encounter was no exception. Signaling by its very occurrence the final breakdown of the Western policy embodied in the Tripartite Declaration, the 1956 war was followed by a massive Egyptian effort to replenish stocks and, if possible, gain an edge over Israel. From the Israeli point of view, even parity with Egypt was unacceptable, let alone an Egyptian advantage. Israel started from the assumption that it had to have an army strong enough to obtain a decisive victory within a few days even if the Jewish state were attacked simultaneously by all the Arab states combined. Hence the Egyptian drive for strategic parity forced Israel to double its own efforts. In turn Israel increasingly became a menacing military reality from the point of view of every one of its neighbors, who—following the same maddening reasoning—had no logical alternative but to increase their own arms buildup still further. The Arab–Israeli arms race during this period, therefore, was of breathtaking proportions because of a critical structural feature: Israel sought deterrence through an equilibrium as if there were only two adversaries in the conflict system. But since Egypt, Syria, and to an extent Jordan all acted on a similar assumption (of a bilateral encounter between each one of them alone and the Jewish state), an Israeli lead could never really be either acheived or, indeed, maintained.

If from this perspective the Arab–Israeli arms race was of a compound variety, then inter-Arab relations turned it into a doubly compounded race. Egypt, for one, had adopted a vocation—namely, the search for a role of leadership in the Arab world. In pursuit of this goal, it had to be able to exhibit the largest military profile. Thus if Syria and Iraq bought arms in increasing quantities and of a growing sophistication, Egypt could not afford to lag behind. But the reverse was also true: if Egypt was willing and able to commit 50,000 troops to a war in the Yemen, it constituted a formidable menace to virtually any other force in the Middle East. Accordingly, Saudi Arabia had to arm itself to the teeth, Jordan could not afford to lag behind, and the vicious cycle of armament and counterarmament among the Arabs themselves—not to mention the Arab–Iranian arms race—added fuel to the overall Arab–Israeli arms race. Perhaps the most effective way to demonstrate the quantitative change that resulted from this doubly compounded arms race is not merely to compare the Israeli and the Arab buildup but also to compare Israel's capabilities at the beginning of the period with those on the eve of the Six-Day War and to perform a similar comparison between Arab capabilities at either end of the period under review (see figures 3–1 and 3–2).[6]

The extent of the quantitative transformation, spectacular as it may have been, was not as dramatic as the qualitative change that took place simultaneously. The mainstay of the IDF in the 1956 war were four (out of a total of five) infantry divisions. Consisting of roughly three brigades each, this force was partly mobile. Most of it, however, was trained to approach an enemy target in "soft" vehicles and then disembark and launch the attack on foot. By 1967 the mainstay of the IDF had become the armored, roughly division-size, formation. To the extent that infantry had survived this dramatic transformation, it had become primarily specialized, an effective and highly respected ancillary.

The IDF still had sizable elements of both airborne and nonairborne infantry. These were elite units with first-rate personnel and a particularly high spirit. They had some training in battlefield cooperation with armored formations. Their main task, however, was to carry out special "pinprick" operations, such as helicopter or traditional airborne landings behind enemy lines, combat in built-up areas, or the mopping up of enemy pockets left behind by the advancing armored "fists" or "razor blades." The main element in any operation would thus be the armored task force (*utsba meshuryenet*). Its size would be determined according to the objective. It could be sub-battalion, brigade-size, divisional-size, or even larger. Regardless of size, it would concentrate a great deal of firepower and then rush head-on in deep thrusts through enemy lines. The purpose would be quick decision. The method to acheive this would be a deep "vertical" maneuver in search of a decisive battle. The means would be the combination of mobility and firepower as embodied by the armored formation.[7]

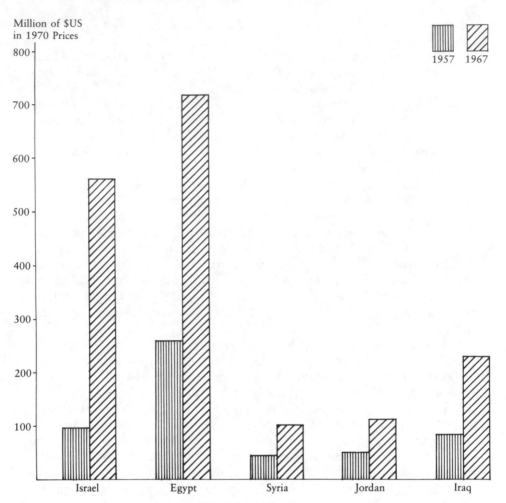

Million of $US
in 1970 Prices

Source: Based on data in *SIPRI Yearbook 1975, World Armament and Disarmament* (Cambridge, Mass.: MIT Press, 1975), p. 126, as quoted by Yair Evron, "Two Periods in Arab–Israeli Strategic Relations," pp. 112–113.

Figure 3–1. Selected Comparisons of Arab and Israeli Military Outlays, 1957 and 1967

Such an image of the most desirable force structure went hand in hand with a similar concept of air warfare. In addition to intelligence and transport, the purpose of the IAF would be, first, to protect the state's air space; second, to shelter and assist ground forces fighting on enemy territory outside the boundaries of the state; and third, to protect the nation's air contact with the rest of the world. The means by which these tasks were to be carried out were first

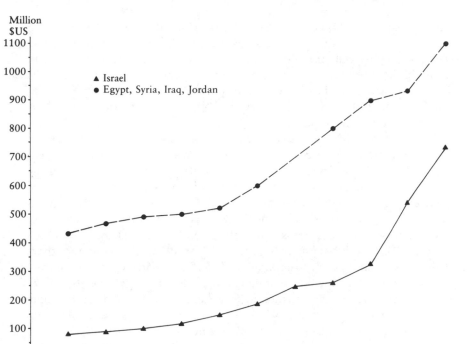

Source: Based on data in Evron, "Two Periods in Arab–Israeli Strategic Relations," p. 103. In constant $US.

Figure 3–2. The Arab–Israeli Arms Race, 1957–1967

and foremost a supersonic strike force. Instead of the hodgepodge of subsonic and piston-engine planes in ground-support roles that had prevailed in 1956,[8] the IAF had become, by 1967, an impressive supersonic air-striking arm. It was still weak in transport planes and in helicopters, although 96 aircrafts of both types had been purchased (16 piston-engine DC-3 Dakotas; 23 piston-engine Nord-2501 and 7 turboprop Stratocruiser transporters; and 5 Super-Frelon, 13 Bell, and 28 Sikorski S-55 and C-53 helicopters). By deliberate decision the IAF eschewed entirely the capacity to carry out long-range bombing operations.[9] But it had 205 French-built fighters and fighter-bombers (50 Ouragan, 35 Mystère, 35 Super Mytère, 20 Votoure, and 65 Mirage) and even its fleet of trainers had been entirely converted to jets with the introduction of 45 Fouga-Magister (a French aircraft built by license in Israel and fitted especially for strafing and other ground-support tasks).[10]

The change in the IN was less impressive. On June 4, 1967, it had 9 patrol and torpedo boats; 3 destroyers (*Yaffo, Eilat,* and *Haifa*); and 3 submarines (*Tanin, Rahav,* and *Livyatan*). It was arriving at the conclusion that in the future its main task should be coastal and off-shore defense and support for the ground operations of other IDF arms. In turn this suggested the purchase of compact, high-speed missile boats rather than larger, more expensive vessels. Because of the steeply rising outlays on weapon purchases for other arms, the actual implementation of the new concept was very slow to take shape. In fact, the real change in the order of battle of the IN would be apparent only in the aftermath of the 1967 war.[11]

The rapid move into recent-vintage late-twentieth-century weapons caused a steep rise (approximately 3 to 5 percent, or from an average of 6 to 7 percent per year during 1949–56 to an average of 10 to 12 percent per year during 1957–67) in that chunk of the Israeli gross national product directly devoted to defense. Since the GNP itself grew about 10 percent per year throughout all but the last year of the decade under investigation, this relatively sharp rise was enormous in absolute terms. The defense budget in terms of U.S. dollars is difficult to establish accurately because until the 1970s it was not published. But it seems to have been in the range of U.S. $200–650 million annually— roughly the size of the then-current deficit in the balance of payments. Subsequent analyses revealed that despite the fact that the rise in the defense budget was larger than the net rise in GNP, the country's standard of living also continued to rise. How did the government close this gap? Apparently it did so by borrowing from abroad as well as from the public at home, by allowing a certain degree of inflation, by permitting a slow erosion in the rate of investment, and—when all these stopgap "tricks" proved inadequate—by introducing a planned recession a year before the 1967 war.[12]

Against such a background, there was no escape from a stringent effort on the part of the IDF to economize as well. The main victims proved to be the Civil and Spatial Defense systems. Whereas during 1949–56, or at least until the Egyptian–Czech arms deal, these were considered important pillars of the national strategic posture—a kind of solid "shield" complementing the IDF's mechanized and air-strike "sword," both had become by the mid-1960s depleted appendages of a vast war machine geared almost exclusively to an offensive modus operandi. Whatever assets had been accumulated in the armories of HAGA and HAGMAR (the Hebrew acronyms for the Civil and Spatial Defense branches of the IDF) in the course of the 1950s were left there in reasonable condition. Resources for modernization and training were reduced to a mere trickle, however, and the manpower resources of both organizations had been so downgraded that in comparison with the rapidly modernizing IDF main force they had become an Israeli version of what the British called "Dad's Army."

Another clearly significant development that went hand in hand with Israel's struggle to keep abreast of the runaway regional arms race was the Israeli decision to embark on an independent nuclear program. The soaring costs of purchasing arms and the persistent refusal of the United States or even France to offer a security guarantee convinced Ben Gurion and his disciples Dayan and Peres that in the long run Israel might not be able to hold its ground. How much time the Jewish state still had before this nightmare became a reality could not be guessed. It was not an immediate threat but, rather, something that, in the estimates of Ben Gurion, Dayan, and Peres, would probably take several decades. Developing an independent nuclear program also takes time, however, especially when obtaining the knowhow and some of the most crucial materials is made difficult by the great powers' determination to prevent nuclear proliferation. Hence it was logical from the Israeli point of view to embark secretly on an independent nuclear program. Its ultimate purpose would be to provide the Jewish state with a weapon of last resort. It would not be a substitute for conventional firepower ("a bigger bang for the buck"), and it would certainly not be a regular instrument for conducting "routine" foreign policy. Rather, it would constitute an instrument to offset the Arabs' quantitative superiority in a moment of extreme emergency. It was hoped that the availability of a small nuclear capability would achieve this in one of two possible ways: either as a means of obtaining U.S. support against the Arabs on an ad hoc basis—if and when, *and only if and when*, the latter were on the verge of a victory in a conventional war—or, if that support proved impossible to obtain and Arab armies were to break through Israeli defenses, as a means of threatening the Arabs directly.[13]

Threats, "Red Lines," and Casi Belli

U.S. pressure on Israel to evacuate the Sinai following its occupation in the course of Operation Kadesh created a distinct possibility that Ben Gurion's government would have nothing to show for the economic cost of the war, for its 190 casualties, and for the struggle in the United Nations that followed it. Moreover, if Israel agreed to withdraw from the Sinai empty-handed, it was possible that not only Nasser but the whole of the Arab world would be greatly emboldened by the results of the war. The operation would then have undercut whatever deterrence Israel had had before launching it—which was not much—or else the war would not have been initiated. For considerations such as these, Ben Gurion would not accept a unilateral withdrawal unless and until at least something more tangible could be extracted, if not from Egypt— with U.S. help—then at least from the United States itself. The result was a tacit U.S. approval of the principle that if and when Israeli navigation through the Straits of Tiran was threatened again, the Jewish state would have the right "in accordance with Article 51 of the Charter of the United Nations," to solve the problem by its own means, including the use of force. Israeli Foreign Minister Golda Meir stated this in the General Assembly, and Prime Minister Ben Gurion reiterated the statement in the Knesset, adding that this principle was endorsed by other maritime powers. The main reason that Israel went to war in 1956 in the first place was thus declared publicly to be what it had already been in effect, a casus belli.[14]

The fact that Israel had also gone to war in order to stop the sabotage actions across the Israeli–Egyptian armistice demarcation lines clearly suggested to all interested parties—mainly Jordan and Syria—that there would be a limit in the future, too, to Israel's tolerance of such actions. Nevertheless, neither this nor the concentration of forces on the borders nor any other type of threatening provocations or moves were clearly stated, along with the statement concerning passage through the straits, to be casi belli. The preference for ambiguity, for avoiding clear commitments, for signaling intentions through actions or discreetly through third parties, lingered on.

This was noticed, and soon criticized, by Yigal Allon, one of Israel's leading military experts. A general in the 1948 war, he was, in effect, forced to retire from the IDF at the peak of his career because Ben Gurion suspected that he would politicize the armed forces. Allon, who was clearly associated with the left-wing, hawkish, Achdut Haavodah party, returned to his kibbutz, Genosar, and then spent time as a graduate student at Oxford University. Before completing his studies, Allon returned to Israel, entered politics, and became a leading commentator on strategic and political affairs. In 1959 he published a book-length essay on Israel's position in the Arab–Israeli conflict, in which he advocated an unambiguous enunciation of casi belli. Allon's catalog of Arab actions that Israel should declare casi belli included the following items:

An offensive deployment of enemy forces

The incorporation of Jordan and/or Lebanon in a wider Arab union with a unified military command, especially if accompanied by entry into the West Bank (in the case of Jordan) or south of the Litani River (in the case of Lebanon) of the armed forces of other Arab governments

The establishment of a Palestinian political entity and the formation of an army under the official control of such an entity, especially if it was supported by one or another Arab government

Any Syrian attempt to thwart Israeli development projects in the Huleh area and/or concerning the utilization of the water of the Jordan River

Further Jordanian interference with Israeli traffic through the Latroun enclave and across east Jerusalem to the Israeli enclave on Mount Scopus, both passage being sanctioned by the armistice agreement

Any Egyptian attempt to reintroduce the naval blockade in the Straits of Tiran

The continuation of the Egyptian boycott of Israeli shipping through the Suez Canal[15]

When Allon's book was published, the author was a member of an opposition party in the Knesset. Given his prominent military background and numerous high-level contacts in the IDF and the Ministry of Defense, he may have been occasionally briefed concerning current military and political thinking. But he was not close enough to the center of power to be regarded as an official spokesman. This is not to say that anyone within the inner circle of decision making would have argued with this list of casi belli. They were all prime reasons for Israeli concern and were widely regarded as likely precipitants of military action, especially if several of them took place simultaneously. The difference between undeclared, perceived *precipitants* and publicly enunciated *casi belli* was important, however. A precipitant does not entail an open, binding commitment to act, a declaration staking the nation's credibility in advance. A casus belli most definitely does so. Allon advocated that widely agreed precipitants would be declared casi belli. His advocacy, however, failed to bring about a change in policy.

This reluctance to announce clear, irrevocable commitments persisted even when events seemed to suggest that the avoidance of commitment was encouraging Israel's adversaries to resort to prodding actions. One area where this was clearly the case was the Israeli–Syrian border, which, relatively tranquil since the massive Israeli raid of December 10, 1955 (Operation Olive Leaves), was gradually coming alive in the late 1950s. The immediate cause was the Jewish state's intention to carry out a number of development projects, all of which were connected to the area's water resources. This had begun in the spring of 1951, when Israel began to reclaim the land of the Huleh swamps. A tiny part of this area was within a DMZ in which, the Syrians argued, Israel was not permitted to effect any significant changes.[16] The tensions with Syria gathered momentum when Israel began the works that would culminate in the National Carrier (*hamovil haartzi*), a massive pipeline carrying fresh water from the Jordan River to the arid Negev desert many miles away. Concerned with preventing a conflagration that might jeopardize its attempts to create an anti-Soviet defense organization in the Middle East, the Eisenhower administration demanded that Israel stop the works until an agreed formula for sharing this precious water was worked out. A plan based on the Tennessee Valley Authority (TVA) concept and designed to turn the project into the beginning of a cooperative venture among all the parties concerned (the Johnston Plan) was negotiated for two years; accepted by Israel, Jordan, and Lebanon; but rejected by Syria late in 1955, when Damascus signed an arms deal with Czechoslovakia.[17]

Israel then proceeded to continue the project in a different location, further away from the Syrian border. Frustrated but powerless to stop the Israelis through a headstrong move, the Syrians began to build up military pressure along the entire border. This was manifested in a great number of small incidents, such as firing on farmers and occasional shelling of Israeli villages. Had Israel explicitly declared all this a casus belli—had Ben Gurion's government stated in the form of an ultimatum that if Syria did not stop forthwith, a severe punishment would be administered—the Syrians might have complied. After all, the fact that Syria resorted to small-scale subwar violence signaled, in itself, a tacit Syrian admission of an inability to resort to more dramatic forms of warfare. Syria, then, *was* partially deterred even without an Israeli ultimatum and might have been further deterred from carrying out even small infringements on the status quo if only Israel had singled out this low-level violence as a casus belli. Conversely, the evident Israeli reluctance to make such a declaration may well have encouraged the Syrians to believe, despite all the evidence of past Israeli conduct in such matters, that they could continue such actions without suffering an unacceptable punishment.

Israel continued to show restraint until the winter of 1960. Late in January the government decided that the time had come to inflict on the Syrians a blow that would impress upon them how seriously Israel regarded the constant disruption of normal life in the area. This reprisal took the form of an infantry attack on the Syrian position in and around the village of Lower Tawfiq, overlooking the Sea of Galilee. Evidently shaken, the Syrians turned to Egypt (since 1958 Syria's twin within the United Arab Republic) with an urgent request for help. Given Egypt's pretensions for leadership in the Arab world, its patronage of Syria under the aegis of the United Arab Republic (UAR) and its leadership of the Arabs in the struggle against Israel, President Nasser could ill afford to seem evasive regarding this urgent Syrian plea for help. He had to do something that would be spectacular enough to prevent criticism in the Arab world but not so substantial as to induce the Israelis to overreact. As far as can be judged, some such calculus, suggesting that Egypt was deterred by Israel but also that it had great difficulties in warding off pressures from the Arab world, led Nasser to order 50,000 troops with 500 tanks into the Sinai peninsula.

The Egyptian force was detected only when it was already deployed between Jebel Libni and El Arish, very close to the Israeli border. This was clearly a serious failure of Israeli intelligence, and it caught the IDF with only twenty or thirty tanks in close proximity to the border. If the Egyptians were to launch an attack, Israel would have to rely for the first twenty-four hours almost exclusively on the IAF. The IDF was caught, in the words of a note General Rabin passed to General Weizman during an emergency General Staff meeting, "with its pants down."[18]

Beyond the problem of intelligence failure and the inadequacy of Israeli forces-in-being, the Egyptian move demonstrated the shortcomings of Israel's ambiguous posture. Both the Israeli and the Egyptian political-military elites had known since 1956 that the foreward deployment of Egyptian forces of such a magnitude in the Sinai would turn on red lights in Israel and might precipitate a crisis. Yet although this was virtually common knowledge, Israel desisted from tying its own hands in advance by undertaking an open, and thus irrevocable, commitment to administer a punishment. This was a prudent policy in the sense that Israel retained its freedom of action. The price, however, may have been a less effective deterrence than Israel should have projected, given its actual capabilities.

Egypt may well have been tempted to move by the ambiguity of the Israeli position. It did not know the precise limits of Israeli tolerance in this regard because Israel did not state what these limits were. Therefore—under the pressure of the Syrian request for help—the temptation for Egypt to explore what these limits were through actual action was probably irresistible. The Israeli response was secretly to mobilize the thirty-seventh reserve armored brigade, deploy it together with the regular seventh armored brigade near the Egyptian border, but avoid any acts or utterances that could escalate the crisis.

To the Egyptians, the Israeli mobilization may have indicated that Israel would not allow Egypt to go any further. It also betrayed Israel's pervasive reluctance to allow the matter to escalate. Under these circumstances, Nasser could decide—if he was in a mood to run greater risks—simply to order the forces to settle down in the El Arish–Jebel Libni area. This would have erased one of the most glaring consequences of the 1956 war and thus would have endowed Nasser with a badly needed victory. The fact that he did not choose to do so suggests that he was afraid of Israel's reaction—in other words, that he was deterred. Yet although from this point of view Operation Rotem (as the incident was code-named in Israel) was a reassuring success, in the final analysis it would have been better from the Israeli viewpoint to act in a way that would deter the Egyptians from crossing into the Sinai in the first place. To achieve this Israel would have to draw clearer "red lines" than it had done. For reasons that will be explored later, this was more than it was prepared to do.

If Israeli policy prior to the Rotem crisis was not optimal, Israel's conduct in the course of the crisis was exceedingly effective. For one thing, although Ben Gurion's government did not take Nasser's action lightly, it also did not panic and was not tempted to read into the Egyptian leader's move more than there was to it. Since 1956 Nasser had become the main apostle in the Arab world of the assiduous argument that, on the one hand, Israel was an implacable enemy that had to be restrained and perhaps eliminated; but that, on the other hand, Israel was too formidable to be assaulted without intensive, meticulous, and hence long-term preparations. This was Nasser's way of telling his radical rivals in the Arab world (especially in Syria and Iraq) that he was every bit as determined as they were to fight Israel, but that he would not be dragged into war prematurely and suffer yet another defeat.[19]

An anxious and isolated Israel, as it had been before the 1956 war, might have failed to read this double message between the lines of Nasser's numerous speeches. Such a failure could have easily led to a serious conflagration as early as February 1960. But the newly acquired self-confidence of the Israelis after their 1956 success made some of them, paradoxically, more cautious. Indeed, the reluctance to become openly committed to sharply drawn casi belli persisted, despite telling episodes such as Operation Rotem, until the end of the 1957–67 period.

An excellent example was provided by Shimon Peres, then deputy minister of defense, in an article published in the IDF monthly, *Ma'arachot*, late in 1962. Addressing himself to the "time dimension" in the Arab–Israeli conflict (a euphemism for the question of whether Israel or its adversaries had time on their side), Peres enumerated five changes (which he defined as *ilot*, Hebrew for "pretexts") in the situation that would make another Arab–Israeli war likely:

> The first pretext—if Egypt blocks the straits of Eilat [sic]—Israel will fight to open them.
>
> The second pretext—if Egypt conquers Jordan—Israel will not remain idle.
>
> The third pretext—if the Arabs build up a force large enough to jeopardize the existence of Israel in an immediate sense, or if they concentrate such a force in an intimidating proximity [to Israel]—such a concentration might lead to a confrontation.
>
> The fourth pretext—if Israel seizes water that are not its own—according to its neighbors—the Arabs will react vehemently.
>
> The fifth pretext—if Israel acquires an unpredictable power—real or imagined—the Arabs will react vehemently.[20]

The language of this statement of casi belli is interesting. It does not specify how much Arab military strength would be too much from the Israeli point of view, or how close a concentration of Arab forces would be regarded as too close. In addition, Peres adds to three casi belli from the Israeli point of view two casi belli from the Arab point of view, but again leaves them very vague. Finally, as if to leave no doubt that he intends no irrevocable commitment, the deputy minister of defense employs the inappropriate but suggestive term "pretexts" while time and again stating that all these changes in the status quo are "pretexts" according to "foreign sources" that he left unspecified.

A not dissimilar list of "Arab acts which would constitute an automatic casus belli for Israel" was related to a leading scholar in private by Gideon Rafael, a senior Israeli diplomat, some four years after the publication of Peres's list. Rafael enumerated four acts belonging in this category: "two are on water, two on land, north, south, east and west; one is the attempt to divert the waters of the Jordan, another the closing of the Straits of Tiran; a third is the control of the Jordan 'bulge' [the West Bank] by a state or a united command more powerful than Amman [Jordan]; and the fourth is the concentration of Egyptian military power in the Sinai desert."[21]

This was clearly far more explicit than any previous official statement, and it certainly represented accurately the Israeli concept of precipitants. The fact that it was not published until 1972, some four years after the crisis in which most of these events happened and did indeed lead to war, underlines once again the main point in this part of the discussion—that Israel had a clear concept of what changes in the status quo would precipitate military action. Under the leadership of David Ben Gurion (who finally retired in 1963) as under the leadership of Levi Eshkol, who succeeded Ben Gurion as prime minister, Israel persisted, however, in its reluctance to state these precipitants boldly and thereby turn them into effective instruments of deterrence.

Aware of this, Allon, who meanwhile had become minister of labor and a leading member of the cabinet security committee in Levi Eshkol's ministry, apparently continued vigorously to advocate a change in policy. Addressing a closed meeting of the MAPAI Young Guard (*Hamishmeret Hatseira*) on February 22, 1967, Allon repeated the essentials of his thesis in his previously mentioned 1959 book, *A Curtain of Sand*. This time, however, he went beyond the original version in his statements concerning casi belli, which he no longer prefaced with caveats. Instead, he spoke explicitly of casi belli, which he had not done in the published 1959 version. Moreover, he added to the list a number of new items while dropping some of those on the original list. "In six possible cases," Allon said, "Israel will be entitled and perhaps obliged to go to war":

a. In the event of a dangerous concentration of offensive [Arab] forces.
b. When it transpires that the enemy is preparing a surprise air attack on Israel's air bases.
c. If the Israeli nuclear reactors [at Nahal Sorek and Dimona] are attacked from the air.
d. If guerrilla warfare, mining and shelling reach a level at which it can no longer be dealt with effectively through passive defense and reprisals.
e. If Jordan enters into a military alliance with another Arab state and permits the deployment of foreign troops on its territory, especially west of the Jordan [River].
f. If Egypt blocks the Straits of Tiran.

Given Allon's official position at the time of this important statement, there can be little doubt that he expressed in this presentation a prevailing concept of war precipitants. But the fact that the lecture was delivered behind closed doors and was published for the first time only in the fall of 1967—three months after the Six-Day War, in which most of these casi belli were rendered obsolete—leaves little doubt that this was still an advocacy rather than an official policy.[22] Allon had persistently favored a vigorous posture of deterrence. He saw clear and unambiguous proclamation of casi belli as an important element in such a national posture. His colleagues, however, saw matters differently. There was little doubt among them that if one, and certainly if several, of the scenarios on Allon's list materialized, the Jewish state would have to resort to force again. But either because of their dilletantism in strategic thinking (at least in comparison to Allon), or because of their apprehensions concerning Arab, great power, and/or domestic reactions, Allon's cabinet colleagues would not endorse in an authoritative, binding manner (such as a speech in the Knesset and a vote on it thereafter) any statement of casi belli. The policy in this regard remained as ambiguous as it had been before the 1956 war.

Patrons and Partners

The French connection that Israel forged on the eve of Operation Kadesh went beyond anything the Israelis had dreamed of during the preceding years of isolation. France supplied Israel with all the arms it needed, with scientific know-how, with access to advanced nuclear research and technology, with the foundations of an important aviation industry, and above all with a sense of pride and self-respect that had been badly shaken by repeated rebuffs from other major powers. Although Israeli–French relations continued to gather momentum in the years following the joint war against Egypt—although, in fact, they reached their peak somewhere between 1958 and 1962, when General De Gaulle was prepared to hail Israel as France's "friend and ally"—it gradually dawned on the Israelis that this tacit alliance had its limits. The French would not turn it into an open alliance based on a contractual commitment for mutual aid in the event of war and ratified in the legislatures of both countries. In fact, France began to move in another direction once the main cause of the alliance, the Algerian rebellion (and France's consequent conflict with the Arab world) came to an end.[23]

Realizing these limits of the French connection, Israeli policymakers came to a variety of different conclusions about the prospects for securing worthy alliances. Dayan stood for the most pessimistic view in this regard and, in fact, advocated something that can best be described as defiant self-reliance. Israel, he said, would not be saved by others simply because it was a Jewish state with such a history of suffering behind it. To ensure its security and survival, the Jewish state should assume the posture of a "detonator" or a "biting beast." Anyone in the world, including the great powers, should know that if they attempted to disregard Israeli interests, there would be such an explosion that their own interests would also be damaged. Circumstantial evidence suggests that this view led Dayan, as early as 1957, to advocate an Israeli nuclear program.[24]

The up-and-coming Yigal Allon, whose background and upbringing were not dissimilar to Dayan's (both of them were *sabras*—Jews born and bred in Palestine), did not share Dayan's view that a last-resort nuclear weapon was an urgent necessity. Much like Dayan, however, Allon too advocated self-reliance.[25] He would not oppose a formal treaty of alliance with a great power if that were feasible, Allon wrote. But this was not the case. Israel was unique in the world in the sense that neither bloc would accept it into their ranks. To plead with them would not only be disgraceful, Allon argued, but positively harmful. A constant refusal by the great powers to extend their protective patronage to the Jewish state would merely serve to underline Israel's basic weakness in Arab eyes. Hence Israel should assume a posture of self-reliance and try to make the most of it.[26]

By contrast with both Dayan and Allon, Abba Eban, always the staunchest advocate of an alliance with the United States, was convinced, as of the 1958 U.S. intervention in Lebanon, that the Eisenhower administration had already come round to the idea that Israel was an important strategic asset. Sooner or later, Eban thought, Israel would be able to cash in on that and obtain formal U.S. patronage.[27] Peres, the indefatigable architect of the French connection, continued to believe in its viability but also shared the views of Dayan and Ben Gurion regarding a nuclear program; in addition, he invested a great deal of effort in attempts to cast Israel's net wider. Peres succeeded in establishing a security liaison with the Federal Republic of Germany (with which Israel had no diplomatic relations); he explored the possibility of an Israeli membership in the North Atlantic Treaty Organization (NATO) as well as in the European Economic Community (EEC), then in the planning stages. He also laid the foundations for Israel's policy of dynamic involvement in black Africa.[28] The resourceful and largely successful efforts of Peres, coupled with the fact that he had become Ben Gurion's right-hand man, greatly frustrated the new foreign minister, Golda Meir. The latter developed a vindictive grudge against Peres that survived until her retirement from politics in 1974. With the exception of the nuclear program, however, a question on which Meir apparently disagreed with Peres, Ben Gurion, and Dayan, she found herself enacting many parts of Peres's other foreign policy advocacies. Chief of these was the attempt to circumvent Arab hostility through an extensive Israeli network of close relations with the emerging continent of Africa.[29]

Arguing the case for these sometimes conflicting foreign policy orientations, these and other key policymakers were united in four underlying assumptions. First, there still was no military equivalent to political understandings with Israel's adversaries. If such understandings could be reached, they would greatly strengthen Israel's security. After more than a decade of failed attempts to establish contact with leaders of the Arab world—from Abdullah, Hosni Zaim, and Nuri al Said to Nasser and Hussein—the bulk of Israel's foreign policy decision makers had become somewhat cynical. Imperceptibly—indeed, contrary to their own declared ethos—they had gradually shifted the emphasis from a search for a political settlement, or at least a détent, to a policy of containment—namely, a search for political arrangements that would act as effective countervailing forces to the Arabs and their Soviet allies.

Second, the demonstration of Israel's military prowess in the Sinai campaign had changed the nature of the problem of alliance affiliation. Henceforth Israel could act on the assumption that both friend and foe were sufficiently impressed to change their approach toward the Jewish state. Israel was no longer a weak and dependent irritant for friends and an easy prey for foes. It had become a regional power to reckon with.

Third, Israel could strengthen its deterrence, as well as its terms of collaboration,[30] with great powers by engaging more forcefully in the regional balance-of-power game.

Fourth, as a consequence of the combination of the previous three factors, Israel could make do for the time being with secondary or even tertiary types of alliances—that is, far less formal and far less public types of alliance connection than the standard primary type. The urgency of obtaining the contractual and public protective patronage of a great power had declined. It was still crucial to ensure the uninterrupted flow of arms and any other types of strategic supplies, ranging from wheat (which Israel did not have) through oil (of which Israel had only a fraction of what it needed) to uranium (which it also lacked). However, the protective political and strategic dimension of the problem had become less acute.

The practical implication of the first two of these assumptions was that for the short- and medium-term future, deterrence could be obtained on the basis of, primarily, a conventional war-winning military capability. This conclusion was reinforced anyway by the rapidly changing force structure of the IDF, from an infantry-based defensive force to an armor- and air force-based instrument for a blitzkrieg. The practical implication of the third assumption—that Israel should engage more forcefully in the regional balance-of-power game—took some time to gel into a concrete concept.

In the 1920s and 1930s Ben Gurion often spoke of the need for an Arab–Jewish alliance. The improbability of the idea did not take him very long to realize. One result was that he began to wonder, occasionally, whether the Zionist movement should not attempt to align itself with other forces in the Middle East that also had a fundamental conflict with the (mainly Sunni Moslem) pan-Arab movement. This led to an on-again, off-again dialogue between Zionist leaders and a variety of leaders of the Maronites in Lebanon. Having investigated the value of this Maronite connection, the Israeli Foreign Ministry reached the conclusion by the very beginning of the 1950s that the Maronites were a hollow reed. Ben Gurion and Dayan, on the other hand, were not entirely convinced. Thus, when the noose seemed to be tightening on Israel as a result of the meteoric rise of Nasserism, Ben Gurion and Dayan proposed to Prime Minister Sharett to establish a link with the Maronites; engineer a coup d'état in Lebanon; and help to establish a small, Maronite-dominated state that would be in alliance with Israel. Their main motive was, it seems, to prevent Lebanon's turning into an active confrontation state. If Israel did not turn Lebanon into its proxy, or buffer, somebody else would turn it into a launching pad for operations against Israel.

Sharett thought that the whole idea was a recipe for disaster—indeed, that Israel would get itself into a quagmire if Ben Gurion's scheme were carried out. He vetoed it, and Ben Gurion, who was out of office, accepted the verdict.[31] But the germ of the idea that Israel could gain tangible strategic advantages from a balance-of-power-oriented response to the regional political process did not die. It did not materialize in the context of Lebanon, nor did anything come out of it when Israeli emissaries established contacts with representatives of other non-Arab and/or non-Moslem governments, such as Turkey, Iran, and Ethiopia. Some Israeli policymakers, however, among them Ben Gurion and Dayan, were convinced that the convergence of the interests of these powers with Israel's was real and that the main reason for these states' lack of enthusiasm was Israel's image of weakness in the 1949–56 period. The corollary to such a perception was that the demonstration of Israel's vitality—its spectacular performance on the battlefield in the course of the 1956 Sinai campaign—should have transformed the evaluation of Israel by these same regional forces. What was difficult to obtain before the 1956 war, supporters of this thesis contended, might have become attainable in its aftermath.

Such thinking was reinforced by events in the Middle East during 1957–58, especially the Eisenhower Doctrine; the near collapse of Lebanon and Jordan; the bloody coup in Iraq; the Egyptian–Syrian union; the growing friction between Syria and Turkey, Iraq and Iran, Egypt and Ethiopia; the growing Soviet involvement in the affairs of leading regional powers like Egypt, Syria, and Iraq.[32] In turn several Israeli policymakers, chief of them Ben Gurion, became convinced that the moment was ripe for an imaginative diplomacy that would extract for Israel the utmost advantage from this state of regional affairs. Specifically, the idea was to develop a three-tier system of regional alignments with Israel as the linchpin holding them together and deriving the utmost benefit from such a pivotal role.

The overt dimension of the scheme would be an alliance between Israel and Turkey, Israel and Iran, and Israel and Ethiopia. This tier, tying together countries that were at conflict with the Nasser-led militant part of the Arab world and with the Soviet Union, would be buttressed by another overt tier binding all these countries with the West in general and with the United States in particular. In addition, however, there would be a third, covert tier involving non-Arab and/or non-Moslem minorities, such as the Christians in Lebanon, the Druzes in Syria, the Kurds in Iraq and the Christians in southern Sudan.[33]

The potential benefits for Israel from such a regional architecture seemed enormous. The scheme would stengthen the Western interest. It would hold at bay the resurgent pan-Arab movement with its radical ideas, violent choice of means, patently Islamic coloring, and limitless ambitions. Moreover, the proposed regional structure would turn Israel into an important asset instead of the liability the Jewish state appeared to have been before. Rather than retaining its image as an isolated focus of Arab hostility, Israel would be integrated into a stabilizing, structurally reliable component of a global camp of nations. Rather than pleading in vain to be incorporated into a Western brainchild such as MEDO, which in any case was abortive, Israel would be the initiator of a regional structure, act as its linchpin, and proceed to reap a rich harvest of Western gratitude and assistance. Above all, if such a scheme ever took shape, it would imply that whenever the Arabs considered war against Israel, they would have to take into account the possible reactions of all the other participants in the scheme, both in the Middle East (Ethiopia, Iran, and Turkey) and beyond (in particular, the United States). Israel's deterrence would thus be enormously strengthened.

The impact of the third, covert, tier of the scheme on the ultimate outcome would be similar. If the Christians of Lebanon had an alliance with Israel, the very existence of such a bond, it was thought in the late 1950s, would be sufficient to draw the attention and pin down some of the resources of the Syrians. If the Kurdish minority in Iraq were helped in its struggle with the regime in Baghdad, the Iraqi army would be unable to commit extensive forces to another Arab–Israeli war. If Sudan had a mutiny or even near-mutiny of the Christians in the south, it too would be unable to reinforce the Egyptian war effort against Israel.

In addition to this strategic perspective, the scheme as a whole, and in particular its minority tier, had a quasi-ideological attraction. The main villain of the Middle East piece, the source of trouble for all, appeared to be the militant, anti-Western, Sunni Moslem, pan-Arab drive for fulfillment. What it seemed to be striving at was the recreation of a huge Arab superpolity, stretching (as in the seventh and eighth centuries A.D.) from the Persian Gulf to the shores of the Atlantic. What this superpolity would inevitably entail, some Israelis argued, was intolerance toward anything that did not entirely fit into it. Every non-Moslem, non-Sunni, or non-Arab minority in the region was thus a thorn in the flesh of this pugnacious movement for unity. Its ethos was predicated on the assumption that the Middle East was a Suni Arab ocean. Therefore, it was in the interest of all those factors in the Middle East that did not fit into this description to emphasize the pluralism, the mosaiclike heterogeneity of the region—the fact, in Ben Gurion's words, that it "is not an exclusively Arab area"; that "on the contrary, the majority of its inhabitants are not Arabs"; that the "Turks, the Persians and the Jews—not to mention the Kurds and the other non-Arab minorities in the Arab states—are more numerous than the Arabs in the Middle East."[34] An alliance of minorities and states that did not fit into the pan-Arab vision would do just that.

In retrospect it is difficult to avoid the impression that the key to the success of the entire edifice was the cooperation of the Western powers, in particular the United States. If the latter were to strengthen Ben Gurion's hand, if they were to lobby the Middle Eastern governments in question and perhaps apply some pressure on them to go along with the Israeli plan, it could well have materialized, at least in part. Conversely, the polite but firm refusal of the U.S. government to endorse the plan doomed it from the very beginning, since the incentives for Iranians, Turks, and Ethiopians to go along were not great to start with. They could see the limited but real convergence of interests between them and the Israelis. They did not object to cooperation with the Israelis whenever that coincided with their immediate interests. But the far-flung vision of the plan left most of them cold. Some of the details of this Israeli search for Middle East partners are worth recalling in greater detail.

Israel had had diplomatic and trade relations with Turkey since the 1950s. When U.S.–Israeli relations were at a low ebb during the first half of the 1950s, Israeli's relations with Turkey suffered, too. When, following the Suez campaign and the U.S. intervention in Lebanon, Israeli relations with the United States began to improve, the Jerusalem–Ankara axis, which Ben Gurion sought to establish, increasingly appeared feasible as well. Impressed by Israel's swift and decisive victory in the Sinai and apprehensive about the effects that the Egyptian–Syrian union and the Qassim coup in Iraq could have on their own position (given the fact of Turkey's common border with both Iraq and Syria), the Turks themselves indicated an interest. Ben Gurion suggested to President Eisenhower that the United States should further encourage Turkey (and Iran) to cooperate with the Jewish state. But although the Americans were evasive, Ben Gurion moved ahead and, on August 28, 1958, flew secretly to Turkey for a meeting with Prime Minister Menderes.

The talks showed a clear meeting of the minds between the Israeli and Turkish prime ministers. The practical results, however, turned out to be meager. Even under the Menderes–Bayar regime, the Turks showed little interest in pursuing links with Israel beyond a certain amount of trade. This attitude was also upheld by the Girsel regime following the coup d'état of May 1960. Thereafter, Turkish–Israeli relations basically stagnated. The threat of Nasserist and Soviet pressure from Syria and from the Soviet Union itself subsided. The U.S. attitude toward Turkey in the course of the Cyprus crisis of 1963 strained relations between them and drove the Turks to a rapprochement with the Soviets. And the combined effect of these two separate trends was to render Israel an essentially marginal factor in the overall Turkish foreign policy calculus.[35]

A far more rewarding pattern gradually emerged in Israeli–Iranian relations. Though reluctant at first to recognize the Jewish state, Iran extended de facto recognition and established a diplomatic legation in Tel Aviv as early as March 1950. Six months later an Israeli diplomatic delegation seeking a de jure recognition and more extensive relations arrived in Teheran. The Israeli requests, however, were turned down. Several months later, following the rise of Mossadeq, the Iranian legation in Tel Aviv was closed. There were even demands by influential Iranians such as the Speaker of the Majlis, Ayatollah Kashani, that Iran's relations with the Arab world should be improved and that the ancient Iranian Jewish community of hundreds of thousands should be expelled en masse. Nor did the eclipse of Mossadeq herald any significant improvement. There was, to be sure, a slight improvement in commercial links. By 1953 Israel had begun to receive small quantities of Iranian crude oil, which were shipped to the new port of Eilat, but this was not accompanied by any significant development on either the military or the diplomatic front.

Iran's reaction to Israel's military victory in the 1956 campaign was ambivalent. On the one hand, echoing the exceedingly harsh reaction of Washington and reflecting some deference to Arab indignation, Iran issued a sternly worded note of censure condemning the venture. On the other hand, Iran was duly impressed with Israel's performance, apprehensive about the political gains of the Soviets, and concerned about the potential ramifications in the Middle East of Nasser's evident success in turning this military defeat of Egypt into a political gold mine. The first sign of this latter attitude was a secret request, early in 1957, for a meeting of the Iranian deputy premier, General Bakhtiar, with a high-ranking Israeli. Within several months Bakhtiar had established working relations with Ya'akov Karoz, a political officer (apparently a Mossad agent) in the Israeli Embassy in Paris. The two met several times, and Karoz was subsequently invited to Teheran. The result was an Iranian invitation for Israel to set up an undercover liaison office in Teheran. Iran also increased the flow of oil to Eilat. Solel Boneh, the Histadrut (trade union) construction conglomerate, began to operate in Iran, and El Al, Israel's national airline, inaugurated a line from Tel Aviv to Johannesburg with a stop in Teheran.

By the summer of 1958, Iranian–Israeli relations had gathered further momentum. Iran became increasingly worried by the coup d'état in Iraq, the Syrian–Egyptian union, the attempt by Arab radicals to destabilize the regimes of Jordan and Lebanon, and above all the evident involvement in all these developments of Iran's great neighbor to the north—the Soviet Union. Noting that Washington was not averse (though it was not enthusiastic, either) to the Israeli scheme of regional alliances, and tending to exaggerate Israel's ability to wield influence in Washington through the so-called Jewish lobby, the shah seemed to have reached the conclusion that the emerging link with Israel should be boosted further. Ben Gurion and the shah began to correspond. Eshkol, the Israeli minister of finance, paid a visit to Iran and met the shah. Israel constructed a pipeline from the port of Eilat on the shores of the Gulf of Aqaba to the port of Ashdod on the Mediterranean. The line not only helped Israel to purchase more crude oil in Iran but also provided an alternative route for Iranian oil, thereby decreasing dependence on Nasser's goodwill concerning the use of the Suez Canal. Iran reopened its diplomatic legation in Tel Aviv, at first as a section in the Swiss Embassy but later as an independent mission. Abba Eban, who had just completed a long tour of duty in Washington and New York as Israeli ambassador to both the United States and the United Nations, paid a visit to Teheran as well.

On July 23, 1960, the eighth anniversary of the Egyptian revolution, the shah announced that Iran was recognizing the state of Israel de facto. President Nasser of Egypt reacted with a sharply worded diatribe, and Egypt severed diplomatic relations with Iran. The shah, however, remained unperturbed. Indeed, not only did he authorize the continued expansion of Iranian–Israeli relations, but in December 1961 he also hosted the Israeli prime minister and minister of defense, Ben Gurion, in Teheran. This was an affront that Nasser could ill afford to ignore. He therefore launched simultaneously a propaganda campaign and a wave of well-orchestrated subversive activities in the Khouzistan region. Although the shah persisted in his refusal to upgrade relations with Israel to the exchange of embassies, he also refused to yield to Nasser's heavyhanded pressures. Following the visit to Iran of Moshe Dayan, the former IDF chief of staff, who was widely regarded as the chief architect of the Israeli victory in the Sinai campaign and who, since 1959, had been minister of agriculture in Ben Gurion's government, Israel launched a major reconstruction project in Iran's earthquake-damaged province of Khazvin. Even after Ben Gurion retired from public life in June 1963, Iranian–Israeli relations did not change course. The new Israeli premier, Levi Eshkol, who as minister of finance was one of the first high-ranking Israelis to visit Iran, sent his own minister of finance, Pinchas Sapir, to Teheran as well.

Soon relations between the two countries began to spill over from civilian to military cooperation. In January 1964 the Israeli chief of staff, Lieutenant-General Tsvi Tsur, and the director-general of the Ministry of Defense, Asher Ben Nathan, stopped in Teheran for two days of talks with the Iranian chief of staff, General Hijazi, and senior members of this staff. This meeting led to the sale to Iran of Uzi submachine guns, to Israeli instruction and training of Iranian army units, to intelligence sharing, to Israeli involvement in the establishment of the SAVAK (Iran's secret police) and to Israeli–Iranian cooperation in assisting the Kurdish rebels of Mula Moustafa al-Barazani's in their struggle against the Iraqi central government.

Though considerable, these Iranian–Israeli links were still a far cry from Ben Gurion's grand design, in which the emphasis was on the public commitment of the partners to come to each other's aid in the event of an attack by a third (Arab) party—namely, on the deterrent aspect of the alliance. Nevertheless, Israel and Iran seemed to be moving toward an alliance that would add important increments of security to Israel by increasing the burden on the Arabs and thereby forcing them to be more preoccupied with their security.[36]

Israeli–Iranian relations were sometimes presented in a broad historical perspective that traced their origins to the fifth century B.C., when Cyrus the Great issued a proclamation calling on the Judaic exiles in Babylon to return to the Land of Canaan and restore their Temple on Mount Zion. A similar motif sometimes appeared in analyses of Israeli relations with imperial Ethiopia, the third angle in Ben Gurion's triangular grand design. The Ethiopian emperor, according to one tradition, was a descendent of Menelik the First, who is said to have been the first fruit of King Solomon's lovemaking with the Queen of Sheba. Historical myths notwithstanding, modern Ethiopian relations with Israel have followed a balance-of-power, interest-based pattern no less than have the Jewish state's relations with Turkey and Iran.

During the occupation of the country by Fascist Italy, the Ethiopian emperor, Haile Selassie, who called himself the Lion of Judah, found refuge in Jerusalem, where he was well received by the Jews and was looked after by the local congregation of Church of Ethiopia clergy. When Israel was established, however, the emperor, who had been returned to power in Addis Ababa by the British, refrained from establishing diplomatic relations with the Jewish state until as late as 1953. Thereafter a great improvement took place. Ethiopia's tense relations with Nasserist Egypt probably help to explain the shift, as does Israel's Sinai victory in 1956. On the other hand, the Ethiopian government—much like the Turkish and Iranian governments—remained aloof toward Israel in its public utterances. There were probably two reasons: concern over further isolation in the Middle East and sensitivity to the reactions of Ethiopia's large Moslem population.

The most important turning point occurred in 1960, precisely when Ben Gurion's drive to implement his grand design was at its peak. There were, again, two important reasons for this—an escalation in Ethiopia's conflict with Somalia over the future of the Ogaden Desert, coinciding (perhaps not by accident) with the intensification of the revolt of the Shifta tribes in Eritrea, and with Nasser's intervention in the Yemen—across the Red Sea. All three events must have created a sense of intimidating isolation in the Ethiopian capital. Ethiopia needed arms and military advice. It also needed development projects that could improve the standard of living (and with it the waning popularity of the aging emperor). Israel could provide both, as it had demonstrated elsewhere in Africa as well as in Iran. Israel itself was also eager to engage in cooperative ventures with the Ethiopian regime for the general reasons already explained as well as for very specific strategic reasons: preventing the turning of the Red Sea, the only sea route to the port of Eilat, into an Arab lake. If Nasser succeeded in his intervention in the Yemen, as seemed certain in the early 1960s, he would be able to deny Israel access to Eilat and thus, in effect, undo the results of the 1956 war. Accordingly, Israel needed an access to Ethiopia's long Red Sea coast; to obtain this strategic advantage, it needed close relations with the Ethiopian regime.

The second reason for the turning point in Ethiopia's relations with Israel in 1960 was more directly connected to the fortunes of the emperor himself. On December 14, 1960, while paying a visit to Brazil, the emperor heard of a coup d'état in Addis Ababa. His supporters transmitted radio appeals for help—specifically, for Israeli help. The emperor flew back at once but, for good measure, stopped in Liberia on his way. While in Monrovia, he requested that the Israeli embassy pass on to Jerusalem a request for help.

This presented the Israeli government with a dilemma. Some of the rebels were on very good terms with the Israeli mission. Should they be helped and the emperor forsaken? Or would it be more advisable to do the reverse? Ben Gurion decided to help the emperor, and the coup was quelled. Thereafter, Ethiopian–Israeli relations moved rapidly toward the implementation of Ben Gurion's grand design. Economic relations were expanded. Israeli experts established a variety of plants in Eritrea and in Ethiopia proper. Sea links between Eilat and Asmara were expanded. Israeli experts established a national university in Addis Ababa. Israeli military personnel trained Ethiopian soldiers to fight counterinsurgency warfare in Eritrea and more conventional warfare in the Ogaden. Israel set up observation posts on the ethiopian Red Sea coast to monitor Arab and Soviet shipping through the Bab-el-Mandeb Straits and in the Red Sea. Last but not least, the Ethiopian government permitted Israeli experts to cross the border to Sudan and establish links with the Christian guerrillas who were fighting the central Sudanese government.

These important links in the Horn of Africa and the Sudan, like the Iranian connection and the involvement with the Kurdish rebels, came close to what Ben Gurion had in mind. They constituted an attempt to circumvent the Arab noose dangling around the Jewish state. They forced the Arabs to commit their attention—and sometimes their forces—to areas that were far from Israel, thereby dispersing the Arab war effort and making it less dangerous. All these links, however, never quite matured into the formal alliance structure Ben Gurion had hoped for—an alliance involving commitments to act whenever one of the allies became subject to attack. Israel, as one Ethiopian put it, remained a "mistress" rather than becoming a "wife." Nevertheless, the sum total of these developments was quite positive from the Israeli point of view.[37]

While developing these important links, Israel also made important strides in its efforts to develop bases of support in Africa, Latin America, and south Asia. Hundreds of Israeli experts were involved in development projects throughout the third world. Thousands of Africans and Asians were training in both civilian and military centers in Israel. A large and lively diplomatic community established itself in Jerusalem and Tel Aviv. Israel's position in the United Nations seemed secure and respectable. Its relations with France were intimate, with the EEC and with the United States quite close. Even its relations with the Soviet bloc were cordial. Consequently, the urgency of eliciting explicit commitments from great powers seemed to have subsided; even the regional dimension of the grand design no longer assumed the same urgency as it had in the late 1950s.

To be sure, Israeli emissaries continued to apply what pressures they could on the Iranian and Ethiopian governments to upgrade the formal and public level of their relations with the Jewish state. They also occasionally raised the question of a formal alliance with U.S. leaders, including Presidents Kennedy and Johnson. For several reasons, however, Israeli leaders lowered their sights in this regard: they fully realized that such formal commitments, which could have constituted a crucial element in Israel's ability to deter its Arab adversaries, would not be offered; they were greatly reassured by the tacit U.S. security guarantee; they were increasingly aware of Israel's enhanced leverage vis-à-vis the United States ever since the latter had discovered the military significance of the Jewish state's independent nuclear program;[38] they remained somewhat reassured by U.S. and French public references to Israel as an "ally"; they were flushed with a strong feeling that theirs had been a success story; above all, they were filled—especially after the departure of the ever-anxious Ben Gurion—with a new sense of security, strength, and self-confidence. Formal deterrence-strengthening alliances continued to be upheld as a long-term foreign policy goal, but they ceased to be regarded as an urgent short-term "must."

The Diplomacy of Violence

The single most important factor contributing to Israel's new sense of relative security was the IDF's performance in the course of the five-day campaign of 1956.[39] Before this operation, the Egyptian army had seemed more formidable, and Israel's perception of the need for outside support had been correspondingly stronger. It was for this reason that Ben Gurion was so adamant about the need for French and British involvement in the attack on Egypt. By the same token, once the crisis was over, the Israelis could look back and marvel at their achievement. Britain and France, hitherto considered world empires, appeared weak and beaten. Egypt seemed to be making the utmost of the political success that it had no doubt obtained in this crisis (thanks to U.S. miscalculations and British weakness). Beyond this, the Israelis could not fail to recall that no Arab state had come to Egypt's rescue and that the Egyptian army had been served a stunning defeat by the IDF.

The impact of this perception of the 1956 crisis on Israeli military and political thinking was far-reaching and profound. In the first place, the military and political elite of the Jewish state became increasingly reassured concerning their nation's ability to go to war alone and achieve its objectives. Second, the advantages of a preemptive, first-strike posture seemed to have been irrefutably reaffirmed. Such a posture gave the IDF the initiative; it maximized the element of surprise and shock; it endowed the IDF with a tremendous momentum that made it, in a way, a stronger, more effective military force in the last day of fighting than in the first. Above all, Israel's initiation of the operation enabled it to concentrate all its force on one Arab state. Whereas in 1948 the Arab world had united and then initiated war in accordance with its own choice of time, scale, and location, in 1956 the Arabs were so surprised by the Israeli attack that no confrontation state would join Egypt unless and until it became clear that the latter was winning, or at least not losing. Thus the fact that Israel had initiated the war acted as a formidable multiplier of its force. The IDF could focus on Egypt and, by serving a knockout blow to this pivot of the Arab world, could also virtually ensure that no other Arab state would join the fighting.

Seen in more or less these terms, the 1956 victory constituted a triple strategic gain from the Israeli point of view:

1. It put a stop to the harassment and attrition of the 1953–56 period.
2. It constituted such a tour de force that it endowed the Jewish state with new—and seemingly very important—increments of deterrence.
3. It seemed to offer an excellent recipe for the future.

The main ingredients of this recipe may have begun to emerge about a year before the 1956 campaign, but that success seemed so remarkable that it removed all doubts about the preferable strategic posture. From now on Israel would abandon all attempts to rely on a defensive posture. The key to national security would be, instead, a defensive posture executed (in the words of Lieutenant-General Chaim Laskov, one of the IDF chiefs of staff during the 1957–67 period) *offensively*[40]—namely, what has been defined in the present discussion as quintessential deterrence. Starting from an unequivocal acceptance of the status quo since the completion of the IDF's withdrawal from the Sinai, the macro strategic-political purpose was as defensive as it had always been. The micro military-tactical method of working toward this purpose, however, would be decidedly offensive.

More specifically, this posture implied two fundamental preferences with respect to the employment of force, one relating mainly to so-called basic security (all-out war) and one relating primarily to current security (subwar violence). The first was as simple as it was harsh: Israel would never allow its adversaries the luxury of a first-strike war. In 1948 the Arabs had begun the war, and Israel had lost 8.9 percent of its population (7,000 casualties out of a population of some 650,000). In 1956 Israel had initiated the war (on the assumption that a full-scale confrontation had become inevitable in any case) and had lost only 190 lives at a time at which its population was already greater than 1.5 million. Permitting the Arabs to initiate war could lead again to a heavy toll. Since in the Israeli perception minimizing IDF casualties was the single most important factor in the national strategic calculus, the conclusion was simple: an Israeli first strike—either a preventive or a preemptive/interceptive strike—was inescapable, a "must."

If, however, Israel failed to initiate or (more likely, in the Israeli perception) if and when the Arabs resorted to attrition practices of the type that had largely precipitated Operation Kadesh, Israel's response would be massive punitive retaliation. As General David Elazar explained, with reference to Syria:

> Israel must always escalate in order to deny . . . [Syria] the game of false peace, while they carry on a permanent guerrilla war. The Syrians had to learn that even if they knew when and how a confrontation would commence—they would never be able to tell how it would end. . . . Israel should be able to dictate the end of such incidents. . . . For the quicker the escalation, the earlier the moment in which Israel brings to bear its main advantage, namely, its ability to use heavy and sophisticated weapons such as tanks and planes.[41]

The fact that the escalation during the 1953–56 period did not bring about deescalation but, contrary to Israel's earlier expectations, further escalation and ultimately war evidently did not lead to an Israeli reappraisal. Dayan's fundamental argument that a showdown was preferable to slow bleeding had, in fact, become orthodoxy. The Arabs, in this view, could afford low-level violence ad infinitum, but Israel could not. If the IDF escalated quickly, the Arabs might be more cautious. They would have to take into account the possibility of a full-dress war even if all they intended was a small, seemingly isolated incident. Hence they might be deterred. If, on the other hand, they were not deterred and a showdown did result, it would still be more acceptable from the Israeli point of view since it would be fought on Israel's terms and in a method of warfare that maximized the advantage of the party with an edge in striking (rather than staying) power—or so argued Elazar and the rest of the IDF General Staff.

Acting on the assumption of a first-strike and massive retaliation posture, however, did not necessarily mean thrashing out an explicit doctrine or specifying all this in public declarations. The reliance on first strike could be assumed but could not be declared for fear of foreign—U.S., French, and even Soviet—reaction. The hope, evidently, was that the Arabs would understand the existence of such a predisposition on the part of Israel simply because Israel had acted in such a fashion in the 1956 war. Moreover, indicating and signaling time and again a disposition toward massive retaliation did not mean specificity in the promised punishments. Indeed, in the emerging Israeli doctrine, leaving unspecified the timing, the location, and the scale of ripostes was elevated to the rank of a cardinal operational principle. "Except in very rare cases," wrote Yigal Allon on this topic, "it is better to leave the enemy in the dark as to our intentions." The reason, he argued, was that this would force the adversary to guess which of an infinite number of possible Israeli retributions would actually be administered, as well as when and where. Facing such a situation, the adversary would find it more difficult to take defensive precautions or preemptive actions.[42]

Both theoretically and in practice, the choice of a posture of massive retaliation was reversible. The IDF could withdraw from such a method of retaliation to a more flexible, tit-for-tat approach if only it—or the government—saw fit to do so. The change of strategy in this regard would not necessitate any corresponding modification in the order of battle. Not so, however, in the case of the preference for first strike. Insofar as this part of the emerging strategic package was concerned, the choices were irreversible because of their ramifications in terms of weapons procurement and, more generally, allocation of resources.

Two seemingly unrelated and equally far-reaching decisions taken in the course of the 1957–67 period illustrate this irreversible nature of the drift toward an exclusive first-strike posture. The first related to the proposition that Israel should construct a defensive line along the Egyptian border. From a topographic point of view, the access from the Egyptian Sinai to the heart of Israel is confined to a relatively narrow opening of roughly forty miles somewhere between Auja and Rafah. Such a line touches on the Mediterranean at its northern end and on a rocky massif at its southern end. Hence this gateway can be blocked quite effectively with fortifications. The idea came up for discussion toward the end of the 1950s but was ultimately rejected.[43] One reason for the rejection was, presumably, that Egyptian control of the Gaza Strip meant that an Israeli defensive line would not be able to reach the Mediterranean. This would leave such a large hole that it would greatly reduce the line's efficacy.

This, however, may have been a relatively minor reason for rejecting the idea of an Israeli Maginot line. A far more important reason seems to have been the estimate that the cost-effectiveness of a defensive deployment based on a massive line of fortifications was significantly inferior to that of a war-winning armored force. It seemed self-evident that Israel's limited resources would not permit both a defensive line and a war-winning armored capability. The choice, in fact, was between an almost exclusively defensive posture and an almost exclusively offensive one. That the spokesmen for the armored corps would reject the notion of a fortified line could be expected. Since there are no traces of any great debate on this issue, it may plausibly be assumed that most of the participants in the debate concurred. Indeed, to the extent that can be judged, the arguments in the late 1950s for preferring an offensive, armored posture to a defensive one relying on a line of fortifications were compelling.

It was generally agreed that as long as Egypt desisted from launching a war, no other Arab state would dare to do so, either. Hence blocking the entry of the Egyptian army into Israel could ostensibly solve Israel's national security problem. But could it? Would such a line take care of Israel's long and exposed coast? Would it take care of Arab air forces? Would it be able to prevent airborne and helicopter landings of Egyptian commandos? Would it not lead to a situation in which the IDF became bogged down in protracted exchanges of the attrition type, which would play straight into the hands of the Arabs? Of course, if it were possible to construct such a line without a corresponding reduction in allocations for the building of an offensive armored corps, the idea would be far more acceptable. Indeed, it would endow Israel with a balanced combination of, so to speak, a shield and a sword. Given the insurmountable constraints on the IDF's budget, however, this was not possible. Consequently, all available resources went into the procurement of tanks, armored personnel carriers (APCs), artillery pieces, and the enormous logistic tail that goes along with them. The IDF, by moving in this direction, in fact eschewed a defensive option altogether.

A not dissimilar problem was encountered during 1960–63 in regard to the question of air defenses. President Kennedy offered Israel Hawk missiles in virtually unlimited quantity. Although this could be considered a major departure in U.S. policy—the first-ever occasion on which the United States offered Israel major arms (on a previous occasion the Eisenhower administration had offered a consignment of about a hundred jeep-mounted recoilless guns)—it was motivated by a shrewd assessment of Israel's strong disposition to rely on a first-strike doctrine.[44] If Israel were to take care of its air defenses by relying on these missiles, it would have to shift the emphasis away from building a large air-striking force. In the event, the Jewish state might gain a nearly foolproof defense against any Arab attempt to launch a disarming first strike, but the corollary to this uncertain gain would be that Israel would then be denied the most important instrument with which to launch a disarming first strike of its own.

President Kennedy's offer occasioned a major debate in the Israeli defense establishment. Those who supported acceptance of the U.S. offer argued that Israel could, with these missiles, project an effective deterrent. Those who disagreed argued that this was impossible. Again, as in the case of the proposed Auja-Rafah line, there was no doubt that if Israel could afford both a fleet of fighter-bombers and a massive shield of missiles, it would be better off. It would be a few notches closer to possessing the conventional equivalent of a strategic nuclear second-strike capability. Since it could be taken for granted that the Arabs would try, probably successfully, to obtain similar systems, the chronic instability of the Arab–Israeli conflict would be significantly reduced. Differently stated, if it were assumed that the evident Israeli preference for preemption was the outcome of the fact that both Israel and its adversaries had only first-strike capabilities, then the introduction of an approximation of second-strike capabilities on both sides of the Arab–Israeli divide could be a major step toward, at least, freezing the conflict at its level of the early 1960s.

If such were the arguments of the Kennedy administration—and of Israeli supporters of reliance on Hawk missiles—the main counterargument was that an absolutely reliable defense was simply inconceivable, especially without nuclear weapons. "President Kennedy's generosity," mused Ezer Weizman, commander of the IAF, "will cost Israel a lot of money. The exchequer is empty and every dollar has at least ten claimants. If this paupers' purse would have to be called upon to pay for Hawk missiles, it will mean procuring fewer planes." But, asked Weizman, would a smaller strike force be sufficient? His own answer was emphatically negative,[45] and he seems to have succeeded in persuading the prime minister as well. As Ben Gurion wrote in a confidential telegram to President Kennedy, "Hawk is appreciated but GOI [the government of Israel] regrets that in light [of] new offensive weapons being prepared by Israel's neighbors, Hawk alone is not a deterrent."[46]

The result was that the IAF purchased five batteries of Hawks for the protection of major installations (air bases, nuclear reactors, ports, and the like) but invested the bulk of its resources in building a first-rate air-striking arm. As in the choice of mobile armor rather than a static line of defenses, this was an irreversible decision. It provided Israel with a formidable offensive capability, but at the price of foreclosing all options except the all-out offensive one.

The war scenario on which the expansion of the IAF during the 1957–67 decade was predicated went roughly as follows. A major change in the status quo—either an infringement of Israel's system of casi belli or, alternatively, intelligence information suggesting an imminent Arab attack—would impel Israel to launch a preventive or (as in the latter case) preemptive strike. This would begin with a disarming attack on the military airfields of the main adversary (probably Egypt). Such an attack would take several hours of maximum peril, since in its duration Israel's air space would be virtually exposed. If this gamble during the initial half day was successful—and since the Arab air forces

did not seem to be prepared for this, the IAF had no doubt that it would be—
the advantages would be enormous. In the first place, it could be expected that
other Arab parties would be deterred from joining. If they desisted from joining, the bulk of the IDF's armor could concentrate on one major adversary
that, moreover, would have no air support. If, conversely, another Arab party
were to join the war, the IAF could hold it at bay while the ground operations
continued against the first victim of the initial strike. The purpose of this
fighting on the ground would be to break through enemy fortifications and
force the adversary into a major battle of decision. This decisive battle should
be of sufficient magnitude virtually to obliterate that adversary's ability to carry
on the fight. Once this objective was achieved, the IDF could shift its main
force to other fronts and deal with other adversaries more or less one at a time.

All this was clearly designed to overcome Israel's numerical inferiority and
dependence on a mainly reserve force, to achieve a quick victory before any
great power had a chance to intervene, to demolish the adversary's ability to
fight, to "kill" (in Weizman's words) "the maximum number of Arabs in the
minimum amount of time,"[47] to capture some territory for political bargaining, to improve the IDF's deterrent image—and to do all this at the lowest possible cost in blood from the Israeli point of view. The main weakness of this
perspective on the next war that guided IDF training, weapons procurement,
and tactics—in fact, all its activities—was that it precluded from the outset the
possiblity of leaving to the Arabs the tormenting choice of whether or not there
would be another war. Israel decided in this manner that if it had a clear war-
winning capability, this in itself would act as a sufficient deterrent until some
time in the early 1970s. What would happen if this expectation were not
fulfilled—if the Arabs were to make a move earlier than the 1970s that would
seem to render an Israeli first strike a virtual imeprative—does not seem to
have been adequately considered.

Another major flaw in the emerging Israeli reliance on an all-out first-strike
posture was that it provided no intermediate alternative between all-out confrontation and undisturbed stability. Either the Arabs would move in a way
that would almost automatically switch on the Israeli war plan, or they would
do nothing. What seems to have remained unclear until the crisis of May 1967
was what Israel would do if the Arabs did not play their part in the script precisely as expected. The answer to this question was evolved incrementally, too.
It boiled down to a piecemeal, almost reflexive, series of decisions to rely on
massive retaliation as the principal instrument for deterrence against subwar Arab
harassment. To be sure, this was not the policy concerning the Egyptian–Israeli
border, since this area was utterly pacified as a result of the consequences of
the 1956 war, Nasser's troubles in the Arab world, and in particular the near
demilitarization of the Sinai and the presence of UNEF. Nor was this the
policy—for most of this period—on either the Jordanian or the Lebanese border.
In both these cases the governments in question seem to have been adequately

deterred by past experience with the Israelis. If Egypt, the Arab world's "big brother" in the course of this decade, were deterred from allowing any military activity against Israel from its territory, Jordan and Lebanon could feel free of any obligation to do more. They had learned that Israeli punitive action could be very painful; they knew, since the crises of the summer of 1958, that the Israeli policy of maintaining the status quo by declaring their borders with Syria and Iraq a red line boiled down to a tacit guarantee of their independence and territorial integrity.[48] They had no real territorial or other grievance against Israel, and they were not particularly enamored of either the Nasserist or the Ba'thist visions of Arab unity—in which these two states would be regarded as shameful, illegitimate reminders of the *ancien* (colonial) *régime*. For all these reasons they had every incentive to play by the Israeli rules of the game while noisily maintaining a pretense of being faithful to the inter-Arab rules. In a word, neither Jordan nor Lebanon would easily be dragged—or so the Israelis thought—into a confrontation with the Jewish state.

This did not apply to Syria. Plagued by deep ethnic and regional divisions; frustrated by a glaring gap between the abiding myth of a golden past and the depressing reality of a squalid present; torn between resignation to its shape and size, a yearning for leadership of a large Arab world, and a competing fascination with an elusive vision of a Greater Syria; and irresistibly titillated by various contemporary radical ideologies, Syria emerged during the 1957–67 decade as a scene of perpetual turmoil and a hotbed of regional instability. It rapidly became an irritant to all its neighbors, including Turkey; a source of constant embarrassment for Nasser's Egypt; and the wellspring of ever-escalating subwar threats against Israel. The last gradually spilled over to the territories of Lebanon and Jordan and ultimately brought about the 1967 crisis.[49]

If Syria's domestic turmoil constituted the main background factor accounting for escalation in the Arab–Israeli conflict, the immediate cause of friction was Israel's vigorous endeavor to complete the National (water) Carrier project. Having given U.S. intermediary Eric Johnston all the time he needed to seek a multilateral agreement among Israel, Syria, Jordan, and Lebanon concerning the equitable distribution of the waters of the Jordan River, having seen Johnston's plan rejected by Syria, Israel was determined to push ahead with the project. To be sure, since both Lebanon and Jordan were prepared to endorse the substance of the plan but not to sign an agreement unless and until Syria did so, Israel proposed to the United States to carry out its own part of the unsigned overall agreement.

Since Syria was increasingly becoming part of the Soviet orbit in the Middle East—and, during 1958–61, a virtual province of Nasser's United Arab Republic (UAR)—and since the project was objectively important for the Israelis, the United States approved the Israeli approach. This approval was facilitated by the fact that Israel proposed to move the site where the water would be pumped from the Jordan to the northwestern corner of the Sea of Galilee, a place called Eshed Kinrot. The catalyst of the reaffirmation of U.S. support, according to one exceedingly well documented study,[50] was Jordan's approach to the World Bank in September 1961 for a loan with which the Jordanian government proposed to carry out its own irrigation project.

Israel cautioned that approval of the loan to Jordan might lead to the undermining, through Jordanian action, of the understandings within the framework of the Johnston Plan. Anxious to help Jordan and Israel while still preserving the main elements of the Johnston Plan, the U.S. State Department offered to reiterate in writing Dulles's assurances to Israel back in 1955, which the late secretary of state had also reaffirmed in 1958. Still not quite satisfied, Israel sought a commitment to these principles from an even higher authority. In November 1962 President Kennedy wrote to Prime Minister Ben Gurion and reaffirmed all previous commitments.

While this exchange was unfolding, Israel had already carried out a major part of the project. This alarmed Syria, which feared that its empty-chair policy concerning the Johnston Plan might backfire: Israel and Jordan would get their share, but Syria would be left out on a limb. Syria alerted other Arab governments, and as of the spring of 1959 the topic was on the agenda of the Arab League. Three courses of action were proposed. The first was a military operation, the second a scheme to divert the water of the Jordan at its sources (the Jordan river derives most of its water from three separate springs, the Hasbani, the Banias, and the Dan; the first two were under Syrian and Lebanese control, whereas the last was on the Israeli side of the DMZ). The third option was a demarche in this regard to the United Nations.

Syrian radicals supported the first, military, alternative. Nasser, however, would not go along with this, since he was evidently aware of the possibility of a harsh Israeli reaction. Indeed, it seems that Nasser deliberately dragged his feet on this issue, as apparently reflected by the fact that it took the Arab League Political Committee more than a year—from late 1959 to early 1961—to adopt an official position in this regard, and that the alternative that was embraced was the second—namely, a diversion scheme. Reinforcing the impression that Nasser was averse to any provocative action is the fact that three more years passed before the January 1961 decision of the league's Political Committee was translated into an operational directive, complete with a budget allocation. Thus only in the Arab summit conference of January 1964 was it finally decided that Syria should begin the diversion project, to be completed within eighteen months, and that the total budget would be somewhere between $168 and $235 million in U.S. dollars.

Strictly speaking, the Arab summit decision was not an act of war. It entailed the rejection of a military option, and it concerned itself with actions to be taken well within Syria's sovereign territory. But such reasoning would also mean that Egypt—which depends on the Nile as much as Israel depends on the Jordan—has no say whatsoever when it comes to Ethiopian or Sudanese action relating to the sources of the Nile. If Israel were to allow Syria to abort the already completed National Carrier project, its economy would suffer irreparable damage. From the Israeli point of view, therefore, any attempt to implement the decision of the Arab summit meeting would be a casus belli.

The question was what could Israel do to prevent the Syrians from carrying out their diversion project. Within days of the summit meeting, Eshkol, the incumbent prime minister and minister of defense, issued a reassuring statement promising that Israel (in accordance with the multilateral Johnston Plan) would not use more than its fair share of the water. Eshkol concluded his statement, however, with a stern but ambiguous warning that Israel would not allow its neighbors to "deny" it the right to exist or attempt to cause it any "injury." This warning was repeated in a Knesset resolution passed in September 1964, when Syrian earth-moving equipment began to appear in the vicinity of the diversion site.

Eshkol's careful combination of soothing and threatening words reflected a decision to avoid anything that might increase tensions. In fact, the prime minister spoke after a careful evaluation of the alternatives at the IDF General Staff. Some participants in the debate suggested that the only way to thwart the diversion scheme was simply to move in force and capture the diversion site. Lieutenant-General Yitzhak Rabin, the chief of staff, was far more cautious. He pointed out that the problem was not Syrian shooting at Israelis but the presence of Syrian earth-moving works on the Syrian side of the border. Hence, Rabin argued, from the Israeli point of view it would be quite enough to take steps to stop the Syrians from working. This could be done heavy-handedly through the use of massive firepower, or it could be done surgically: every bulldozer entering the diversion site would be shot at in a manner that would scare its operator and dissuade him from carrying on. Of course, it could not be taken for granted that the Syrians would not move to protect the works. But the decision whether or not to escalate would fall squarely on Syria, not on Israel.[51]

This advocacy by the chief of staff of what amounted to a strategy of flexible response appealed to Prime Minister Eshkol, who, by inclination and temperament, was a moderate man of compromise and good humor.[52] When this strategy was applied, however, it became immediately clear that the Syrians were determined to return fire and even to escalate. In fact, they shot back not only at Israeli military positions but also at the civilian population in the densely populated area known as the Galilee Finger—an elongated valley lying between the Syrian-controlled Golan Heights to the east and the Lebanese Arnoun Heights on the west. Differently stated, Syria chose to escalate both vertically (in terms of the choice of weapons) and horizontally (in terms of the area to come under fire). As a result, Israel was forced to abandon flexible response and fall back on massive retaliation. The weapons involved in this encounter, which reached its peak in November 1964, included at first light firearms, then mortars and medium-size machine guns, then artillery and tanks. When even this escalation failed to deescalate, Israel ultimately turned—for the first time since 1951—to air power.

Could all this have been prevented? Probably not. Having obtained an Arab summit mandate to carry out the project after years of chiding Egypt for not doing its utmost to fight the common enemy, Syria could ill afford to back down unless and until it could prove it had done everything in its capacity to be as good as its word. Israel's initial attempt to defuse the situation through flexible response thus came up against a determined opponent, whose order of preferences was the obverse of its own: Syria was eager to have a static encounter, whereas Israel wanted to avoid one. Hence Israel's only way out of the trap was to raise the level of fire to air power—namely, to Syria's level of military incompetence.[53]

Syria, however, could not accept defeat. The stakes for the regime at home and for Syria in the Arab world were too high to be risked by conduct that would elicit charges of cowardice. The Syrians therefore resorted to an indirect alternative: helping a number of Palestinian organizations to get together and form a body called al-Fateh (Arab acronym for Movement for the Liberation of Palestine: *Charakat at-Tachrir al-Philastin* in reverse). Syrian military intelligence encouraged small parties of members of this newly created body to launch small, pinprick raids inside Israel.[54]

As on previous, comparable occasions, Israel held Syria directly responsible and launched counterattacks in a variety of forms. The common denominator of most Israeli retributions during the last two years before the Six-Day War was the emphasis on larger and more sophisticated weapons. Instead of relatively surgical infantry raids (The Sea of Galilee in December 1955, Tawfiq in January 1960, and Nuqeib in March 1962), the IDF relied increasingly on artillery fire, armor fire, and air strikes.

This new style of retribution was the result of a variety of factors. First, Syrian fortifications, based on the Soviet model and constructed with the assistance of Soviet experts, had become far more sophisticated than in the past, and infantry raids would be more hazardous than they had been up to the 1962 Nuqeib raid. Second, the OC Northern Command during this period was General David Elazar, formerly OC of the armored corps (*Ha Gayis*). It was thus not entirely surprising that he would prefer to rely increasingly on armor—not least, according to some evidence, because he was anxious to exercise the IDF's concepts of armored warfare.[55] Third, as of April 1966, the head of G3 (Operations) Branch of the IDF General Staff was Ezer Weizman, whose previous position had been commander of the IAF. As he related later, his advice to his colleagues on the General Staff was to escalate vigorously. "In 1966 we cannot carry out reprisals of the 1955 style," he argued. The days in which a small force would "enter [an Arab village or police station] at night, lay a few pounds of explosives, demolish a house or a police station and take off" were over. "When a sovereign state decides to punish those who hurt it, it must act differently. We have armor and we have an air force. We should enter in broad daylight and act forcefully."[56]

Last but not least, Ezer Weizman's opposite number on the Syrian side, Hafiz al-Assad, seems to have been impelled by the exigencies of his domestic position to advocate a similar strategy of escalation. Assad was, as of the coup d'état of February 1966, number two in the Syrian power structure. A tough-minded member of the Alawi minority, he was the commander in chief of the Syrian air force and was said to be in fierce competition with Damascus strong man, Salah Jedid, another Alawi. Thus it is not inconceivable that the rivalry between these two at the apex of the Syrian regime bred an increased tendency to escalate the conflict.[57]

It seemed clear that Assad's domestic position would be jeopardized if he allowed the IAF to continue to roam freely over Syrian airspace and to pro-duce provocative, window-breaking sonic booms over the capital, Damascus, as the IAF had begun to do regularly since the National Carrier skirmishes in late 1964. Hence, as of August 1966, Syria declared its intention to employ air power for strikes at the Israeli rear, too.[58] The result was rampant escala-tion, a succession of dogfights between Israeli and Syrian planes in the fall of 1966 and the spring of 1967 in which the Syrians kept losing planes while Israel suffered no losses. The Syrians responded by increasing the fire against Israeli civilians in the Galilee Finger. This prompted Israeli leaders to issue stern threats of retribution. Tensions had reached a new peak in the autumn of 1966. Sensing this, Prime Minsiter Eshkol attempted to stabilize the situation through soothing public statements emphasizing Israel's desire to "stop shooting and start talking."[59] Although a number of meetings of the Israeli–Syrian Mixed Armistice Commission did take place during January and February 1967, however, the tensions did not really subside, and the entire system continued to grind toward a full-scale confrontation.[60]

Thus despite the enormous improvement in Israel's overall situation, the Jewish state became once again a prisoner of a nearly deterministic war trap. The breathtaking pace of the arms race drove it to rely exclusively on a first-strike posture as the means of deterring the Arabs from launching a general war and of dealing with such a war situation if and when it developed. The pressure of the Syrians led, after a short-lived attempt to play flexible response, to ferocious massive retaliation as the main instrument for countering subwar threats. As during the 1953–56 period, the upshot was rapid escalation on the level of subwar confrontation pushing the system more or less deter-ministically toward a major showdown. Moreover, also as during the 1953–56 period, the driving force behind the scenes was the upper echelon of the IDF. The difference, however, was that on the road leading to the Sinai campaign, the IDF had had a formidable civilian boss, David Ben Gurion, whereas on the road to the Six-Day War, the prime minister and minister of defense was Levi Eshkol, a far friendlier and, in a way, more humane character than his stern, almost demonically dedicated, distant, and enigmatic predecessor—but also a far less astute master strategist.

The Domestic Politics of Escalation

The most common Israeli interpretation of the origins of the Six-Day War puts the blame entirely on Syria. The Ba'ath republic, most Israelis believed at the time, was internally in a state of crisis resulting from a fierce struggle for power. This drove it to an external radicalism that focused in particular on relations with Israel. The Jewish state was thus a hapless victim of straightforward aggression. In the words of one study, the

> violence [along the Israeli–Syrian border] no longer could be related simply to territorial claims and counterclaims. Much of it reflected the unique nature of the Syrian Ba'ath regime. Advocating a curious melange of Leninism and pan-Arabism (although with increasing emphasis upon the latter), the junta of Syrian officers who had seized power in 1962 soon revealed themselves as the most grimly chauvinist government in the Middle East. Their diatribes on behalf of the Viet Cong, the Maoists and the Guevarists, and against the United States and Israel, were splenetic and at times psychotic. The truth was that the Damascus cabal enjoyed little popular support, and barely survived two armed revolts in September 1966 and February 1967. It was this very weakness which propelled the regime's strongman, Colonel Salah Jedid, and his colleagues into an uncompromising stance on the one issue that was universally popular—a war of liberation against Israel.[61]

Apologists for the Arab cause tend to offer the same interpretation in reverse—namely, that domestic trouble in Israel spurred Israeli adventurists to seek an outlet in another war with the Arabs and that the helpless Syrians fell victim to a cold-blooded, premeditated, and meticulously planned grand Israeli maneuver. "In early 1967," according to one widely read account by a journalist of clear anti-Israeli persuasion,

> Israel's congenital militancy was pushing it towards . . . a decision [to launch another war]. In a sense it needed the war. It was suffering the severest economic crisis of its existence; unemployment stood at ten percent; the growth rate had plummeted; subventions from the diaspora were drying up; worst of all, emigration was beginning to exceed immigration—a yardstick which of course indicated, more than any other, that the economic crisis was a crisis of Zionism itself. What this portended [had been forecasted already in 1962]. . . . Israel's leaders have the habit of putting down her economic difficulties to the boycott of all trade and economic relations maintained by the Arab states, and the

pressure they exercise on other countries to limit trade with Israel. In such circumstances there seems . . . to be a great temptation to find some excuse to go to war and thus break out of the blockade and boycott—to force peace on Israel's terms.[62]

Both the pro- and the anti-Israeli arguments contain important nuggets of truth. The former is correct, according to all studies on the topic to date, in arguing that Syria's internal instability increased its propensity to adopt a militant posture vis-à-vis Israel.[63] The latter is certainly correct in stating that Israel was in the throes of a severe economic recession when the Six-Day War broke out. Yet both approaches were quite unsuccessful in drawing credible inferences from the correct data they present.

A realistic appreciation of the process of escalation that led to the 1967 crisis must begin with the acknowledgment that both Syria *and* Israel were impelled to act the way they did by a combination of standard, somewhat shortsighted, strategic calculations as well as by the exigencies of their domestic political processes. This is not the same as a Machiavellian conspiracy theory suggesting that decision makers were consciously and openly seeking to solve their domestic problems by dragging their countries into war. Such an interpretation, however, does accept the argument that, at least insofar as Israel was concerned, strategic-military decision making during the 1957–67 period was not conducted with as much autonomy from domestic politics as is sometimes argued.[64]

The decade can be divided in this respect into two parts: the 1957–63 period, in which Ben Gurion was still prime minister and minister of defense, and the 1963–67 period, in which his positions were taken over by Levi Eshkol. During the first five and a half years, the insulation of strategic and military decision making from domestic politics was more or less complete because of the preponderance of *ha-zaken*, the old man (or what the Germans at the same time called the aging Dr. Adenauer, *Der Alte*). Ben Gurion restrained public debate about national security affairs, limited discussion of these matters at the cabinet, kept briefings to the Knesset Security and Foreign Policy Committee to a bare minimum, and did not hesitate to impose strict censorship on the press.

Although this amounted to an undemocratic politicization of defense matters, it also proved an effective way of conducting the nation's most important business. Israeli national security policy during this period was conducted (relatively speaking) smoothly, effectively, and consistently. There was a clear guiding formula establishing a logical balance among various subfields of the national security sphere. There was a clear, consistent projection of a measured balance between a policy of strength, on the one hand, and a policy of restraint on the other. The defense budget was kept under tight control. The IDF's top echelon were treated by the minister of defense (who was almost twice their average age) with affection—but they also knew their place. Their job was to offer professional military advice. Their superior's job was to make the ultimate strategic-political decision.

Halfway between the retreat from the Sinai and Ben Gurion's retirement, this model of autonomy of the security sphere began to come under domestic political fire. The roots of the change seem to have been connected with the beginning of what was presented at the time as a conflict of two competing world views (socialism versus statism), but they might be more properly described as a struggle for succession. Conscious of his own advanced age, Ben Gurion sought to cultivate a cohort of younger people to whom the management of national affairs could be entrusted. Although the Old Man was surrounded by a coherent group of experienced veterans about ten years younger than himself, including such high-powered individuals as Levi Eshkol, Golda Meir, Zalman Aran, Dov Joseph, Mordechai Namir and Pinchas Sapir, Ben Gurion was apparently determined to pass the reins of power to a younger generation. Fascinated by youth, especially if and when it went along with being a native of Palestine and not an immigrant from an eastern European Jewish *shtetl* (small town), he apparently sought to install in positions of influence individuals such as Dayan, Peres, Eban, and others of their age group.

This transpired gradually through the 1950s but took a major step forward after the 1959 elections, when Ben Gurion promoted to cabinet membership a number of well-known disciples of his: Moshe Dayan (as minister of agriculture), Shimon Peres (as deputy minister of defense), Abba Eban (as minister without portfolio and later minister of education), and one or two of their internationally less well known allies. The result was a political tug of war, not only between the new appointees and their older rivals in the cabinet but also, inescapably, between the latter and David Ben Gurion. As Israel Yesha'ayahou, a frustrated ministerial hopeful of the older generation, bitterly complained to Ben Gurion on one occasion, the "question is entirely that of the coat of many colors. [As in the biblical story of Joseph and his brothers,] all those present here are your sons, and you have chosen Josephs of your own, robed them in coats of many colours, and aroused the great jealousy of those whom you have left coatless."[65]

The pressures that this emerging struggle generated were not connected directly to the sphere of national security at first, but they soon impinged on it, too. The first phase was the public debate concerning the 1954 Lavon affair. When Ben Gurion was in retirement, Lavon, Ben Gurion's choice for the Ministry of Defense, apparently authorized activation of a dormant military intelligence network in Egypt. The purpose was sabotage, with a view to inducing discord between the then-new Nasserist revolutionary regime, on the one hand, and Britain and the United States, on the other hand. This ill-conceived and ill-fated scheme was clearly the stillborn child of a state of mind of isolation and despair that typified Israel's attitude at that time. It failed abysmally; the ring, consisting mainly of Egyptian-born Jews, was captured, tried, and severely punished (two of its members were hanged).[66]

Israeli military censorship kept the entire issue from the public for six years. Then it exploded into a public issue because Lavon, who retired in 1954 and subsequently became secretary-general of the Histadrut, demanded complete exoneration of any responsibility for the affair bearing his name. Ben Gurion, however, maintained that only a judicial body could either exonerate Lavon (and thus place the blame on others) or, conversely, reaffirm Lavon's culpability. Lavon, not satisfied by this, threatened to launch a public campaign for his acquittal. Since this would jeopardize the public standing of MAPAI—the precursor of what later became the Labor party, of which all these poeple were top leaders—the second-echelon leadership (Eshkol and Meir, among others) tried unsuccessfully to prevail on Ben Gurion to accept the verdict on the issue of a committee of seven cabinet ministers. Hence despite the prime minister's boycott of the vote of this committee, the cabinet proceeded to appoint it.

The so-called Committee of Seven conducted only a limited inquiry and then, somehow, acquitted Lavon. Ben Gurion, however, would not accept its verdict. In a vain attempt to mollify him, the MAPAI top leadership forced Lavon to retire. Nevertheless, Ben Gurion would not withdraw his demand to initiate judicial investigation. The upshot was such a fierce conflict between the prime minister and his own party's leadership that MAPAI lost five seats in the next election. The new cabinet, Ben Gurion's last, was negotiated and brought together, not by the prime minister but by Eshkol acting on his behalf.[67]

The implications of these events for Israeli national security were far-reaching. It was the first time that the very core of the most secret part of national security policy had been aired in public. The disorder, incoherence, and power struggles within the national security elite that were made public suggested a far less reliable, rational, and effective management than had been the image of Israel before. The cohesion of the incumbent cabinet was gravely disrupted, thus giving Israel an image of weakness. Above all, the decline of Ben Gurion's stature as a result of the scandal was underlined by the fact that the old guard of his party succeeded in forcing him to accept into his cabinet after the 1961 elections three ministers (Allon, Carmel, and Ben Aharon) from Achdut Haavodah, the left-wing, hawkish party that Ben Gurion had kept out of government since 1948.

Before long this new power structure had manifested itself in significant changes in Israel's national security preferences. The tenuous alliance between Ben Gurion and the MAPAI old guard collapsed. The old man retired from office and, on the eve of the 1965 general elections, broke away from the party which he had founded and had led for two generations. Taking Dayan, Peres, Teddy Kollek, Yitzhak Navon, and others of his disciples with him, Ben Gurion formed a new party called RAFI (Hebrew acronym for "the workers of Israel list" but also a popular diminutive for Rafael). Its platform showed a clear statist emphasis—namely, advocacy of an ethos of modernization, liberalization, the promotion of a vision of advanced science and technology, and above all a change in the electoral system that would turn Israel into a cross between the British two-party parliamentary and the French Fifth Republic presidential systems.[68]

Contrary to Ben Gurion's hopes, RAFI gained only ten seats in the 1965 elections. Thus the founder of Israel and the godfather of its national security system found himself in the opposition, while the veteran leadership of his own former party set up a new coalition government based on a MAPAI/Achdut Haavodah axis. In terms of national security policymaking, this meant that the inner core of decision makers was dramatically transformed. Eshkol, whose strength had always been in economic affairs, became prime minister and minister of defense. Golda Meir, whose impact on foreign policy had been greatly restricted when Ben Gurion was prime minister and Peres deputy minister of defense, now came to occupy a central role in foreign policy decision making. But the most dramatic change in the setup was the fact that after fifteen years in which they had been ruthlessly denied access to national security policymaking, Yigal Allon, Moshe Carmel, and Israel Galili of Achdut Haavodah were suddenly a preponderant force in the formulation of national security policy.

This led to two important changes of emphasis in policy preferences. First, unlike Ben Gurion, Dayan, and Peres, who felt that a vigorous bid for a last-resort nuclear program was an urgent imperative, Allon in particular was sanguine about Israel's ability to hold its own on the basis of a purely conventional order of battle. Apparently Allon succeeded in carrying Eshkol and Golda Meir along with him. Consequently, faced with further U.S. pressures to slow down the nuclear program, Eshkol yielded. He requested U.S. supply of greater quantities of more sophisticated conventional weapons and, when the Johnson administration agreed to supply them, he undertook to permit U.S. inspection on an ad hoc basis of the 24-megawatt Dimona nuclear reactor and promised to slwo down the drive toward a nuclear capability for military purposes.[69]

Although the details of this agreement remain unknown to this day, the fact that it took place became known at the time throughout the Israeli national security elite. It elicited acrimonious charges from Ben Gurion of a "major blunder" and led the former prime minister to declare that Eshkol, his own choice for successor, "would have been a great leader and an excellent prime minister if only he were not so lamentably lacking in foresight" and that he was "unfit to govern."[70] Although this episode could not possibly have strengthened Israel's deterrence in the minds of the Arabs, it may have had an important impact on Eshkol's management of two cardinal aspects of national security: the defense budget and the escalating crisis with Syria.

Under Ben Gurion, Israel kept the defense budget within a very rigid framework of not more than roughly 12 percent of GNP. In 1951 this caused

Chief of Staff Yadin to resign his post. Although Ben Gurion liked him and wanted him to stay on, the old man finally accepted the resignation because maintaining the framework of defense outlays was more important. Later this converged with Ben Gurion's existential fears and led him to launch Israel's nuclear program and to resist all U.S. pressures to halt it. By yielding to the pressures of the Johnson administration in this regard, Eshkol, in fact, accepted for the first time in Israel's history a major deviation from the iron rule that economic solvency was just as important as any other, more conspicuous dimension of national security. The repercussions did not surface right away, but in the long run they were of historic magnitude.

Eshkol's second deviation from the Ben Gurion formula for national security had more immediate ramifications. Under Ben Gurion, Israel's use of force against Syria since 1957 had become relatively limited and controlled. Although Syrian shelling and mining in the Galilee Finger and in the vicinity of the Sea of Galilee was quite extensive, Ben Gurion kept a tight rein over Israeli reprisals, apparently in the hope of preventing runaway escalation. In a period of six years he authorized only two important raids on Syrian positions (Tawfiq in January 1960 and Nuqeib in March 1962). Above all, not only did Ben Gurion resist all suggestions of employing air power, but he was even "stingy" (in Ezer Weizman's words) when it came to the authorization of sorties for intelligence purposes.[71]

Under Levi Eshkol, a seemingly far less pugnacious leader than Ben Gurion, this policy changed markedly. Eshkol may have pleased all those Israelis who lamented Ben Gurion's somewhat authoritarian control of the national security system. He was, indeed, a far more democratic leader. But this led to the withering away of the insulation of strategic-military decision making from political debates and, more immediately, to a far greater influence of the military over policymaking. Yitzhak Rabin, the chief of staff; Ezer Weizman, as OC of the IAF and subsequently head of G3 Division (operations) in the General Staff; David Elazar, as OC of the *Gayis* and subsequently of Northern Command— all of them admired Ben Gurion but liked Eshkol. They found him more attentive and, apparently, far more receptive to their policy recommendations.

The policymaking setup, then, had built into it a number of ingredients that must have led, in their ensemble, to a drift toward a far less effective escalation control than during 1957–63. Eshkol's mainstay of support in the cabinet included Golda Meir; the hawkish and opinionated foreign minister, Yigal Allon; the hawkish former commander of the PALMACH who, after fifteen years in the political wilderness, was seething with desire to have an impact on foreign policy and security; and the latter's Achdut Haavodah colleagues. At the same time, Eshkol was constantly attacked by Ben Gurion, Dayan, and Peres for his alleged ineptitude in conducting the nation's security affairs.

Finally, if this cross fire of relativley hawkish advocacies pushed Eshkol to a greater activism than he would have preferred by natural disposition, he was also constantly advised to act vigorously by the IDF General Staff. The officers, to be sure, were honestly convinced that they were doing their very best to advance the national interest. In formal terms they acted properly and honorably. Indeed, they could not even be chided for offering activist advice, since it was their duty to offer the best *military* advice on the assumption that it was the duty of the government, not of the armed forces, to weigh the political pros and cons of military action. An army, after all, should be imbued with an aggressive spirit, or else it cannot be effective on the battlefield. In this sense the IDF General Staff functioned well; the culprit was the prime minister and minister of defense. Unwittingly, no doubt, Eshkol abdicated his responsibility. His understanding of the full political and strategic significance of the IDF's reprisals against Syria seems to have been inadequate. He was unsuccessful in acting as devil's advocate to the suggestions of his military advisers. As a result, he may have authorized actions that—against the background of a conflict with an escalation-prone Syria—only made things worse. To put it even more bluntly, whereas under Ben Gurion—the pugnacious warrior—the IAF had not been authorized to operate ever since April 5, 1951, as soon as Eshkol—the moderate, by all accounts—was at the helm, the IAF was virtually let loose. Whereas under Ben Gurion reprisals against Syria were carried out sparingly by infantry with some artillery support (with the notable exception of the December 10, 1955, attack on Kursi, in which Ben Gurion intended ten or twelve Syrian casualties but Ariel Sharon caused fifty-six to lose their lives),[72] under Eshkol the emphasis was shifted to the awesome triad of artillery, armor, and air power. Finally, whereas Ben Gurion was brilliantly successful in managing the January 1960 Rotem crisis, so that it passed almost unnoticed and is hardly remembered a generation later, Eshkol's mismanagement of the May–June 1967 crisis, his failure to convert the considerable assets of general deterrence that Israel had painstakingly accumulated over the years into effective instruments of specific deterrence, resulted in an epoch-making war.

Deterrence in Crisis: May 1967

On April 7, 1967, following the mounting tensions of the previous years, Israeli and Syrian planes engaged in battle. Six Syrian Migs were shot down. From the Israeli point of view, the main implication was that Syria would be effectively deterred. The logic of this perception appeared flawless: without air cover, the Syrians could not seriously challenge the IDF. An air battle like this constituted a massive demonstration of the fact that Syria had virtually no air cover. If, in addition, Israel would in the future prove to the Syrians time and again in the most abrasive way that they had no air support, the Syrians would remain deterred, and a general war (which Israel did not want) would be averted. Frequent flights over Syria, especially over Damascus, the capital, by French-built Mirage fighter-bombers with blue stars of David on their wings would underscore Syria's vulnerability and, simultaneously, reinvigorate Israeli deterrence.

In the course of the 1960s this had become, increasingly, the most typical way in which Israeli policymakers came to look at the problem. Unfortunately, what made sense to the Israelis failed to elicit from the Syrians the kind of response that this perspective expected of them. From a Syrian point of view, this situation amounted to a daily reminder of their relative inadequacy vis-à-vis the Israelis. At least as proud as the Israelis, and just as obstinate, the Syrians could not simply yield. What could they do instead? A headstrong military confrontation with Israel without any guaranteed support from other Arab states would lead to a catastrophe. From this point of view, the Syrians were clearly deterred.

But there were other things the Syrians could do in order to demonstrate to the Israelis that they were determined not to give way (in other words, that they were not *entirely* deterred). They could, for example, intensify their small-scale attacks on Israeli civilians in the Huleh valley right below the Golan and thus, in a sense, signal to Israel that this population was hostage to Syria—a means by which to force Israel's hand despite Syria's military inferiority. Experience had demonstrated that for all its military might, Israel had no simple means by which to deter Syria, or anyone else, from employing such a strategy. The maximum Israel could do would be to escalate. If the Jewish state chose to do so, Syria could turn to the rest of the Arab world for support. If the Arab allies, especially Egypt, failed to come to Syria's rescue, Syria could back down from the collision course with Israel and put the blame for that on the rest of the Arabs. If, on the other hand, Egypt and the rest came to Syria's rescue, the escalation could be contained through the creation of a clearly underlined equilibrium. If it came to the worst and there was a war, Syria would not be alone. Indeed, the Syrians might have reasoned that from their point of view it was a "heads I win, tails you lose" situation. They would not fight a war on their own; if there were a war, it would involve Egypt as well. In turn it could be taken for granted that Israeli attention would be focused primarily on Egypt and not on Syria.

Although it cannot be clearly established that these were precisely Syria's calculations during April and May of 1967, Syria clearly did choose to intensify its harassment of the Israeli population near the border, thereby challenging the credibility of the repeated Israeli warning that turning the population into hostages would be unacceptable. Eshkol's cabinet, therefore, decided first to resort to new threats and, if these failed, to initiate some kind of limited tour de force.

The question of which kind of threats to issue was more complicated than was first apparent. The choice was essentially among four types of threats: ominous in tone but vague as to the precise punishment to be administered if the threat were ignored; ominous in tone and specific about the retribution;

mild in tone and vague as to the retribution; or, finally, mild in tone but specific about the retribution. Given the background—given, specifically, that milder threats in previous months and years had failed to elicit a satisfactory response from the Syrians—it was clear that if further threats were to be issued, they would have to be stern. At the same time, there were very good reasons for avoiding specificity concerning the nature, scope, location, and timing of the Israeli military action if Syria did not yield to the threats.

For one thing, specificity could lead to pressures from the United States, France, the Soviets, and/or the United Nations to avoid action. Second, it could alert the Syrians and the rest of the Arabs, not only enabling them to prepare but also indicating to them *what* they should prepare in order to thwart any Israeli attempt to "teach Syria a lesson." If Israel were, for example, to offer Syria a specific "price list," indicating what kind of action would follow, say, a small mining incident, a large mining incident, a small shooting incident, or a large one; if Israel were to promise that the punishment would be administered instantly and at the same locations in which the precipitating Syrian action took place, this price list could only make the Syrian task easier. All the Syrians would have to do would be to evaluate in advance which types of actions against Israeli targets were worth their while and which were not. Conversely, if the Syrians were left utterly in the dark as to the timing, location, and scope of possible ripostes, they would have to prepare for a large number of contingencies and would have to assume the worst—namely, that even a small provocation might elicit a large Israeli retribution.

Such were Israel's operational reflexes. The government and the IDF never held elaborate discussions or ever ordered intensive position papers. A brief, almost perfunctory discussion—sometimes even on the telephone—between one or two ministers, the prime minister, the chief of staff, and one or two of his subordinates on the General Staff was more often than not the manner in which a calculus such as this was gone through. In this particular case it led to the issuing by the prime minister and by the IDF spokesman of stern but vague warnings. The former's language in particular was typically oblique. He told the Syrians merely that "the notebook was open and the hand was writing." This seems to have suggested that Israel was keeping count of the incidents and that, ultimately, if and when the Syrians were to initiate more than some unspecified number of incidents involving some unspecified number of casualties or unspecified material damage, Israel would carry out a reprisal on an unspecified scale in an unspecified location. In addition, Eshkol also authorized a limited reinforcement of IDF forces on the Syrian border.

The Israeli moves were undertaken within a more or less routine frame of mind. Egypt was bogged down in the Yemen, and the Syrians did not appear to be a real threat (in terms of basic security) on their own. The worst that could happen, thought the Eshkol government, was a small flare-up of the type that had become almost routine along the Israeli–Syrian armistice lines. This proved a gross miscalculation. The Syrians apparently feared a more vigorous Israeli response than Israel itself was contemplating. Their apprehensions were reinforced by the Soviets, who—for reasons that have never been explained—also proceeded to alert Egypt. Nasser, in turn, faced a dilemma of his own. On the one hand, this was a golden opportunity to extricate the Egyptian expeditionary force from the Yemen quagmire in which it had been bogged down since the coup d'état of 1962. Egypt could claim a more pressing emergency closer to home and pull out of this hopeless, misguided adventure in the south of the Arabian peninsula.

On the other hand, moving forces into the Sinai could lead to a confrontation with the hypersensitive yet also arrogantly self-assured Israelis (as they may have appeared to the Egyptians). If for fear of this Egypt would not send forces into the Sinai, its position in the Arab world would suffer. Syria would have to back down and would most probably blame this act on the refusal of the Egyptians to offer a helping hand. Hence the most logical move from the Egyptian point of view would be a limited replay of the January 1960 Rotem crisis. A large Egyptian force would enter the Sinai but would stay some distance from UNEF. Israel would then be placed in a difficult situation. If it were to attempt to eject Egypt from the Sinai by force, it would have to cross through UNEF lines and would then be taken to task by the whole world. It was logical to assume, therefore, that the IDF would not move and that the Egyptian army would remain in the Sinai behind UNEF lines. If this could be achieved, Egypt would not only extricate itself from the Yemen but would also appear as Syria's savior; further, it would erase the least palatable consequence of the 1956 war—the de facto demilitarization of the Sinai. In a word, it was not difficult, and certainly not irrational, for Nasser to conclude that the Soviet–Syrian challenge was an opportunity to boost Egypt's declining status without firing a single shot. Accordingly, Nasser ordered the Egyptian army on May 14, 1967, to move a force of several divisions across the Suez Canal into the Sinai.

In the next seventy-two hours Israel missed an opportunity to contain Egypt without war. The tragedy, however, was that this mistake was made not because Eshkol's government wanted a war (as apologists for the Arab cause often argue), and not because it was unconvinced that Israel could win a war, but precisely the reverse: Israel did not want a war and acted with restraint in order to prevent it. Here, Eshkol's sweet reason backfired. Rather than signaling moderation and strength, it projected weakness and indecision, Israel spoke softly and carried a big stick. To Nasser, however, Israel appeared to be speaking softly because it was carrying a hollow reed.

The specifics of this tragic sequence were roughly as follows. During the first week of the crisis, the Egyptian forces in the Sinai did not appear to be deployed purposefully but seemed to be moving in circles in order to "raise dust." This noisy saber rattling reinforced an Israeli inclination to interpret the move as if it were only a show, a mere replay of the 1960 Rotem incident.

Consequently, it seemed prudent not to make too much of it. The IDF was alerted, and some regular units were moved to the south—precisely the same drill as in 1960. In addition, the IDF was ordered to carry out discreetly a small-scale mobilization of reserves and to prepare the ground for a larger mobilization if and when the situation deteriorated. The Egyptians, moreover, were informed through third parties that Israel entertained no aggressive intentions. Prime Minister Eshkol alerted the Knesset security and Foreign Relations committee and ordered the speeding up of some military deliveries from abroad. He also ordered some emergency fund raising in wealthy Jewish communities overseas.

What impression did all this make on the Egyptians? To judge by Nasser's subsequent actions, it seems that Eshkol's strategy either convinced Nasser that the incumbent Israeli prime minister was made of softer fabric than was Ben Gurion, or unwittingly created situations that made it difficult for Nasser not to escalate the crisis. On the face of it, of course, Eshkol merely replayed Ben Gurion's handling of the 1960 crisis, but with two important differences. First, Ben Gurion's handling of the 1960 crisis was singularly discreet. The alert to the IDF was carried out under strict secrecy. Ben Gurion had not even consulted the Knesset Security and Foreign Relations Committee. All he did was to alert the IAF, move the seventh armored brigade of regulars to the Egyptian border, mobilize the thirty-seventh reserve armored brigade, and deploy it in the south as well. Finally, to calm the Arabs, Ben Gurion, nonchalantly let it be known that he was planning a visit to the United States.

The second factor that may have helped Ben Gurion to achieve more deterrence with less overt pressure was his reputation. In fact, it does not seem farfetched to argue that his manner in the course of the 1960 crisis may have been interpreted by Nasser against the background of eight years of encounter with Ben Gurion, during which the Israeli leader had persistently projected an image of utmost resolve. Hence, in 1960 Nasser ordered his 50,000 troops out of the Sinai barely thirty-two hours after the beginning of the crisis.[73] Conversely, Eshkol was reputed to be a far less formidable leader, and his moderation during the first three days of the crisis may have been interpreted by Nasser in the light of this image.

Beyond the problem of images, however, the publicity that attended Eshkol's moves may have made it very difficult for Nasser to back down without some concrete achievement. The bottom line, then, was that Egypt, in Nasser's definition of the situation, not only could but, indeed, almost had no choice but to "nibble" more—that is, to carry on this short-of-war mischief in order to extricate itself from the collision course with more substantial gains. In practical terms, it led Nasser to demand, at 10:00 P.M. on May 16, that UNEF be removed forthwith.

This was Nasser's most critical decision in the course of the entire crisis. Had he avoided this move, his forces might well have stayed in the Sinai, since it is clear that Israel would not have gone to war in order to evict them from their positions during May 14–16 (Eshkol briefed his government that the 35,000-strong Egyptian force that had crossed the canal on May 15 was deployed in a "defensive" form). Apparently, Nasser counted on the inefficiency of the U.N. decision-making process. Nasser probably believed that the commander of UNEF, General Rikhye of India, would drag his feet. He would pass Nasser's demand on to Secretary-General U Thant. The latter would consult the Security Council. All this would take time, which would enable Egypt to bargain: it could agree to withdraw the demand for UNEF's removal in return for an international legitimization of all the changes in the status quo that his moves since May 14 had created.

If Eshkol had acted with greater vigor but less publicity—initiating a partial mobilization of reserves, concentrating forces along the Egyptian border, and transmitting (through third parties) unambiguous warnings presenting any further Egyptian move as a casus belli—Nasser might have been more careful to avoid such brinkmanship. But Eshkol's cautious, prudent, and conciliatory posture—the fact that he confined himself to precautionary defensive moves and *did not really play deterrence effectively*—turned the Egyptian president's move vis-à-vis the United Nations from a calculated risk into an irreversible slide down the slippery slope leading to war.

Assuming as Eshkol did that Nasser was not ready for war and was merely showing off, U Thant presented Nasser with an all-or-nothing ultimatum: either he was to take back his request for the removal of UNEF or the force would be entirely withdrawn at once. The latter alternative put the onus of the next critical move back on Egypt, which would then have to decide whether or not to move into UNEF's positions.

In reality, because of possible reactions in the Arab world, the Egyptian army was unable *not* to move into UNEF's place. This step, however, would mean the return of the Egyptians to a menacing forward deployment along Israel's border and the reimposition of a naval blockade. Could Egyptian troops sit at Sharm el Sheikh and passively watch Israeli ships sailing right in front of their eyes? How would the Arab world—and Nasser's numerous rivals there—react to that?

Such, apparently, were the considerations that prompted the secretary-general of the United Nations to present the Egyptian president with an all-or-nothing proposition. But could Nasser back down at this stage without suffering serious damage to his prestige? Probably not, unless he could point out that Israel had reacted so vigorously that another move would mean a war, for which—as Nasser had said time and again during the preceding years—the Arabs were not yet ready. Since Eshkol's prudence meant that Israel was acting gingerly, Nasser could not easily extricate himself from this dead end. Indeed, Israel's apparent weakness may have convinced Nasser that he would be able to eject UNEF, erase the shame of 1956, and get away with it without war. To put it very bluntly, if at this moment in the crisis Israel had been less diplomatic and more determined, and had avoided any publicity, it might, paradoxically, have helped Nasser to back down. If, however, it came to the worst and Nasser did not back down even in the face of a spirited Israeli response, then the outcome would have been the same as it eventually was—all-out war.

By the time Eshkol and his colleagues discovered that a more vigorous reaction was called for, it was already too late. By May 18, 1967, U Thant already had Nasser's reply to his own ultimatum—namely, that UNEF should leave. The secretary-general decided to comply with the Egyptian request, and within five days, on May 23, Egyptian forces were deployed on the Israeli border again and Nasser had declared the reimposition of the naval blockade.

As these events evolved, Israel called up the bulk of the IDF reserves. At first mobilization was selective and undeclared. Within this five-day period, however, it ceased to be a secret and more or less ceased to be selective. The trouble was that despite the great emphasis in the rhetoric of the Eshkol government and especially of IDF Chief of Staff Rabin on deterrence, the manner in which the IDF carried out the mobilization of the reserves suggested that it did not really understand the role of a reserve call-up in the pursuit of deterrence. An unannounced call-up of a significant scale during May 14–16 would have presented Nasser with a picture of utmost Israeli resolve before Egypt itself had gone beyond the point of no return. Conversely, the deterrent impact of the mobilization, one of Israel's most valuable instruments of deterrence in crisis, was squandered by the piecemeal, semiannounced manner in which it was carried out.

Thus by the time the IDF was nearly at a wartime level of mobilization, Egypt had already become irrevocably committed. Nasser's declaration of a new maritime blockade and his subsequent signing of mutual defense agreements with Jordan and Syria came when the Egyptian president had already gone so far that he could not back down without an unacceptable loss of face. Hence the most logical thing for him to do was to try to put the onus of deciding whether or not there would be war on Israel and, simultaneously, to try to build as much as possible of a countervailing force. Assuming, apparently, that the point of no return had been crossed, Nasser attempted to neutralize the Israeli deterrence through intimidating moves of his own. Once it had openly become a gigantic test of nerve and resolve, a large-scale game of brinksmanship, a kind of grand encounter of gladiators in a global arena, it was perfectly rational for Egypt to project the most warlike, ferocious image it could produce. Such an image, Nasser may have reasoned, would either deter Israel from launching a preemptive strike (which would have amounted to a great Egyptian victory) or, at least, maximize Egypt's power and prop up Arab morale to a pitch that would lessen the prospects for an unacceptable Arab defeat.

According to all available accounts, Nasser's reimposition of a maritime blockade turned war—from the Israeli point of view—into a more or less foregone conclusion. Indeed, as of May 24, 1967, Israel acted on the assumption that deterrence had failed. If Israel had had a defensive second-strike option, the entire picture might have looked different. In the absence of such an option (attributable to Israel's own choices in the realm of force structure and capabilities during the previous decade), the logical corollary to the diagnosis that deterrence had failed was either that the reserves should be demobilized as a means of defusing the crisis (as Ben Gurion proposed) or that first, preemptive, strike was the only method of resolving the crisis in a satisfactory manner from the Israeli point of view (the opinion of the overwhelming majority of the Israeli political elite). Since Ben Gurion was out of power and, in fact, represented a minority of one, the prevailing view, almost without any further deliberation, was that a preemptive strike within a matter of days had become unavoidable.

Accordingly, the rest of the crisis—namely, the period May 24–June 5—shifted the emphasis in Israel to an entirely different focus, which in a sense falls outside the purview of this discussion. One cardinal issue that came to the fore as soon as a preemptive strike was taken for granted was how to maximize international support. This boiled down to two critical desiderata that had not been fulfilled in Israel's previous war (1956). First, when war broke out, it would be important to ensure that Israel's military effort would not be undercut by international pressures. Second, after the fighting it was imperative that the (expected) military victory be converted into a satisfactory political outcome.

Another issue, once the assumption that deterrence had failed was embraced as a starting point, was how to define the war's objectives. Should it be a modest operation designed to lead to the limited acquisition of Egyptian territory, which would subsequently be returned to Egypt in exchange for the retreat of the Egyptian army from the Sinai (as proposed by Chief of Staff Rabin)? Or should the main purpose of an Israeli first strike be to break the back of the Egyptian army as a means of deterring both Egypt and any other Arab state from repeating Nasser's challenge in the future (as proposed by Moshe Dayan)? Or, finally, should it be a combination of both approaches (as proposed by Yigal Allon)?

What ultimately determined the definition of the war's objectives, though not all its actual results, was yet a third topic of intense preoccupation after May 23, 1967—namely, building a domestic array of forces that would undertake to define the objectives of the war, take the onerous decision to launch it, and share the blame if it failed or the domestic political spoils if it was a success. In the course of an intense struggle, Eshkol of MAPAI was forced by grass-roots pressures and anxiety to cede the Ministry of Defense to Dayan of RAFI; Allon of Achdut Haavodah was made to realize that he was no match for Dayan in terms of public esteem; Menachem Begin, hitherto the pariah of Israeli politics, suggested that his lifelong foe, the octogenarian Ben Gurion, be recalled from his Negev retreat; GAHAL (Gush Herut Liberalim, Hebrew for Henut-Liberal bloc), Begin's Knesset following, was invited for the first time in Israel's history to join the cabinet; Golda Meir and the MAPAI old guard suffered a major political defeat; a number of ranking IDF officers were close to resigning their posts in protest against Eshkol's performance; Eban discovered that his own colleagues did not entirely trust his poltical judgment; Rabin, the chief of staff, suffered a nervous breakdown; and, to everyone's great surprise, Ben Gurion, widely regarded as the epitome of the warrior, cautioned against military action. Thus even before the war itself had begun, the Israeli domestic political scene had been dramatically transformed. Israel was clearly on the verge of an entirely new era.[74]

The Second Strategic Package

Compared to the Israeli strategic package of the 1949–56 period, the situation in the decade that elapsed between the Sinai compaign and the Six-Day War clearly constituted a great improvement. The IDF's capabilities kept abreast of the Arabs' despite the breathtaking pace and enormous scope of the regional arms race. Having discovered in the Sinai war of 1956 a doctrine that suited its ethos, mentality, structure, and shortcomings, the IDF proceeded to develop that doctrine to the best of its ability. The most important implications were that a defensive posture was beyond Israel's means, that the only available option was a first-strike posture, and that in the long run even this would not suffice. There might be no escape from a tacit reliance on a last-resort nuclear weapon.

An important reason that these were the most prominent conclusions of Israeli policymakers during this period was the continued failure to integrate Israel into a solid system of alliances. Although the performance of the IDF in the Sinai campaign and Nasser's regional policies together helped change Israel's image from that of a vulnerable liability to an able asset, the Israelis discovered that primary alliances capable of offering a reliable strategic shield were unattainable. Israel could obtain only so-called secondary and tertiary alliances—that is, bonds that ensured a continuing and adequate flow of weapons and strategic materials and that coordinated Israel's efforts to contain the Arabs with the parallel efforts of other powers. Although this was a great improvement in comparison to the pre-1956 period, it was not sufficiently extensive to enable the Jewish state to relax, to decrease its reliance on military power for deterrence purposes, or for that matter to abandon the quest for unconventional forms of strategic insurance.

The failure to enter into solid alliance structures also had an impact on Israel's posture regarding casi belli. Still constantly preoccupied with the impact of their every step on relations with great power patrons, the Israelis had not advanced very far beyond their cautious, suboptimal reliance on this instrument of deterrence in the previous period. The government had a clear idea of which changes in the status quo would constitute a threat. Government spokesmen would make these casi belli public. But although a bold publication of the entire inventory was incessantly advocated (by Allon, for example), such a step was not taken prior to the Six-Day War. The Arabs were led to understand what would be unacceptable, but Israel would not tie its own hands to irrevocable commitments. Small wonder, then, that the Arab confrontation states constantly prodded Israel's resolve in a variety of ways. In the case of Syria, this resulted in rampant escalation. Egypt also tried once, in 1960, and, having established the limits of Ben Gurion's patience, was irresistibly tempted to try again in 1967 in order to find out what Eshkol's threshold would be.

The same reluctance to announce a clear position was also apparent in Israel's stance concerning the use of force. The IDF's capabilities left the Jewish state without a defensive second-strike option. Instead of turning necessity into a virtue—instead of announcing a first-strike posture boldly and repeatedly as a means of deterring the adversaries from any hasty moves—Israel left the issue undetermined until a moment of crisis. The political and national security elites of Israel, its friends in the West, and almost certainly the Arab states knew after the 1956 war that if Israel's security margins were infringed on, an Israeli first strike would be almost automatic. Since this posture was deliberately muffled, a dangerous residue of ambiguity and doubt remained in the minds of all concerned—first of all the Arabs. This, arguably, did not strengthen the Israeli deterrence but somewhat compromised it.

Not so with regard to Israel's clear preference during this period for a strategy of massive retaliation. This had become almost an instinct with the Israelis. The Arabs were fully familiar with it in the course of the 1953–56 period were not allowed to forget it in subsequent years. Did this strengthen Israel's deterrence? The answer seems to be that it did so far less than many Israeli policymakers had led themselves to believe. On many occasions such a strategy was virtually unavoidable because Israel could not allow its adversaries a strategy of slow bleeding. In this sense the Israeli preference for a large-scale showdown over protracted attrition remained as logical as it had been before. During the 1957–67 decade this logic was often carried to an unnecessary excess, for which Israel itself was the first to pay the price.

In this respect there was a clear difference between the first six years of the package and the remaining four. Under Ben Gurion, escalation control was apparently more effective than under Eshkol. In this sense the domestic political setup seems to have exerted a far-reaching impact on strategic choices and performance. As a result of the changing decision-making structure after Ben Gurion's retirement from the premiership, Israel's own policies hastened the escalation that led to the crisis of May–June 1967. When it came to managing the crisis itself, domestic politics once again influenced strategic behavior more than was either necessary or, indeed, beneficial. Thus the period since the retirement of Ben Gurion foreshadowed many important developments in the post-1967 era.

4

The Perils of Victory: 1967–1973

A s in 1956, Israel went to war in June 1967 in order to reverse a process whereby, according to the perceptions of its key decision makers, its deterrence was rapidly becoming perilously depleted. Six days later, with close to 900 Israelis and some 15,000 Arabs dead, the main purpose of the war seemed to have been achieved. The Egyptian army, which only a few days earlier had been celebrating what seemed (even to many Israelis) an inevitable victory, was virtually annihilated. Nasser, whose rhetoric and self-confidence had been instrumental in bringing about this calamity, seemed a broken man. He himself proposed to resign, and his minister of war, Field Marshal Abdul Hakim Amar, committed suicide. The Jordanian army suffered an equally humiliating defeat and lost the West Bank, for the acquisition of which it had gone to war in 1948. The Syrian army, whose nagging encounters with the Israelis in the years immediately preceding the Six-Day War had been the principal immediate cause of the war, retreated ignominiously from the edges of the Golan plateau, a huge, heavily fortified citadel that until June 10, 1967, had seemed virtually unconquerable.

The magnitude of the defeat and the fact that it was the third consecutive military humiliation of Arabs by Israelis shook the very foundations of Arab self-confidence. After the *naqba* (Arabic for "disaster") of 1948, the Arabs could blame their failure on the assumption that their regimes were corrupt and that the Jews were tacitly helped by an unholy alliance between these regimes and European imperialism. In 1956 the Egyptians could still invoke the Arab disunity resulting from corruption and imperialist machinations and, above all, the fact that the Israelis were open cohorts of Britain and France. In 1967, however, such excuses were no longer effective. Most Arab regimes had been progressive (in Arab eyes), young, and implacably anti-imperialist. The Arabs went to war united under the leadership of a person who was widely seen as a latter-day Saladin. The evidence of Israeli weakness and isolation before the war was compelling. The Arabs had ample support from the Soviet Union, one of the world's two largest military and political powers.

Against such a background, Nasser's attempt to blame the United States for assisting (and thus, by implication, facilitating) the Israeli victory was not taken very seriously. The resort of this once-proud Egyptian to such arguments appeared pathetic. The reasons for the *naqsa* ("catastrophe") of 1967, some Arab intellectuals argued, had to be sought in Arab politics, education, way of life, perhaps even psyche. The Israelis were successful because they had proved to be superior in these respects. Few Arabs would dare say such harsh things. By suggesting the components of the malaise, however, Arab writings implied also (perhaps inadvertently) what qualities made it possible for the Israelis to succeed so brillantly.[1]

The Israelis, for their part, followed this process of tormented Arab soul-searching with avid interest and barely concealed satisfaction.[2] Here was affirmation by the Arabs themselves of their own culpability for the conflict. Here, too, was a reassuring torrent of evidence suggesting that quality of spirit, social organization, technology—in fact, all those virtues that the Israelis wanted to see in themselves—could overcome quantity. *The Power of Quality* was the title (in Hebrew, *Otsmata Shel Eichut*) of one widely read book that spelled out the new Israeli gospel of strength based on qualitative superiority.[3] *David's Sling,* Shimon Peres's combination of memoir and political program, was another title that essentially preached the same creed. Such books—and there were many more—contained warnings against euphoria, against complacency, and against condescension toward the Arabs. Mentally, however, such admonitions amounted to little more than prudently going through the motions. After centuries of persecution by Europeans and decades of intimidation by Arabs, the Israelis were incurably possessed by an insatiable, almost overpowering, urge to feel strong. "I feel strong, therefore I am strong" would have been an appropriate epitaph encapsulating the Israeli state of mind during the six years from June 1967 to October 1973. But although such a state of mind is an important source of fortitude, it can also be, and clearly was in this case, the wellspring of self-delusion.

To be sure, not only the Arab defeat in this third round (1948 being the first and 1956 the second) but also important elements in the postwar strategic realities seemed to support the newfound Israeli confidence. The occupation of the Sinai, of the West Bank, and of the Golan seemingly gave Israel one of the assets of deterrence that the Jewish state had lacked most—namely, strategic depth, the advantage of formidable physical barriers, a substantially extended lead time in terms of alert, a priceless inventory of bargaining chips. Moreover, in the same way that the demonstration of military prowess in 1956 had lost Israel a few friends but gained it a larger number of admirers, so the even greater victory of 1967 caused a visible reappraisal of the Jewish state as a strategic factor the world over. Israel lost the friendship of France and formal diplomatic relations with the entire Soviet bloc. At the same time, the United States moved steadily closer to Israel and offered assistance in matters that previously had seemed not merely unattainable but perhaps even undiscussable. The peripheral powers of the Middle East, whose cooperation had been sought for two decades, were now prepared to tighten relations with Israel further. World Jewry, in Israeli perception the only truly reliable external ally, was virtually overwhelmed with joy and pride and was willing to mobilize substantial resources (financial and otherwise) to support the further strengthening of the emerging Jewish regional power. With its support, the Israeli economy emerged from an agonizing depression and resumed its buoyancy and breathtaking growth.

Yet side by side with these important reasons for reassurance, the Israelis were confronted in quick succession with a host of equally powerful reasons for grave concern. Egypt was not prepared to enter into negotiations under the shadow of a humiliating military defeat. Instead, it led the Arab rejection of a search for a settlement and engaged Israel in a costly, dangerous war of attrition. The Palestinians, who during 1949–67 had ceased to exist in the Israeli cognitive map of the Arab–Israeli conflict, reemerged (to Israel's suppressed but nonetheless palpable chagrin) as a troublesome source of both military and political threats. The Soviet Union deepened its involvement on the side of the Arabs and its commitment to back them up in the event of another war. Gradually, at first imperceptibly, the Israelis were forced to recognize that the Arab oil weapon—for decades a mere bogus—was coming into its own. The spectrum of threats with which Israeli deterrence would have to cope was, in other words, steadily expanding.

In the pre-1967 period, that spectrum could be neatly divided into basic and current security. By contrast, during the 1967–73 period it turned into a complex range. Its less awesome end included guerrilla warfare in occupied territories, small-scale harassment across the boundaries, air piracy in the world's skies, and attempts on the life of Israeli diplomatic and commercial emissaries. Its intermediate level of potential harm included the familiar but ever-more-complex range of conventional threats, attrition strategies, and full-scale surprise attacks. Finally, the most alarming end of this range of threats with which the Israeli deterrent might have to cope included the once remote but suddenly more palpable specter of a nuclear threat, either directly, through Arab acquisition of such weapons, or indirectly, through Soviet extension of a nuclear canopy to Israel's main Arab adversaries.

The calculus of Israeli deterrence, furthermore, became more complicated during the 1967–73 period with two more novel factors. First, the cold war had given way to détente, an occasionally mystifying concept suggesting a less predictable—but not necessarily less dangerous—pattern of superpower relations. From Israel's point of view, the implications were not entirely clear. On the one hand, the United States was drawing ever closer to Israel in ways that had previously been undreamed of. On the other hand, détente implied a mixed-motive U.S. posture—in fact, a degree of mutual interest with the Soviets that set the two superpowers apart from all other nations on earth.

The second factor related to the course of Israeli domestic politics. Israeli society was changing in a manner that increased the inevitable tension between domestic demands and external needs. With a significant change in the social basis of politics also came a gradual change in the political array of forces, in the rules of the game, in the texture and pace of domestic politics. It all added up to an immeasurably greater difficulty in insulating national strategy from the warp and hoof of the domestic political process.

Against such a background of growing strength—but also of breathtaking growth in the complexity of the issues, in the weight of decisions, and in the constraints on rational decision making—the strategic posture that evolved during 1967–73 was less coherent than it was boldly claimed to be. It entailed a gigantic, yet somewhat unimaginative, growth in capabilities; a bolder reliance on threats, but a far less coherent concept of casi belli than before; an abrasive, often self-righteous celebration of the virtues of self-reliance amid a growing dependence on the United States; a lingering preference for first strike and massive retaliation without a levelheaded evaluation of the *political* feasibility of such a posture. The net result of the greatest victory in Israel's history was, accordingly, confusion, conceptual inertia, a visible decline in the quality of strategic thought, and—contrary to the intuitive appraisal of most Israelis at the time—significant depreciation of the efficacy of Israel's conventional deterrence.

Force Structure and Capabilities

In retrospect it appears that four factors shaped the main trends in IDF growth policies during the 1967–73 period. The first was intellectual inertia. The force structure that had brought about the victory of 1956 for the loss of 180 Israeli lives and the more mature and far larger force that obtained the victory of 1967 for the loss of fewer than 900 lives inevitably seemed ideal for the post-1967 period. Large, bureaucratized, and technologically intensive armed forces, to put it bluntly, tend to be conservative. They resist change and very often do not encourage imaginative, unorthodox thinking. This tendency is to be expected when things do not go as well as they should—but even more so when things *do* go well. In this sense the worst thing that can happen to any army is, paradoxically, a total and relatively easy victory, which is almost bound to lead to a strengthened conceptual conservatism.

The IDF was no exception to this iron law. Having won the previous two wars with such ease, it had no readily discernible reason to discard what appeared to be a certain recipe for unqualified success. Accordingly, it was inclined to assume, almost without real questioning, that what would be needed in the future was merely more, and ever more, of the same. In 1967 the IAF had a relatively aging fleet of 460 French-built, Fouga-Magister, Ouragan,

Mystère, Votour, and Mirage III trainers, fighers, and fighter-bombers, as well as 35 transport planes and 40 helicopters; by 1973 it had 432 relatively modern, mainly U.S.-built Phantom F-4s and Skyhawk A-4s, as well as 30 transporters and 72 helicopters. In 1967 the armored command of the IDF had at its disposal 990 tanks, 250 cannons, 50 antiaircraft batteries, 4 ancient submarines, 2 obsolete destroyers, and 20 other vessels; by 1973 it could boast of 1,700 tanks, 1,000 APCs, 352 artillery pieces, 48 antiaircraft batteries, scores of short- and medium-range surface-to-surface missiles, 12 latest-model missile boats, 2 submarines, 1 destroyer, and 26 other boats. As a result, the IDF as a whole grew by 10 percent, from a total (regular plus reserve) army of 275,000 to a total of 300,000 soldiers; the defense budget grew (in fixed shekel values) from 3,615 billion shekels in 1967 to 15,980 billion shekels six years later.[4] Yet for all the growth in size, the underlying doctrine guiding training, emergency, and contingency planning remained essentially the same.

To be fair to the IDF, the scope of the growth—as distinct from its content—was largely due to the regional arms race (and to the ever-spiraling price of late-model weapons systems). The routing of the armed forces of Egypt and Syria; the painful wounds inflicted on the Jordanian army; the ripples sent across the Middle East by the spectacular demonstration of Israeli superiority; inter-Arab rivalries; Soviet, French, and—with the rise in oil prices—British, Italian, and U.S. pushing of arms sales to the Arabs; and, finally, the exceedingly escalatory war of attrition between Israel and Egypt along the Suez Canal during 1969–70—all these added a stupendous impetus to the regional arms race. Israel could not escape this trap. It had to struggle to keep a composite, overall approximation of 1:4 ratio—the bare minimum for defensive purposes— between its own capabilities and those of a steadily growing list of adversaries. Thus if in 1967 the military manpower total for Lebanon, Syria, Jordan, Saudi Arabia, Egypt, and Iraq together, according to Israeli sources, was 370,500 (less than 100,000 more than Israel's, or approximately 5:6 ratio), in 1973 the total for the same countries was 650,000 compared to Israel's 300,000, or approximately a 1:2 ratio. In 1967 these (in Israeli eyes) confrontation states had 680 fighters and fighter-bombers, 73 helicopters, and 1,700 tanks; by 1973 their armories already contained 1,100 fighters and figher-bombers, 300 helicopters, 4,770 tanks, and 4,000 APCs.[5] (See figures 4–1 and 4–2.)

The third factor that had an important bearing on the main trends in the IDF's evolving force structure was, to an extent, fortuitous. Whereas the IDF that fought in the Sinai campaign in 1956 was dominated by infantry officers, the IDF of the mid- and late-1960s became conspicuously dominated by tank experts. To a significant extent, this was the result of the vicissitudes of career patterns in the IDF. The growing emphasis on armor by the late 1950s had created a glittering field of opportunities for up-and-coming officers in the armored corps and related units, such as artillery, ordnance, and communications. This was not the case with the infantry, where the total size of the corps

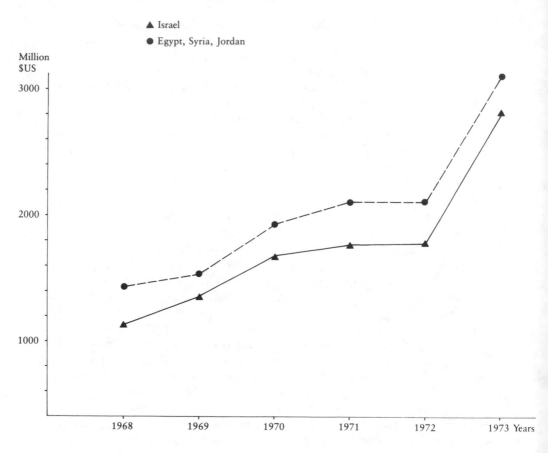

Source: Based on data in Evron, "Two Periods in Arab–Israeli Strategic Relations," p. 115.

Figure 4–1. Selected Comparisons of Arab and Israeli Military Outlays, 1968 and 1973

did not significantly change for years. Bright infantry officers who wished to advance, therefore, had little choice—even if they detested the thought, as some of them did—but to convert to armor. In turn the preponderance of somewhat schematic and unimaginative armored thinking in the IDF was reinforced as was, inevitably, the tendency to cut appropriations for other arms.

Then came the Six-Day War, in which armor was the very spine of all offensives, including—against all the orthodox rules of warfare—the steep and rocky Golan Heights. The reliance on daring, headstrong, and fast-moving armored fists as the backbone of any significant military operation, the simpleminded assumption, in the words of Major-General Yesha'ayahou ("Shaike") Gavish, that an "armored brigade or division could break through [virtually] anything"

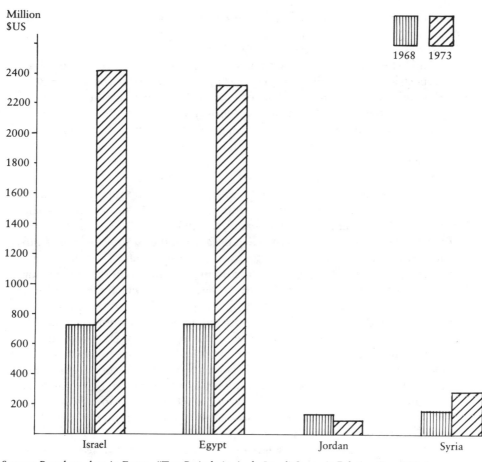

Million
$US

Source: Based on data in Evron, "Two Periods in Arab–Israeli Strategic Relations," p. 115.
In constant $US.

Figure 4–2. The Arab–Israeli Arms Race, 1968–1973

and that for this reason there was no longer any need for "ingenious and unorthodox maneuvering," was seemingly further vindicated.[6]

Going along with this transformation was the growth of a romantic ethos exalting the bravery and nonchalant manliness of tank crews—especially of tank commanders, standing, half their bodies exposed, in the turrets of their powerful machines.[7] It was thus hardly surprising that by 1968, the chief of staff, Lieutenant-General Chaim Bar-Lev; his deputy, Major-General David Elazar; members of the General Staff such as Major-Generals Israel Tal, Shlomo Lahat, Shmuel Gonen, Avraham Adan, Dan Lanner, Moshe Peled, Hertzel Shafir, and Menachem Marom (in other words, nine out of a total of eighteen members of the General Staff); and, beyond them, a burgeoning phalanx of brigadier-generals and colonels were all products of, or at least converts to, *Gyasot Hashiryon*—the armored corps.

The ascent of armor was accompanied by a stagnation of infantry. Exotic, special-operations, air- and helicopter-borne commando-type infantry was further cultivated. A substantial element of APC-mounted infantry as an integral part of the armored task force was introduced, as well. But autonomous infantry formations of the standard type, previously the backbone of the IDF, were gradually relegated in terms of both doctrine and resources to a humble, auxiliary status.

Since this could not but be reflected in the composition of planning bodies at general headquarters (GHQ)-level, both the overall doctrine and the arms procurement philosophy that flowed from it were significantly affected. The next war, it was assumed unquestioningly, would be a vastly expanded version of the previous one. The IAF, which had devastated the air forces of four Arab countries in three hours on June 5, 1967, would have no difficulty in guaranteeing clean skies. Vast, roaring armored columns would smash through enemy fortifications in eager pursuit of a battle of decisions, in which the main force of the adversary would be obliterated. Infantry would follow the advance of armor, deal with built-up areas, and offer the armored columns protection against enemy infantry—as it had done during the Six-Day War in the Gaza–Rafah–El Arish axis. Otherwise infantry had no serious role to play. The tendency that had begun in 1956–55 had thus run its full course. An army that had been at first an infantry force with armor in an auxiliary role had been transformed within a decade (and two campaigns) into a mainly armored force with small relics of infantry, whose exact position within the prevailing war scenario was not entirely clear.

The fourth and last factor affecting the emphases in the development of the IDF's force structure and deployment preferences was a direct consequence of the Six-Day War—namely, the new tasks facing it as a result of the changing geography of Israeli national security with the occupation of vast new territories. Since the topic is too complex to be dealt with in general terms, the discussion that follows will focus separately on each of the fronts—Egyptian, Jordanian, Syrian, and Lebanese.

The Egyptian Front

Apart from helping the IDF restore its declining morale during the waiting period preceding the 1967 war, Dayan's return to power resulted in an important change in the war plan. Rabin had strongly supported the idea that Israel should seize the Gaza Strip and hold on to it as long as Egypt refused to lift the naval blockade and withdraw its forces from the Sinai. Dayan, who had an acute sense of an immeasurable loss of credibility (and, therefore, of the power to deter) argued for a dramatic *spectacle,* an all-out strike leading to the destruction of the fighting ability of the Egyptian army of the Sinai; to the seizure of the Straits of Tiran and Sharm el Sheik; and, as a net result, to the recovery and even the further reinvigoration of Israel's deterrence. Having won the debate on this, Dayan added an important caveat: under no circumstances should the IDF approach the Suez Canal area. The canal should remain open for shipping, and Israeli forces should stop more or less on the western approaches of the Mitle and Gidi passes, some 15 miles east of the canal.

Dayan's orders not to "approach the water" were, however, rescinded. One reason was that Israel anticipated a U.N. order for the forces of both sides to disengage, and, in Dayan's own words, "It was desirable to have what to disengage from."[8] Another, probably more important, reason for the change was the IDF's momentum of hot pursuit of the Egyptians. Captains, lieutenants, sergeants, and corporals competing to see who would reach the canal first engaged in an unruly race during the final chase after the fleeing Egyptian army until they reached the canal.[9] Carried away by the general euphoria that followed the war, the minister of defense simply resigned himself to this outcome. Unbelievable as it may sound, this may have been the most important factor in ultimately determining where the 1967 cease-fire lines would be.

Once the IDF was on the banks of the Suez Canal, two arguments for keeping it there were advanced. The first was political. Israel should hold on to the canal's bank and thus cause Egypt a major loss of revenues. Surely Egypt would want to see the canal reopened and, to obtain this, would agree to deal with Israel. More broadly, the argument was that Israel should hold on to the cease-fire lines on the canal for political bargaining purposes. Once the area was set ablaze by the war of attrition, however, this political-bargaining argument turned into a logical trap. As long as the Egyptians were shooting, Israel could not yield if it was to avoid looking weak. Once the shooting stopped, however, Israel had no reason to withdraw unless and until Egypt agreed to a political settlement. In other words, whatever happened, the IDF should stay on the banks of Suez.[10]

A second argument for staying on the banks of Suez was strategic-military. The canal was a formidable barrier against an Egyptian counterattack. It was, some armor experts argued, a superb tank ditch, capable of making an Egyptian attack so costly that its very possession greatly improved the efficacy of the Israeli deterrent. The other side of the same coin was that by sitting on the exposed banks of the canal in close proximity to the Egyptians, the IDF raised both the Egyptians' ability and (partly as a result) their incentives to keep up their military pressure. Based on a small regular force, the interwar (for peacetime it certainly was not) IDF was too small to be able to hold the line from Kantara on the Mediterranean to Sharm el Sheik at the tip of the Sinai peninsula against an all-out Egyptian attack. If the Egyptians decided to launch a major attack based on an attempted crossing of the canal by the two army groups that they had between the canal and Cairo, they would be able to seize substantial territory before Israeli reserves could reach the front. Most members of the Israeli strategic political elite considered this argument valid even after the IDF stretched its manpower reserves to the very limit. It extended compulsory military service by six months (to three years); it quadrupled the size of the regular armored force (from five to six battalions to the equivalent of five to six brigades); and it committed permanently 60 percent of this armored force (or a whole armored division) to the Suez front. Nevertheless, even after this gigantic effort (considering Israel's limited resources), the IDF units in forward deployment along the canal were still vastly outnumbered, outgunned, and arguably less capable of deterring the Egyptians than the one regular armored brigade that the IDF had had in rear deployment between 1957 and 1967.

That this was the case was indirectly demonstrated by the difficulties the IDF encountered in its search for an appropriate deployment formula for the supposedly ideal Suez line. Broadly speaking, there were three contending advocacies: static deployment in forward positions, mobile deployment from rear bases, and a partial withdrawal from the waterfront. Concerned with preserving the flexibility and mobility of the IDF, members of the General Staff like Israel Tal and Arik Sharon proposed the concentration of the bulk of the IDF force somewhat in the rear, away from the waterfront. From that vantage point they proposed to employ the IDF for bold strikes in the rear of the Egyptian army across the canal. If an Egyptian intention to launch a major attack was detected, it should be thrown off balance as soon as it began. If there was not enough force to do so, the Israeli force on the east bank of the canal would wait until the main thrust of the Egyptian crossing was detected and then encounter it with vigorous fire and movement by an armored attack in the best IDF tradition. Meanwhile, of course, enough time would be gained to permit the reserves to be called up and transported from the rear to the battlefield.[11]

Temperamentally, Dayan, the minister of defense, sympathized with this concept of rear and flexible deployment. He appears, however, to have extended it to its logical conclusion—namely, a partial withdrawal from the waterfront. In fact, Dayan argued for a return to the original plan on the eve of the 1967 war. The waterfront line of deployment, he thought, was poor strategically and costly politically. Therefore, he contemplated a partial Israeli withdrawal within the framework of a partial agreement with Egypt. As long as Nasser was alive and at the helm, it was clear that there was no partner to any such understanding on the Egyptian side. The war of attrition was raging, and to offer a unilateral withdrawal under the pressure of Egyptian fire made no political sense. But the rise of Sadat after the termination of the war of attrition and the death of Nasser convinced Dayan that the time had come to put forward his proposal.

The Egyptians, with Soviet help, had advanced surface-to-air (SAM) missiles to the waterfront on their side of the canal. That meant that the IDF units deployed on the east bank waterfront would be exposed to superior Egyptian artillery. The Israeli flying artillery—the IAF—would find it difficult to protect them because of the presence of the Egyptian missiles. Ever conscious of the danger of a clash with the Soviets, Dayan, moreover, was eager to effect a disengagement agreement of some sort that would lessen the danger of such a confrontation. Finally, an Israeli withdrawal to the Mitla and Gidi Passes would greatly improve Israel's ability to deter the Egyptians from launching a major attack.

The passes formed two critical bottlenecks controlling the land access from Egypt to Israel. Because of their physical features, the passes could be held effectively by a small force for as long as it would take Israeli reserves to be mobilized and transported from the Israeli rear. In other words, the same armored division that was too small alone to hold the long and exposed Suez Canal/Gulf of Suez line would be more than adequate if it were deployed in the passes instead of being deployed in the wide open space stretching between the passes and the Suez Canal. If only the Egyptians were to agree to an effective demilitarization of the space lying between the canal and the passes, the IDF would have every reason to withdraw to the passes.

To be sure, this would entail an Egyptian concession in that Egypt would have to agree not to reoccupy the sovereign Egyptian territory that the IDF would evacuate. On the other hand, the Egyptians would be able to reopen the Suez Canal, to restore the cities and villages along the canal that had been destroyed by the war of attrition, and to resettle a population of some 600,000 people who had become refugees in their own land in the course of the fighting of 1968–70. As a result, Dayan apparently figured, the military interface between the Egyptian and Israeli armed forces would become significantly smaller, and the conflict between the two countries would be reduced. There would be a calmer atmosphere in which, he hoped, further negotiations ultimately leading to peace could be conducted. Indeed, the negotiations leading to such a limited agreement could in themselves create the precedent for and the procedure with which to pursue further negotiations in the future.

Dayan's plan for an interim settlement along these lines was presented in March 1971 but was aborted within a few weeks, for complex reasons. In the first place, the Egyptians would agree to a scheme like this only if their troops were allowed to follow the footsteps of the retreating IDF or, alternatively, if Israel agreed to a withdrawal from the banks of Suez to the passes 15 miles to the east only within a larger timetable for withdrawal from the rest of the Sinai. Israel could not possibly agree to either alternative. If it accepted the first option—that the Egyptian army would cross the canal and deploy in the area the IDF would evacuate—the whole idea of a demilitarized belt between the two armies would be compromised. In fact, Egypt would simply be stripping Israel of territorial assets in exchange for nothing of value.

Nor was the second option offered by the Egyptians—encasing an Israeli withdrawal to the passes within a predetermined time frame—any more acceptable. Israeli thinking on this matter was colored by the experience of 1956, when Israel had withdrawn from the Sinai without any political agreement terminating the state of war between the Jewish state and Egypt. Within a few years the Egyptians had redeployed military forces close to the Israeli border and reimposed a naval blockade. This time the Israelis were determined not to allow that to happen again. Israel would hold the Sinai unless and until Egypt agreed to a full peace agreement. It would not accept an Egyptian demand to view the withdrawal from the pennisula as a precondition to the possible negotiation of peace thereafter.

Because of such dispositions on the Israeli side, which Dayan himself fully shared, the fact that this was the maximum Egypt would contemplate in response to the idea of an interim agreement was the main obstacle to any serious negotiations. Even if the Egyptian response were more flexible than it actually was, Dayan's advocacy of an interim agreement leading to a unilateral Israeli withdrawal from the banks of Suez to the Sinai passes still aroused an unenthusiastic response in the Israeli cabinet. His colleagues' reasoning went roughly as follows. Without Egypt, the Arab world would not dare launch a war against Israel. Emasculating Egypt, therefore, was the most important element in Israel's search for deterrence. How, then, could Egypt be emasculated most effectively? Dayan thought that deployment in the passes would be more effective than deployment on the banks of the canal, but many of his cabinet colleagues did not share this view. The canal, they thought, was virtually impassable. The Egyptian army had lost the war of 1967 as well as the war of attrition, at the end of which the whole area between the canal and the Egyptian capital was in ruins. Nasser in his last years in office was a ruined man, and Sadat, who replaced him, was a weak leader, perhaps an interim appointment pending the emergence of a more dominant figure. The IDF, on the other hand, was in excellent shape and could hold onto the canal banks for as long as was politically necessary.

Tacitly, this last assumption was obviously based on an exaggerated sense of superiority—the notion that the IDF was invincible, certainly vis-à-vis the Egyptian army. Dayan's apprehensions that the small force along the canal would be inadequate were not taken too seriously. Since he himself would not stake his career on this issue, his colleagues in the cabinet, led by Prime Minister Golda Meir, Deputy Prime Minister Yigal Allon, and Minister without Portfolio Israel Galili—and, above all, supported by the expert opinion of the chief of staff, Bar-Lev, and his deputy, Elazar—saw no reason to embrace Dayan's proposals.[12]

In the two and a half years that elapsed between the discussions concerning the interim agreement and the 1973 war, the Egyptian front sank into a deceptive tranquility. Sadat's repeated threats that a prolonged impasse would lead to renewed hostilities were not taken very seriously. The IDF, after intensive deliberations and extensive exercises, was led to believe that it had an adequate solution to the deployment problem with which the Sinai had faced it. The main force would remain one armored division. In the event of an Egyptian attack, its task would be to hold the line alone for about seventy-two hours—enough time for two more armored divisions, consisting primarily of reserves, to be mobilized and deployed close to the canal. The permanent armored division itself would be deployed astride the canal, with two brigades in the rear and one brigade in forward positions. The tanks of the last would constitute an emergency reinforcement for about one infantry battalion, which would man a line of seventeen fortified positions (*maozim* in Hebrew) right on the waterline. These forces would be able to gather information about Egyptian moves, show the Israeli flag along the canal, prevent small-scale Egyptian encroachments on the east bank, and sustain the initial wave of any large-scale surprise attack.

If it transpired that the Egyptians were planning a truly massive operation, one more of the three armored brigades in the area would be moved forward. Thus, in an emergency, two armored brigades and one infantry battalion, plus one more armored brigade (or a total of fewer than three hundred tanks) should be able—the Israelis assumed—to hold their ground against an Egyptian army of close to half a million soldiers deployed across the canal at a distance of no more than 200–500 yards away.[13]

The most amazing aspect of this strategy was that its explicit prime intention was to deter. It started from assumptions about what would constitute an adequate defense and then proceeded to the conclusion that a form of deployment capable of defending would also ipso facto be capable of deterring. But how could such a thin line of defense deter such a massive Egyptian force in positions of forward deployment and with such a high motivation to retaliate? Clearly it could not. The fact that the Israelis deluded themselves into believing that it could stemmed from their most central error in analyzing what the Egyptians might do: the assumption that as long as Egypt felt unable to reconquer a substantial part of the Sinai in a single military campaign, it would not go to war.

To be sure, Israeli planners took into account the possibility of small-scale warfare, a replay of the war of attrition. The form of IDF deployment described earlier was meant to deal with such a threat and would most probably succeed in obtaining that objective. The military planners also considered the possibility of an all-out Egyptian attempt to reconquer the bulk of the Sinai. But on the assumption that the Egyptians felt—and would continue for a long time to feel—unable to perform such an operation successfully, the Israeli planners did not really prepare for such a scenario. At any rate, they acted on the high-risk assumption that intelligence would offer enough lead time for mobilizing reserves, deploying them close to the Egyptian lines, and thus either deterring the Egyptians or thwarting their design as soon as hostilities began.

What Israeli thinking prior to the 1973 war failed to take into account was the possibility that the Egyptians, precisely *because* they assumed that the

IDF was a mighty military machine, precisely *because* they had been so impressed by the IDF's power of decision, would lower their sights and aim at limited military objectives. They would vastly expand their capabilities and then throw into battle almost everything at their disposal. The purpose, however, at least initially, would be limited: to cross the canal and to establish a firm base on its east bank from which no Israeli counterattack would be able to dislodge them. To such a strategy, the IDF with its less than one armored division could not possibly respond. Its deterrence along the Suez Canal was, in other words, less effective than it had been within the supposedly indefensible 1967 borders. Though entailing an unprecedented cost, though leading to the permanent commitment to one front of a force *four times as large* as the total regular armored force on all fronts together before the 1967 war, it nevertheless failed to dissuade the Egyptians. They were not deterred from launching the war of attrition—and, when it came to the test on October 6, 1973, they were not dissuaded from attempting to cross the canal.

The Jordanian Front

On the Egyptian front the familiar Israeli distinction between *basic* and *current* security sank to the continental shelf of the Mediterranean on October 21, 1967, with the Israeli navy flagship *Eilat*. The war of attrition that raged there for two years (1968–70) was sometimes so fierce that it was merely a question of basic security within a static context. The style, in other words, was different from anything the Israelis had experienced before because it did not involve the actual seizure of territory by either side. But in terms of stakes, scope, objectives, casualties, economic costs, impact on morale, and superpower involvement, the war of attrition with Egypt clearly fell into the category of basic security.

Viewed from such a perspective, Israel's pursuit of deterrence along the Jordan River (the cease-fire line of 1967), did entail the two traditional categories of basic and current security. The IDF had to find an optimal method of deployment with which to deter the Jordanian army from any attempt to recapture the West Bank. Simultaneously, it had to find ways and means of deterring a new force, the Palestinian Liberation Organization (PLO), from attempting to ensconce itself in the West Bank or from harassing the Israeli population of the Beit Shean area or from attacking IDF units deployed in the area to deter the Jordanian army. As it turned out, the IDF was exceedingly successful in finding a solution to both problems.

As along the Suez Canal, the formula evolved piecemeal in response to challenges. Immediately after the Six-Day War, the Jordanians appeared so shattered by their defeat, by the manner in which President Nasser had hustled them into the war, and by the extent of their territorial loss (the entire West Bank) that, seen from Israel, they did not constitute a significant threat. As time passed, the Jordanian army (with U.S. help) gradually recouped from the disaster. Increasingly, however, it was facing imminent danger from within as a result of the growth of the putative power of the PLO. As the point of a showdown between King Hussein's fierce, well-armed, and disciplined Bedouin troops and Yasser Arafat's ragtag and unruly PLO militias was drawing nearer, the hidden but ever-present convergence of Israeli and Hashemite interests resurfaced. Israel deliberately accelerated, through a forceful policy of reprisals, the growth of the conflict between the Hashemites and the Palestinians. The Israeli argument was that from Hussein's point of view the showdown was inevitable: sooner or later he would either clip the wings of the PLO or see his own kingdom go under.

In September 1970 the Israeli thesis was substantiated. Faced with a triple hijacking operation on Jordanian territory, King Hussein could no longer defer an open clash with the Palestinians. His troops crushed the PLO almost to the point of total extinction within a few days. Since then, the Hashemite Kingdom of Jordan has become, for all intents and purposes, Israel's tacit ally—a virtual proxy vis-à-vis the PLO. The latter has not been allowed to return to military activities from Jordanian territory; as a result, the Israeli–Jordanian 1967 cease-fire lines have become the scene of peaceful relations in everything but name.

Beyond the question of how to deal with the Palestinians, an issue on which Israel and Jordan have never been very far apart, there has always lurked the hidden but very important element of deterrence. When King Hussein decided to sign a mutual defense pact with President Nasser and to place the Jordanian army under a joint Egyptian–Jordanian–Syrian–Iraqi command in the last week before the outbreak of the Six-Day War, the king evidently assumed that he was risking less vis-à-vis Israel by joining this Arab alliance than he would be risking vis-à-vis the Arab world if—out of fear of Israeli reaction—he were to decline Nasser's invitation. Israel's ability to deter Hussein was, in this sense, fatally depreciated.

Conversely, Hussein's devastating defeat in the Six-Day War recovered Israel's deterrent from the Jordanian perspective beyond recognition. For one thing, having lost so much, Hussein could legitimately argue from then on that he had sacrificed in the name of Arab unity more than any other Arab state. With the force of such an argument, he could ward off pressures for many years to come that Jordan should engage Israel on the battlefield again. Second, Hussein's ability to keep abreast of the arms race was critically affected by the 1967 war. Whereas Israel, Syria, Iraq, Egypt, and—with the beginning of the sharp rise in oil prices—Saudi Arabia all embarked in the aftermath of the 1967 war on a breathtaking arms race, Jordan all but opted out. There were three reasons: (1) shortage of funds; (2) difficulties in obtaining arms from the United States after not having kept a promise to avoid using them against Israel; (3) a mood of near resignation, an unarticulated but strongly suggested assumption that Jordan no longer had any need for arms for the purpose of a major war.

Beyond these political ingredients, the Israeli deterrent against Jordanian participation in a future Arab–Israeli war came to be based, after 1967, on three specific strategic elements. The first relates to the future of Aqaba, Jordan's only port. Any attempt by Jordan to attack territory held by Israel could lead the Israelis—as Hussein may have been told in private—to occupy Aqaba. Israel could probably accomplish this in a matter of hours even at a time of distress, as during the most critical hours of the 1973 war. Jordan would then be landlocked, denied an important outlet for trade, and dependent on the goodwill of not entirely predictable neighbors such as Syria, Iraq, Saudi Arabia, and for that matter Israel itself.

The second strategic source of effective Israeli deterrence against Jordan has been its patent inability, as a direct result of the 1967 war, to inflict on Israel any unacceptable damage through a brief and decisive fait accompli. Before June 1967 Jordan could, at least in theory, cut Israel in half right through the center of the country, and, since Israel's waistline (in the Kalkilya–Herzliya area) was less than 10 miles wide, Jordanian armor could achieve such an objective within an hour. Since 1967, however, the only Israeli soft underbelly from a Jordanian perspective have been the towns of Eilat (opposite Aqaba on the southern tip of the respective countries) and Beit Shean, south of the Sea of Galilee. Otherwise, a Jordanian military thrust would be complicated, costly, protracted, and fruitless because of the physical features of the terrain. Specifically, the most important area lying astride the Jordan valley (where the cease-fire lines have been located since 1967) is the Judea and Samaria massif, a steep rise of more than 3,000 feet (depending at which point), in which armor can move with great difficulty only on three or four axes. The area is predominantly barren, very rocky, exceedingly hot in summer, and very slippery and muddy in winter. It is also predominantly uninhabited.[14]

These features of the Israeli–Jordanian border since 1967 have made it quite possible for the Israelis to obtain a significant measure of deterrence against Jordan for a very limited investment in manpower and other resources. To block the advance of an armored Jordanian thrust, Israel does not need more than a small number of lookouts for early detection along the Jordan River, extensive mining, and a relatively small force capable of blocking Jordanian entry into the three or four east–west axes. What could make a difference would be the deployment of Jordanian SAMS along the Jordan River; such weapons could neutralize, or at least make more difficult, the intervention of the IAF against an invading Jordanian force. Such a move on the part of Jordan, however, can be effectively controlled through a finely tuned system of Israeli deterrent threats.

For reasons such as these, Israel faced no insurmountable difficulty in deterring Jordan from launching any kind of military attack, even during the first ten days of the 1973 war, when there was virtually no Israeli soldier in sight along the cease-fire lines with Jordan. Indeed, from this perspective it seems almost true to say that the 1967 war eliminated Jordan as an adversary except if and when Israel should prove incapable of dealing effectively with a war situation begun by other adversaries. Since the 1967 war Jordan has been expected by the Israelis to sit on the fence and watch. If a war is launched against Israel by, say, Syria and Egypt that the Jewish state finds difficult to contain and bring to a decisive resolution within a few days, then and only then do the Israelis expect Jordan to throw its weight behind the Arab war effort. The key to deterring Jordan, therefore, lies less in the actual Israeli military capabilities allocated by Israel for fighting Jordan than in an effective deterrence of the two pivotal neighbors, Egypt and Syria.

This does not apply, however, to the Israeli view of deterrence against small-scale threats to current security emanating from Jordan. At first the reemergence of the Palestinian issue as a major focal point in Arab–Israeli relations did not appear to the Israelis to pose any undue difficulty. The Jordanians, who in 1948 had forcibly imposed themselves on the West Bank Palestinian population, kept a close watch on Palestinian nationalist agitation within their realm. In June 1967 the Israeli occupation authorities managed to lay their hands on much of the information that the Jordanians had assembled on these elements in the West Bank. Consequently, it did not take long for the Israelis to evolve a reasonably effective deterrent vis-à-vis the Palestinians—namely, to demonstrate to the West Bank population that cooperation with the PLO at the risk of suffering Israeli punishment was more hazardous than collaboration with Israel at the risk of PLO punishment. From this point of view—and in terms of the mechanics, this was clearly a problem of deterrence, too—Israel had only a minor problem with the population of the West Bank during the 1967–73 period.[15]

In the Gaza Strip it proved more difficult to obtain the same results. The area, a small, poor zone in which the Palestinian refugees in the camps outnumbered the Palestinian nonrefugees in the towns and villages, was rife with PLO activists (especially radicals from George Habash's Popular Front for the Liberation of Palestine, or PFLP). Acts of resistance against the Israeli occupation were carried out daily almost from the very beginning of the Israeli occupation. When all this reached a boiling point after a number of particularly vicious killings of Israelis, the Meir government permitted Major-General Ariel Sharon, OC Southern Command, to try a new iron-fist policy in the Gaza area. Moving in bulldozers, which broke open wide avenues in the crowded refugee camps, the IDF and the SHABAK (Hebrew acronym for the plainclothes General Security Service) made hundreds of arrests, carried out numerous manhunts of fleeing PLO activists, and within a matter of weeks had terrorized the population of the Gaza Strip into an attitude of submission that did not wear out even long after Sharon's retirement from the IDF.[16]

The routing of the PLO from the West Bank and the Gaza Strip shifted the weight of the conflict with this organization from the interior of the occupied territories to the cease-fire lines on the rim. Egypt and Syria permitted no free play by the PLO from their territories and, in any case, held the PLO on such a short leash that it did not behoove that organization to seek to base itself on their territories.[17] Conversely, weaker governments such as those of Jordan and Lebanon had far greater difficulty in restraining the PLO, either for fear of critical Arab reactions—including those of countries that would not allow PLO activities from their own territories—or for fear of domestic repercussions. Thus once the PLO had lost its initial ability to operate against Israel inside the occupied territories, it increasingly based itself on the east bank of the Jordan River and in South Lebanon. As a result, Israel faced the old problem of deterrence against small-scale threats in an entirely new setting.

Insofar as Jordan was concerned, solving the problem proved far easier in the context of the 1967–73 period than it had been during the 1949–56 period. The main reason for the difference was that the Jordan valley was uninhabited by Jews, whose presence could provide marauders with conveniently vulnerable targets, and offered a topographic setting that facilitated effective defensive/preventive/denial strategy. In the 1950s, Dayan, as chief of staff, felt that Israel could not defend every tree, house, or well, and therefore that it was imperative to rely on a harsh punitive policy vis-à-vis the Jordanians in order to force them to restrain the Palestinians under their jurisdiction. In the 1960s, and early 1970s, Dayan, as minister of defense, authorized a more sophisticated policy. It blended a powerful incentive for good behavior in the form of the open-bridges policy, which permitted trade between the east and west banks, with severe punishment—virtually a scorched-earth policy against the population on the Jordanian side of the river—and very effective defensive measures that brought PLO casualty rates per attack to above 90 percent while keeping Israeli casualties very low.

The open-bridges policy enabled Israel to turn on and turn off commercial and civil traffic on the Allenby, Damya, and Abdullah bridges across the Jordan River and thus to affect critically life and trade on both banks. Consequently, this policy gave Israel an effective instrument with which to turn both the Palestinians on the West Bank and the Jordanian government against the PLO. The punitive policy of shelling, bombing, and strafing, along with occasional infantry and light-armor raids on the east bank of the river, led at one point to the complete disruption of life in the whole area. Farmers could not work, fields were set on fire, irrigation canals were destroyed. The population ran away into the Jordanian hinterland and created congested and politically dangerous concentrations of refugees. Finally, the combination of small forts (*moutsavim*), extensive mine fields, barbed-wife fencing, tracking roads, patrols, and other devices along the Jordan River created a situation in which fewer than 400 Israeli soldiers could hold a 250-mile-long line from the Sea of Galilee to Eilat; it enabled the Israelis to capture or kill within several hours every PLO party that succeeded in crossing the mine fields, breaking through the fences, avoiding the ambushes, or bypassing the forts. As a result, by 1970, even before the ouster of the PLO from Jordan, the latter country had ceased to be an effective sanctuary for PLO operations against Israel.[18]

Lebanon

Achieving the same result on the Lebanese border, however, proved a far more demanding task. The difficulty began with the difference in terrain. Whereas the Jordan valley is for the most part barren—making surveillance, detection, and accurate shooting very easy—the Israeli–Lebanese border is a hilly woodland where small parties can move quite easily without being detected. In addition, the Israeli–Lebanese 1949 armistice demarcation line—unlike the 1967 Israeli–Jordanian cease-fire line—does not run along one distinct ravine. Zionist plans during World War I advocated that the border should run along the Litani, Zaharani, or even Awali River. The final border, however, bore no resemblance to these plans and in fact resulted from British–French negotiations in which neither the Lebanese nor the Zionist interest was an important factor. In the course of the 1948 war, Israel had an opportunity to rectify this artificial border since the IDF was in control of substantial Lebanese territory. The Ben Gurion government, however, decided to return every inch to the Lebanese; therefore, the final border remained exposed, topographically incoherent, and thus difficult to defend—especially against small-scale infiltration.

The most important factor that turned the Lebanese border into a festering wound, however, was the fact that on the Israeli side there was a large, physically vulnerable, and often socially-culturally infirm Jewish population, whereas on the Lebanese side there was no punishable government against which coercive diplomacy could effectively be directed. The Jewish population on the border constituted a soft underbelly—a victim and a hostage that could be subject to daily hit-and-run attacks by ragtag forces that were neither very big nor very well trained nor even very impressively equipped; they were, nevertheless, a very effective instrument of harassment and demoralization. The absence of a Lebanese government capable of being pushed—through punitive Israeli action—into taking disciplinary action against the PLO turned the south of Lebanon into an almost impregnable PLO sanctuary.

Together, the two elements turned the Israeli–Lebanese border into a scene of ever-increasing violence. To deal with this situation, the IDF essentially applied a different mix of the same methods it applied in the Jordan valley and along the banks of the Suez: a combined system (*ma'arechet* in Hebrew) consisting of a chain of small fortified positions, mine fields, patrols, ambushes, day and night raids across the lines and intermittent fire. This mix exacted a high price from the Arab Lebanese population across the border if and when the latter seemed to offer shelter to the PLO. On the Sinai and Jordan fronts these same methods were quite successful (insofar as they led to a cease-fire on the Egyptian front and to the ejection of the PLO from Jordan). On the Lebanese border, however, the same methods did not quite work.[19]

Syria

Although tensions on the Syrian border were the immediate cause of the 1967 war, the question of whether or not there would be a war between Israel and the Ba'ath republic was left almost entirely up to Israel. The Syrians, to be sure, did launch a small-scale attack on Tel Dan and did step up somewhat the shelling of Israeli villages in the Huleh valley. Nevertheless, the overall impression was that Syria was neither ready for nor interested in a war with Israel in June 1967. And when Syria accepted a cease-fire *before* Israel's counterattack, it became crystal clear that the Israeli deterrence against a Syrian threat to basic security had been largely successful.[20]

As has been shown before, where Israel had failed abysmally prior to the Six-Day War was in dissuading the Syrians from harassing the population of the Galilee—in other words, in deterring Syria from posing a constant, nerve-racking threat of the low-level, current-security variety. Consequently, Eshkol's government in the course of the 1967 war was split into doves and hawks concerning Syria. To everyone's surprise, Dayan, the minister of defense, was a dove in this regard. Fearing a clash with the Soviets, a division inside Israel, and intensified conflict with the Syrians, he advocated the conquest of the DMZs in order to remove this constant source of trouble from the agenda. But he argued vehemently against a move to seize the Syrian Golan plateau.[21]

Dayan's dovish views were contested vigorously by Yigal Allon. A member of a kubbutz near the Syrian border, Allon was sensitive to the views of the population that had suffered from Syrian fire throughout the previous nineteen years. Above all, he did not particularly fear that Israel might find itself clashing with the Soviets. He also entertained far-flung ideas concerning the future of Israeli–Syrian relations. Born in Kefar Tabor, a village in the Galilee, he knew parts of Syria as well as his own birthplace. This familiarity led to a strong conviction that Syria was not an irreversible political fact. The country was, like Lebanon, a mosaic of rival minorities. It was in the Israeli interest, Allon argued, to try to weaken it by establishing enduring links with some of these minorities. In particular, Allon believed that the Druzes of southern Syria would welcome such contact with Israel. Thus when the Six-Day War began, Allon was convinced that this was a unique opportunity to capture from Syria an area astride the Israeli border that could be turned into a security belt, as well as to make a bold attempt to link up with the Druzes further east, in the Hawran. In his own words, "considering Syria's role in fomenting the [Six-Day] war, and its fierce shelling of the [Israeli] villages and attempt to perform an armoured incursion—it was imperative to open an offensive on the Syrian front as soon as the IAF had vanquished Arab air forces . . . in order to uproot Syria from the [Golan] mountain, obliterate her forces, and force the remains of Syrian army to concentrate on the defense of Damascus—without letting the IDF move too closely to [this town]—and conquer the whole of south Syria, including the Druze Mountains."[22]

Though Allon's far-reaching ideas had virtually no support in Eshkol's cabinet, he did succeed in presenting a strong case for an Israeli-controlled security belt on the Golan. Since Dayan opposed this, Allon had to bypass him and twist the prime minister's arm. Leading a deputation of the population of the Galilee Finger virtually into the prime minister's office, Allon succeeded in bringing Eshkol to overrule Dayan's objections and to authorize the conquest of the Golan. What undoubtedly helped this pressure along was the fact that the IDF Northern Command, under Major-General David Elazar, was also pressing for action. Allon and Elazar together advanced many reasons that the conquest of the Golan would contribute to Israel's security. It is difficult to avoid the impression, however that their most important reason for advocating the assault on the Syrian Golan was sheer ambition: General Elazar and his staff, too, wished to participate in what was rapidly developing into a spectacular victory.

Dayan, the main opponent of the idea of expanding the war against Syria, was being surrounded by an ever-growing demand to authorize a redefinition of war aims to which he was opposed. Probably out of fear of domestic criticism if and when the Syrians were to resume their fire some time after the opportunity to seize the Golan had slipped away, Dayan yielded (as he yielded against his own better judgment to the pressure to allow the IDF to reach the Suez Canal); within forty-eight hours the IDF had captured a sizable chunk of sovereign Syrian territory.[23]

This acquisition seemingly strengthened the Israeli deterrent beyond recognition. Deterrence against current security threats was improved, since Syrian artillery and light firearms could no longer shoot at Israelis living and working the valley right below them. Deterrence against basic security threats was also improved because the Syrians lost their immense topographic advantage; because the IDF suddenly was barely twenty-five miles from the Syrian capital; and because the IDF captured Mount Hermon, a ridge rising to more than 6,000 feet at its peak and offering a position from which virtually anything that moved on the Syrian side could be seen. Such a narrowly pitted cartographic-topographic and military calculus of deterrence failed, however, to place the issue in the appropriate psychological context. Specifically, it failed to take into account what the loss of this important piece of territory would do to the Syrians' motivation to participate in future wars with Israel. In 1948 the Syrians noisily advertised ambitious war aims but settled for the conquest of three minuscule enclaves on the Israeli side of the border. In 1956 the Syrians were loud again, but they let Egypt take a painful beating from the French, the British, and the Israelis without lifting a finger to help them. In 1967 Syria dragged Egypt into war, but when it came to the test the Syrian army fought gingerly and seemed far more preoccupied with defending the regime in

Damascus than with engaging the IDF. Nevertheless, eager to settle the score with Syria once and for all, those members of Eshkol's cabinet who advocated the capture of the Golan exaggerated the extent of Syria's involvement in the 1967 war. They won the day but, in the process, created a situation in which Syria was intimidated, but its national pride and its position and status in its Arab peer group were so badly hurt that its commitment to the struggle against Israel may have been transformed from something vague and not entirely serious to a specific, powerful, galvanizing national purpose. By conquering the Golan, then, Israel may have appreciated its *defense* against Syria *in relative terms*. But it almost certainly depreciated its *deterrence in absolute terms*. The full scope of this miscalculation unfolded in October 1973, when a huge Syrian force broke through the Israeli lines on the Golan and stopped only on the edge of the plateau, at a point from which the lush valley below—with its multitude of Israeli villages and towns—could be seen.

Even during the first two years after the 1967 war there were moments at which holding on to the Golan appeared as complex a proposition as holding on to the Suez Canal. Indeed, on the Golan, as along the canal, the Israeli presence led to something resembling a war of attrition. In terms of deployment and force structure, the Israeli response was basically schematic and predictable. Shelter for the forces holding the lines on the Golan was provided by a system of *ma'ozim* very close to the cease-fire lines (as in the Sinai, the Jordan valley, and the Lebanese border). In addition (emulating the Jordan River and the Suez Canal) the IDF dug a deep artificial tank ditch as an obstacle to armored attacks. If such an attack was planned by the Syrians, it would have required special bridging equipment at a number of points, which would inevitably become vulnerable bottlenecks. To make a Syrian attack even more difficult, the IDF laid a large number of antipersonnel and antivehicle mines and deployed elements of artillery, armor, and some infantry at a number of central points some distance from the cease-fire lines. There was, of course, also a fence system against infiltration for purpose of sabotage and intelligence gathering, as well as some awesome-looking early warning and electronic communications centers.

All in all, the Golan front had one-third the size of the force that the IDF had in the Sinai. One armored brigade (60–80 tanks) plus one infantry battalion (about 350 combatants) and some auxiliaries were supposed to be able to absorb an attack by a formidable force of more than 600 tanks, which Syria had deployed in the immediate vicinity of the cease-fire line. Moreover, a substantial part of the Syrian force was concentrated so close to the crossing line that the small IDF contingent would hardly have any early warning. All the Syrians had to do was to take the camouflage nets off their tanks, start the engines, and move them to the crossing line a few hundred yards away. Under these circumstances, unless the IDF succeeded in obtaining hard intelligence data positively proving an imminent Syrian intention to launch a massive attack (which not even the best intelligence service in the world could responsibly promise), the minuscule Israeli force on the Golan—the only force standing between the Syrians and the population of the valley ten miles to the west—would have to fight against a force ten times its size, for at least forty-eight hours, without any significant reinforcement.

How could the IDF planners have been tempted to believe that such a force would deter effectively? The answer may lie in two separate but related sets of assumptions. First, having already become overextended because of the requirements of deployment on other fronts, the IDF had no choice but to make the high-risk assumption that more force could be made available only in a supreme emergency. Hypnotized by the advantages of strategic depth, the Achilles' heel of the Israeli deterrent before June 1967, IDF planners were apparently not entirely aware of the trade-off between strategic depth and other components of deterrence.

The pre-1967 boundaries may have been imperfect, but they were commensurate with the order of battle that Israel could afford to maintain. The post-1967 boundaries greatly improved security from the point of view of strategic depth, but they may have also increased Arab motivation to fight and, despite the colossal expansion of the IDF, led to a worse force-to-space ratio than existed before the 1967 war. To put it bluntly, one regular armored brigade (the seventh) near the town of Ashkelon in the center of Israel as a strategic reserve offered a better deterrent within the more compact 1967 lines than did a whole armored division in the Sinai, plus an armored brigade in the Golan, plus numerous other smaller elements of armor spread over a great variety of locations along the new—and far longer—boundaries. What was gained in size was undercut by the combination of far longer internal lines, with a shift to—in essence—forward deployment, a method reducing Israel's early warning and underlining its abject numerical inferiority.

The IDF, then, started its calculus from the assumption that the forces in the Golan could not be substantially augmented unless and until a supreme emergency was positivley identified. Thus it was only natural for the planners to assume that this entailed no unacceptable risk. But how could it be assumed that there was no unreasonable risk when the Syrians were engaged—right in front of Israeli eyes—in the most vigorous arms buildup in their history? The explanation may be traced in standard Israeli assumptions concerning the Syrian calculus. Syria, it may have been assumed, would not go to war without Egypt. Egypt would not go to war unless it could recapture a substantial part of the Sinai. But since—at least in the Israeli perception—the Egyptians would remain unable to do so for a long time to come, a large-scale Syrian attack was highly unlikely.

This reasoning is not the same as saying that the Israelis did not anticipate any kind of threat. Although a full-scale Syrian assault was considered only a remote possibility, contingencies such as a renewed war of attrition or a

Syrian attempt to grab a piece of land on which the Syrian flag could be proudly hoisted were held to be likely, even very likely. Against such limited threats, the forces allocated for the Golan would be quite enough, especially if their backbone, the 188th armored brigade, were deployed somewhere in the rear as a local, concentrated strategic reserve capable of deploying quickly at any point along the cease-fire lines where a Syrian intention to perform a *mechtaff* ("grab" in Hebrew) or any other hostile move was detected.

The Decline of Casi Belli

One of the most paradoxical aspects of the Israeli experience with casi belli as an instrument of deterrence is that most of the changes in the status quo that would have led Israel, before the Six-Day War, to initiate hostilities became obsolete before they were fully spelled out. Allon's comprehensive definition of Arab acts that would be regarded by Israel as a grievous breach of the status quo, and thus as a potential cause for resorting to force, was published in the summer 1967 issue of the hebrew language magazine *Molad*. When the article was published, Israel had already gone to war in order to undo the consequences of Nasser's challenge and thus ipso facto exhibit the credibility of its deterrence. The consequences of the war, however, robbed the concept of deterrent casi belli of much of its policy relevance. If a naval blockade was a casus belli, Israel's conquest of the Sinai peninsula endowed it with effective control over the Straits of Tiran. If the concentration of Egyptian forces in the Sinai in close proximity to the Israeli border was a casus belli, the Israeli control of the peninsula, again, ensured that the Egyptians would not be able to concentrate their forces there except by actually launching a war. If the passage of Israeli ships through the Suez Canal had been a grievous wound since the early 1950s, Israel's control of the Sinai created a situation in which the canal was open either to both countries or to neither. If the stationing of Jordanian troops in great concentrations on the West Bank was a casus belli, the Israeli conquest of this territory removed it from the list as well. Last but not least, if Israel considered Syrian interference with the use of the water of the Jordan River a casus belli, Syria could no longer interfere while the IDF controlled the Hasbani, the Banias, and the Dan, the three main tributaries of the Jordan.

The sudden irrelevance of Israel's casi belli had more profound implications than the Eshkol and Meir governments realized. It boiled down, in fact, to nothing less than a fundamental shift in overall strategic posture from deterrence to defense; from a strategy of war prevention through a threat of punishment to a strategy of war prevention through the declared intention of denying the adversary any military or territorial gains; from, in the final analysis, a strategy that was commensurate with Israel's size and resources to a strategy that was more aligned with Israeli dreams.

The full extent of the shift can best be understood through the perspective of what is known as *strategic depth*. Before the 1967 war, Israel relied on a strategic posture that sought to compensate for the lack of *endogenous* strategic depth by creating through the enunciation or signaling of casi belli an envelope of added, *exogenous*, shock-absorbing capacity. This entailed both spatial and functional dimensions. In spatial terms the added absorptive capacity of enemy attack would be gained through the unilateral definition of security margins outside the sovereign territory of the state. Differently stated, if the boundaries of the state delineated the domain of its intrinsic, vital interests, then declared, semideclared, hinted, signaled, or even only mooted casi belli constituted a desperate and not entirely successful attempt to delineate a wider strategic perimeter. In functional terms, the added increments of security would be gained through the unilateral designation of specific limitations on the adversaries' capabilities.

From a legal point of view, this was an outrageous practice. It entailed an Israeli demand from neighboring states to accept restrictions on their freedom of action in matters that were entirely within their sovereign rights. Thus if Israel declared that it would not tolerate the arming of the Arab world beyond a certain level, or if it threatened that the concentration of Egyptian forces in the Sinai or of Jordanian forces on the West Bank or of Syrian forces in Jordan or in Lebanon would constitute a casus belli, the Jewish state would, strictly speaking, be interfering with the internal affairs of these countries. Such anticipatory deterrent threats constituted, in other words, a *Diktat*, a challenge—an intolerable affront. They were uncivilized, brigand, unlawful, and above all provocative.

Nevertheless, even if the Israelis were fully aware of this—and it is not entirely clear that they were—they could argue two things in defense of this policy. First, they could say, the Arabs had brought such a predicament upon themselves by declaring and maintaining a state of war. Second, the alternative could be worse; namely, if Israel could not protect itself through threats, if its admittedly provocative demands were not heeded, it might have to protect itself through execution. From the Arab point of view, the result would be worse: ever more frequent Israeli preemptions leading to an Israeli occupation of Arab lands. This was what Israel had tried to prevent throughout the nineteen years preceding the Six-Day War. Having failed (by its own perception more than by Arab perceptions), it shifted its strategy from threats to their execution, from deterrence to active defense. This was the story of the reprisals before the 1956 war and of the 1956 campaign itself. The outcome was an Israeli withdrawal in return for a vague U.S. assurance that the Egyptians would tacitly agree to regard any return to the pre-1956 war status quo ante a legitimate casus belli.

Egypt had complied with this voluntary agreement, but it evidently continued to regard this state of affairs as an open wound, a score that a proud and ambitious nation like itself could not afford to forego. In February 1960

Nasser attempted to settle this score for the first time; in May 1967 he tried again. In the first instance Israel's response succeeded in deterring; in the second, however, Israel failed to take full advantage of its very real deterrent power and was consequently impelled to execute its deterrent threats.

Once the threatened punishments had been administered, however, Israel's projected, potential, and exogenous strategic depth was realized. It became actual, internalized, endogenous. What until June 1967 had been perceived as secondary *strategic* interests (for which one *may* fight) were inadvertently redefined as primary, *intrinsic* interests (for which one *will* fight). Although the bulk of the newly acquired territory was seen by Israeli policymakers as a mere bargaining asset, the provisional arrangements made in order to hold on to it, the fortifications, the military air bases and infrastructure, the civilian and paramilitary settlements—all had the effect of transforming the overall strategy. The previous strategy of deterrence based on the threat of punishment was abandoned. Adopted instead was a strategy of deterrence based on a supposedly impregnable defensive deployment. That this defensive form of deterrence was not impregnable the Israelis discovered with a shock in 1973. Meanwhile, however, the novel and immensely satisfying sense of impregnability affected Israel's official attitude toward other elements in its own formula for general deterrence.

The Illusion of Self-Reliance

The first victim of Israel's newly acquired self-confidence was its long-held policy regarding international patronage. Ben Gurion's maxim that a mighty international patron like the United States would greatly augment Israel's deterrence—that the very existence of a formal, public alliance with such a patron would have an important impact on the Arab strategic calculus and willingness to initiate hostilities—was never explicitly challenged. But the harrowing experience of being abandoned by virtually everyone on the eve of the 1967 war, and the heady sensation of victory and omniscience that engulfed the Israelis after the war, soon led to a new calculus of deterrence in which a formal alliance with a great power was relegated to a tertiary level of importance.

This was not the result of a single decision or of a consistent, orderly process of policy evaluation. Rather, it was the outcome of a drawn-out exchange in which the United States confronted Israel with a clear choice: *either* territories *or* a formal alliance. Coauthored by a multitude of policymaking authorities, the U.S. perspective in this regard (as in most others) was not entirely coherent. Its main elements, however, were not difficult to identify. The United States was not unhappy about the Israeli victory in the war (although it was outraged by the mysterious attack on the USS *Liberty*). After all, Israel had administered a stunning knockout blow to the allies of the Soviet Union and had thereby seemingly changed the strategic realities of the Middle East. The Soviet traffic of supplies to North Vietnam through the Black Sea, the Mediterranean, the Suez Canal, the Red Sea, and the Indian Ocean was blocked. The Soviets were not only humiliated but, indeed, forced to spend huge sums to restore the devastated armed forces of their Arab clients.

At the same time, however, the U.S. government was alarmed by the heightened tensions in the Middle East resulting from the war. There was an urgent need to remove some of the sources of imminent explosion that were virtually built into a situation in which Israel occupied such vast Arab lands. Indeed, the U.S. position in the Arab world had suffered greatly as a result of the Israeli triumph, since officially the United States was held to be in collusion with the Jewish state. Accordingly, if the United States could facilitate a constructive Arab–Israeli dialogue, or at least an interim agreement that would lead to an Israeli withdrawal in exchange for partial Arab recognition, U.S. interests would be greatly benefited.

This in a nutshell was the position of the Near East Bureau of the State Department, the main depository of empathy for the Arabs in official Washington. The National Security Council and the White House did not entirely disagree with the main tenets of this thesis, but they also tended to accept elements of the Israeli thesis. In particular, they conceded the logic of the argument that, had Israel possesseed a security guarantee from the United States and had Israel not been pushed by the United States in 1957 to evacuate the Sinai without any Egyptian willingness to make peace, the war of 1967 might have been avoided. It was urgent, President Johnson and his White House staff believed, to defuse the situation. This could be achieved through an Israeli withdrawal, but Israel should not be pushed into withdrawing again in return for no tangible improvement in its basic security situation.

Seen from Washington, the optimal solution would have been an Israeli withdrawal, Arab recognition of Israel, and a formal U.S. guarantee of Israel's security as insurance against sudden shifts in the Arab position. The second-best solution would be an Israeli withdrawal without a full peace with the Arabs but with a U.S. security guarantee. What the United States could not do, however, was what Israel would have preferred—namely, underwrite Israel's security in a formal treaty while Israel still occupied vast Arab lands. Under such circumstances, the danger of a flare-up leading to a U.S. entanglement in another imbroglio (in addition to Vietnam) would be very great, as would the damage to U.S. relations with the Arab and Moslem worlds.

Such a view of U.S. interests presented Israel with a difficult choice. On the one hand, the United States was offering what Israel had craved ever since its inception—namely, a public, unambiguously defined security guarantee. If the Jewish state were to have such an agreement with the mightiest power in the world, especially if it would be not merely an executive agreement but a treaty ratified in Congress, the strategic calculus of its Arab adversaries was bound to be altered. The Arabs would have to assume not only that Israel itself was powerful and quite capable of inflicting painful wounds to them, but also that Israel was supported in a binding manner by the United States; that it had no problem of either economic solvency or military supplies; that if it ran out of manpower, the United States would have to dispatch U.S. troops to defend it; that the actual might and credibility of the great American republic were irrevocably committed to the Jewish state's defense; that the impact of the far-flung Soviet commitment on the side of the Arabs was substantially undercut and neutralized by a symmetrical U.S. involvement on the side of Israel; that, ultimately, the undoing of Israel as a political reality in the Middle East had become an utterly unrealistic proposition.

On the other hand, such a security guarantee was bound to carry a significant price tag. In the first place, Israel would have to accept the notion of a withdrawal from virtually all the territories occupied in the Six-Day War in return for less than what the Israelis perceived as full and normal peace with the Arbas. In a sense, if they accepted the U.S. offer, they might have to go back to the pre–June 1967 status quo ante, in which the Sinai would be under Egyptian control, the West Bank under Jordanian control, and the Golan (possibly excluding the DMZs), under Syrian control. This would mean that Israel would be in fact trading territories, physical barriers, and strategic depth for a U.S. declaration (albeit a written one) as the main shield of its security.

The implications would be profound. An utter lack of exchange of either persons or commodities or ideas between the Jewish state and its neighbors would be endorsed as a normal state of affairs. U.S. arms rather than a complex web of human relations and interdependencies would be the main dam against yet another Arab attack. The Jewish state would largely forego its freedom to decide when and how to use force. Henceforth, every time the Arabs either threatened or actually implemented steps Israel deemed detrimental to its security, it would have to prevail on U.S. hesitations and obtain an executive commitment, backed by Congress, to take deterrent or defensive action. The problem would be serious with regard to threats to Israel's basic security—that is, the probability of an all-out war (as in 1948, 1956, or 1967)—because of the dangers that this entailed. But it would be acute with regard to low-level, current-security threats (such as Israel had to deal with all along). From a U.S. perspective such threats might appear inconsequential, whereas from an Israeli perspective they would be as intolerable as a similar situation on the California–Mexico border would be from the U.S. point of view. Since it could be taken for granted that the United States would always advise caution, prudence, and restraint and that it would always drag its feet in response to any Israeli request for backing, a formal U.S.–Israeli alliance could turn into an endless source of friction between the two countries.

Which of these considerations loomed larger in the Israeli mind is impossible to tell. What is clear, however, is that the Eshkol government never really seriously considered the U.S. offer of a treaty of alliance in exchange for an

Israeli endorsement of the principle of more or less complete withdrawal from the occupied territories. Israel's ability to deter the Arabs by holding onto all the newly occupied territories appeared to be beyond challenge. The United States seemed to have been so favorably impressed by Israel's latest demonstration of military prowess that it was moving rapidly toward an acknowledgment of the Jewish state's value as a strategic asset. Meanwhile, it was supplying Israel with most of the arms and political and economic support it needed. In other words, Israel was reaping most of the tangible fruits of an alliance without paying any real price for it. So why even consider a treaty?[24]

David Ben Gurion might have insisted that in the long run Israel was too small and vulnerable to shun a formal alliance with the world's mightiest power, that the moral and strategic-political impact of such an alliance on Israel's posture vis-à-vis the Arabs should not be taken lightly. His successors, however, acted from a position of greatly invigorated self-confidence. This was already discernible in the attitude of the Eshkol government during Lyndon Johnson's last year in the White House. But it became an unchallenged orthodoxy, an article of faith, an assumption that one acts on and never stops to question, during 1969–73, when Nixon, Kissinger, Golda Meir, Israel Galili, Dayan, Allon, and Rabin were the principal actors.

From the Israeli point of view, what seems to explain this breakaway from the age-old maxim that the Jewish state needed a superpower patron is the combination of personal and situational factors. The personal dimension is as simple as it is difficult to substantiate: the leading team in Israel after Eshkol's death in February 1969 added up to a hard, self-confident group. This started from the personality of the prime minister herself—a pugnacious, self-righteous, courageous, but conspicuously unimaginative person. In turn, all her colleagues—including some, like Dayan, who were occasionally given to doubts—came to share her unshakable conviction that Israel was safe because it was right and its adversaries were wrong.

The conviction that the occupied territories were a more reliable foundation for security than a U.S. guarantee was an article of faith both for Moshe Dayan and for the Achdut Haavodah component in the government, whose two leaders, Israel Galili and Yigal Allon, were very close to Prime Minister Meir. Finally, during the years under discussion (1968–73), the United States was in the process of withdrawing from its commitments to South Vietnam and Taiwan. To advocate a U.S. guarantee under these inauspicious circumstances made no sense. Who could trust a U.S. guarantee if the United States could not make good its own words? On the other hand, who wished to confront U.S. public opinon with a demand for a guarantee that might lead to the stationing of U.S. troops in yet another trouble spot thousands of miles away from the shores of the great American republic?

This rationale for abandoning the search for a formally guaranteed U.S. patronage was strongly reinforced by two more considerations. First, the Israeli nuclear program was drawing closer to a point at which a weapon of last resort could be within reach at short notice. Whether or not this was really the case is still unclear. But there appears to be some credence to the argument that under the impact of the crisis of 1967, in which Israel was—in its own perceptions—abandoned to its fate, a decision was taken to accelerate (along with a conventional-weapons productive capacity) efforts to obtain access to some nuclear device. If this factor was added to the presumably strengthened security owing to the acquisition of defensible borders, small wonder that Golda Meir and her colleagues felt that a formal security guarantee would be a poor substitute.[25]

Second, there was increasing evidence that the Nixon administration, for its own reasons, was heading toward a de facto alliance in any case. Both Nixon and his national security adviser, Henry Kissinger, saw in the Arab–Israeli confrontation an important arena of the East–West struggle, an area where the United States could either offset the damage that Vietnam had done to its credibility or, if it did not play it right, accelerate its decline as a great power. Such a perspective led them virtually to ignore the advice of the State Department's area specialists (who tended to propose a kind of pro-Arab appeasement) and move instead toward a strongly pro-Israel posture.

Israel appeared to be a model U.S. ally because it was both able and willing to defend itself. It made little sense for the United States to punish such an ally and strive to deliver Israeli concessions to the Arabs (and through them to the Soviets). To be sure, it was a supreme U.S. interest to stabilize the Arab–Israeli conflict and consolidate the U.S. position in the oil states. This, however, could be achieved only if the United States retained the ability to influence Israeli policy.

The Arab-affairs specialists in the Near East Bureau believed that U.S. influence on Israeli policy could—in fact should—be gained through pressure. Nixon and Kissinger, on the other hand, believed that the United States should flex its muscles against its foes, not against its allies. Making Israel stronger through arms supplies, economic assistance, and political patronage, the president and Kissinger argued, would be a far more efficient way to gain influence over the Israelis and would not further harm relations with the Arab world.

The area specialists had an opportunity to test the validity of their thesis in 1969–70. Their initiatives (the four-power and two-power proximity talks, the Rogers initiatives, and the various Jarring missions) led to meager results. In fact, the only success the State Department could claim was the August 1970 Egyptian–Israeli cease-fire, which was violated by the Egyptians within twenty-four hours in a manner that gained U.S. diplomacy no laurels. The president and Kissinger, on the other hand, collected handsome dividends for the United States in their management of the Jordan crisis of September 1970, a dramatic demonstration of the potential of U.S.–Israeli strategic cooperation.[26] Small wonder, then, that the lessons of this last experience continued to inform U.S. policy in the Middle East until the 1973 Yom Kippur War.

In practice this boiled down to unabashed, consistent, and high-handed support for Israel in every possible respect—something the Israelis had always dreamed about but had never before succeeded in obtaining (not even during the peak of the honeymoon with France). It was thus to be expected that the Meir government would be further reinforced in its conviction that a formal U.S. guarantee was no longer necessary. Judging by their statements, the Arab confrontation states (Syria and Egypt, in particular) treated U.S.–Israeli relations as an alliance, as did the Soviets and, increasingly, the Americans themselves. Why, then, should the Israelis question this by insisting pedantically on a contractual agreement?[27]

Israel's relations with non-Arab regional powers during this period mirrored the same attitude. Like the United States, Turkey, Ethiopia, and above all Iran would not enter into an alliance with the Jewish state even after the spectacular victory of 1967. Again like the United States, however, these powers, too, were enormously impressed by the Israelis and exceedingly eager to tap some of the strategic resources that the Jewish state seemed to have in order to strengthen their own positions. The result was a marked rise in the intensity and scope of Israeli relations with all three countries. At the same time, and much to the annoyance of the Israelis, all three countries continued to prefer a low public profile for their Israeli connection. This was particularly noticeable—and annoying from the Israeli point of view— in the case of Iran, the other pillar of Nixon's Middle East policy. The Israelis traded with Iran to the tune of close to U.S. $250 million annually; they trained Iranian armed forces and instructed the all-too-powerful Iranian secret service (SAVAK); they built Iranian military bases; they bought Iranian oil and piped it through a special pipeline from Eilat on the Gulf of Aqaba to Ashdod on the Mediterranean that bypassed the Suez Canal (which the Egyptians had blocked); they employed Iranian territory as a forward base for substantial assistance to the Kurdish rebels of Mula Mustapha al Barazani in the northern part of Iraq.

Many of these operations were managed from a burgeoning Israeli mission in Teheran whose head carried ambassadorial rank and had easier access to the shah than did most of the latter's own subjects. Yet Iran persisted in its flat refusal not only to sign a treaty of alliance but even to establish normal and open diplomatic relations—seemingly a mere formality. Its own embassy in Tel Aviv continued to be regarded as a mere section of the Swiss Embassy. Visits to Teheran by Israeli leaders such as Golda Meir, Moshe Dayan, Abba Eban, and Pinchas Sapir (Meir's powerful finance minister) were kept secret. Iranian officials of comparable rank avoided Israel.

More important still was the fact that, while expanding relations with Israel, the shah himself was tirelessly searching for a crack in the wall of Arab hostility toward Iran. Anticipating a dangerous political vacuum in the Gulf area after the British departure from east of Suez, he thawed relations with moderate

Arab regimes like that of Saudi Arabia, invested tremendous efforts in attempts to come to terms with the new Gulf states, and—as soon as Nasser, his foe for two decades, had passed away—hurried to resume relations with Egypt. The political tender with which the shah paid for these major diplomatic strides included signals of a strong willingness to pursue a rapproachement with Arab moderates. In public this posture took the form of an emphasis on positions that would please the Arabs and raise the concern and anguish of the Israelis. Thus he underscored repeatedly Iran's objections to Israel's acquisition of Arab territory by the force of arms, and—though openly hostile toward the PLO (which supported his own Pharsi enemies), he repeatedly upheld the "legitimate rights of the Palestinians."

As a strategic decoy capable of diverting Arab attention and resources away from Israel's own borders, Iran lived up to the Israelis' expectations. Paradoxically, the very fact that so much could be achieved in practice without normal diplomatic relations underlined the inadequacy of these strange relations from the political and strategic viewpoints. The Arabs may have felt that the Iranians were in Israel's strategic pocket, so to speak. Some of them, notably the Iraqis, may have feared that if and when they were to become involved in another war with Israel, Iran might be tempted to take advantage of this in order to encroach on Iraq's own vital interests. From the Israeli point of view, however, such an impact on the Arab strategic calculus could not be too readily assumed. Indeed, the absence of the formal and public dimension in Israel's relations with Iran implied the continued existence in the Israeli mind of an irreducible residue of doubt: if there were another war between Israel and the Arabs, would the Iranians do anything to help? Few Israeli policymakers entertained any illusions about that. In the final analysis, despite the cloak-and-dagger atmosphere in which it was sometimes shrouded, the whole Iranian escapade boiled down, from the Israeli point of view, to little more than a promising commercial opportunity.[28]

Inertia, Brinksmanship, and the Use of Force

Israel's *tactical* employment of force during the 1967–73 period was imaginative, innovative, sometimes almost virtuoso. The IAF, which in the course of the 1967 war had carried out one of the most devastating air strikes in the history of military aviation, continued to startle the world with unexpected coups that set new standards of performance. The Israeli naval commandos, too, began to make an important impression on the emerging picture of warfare. Israeli paratroopers, special reconnaissance units, helicopter pilots, and even a sizable number of less exotic units performed spectacular surgical operations—such as a raid on Beirut's international airport; the killing of prominent PLO leaders in their homes in the heart of Beirut; a raid on a hijacked Sabena aircraft; the seizure and airlifting of a late-model Soviet radar system; a twenty-four-hour hike of a large armored unit (using Soviet-made vehicles and tanks) on the Egyptian side of the gulf of Suez; and the blowing up of highway bridges, dams, and power stations right in the heart of Egypt.

Exploits like these had an electrifying impact on Israelis back home. They projected an ability to carry out almost any task. They demonstrated the vulnerability of the Arabs. They reinforced the conviction of many Israelis that time was on Israel's side and that, small and exposed as the Jewish state may have been, it was capable of coping with the main challenges facing it. Yet such an atmosphere also reinforced a tendency not to see the strategic wood for the tactical trees. Brilliant as all the Israeli tactical effects may have been, Israeli grand strategy during this period was—or so it seems in retrospect—schematic, predictable, unimaginative, lacking in conceptual clarity, full of fundamental misperceptions—in fact, quite poor. It continued to operate within the confines of assumptions that had seemed suitable during earlier periods. It led to a dangerous escalation that brought Israel to the brink of a military confrontation with the Soviet Union. Above all, not only did it fail to deter Egypt and Syria, not only did it fail to lead to a coherent doctrine, but it even had no success in resolving the most important preliminary question relating to general war: under what circumstances the Jewish state would again initiate an all-out war.

One reason for this poverty of strategic thought was quite human: the Israelis were stunned by the magnitude of their own victory in the 1967 war. Having panicked during the crisis preceding the war, they also lost their cool judgment once the war was over. The long-held assumption of vulnerability and limited control over the flow of events gave way to an unrealistic delirium in which almost everything seemed possible. Since the strategy of the past had been so spectacularly successful, its utility for the future seemed beyond doubt.

This, however, was only one—and not necessarily the most important—cause of the stagnation of Israeli strategic thought. Another factor, far more concrete, was the logical trap into which Israeli strategy fell as a result of Israel's acquisition of seemingly impregnable borders. In Israeli policy concerning the occupied territories, the starting point was a cabinet decision on June 19, 1967—a week after the war—that Israel would agree to return the Sinai and the Golan to Egypt and Syria, respectively, if and when the two agreed to sign a normal peace treaty. The Egyptian and Syrian reply came on August 30, when the Arab summit meeting at Khartoum rejected categorically any negotiations with Israel prior to the return of the occupied territories. Simultaneously Egypt, Syria, and increasingly the PLO (operating from Jordan and Lebanon) engaged Israel in a multidimensional war of attrition. The result was a grim change in the Israeli position. The June 19, 1967, decision was never officially rescinded. But leading members of the cabinet—especially after the death of Eshkol and the appointment of Meir (February–March 1969)—spoke increasingly about the need for defensible borders.

It was not easy to determine what were the most defensible borders that the Jewish state could hope for. For the Israeli left, only peace could provide defensible borders, and peace could not be obtained without an Israeli commitment to return all the territories. To the Israeli right, the most defensible borders were those obtained as a result of the 1967 war—namely, the June 11, 1967, cease-fire lines, which included Arab territories four times the size of Israel proper (within the 1949 "green line") and a population of a million and a half resentful Palestinians. To middle-of-the-road Israelis, the most defensible borders corresponded to an elusive break-even point between the non-strategic approach of the doves and the narrowly strategic perception of the hawks. For the time being, this mainstream view led to a grim determination to hold on to the cease-fire lines. Thus, in effect, the majority view was identical with the most hawkish view.[29]

The logic that led to this was simple. Since there was nobody to talk to on the Arab side, Israel should hold on to the territories until the Arabs became convinced that the only way to retrieve their territories was through direct negotiations leading to peace agreements. Until then, however, the Arabs would probably continue to harbor warlike intentions. To deal with this military threat, there were no better borders than the cease-fire lines or something approximating them (such as the Mitla-Gidi line in the Sinai). These lines were thus reified. They were seen as the best lines Israel ever had, as the ultimate solution to Israel's daunting problem of strategic depth and early warning, as an asset that would have prevented previous wars and would prevent major wars in the future.

Such a disposition inadvertently ruled out any possibility of yet another Israeli first strike. This was so both for domestic political reasons and from the point of view of foreign policy. Domestically, the future of the territories was the single most divisive issue the Israeli polity had ever faced. With the growing number of casualties in the war of attrition, the controversiality of this issue only increased. To this the Meir government had only one answer: imagine Israel without the cease-fire lines. The Arab threat would still be there, but the Jewish state would not have defensible borders to shield it. The war of attrition, in other words, was an acute version of Israel's chronic current-security problem: a full-scale war waged in a subwar fashion. Israel's basic security, Golda Meir and her colleagues argued—its ability to deter against and defend itself from all-out war—had been immeasurably improved as a result of the acquisition of the cease-fire lines.

Not surprisingly, this argument gained credibility during the 1971–73 period, when the cease-fire along the Suez Canal was maintained by Egypt and the PLO had been driven out of Jordan. The only serious problem facing Israel during this three-year period was the insecurity along the border with Lebanon. But this was a typical problem of current, low-level security. Thus the argument that, strategically, Israel had never had it so good was as plausible as it was pleasing to the ear of the average Israeli. The trouble, however, was that the same government that maintained that Israel had never had it so good could not uphold a first-strike strategy. If the cease-fire lines provided such absolute security, if they were strategically so superb, they should save Israel the agonizing decision of the past of whether to initiate war. This onus, like that of the decision whether or not to negotiate peace, thus fell conveniently on the Arabs. Israel, in this view, had done enough to show that it wanted peace and was secure enough to absorb a war begun by the Arabs.

If the Meir government had no better argument to defend its policies in the arena of Israeli domestic politics, it also had no better argument to rely on in its efforts to justify the impasse in the arena of international politics. Israel was slow and conspicuously unenthusiastic in its response to U.N. Resolution 242, to the various Jarring missions, and to the various peace initiatives of U.S. Secretary of State William Rogers. The reason was not so much an objection in principle to negotiations or even to the principle that substantial parts of the territories occupied in 1967 should be returned to the Arabs. Rather, it stemmed from a fear—reinforced by the experience of 1956—of being cunningly stripped of bargaining chips and strategic assets without obtaining adequate returns. Whatever the reasons, the most important argument Israeli leaders resorted to during this period was that in the absence of an Arab willingness to make peace, the cease-fire lines at least reduced the likelihood of war.

The Israeli position was predicated on a sequence of assumptions, such as the following. First, exceptionally defensible lines meant a far smaller hope for the Arabs to gain from war. Second, for this reason there was a far smaller likelihood of large-scale Arab attacks. The Arabs might threaten war, but they were incapable of carrying it out. They could resort to small-scale attacks and wars of attrition, but Israel was far better placed to deal with this type of threat as well, within the cease-fire lines. Third, if the Arabs were nevertheless tempted to launch a major military campaign, Israel, again, would be far better placed to meet the challenge. Fourth, the temptation for Israel to initiate wars was greatly reduced. Previously, when it had had to observe Arab threats from the vulnerable position of the armistice demarcation lines, Israel had acted somewhat nervously. Conversely, surrounded by easily defended boundaries, Israel could look forward to the future with greater confidence. Differently stated, the prevailing Israeli view between the war of attrition and the Yom Kippur War was that the defensible cease-fire lines had reduced not only the Arabs' but also Israel's proneness to war.

Against the background of Israel's experience with the Arabs, such arguments were quite persuasive. They were rejected out of hand by the Soviet bloc and challenged by the French. But the rest of western Europe and, in particular, the Nixon administration in the United States could not but concede that the Israelis had a point. Consequently, the Jewish state was permitted to hold on to the occupied territories without any significant international pressure to give them back for much less than what the Meir government would have accepted anyway. The other side of the same coin, however, was that Israel, in effect, eschewed its right to another preemptive strike. The mitigating circumstances that had endowed the Israeli preemtive/preventive/interceptive disposition of the past with an air of legitimacy were thus undone by the Israelis themselves—all the more so since the success of the 1967 war had made Israel look either hysterical or somewhat dishonest. If the danger to Israel's existence had been so great on June 4, 1967, how was it that the armies of its enemies were turned into a smoldering rubble by June 11? Clearly Israel was stronger than it had admitted before the June 1967 war and—by the same token—at least as strong as it claimed after this war.

Adding a great deal of weight to the arguments against the preservation of Israel's first-strike doctrine was the fact that the IDF found it difficult to designate reasonable war aims. Before the 1967 war there were four principal aims of a military operation: (1) to destroy the enemy's fighting capacity; (2) to capture territory for political bargaining; (3) to capture territory for the purpose of improving the Jewish state's own defensive capacity; and (4) to recharge the failing batteries of the Israeli deterrent through a bold rise to an Arab challenge to one or another casus belli and through a spectacular demonstration of both resolve and skill on the battlefield.

After the 1967 war, however, it became far more difficult to define logical war aims. Destroying the enemy's fighting capacity was still a respectable war aim in principle, but it would entail operations over a perimeter that became too wide for Israel's capacity (at least insofar as armored operations were concerned). Capturing more territories in order to bargain made no sense when even the occupation of the Sinai, the West Bank, and the Golan had failed to induce the Arabs to negotiate. Capturing more Arab territories for the purpose of improving Israel's own defensive capacity made even less sense because, *by Israel's own statements,* the cease-fire lines were the very epitome of defensible boundaries. Finally, as a result of the 1967 war, Israel was left with no casi belli to defend. The IDF was deployed on the very lines whose crossing by Arab armies would have constituted casus belli before the 1967 war. Hence the question of using force for deterrence purposes was confined to demonstrative tours de force. This, however, could surely be achieved through spectacular short-of-war operations such as the IDF was carrying out anyway—and with outstanding success.

Israel, then, had ample reason to assume that the next war would be (from its own point of view) a second-strike one. It would be initiated by the Arabs, and the IDF would not enjoy the advantages of either surprise or momentum, but would have to absorb a shock itself without letting this shatter its morale. Despite such an inauspicious start, it would have to pick up the pieces, regroup, mobilize the reserves, and only then return to the modus operandi that had stood it in such good stead in the past—a dashing, mobile combination of the concentration of force and the indirect approach.

That this scenario became highly realistic as soon as the Egyptian and Syrian armies had recuperated from the shock of the 1967 war was widely assumed as a matter of course by Israeli policymakers throughout the 1967–73 period and, increasingly, after the August 1970 standstill/cease-fire agreement with Egypt. It was, indeed, the omnipresence of such a possibility that turned the question of how to deploy along the Suez Canal into a source of a divisive controversy within the IDF General Staff. Nonetheless, to the extent that can be judged, the Meir government did not devote even one orderly session to a discussion of the simple question of how Israel should react if and when there were clear signs of a pending Egyptian and/or Syrian attack. The question was simply left in abeyance, to be discussed if and when circumstances made it urgent. In a word, instead of formulating a policy, a doctrine, at least a contingency plan, the Meir government chose not to decide until a decision would be forced on it by its opponents.

This was, of course, the traditional Israeli approach of muddling through, trial and error, crossing the bridge when we get to it. In this sense the Meir government accurately mirrored a deep-seated principle of government and administration in the Jewish state.[30] But this principle became the origin of a catastrophe because of the prevalence of three critical assumptions in IDF thinking:

1. That intelligence would ensure an adequate advance warning
2. That the government would not desist from a decision to authorize an interceptive strike if and when Arab moves suggested that an attack was imminent
3. That the very least that the government would authorize would be a large-scale mobilizaiton of reserves[31]

What the IDF did not foresee was the possibility that not even one of these conditions would materialize—that is, a scenario in which intelligence estimates were slow and fuzzy; the government did not authorize a disarming first strike, not even a limited one; and the government would authorize only a limited and secret mobilization of reserves. The origins of the Israeli debacle in the first week of the 1973 war, in this sense, should be ascribed not merely to the failure of national-intelligence estimates,[32] but above all to a fundamental incongruity, a truly critical short circuit in the interface between military planning and political purpose. Meir and her colleagues either failed to consider the possibility of an all-out Arab attack or took it for granted that Israel could deal with one effectively even without the benefit of mobilization and a disarming first strike. The IDF, on the other hand, had assumed all along that the government would yield to its demand to initiate hostilities if and when an Arab attack appeared imminent.

Both sides in this tangle discovered the differences between their respective expectations only during the last forty-eight hours before the Egyptian–Syrian attack. The IDF General Staff, in particular the IAF, pressed almost hysterically for permission to preempt. Fearing U.S. criticism and concerned with avoiding a replay of the 1967 crisis—especially the loss of flexibility as a result of the vast scope of reserve mobilization—the Meir cabinet resisted the pressures. It was even reluctant to authorize a limited reserve call-up. Alarmed, the IDF proceeded to alert many more reserve units than the government had authorized, but this was too little and too late; it could not be an adequate substitute either for a preemptive strike or for comprehensive mobilization. It was a last-minute improvization, not a thoroughly considered strategic move such as was expected of a military machine of the size, capability, experience, and technological sophistication of the IDF.[33]

There is no doubt that the IDF General Staff bears much of the responsibility for this debacle because of its smugness, neglect of a variety of logistical aspects, and failure to interpret the intelligence at its disposal. The civilians in the government from whom the IDF received its orders, however, ultimately bear a greater share of the blame. Indeed, whereas the IDF cannot be blamed for being unprofessional, the Meir government can. For all the experience in national security affairs of individuals such as Golda Meir, Moshe Dayan, Yigal Allon, Israel Galili, and Chaim Bar-Lev, their level of strategic consciousness, so to speak, left much to be desired. It was the cabinet's responsibliity, not the IDF's, to attend to questions such as whether or not to act on the assumption of a first strike. The individuals concerned, however, did not seem to have been sufficiently aware of the need to discuss the issue thoroughly in advance; therefore, they placed the IDF in an impossible situation.

A not dissimilar dilletantism, shortsightedness, and muddleheadedness was also reflected in the same cabinet's handling of the problem of retaliation. The war of attrition, especially along the Suez Canal, faced these cabinet members with some very hard choices concerning the fundamental question of whether to follow the path of massive retaliation or the alternative of flexible response. As with the question of initiation discussed earlier, they responded mechanically and showed far more tactical than strategic imagination. The emphasis was on force, but the focus was narrow and amazingly lacking in foresight, and the result was mixed. Israel was successful on the Jordanian and Syrian fronts, utterly unsuccessful on the Lebanese front, and only partly successful on the Egyptian front. The details are worth an examination at some length.

The Jordan Valley

The effective sealing by the IDF of the Jordan cease-fire lines to Palestinian penetration, Israel's success in inducing the West Bank population not to assist the PLO, and the state of interdependence with Jordan on the basis of the open-bridges policy added up to an environment in which escalation could be effectively contained. To be sure, from the Jordanian point of view, the problem was not simple. At stake was not merely the future of the PLO on Jordanian territory but, indeed, the future of the Hashemite monarchy itself. If King Hussein were to restrain the PLO when the latter was the Arab world's favorite son, Jordan would be ostracized in the all-important arena of inter-Arab politics. If, on the other hand, the Hashemite monarch did not restrain the PLO, then PLO attacks against Israel would be stepped up, the Israelis would escalate their punitive countermeasures, and the PLO would gradually seize control over the Hashemite state from within.

Faced with this choice, King Hussein maneuvered very carefully. At first he allowed the PLO to operate against the IDF from a sanctuary on the Jordanian (eastern) side of the valley. Indeed, the PLO received Jordanian army escorts, artillery cover, and assistance in logistics and intelligence. Israel, however, refused to show any forbearance in the face of these attacks. The IDF resorted to an invigorated form of flexible response in which, as in the standard form of this strategy, the link in time and place between fire from the Jordanian side and the Israeli riposte was maintained. In terms of scale, however, the IDF did not confine itself to a strict tit-for-tat. Rather, it tended to escalate by at least one rung as a means of pointing out to the Jordanian authorities that Israel, though wishing to avoid escalation, would not accept intermittent fire as a normal, routine way of life. Either Jordan took measures to restrain the PLO, or it would be made to pay for it.

During the first year of this encounter, the fighting was concentrated primarily in the immediate vicinity of the Jordan River. As a result of the Israeli response the battlefield was gradually expanded eastward into the Jordanian state. At first this horizontal escalation occurred primarily as a result of artillery fire and air strike by the Israelis against both PLO and Jordanian army positions. The Jordanian response, especially Jordanian gunnery, was accurate and quite costly from the Israeli point of view. Hence the IDF escalated vertically by bringing in the IAF. Consequently, the Jordanian relative advnatage in gunnery was neutralized, and its relative disadvantage as a result of having a substantial—and very vulnerable—population in the area was underlined.

This, however, was not enough to stop the PLO from carrying on its operations against IDF positions on the western bank of the river and against Israeli towns such as Eilat in the south and Beit Shean in the north. Barrred from easy access to the river, the PLO resorted to sudden salvos of *katyusha*—multiple rocket fire—an ineffective and inaccurate instrument of warfare against military units but a devastating means of demoralizing and harming civilians in densely populated areas. Given the considerable range of these weapons, all the PLO needed was a very small number of weapons and operators. Since the launching pad of this Soviet-made weapon is highly mobile, it could be employed at night, when IDF fire and reconnaissance cover of the eastern Jordan valley was minimal.

The effect on the civilian population, especially in Beit Shean, was alarming. There were demonstrations and fits of public hysteria, and the government came under pressure to do virtually anything to stop the fire. The result was escalation in two forms. The first was an attack by a substantial armored force on the PLO center at Karameh on March 21, 1968. The second was a devastating bombardment of the Jordanian town of Aqaba several miles east of Eilat on the Gulf of Aqaba. The former operation was carried out under strict orders not to penetrate deeper into Jordan. Jordanian tanks and guns on the hills overlooking Karameh gave massive support to the PLO, with the result that the IDF suffered heavy casualties. The PLO, which fought poorly, later claimed that the IDF's intention was to conquer Jordanian territory and that this design was thwarted by the Palestinians' heroic resistance. The story gained a momentum of its own and greatly assisted the ascendance of the PLO in the Arab world. From the Israeli point of view, however, it was looked upon then, and ever after, as a limited part of an attempt to force Jordan's hand and bring it to discipline the PLO.

By contrast, the riposte in Aqaba achieved its main purpose—namely, to establish a rule whereby neither Eilat nor Aqaba would be part of the fighting zone. This attack, however, was not sufficient to compel Jordan to clamp down on the PLO. As attacks against Beit Shean and its vicinity continued, Israel escalated its response one notch further. Using artillery and air power, the IDF turned the most fertile and most populated part of the east bank of the Jordan valley into a smoldering desert. The Ghor irrigation project, which Jordan had constructed with U.S. and World Bank support, was demolished. Farmers were prevented from tilling their lands and became refugees in the safer hinterland of the Gilead Heights. Jordan's economy suffered, and the pressure on the king to stop Arafat's guerrillas mounted. It was becoming increasingly clear that the choice, from the Hashemites' point of view, was literally existential.[34]

The Golan Heights

King Hussein yielded to Israel's coercive diplomacy in September 1970, and from then on the Jordanian border was quiet and stable. From the Israeli view-point, this was an important achievement, all the more so since a similar situation was obtained on the Syrian front. To be sure, since Syria never allowed the PLO any measure of freedom, it also required a far less problematic policy from the Israeli point of view to stabilize the Golan cease-fire line. Unlike Hussein of Jordan, who to some extent was the PLO's rival, Syria had been the most important champion of the Palestinian cause. Indeed, it was in Syria that Yasser Arafat's Fateh, the mainstay of the PLO, was established, and it was there that it began to train guerrillas and send them into action against Israel.

Yet behind the rhetoric of support for the PLO, Syria was ultimately as much an enemy of the organization as was King Hussein's Jordan. Ideologically, this was manifested by a Syrian tendency to regard what the PLO perceived as Palestine as a mere province of a Greater Syria. Politically, the Syrians allowed

Fateh to come into existence and to begin to operate as part of a complex struggle for mastery in the Arab world. In 1964 President Nasser of Egypt launched an Egyptian-sponsored Palestinian organization under the title PLO. Syria reacted by sponsoring its own Palestinian proxy under the title Fateh (Arabic acronym in reverse for Movement for the Liberation of Palestine). As soon as Fateh showed signs of independence and autonomy, however, the Syrian regime of Salah Jedid—representing as it did the fiercest version of Ba'athist radicalism—arrested the inner circle of the organization's leadership. Recognizing what the Syrians were up to, the Fateh leadership sought to escape the Syrian embrace after the Six-Day War and moved its center of operations to the West Bank and Jordan. When Yasser Arafat succeeded in merging the Fateh into the formerly Egyptian-sponsored PLO, he also had no way of preventing Syria from setting up within the revamped PLO a proxy organization of its own under Zoheir Mohsen, a Syrian army officer.[35]

During the September 1970 encounter between Hussein's troops and Arafat's guerrillas, the Syrian ruler Jedid sent an armored column into Jordan to help the guerrillas. But the Syrian armor was denied air support because Hafez al-Assad, the commander of the Air Force and Jedid's main rival, would not allow the Syrian air force to intervene. Assad's unusual conduct may have been affected by his fierce rivalry with Jedid. Indeed, within several weeks he took advantage of Jedid's humiliation at having to withdraw the force from Jordan and seized ultimate power in the Ba'ath republic.[36]

Assad may also have been influenced by fear of an Israeli and U.S. response. Israel made threatening noises and concentrated some armor close to the Syrian border. This was coordinated quite visibly with the United States, and in this sense Assad may have been deterred.[37] Once in power, furthermore, Assad would not authorize any short-of-war military operations against the Israelis from Syrian territory. This applied not only to the Syrian army but no less so to the Palestinian guerrilla organizations. Thus, unlike the Israeli–Syrian armistice demarcation lines before the 1967 war (which corresponded to the international border), the Israeli–Syrian 1967 cease-fire lines (which ran inside Syria's own sovereign territory) were quite stable from the summer of 1970 until the outbreak of the 1973 war.

Lebanon

In both Jordan and Syria, an escalatory strategy of massive retaliation ultimately led to deescalation, for four principal reasons:

1. The two countries had vigorous governments, which provided Israel with a punishable target.

2. In both cases it was ultimately rational from the point of view of the incumbent regime to play the game by Israeli rules, at least for a while.

3. The Jordanian and Syrian ceasefire lines were sparsely populated on both sides.
4. The Jordan valley and the Golan Heights were topographically easy to defend against small-scale guerrilla warfare.

None of these facilitating conditions existed on Israel's Lebanese front. Nonetheless, Israel resorted reflexively to a strategy of massive retaliation. The purpose, as always, was to obtain *deescalation* through *escalation*. To the dismay of Meir and her colleagues, however, those same methods that had worked so well on the eastern cease-fire lines bore meager results on the northern front.

The first PLO attack from Lebanese territory occurred on June 2, 1965, two years before the Six-Day War. From then until the summer of 1968, the PLO launched twenty-nine additional attacks of various kinds. All this, however, was a mere prelude to a major effort to step up the attacks as of May 1968. The opening shots in the new phase were sudden salvos of Katyusha rockets on Kibbutz Manara (on May 8, 1968) and on Moshav Margaliot four days later. The fire was renewed on June 14, 1968, when ten 2-inch mortar shells landed again on Kibbutz Manara. On September, 16, 1968, a civilian vehicle was ambushed near the village of Zar'it. On October 14, 20, 26, and 28 there were attacks on Kefar Yuval, Kibbutz Malkiya, Kibbutz Dan, and again Kibbutz Manara. Four Israelis, two of them civilians, were killed, and an Israeli vehicle was destroyed.

Up to this point the Israeli response had been primarily defensive. The Lebanese government was urged to stop the activities of the PLO, and on the Israeli side of the border the IDF erected fences, dug shelters, and stepped up its patrolling activities. When the PLO escalated its attacks, Israel had no logical alternative to escalatory counteraction. It was impossible to confine the entire population in the area to shelters and trenches. The Lebanese government did not seem to be either able or willing to do anything about it all. The only hope, therefore, lay in exacting a high price from the PLO itself through direct Israeli action inside Lebanon's own territory. This was done for the first time on October 30, 1968, when a small IDF unit penetrated the territory of south Lebanon and destroyed a small PLO encampment there.

The raid bought Israel's northern Jewish population (a substantial segment of the population on the Israeli side is Arab, but they were never subject to PLO assaults) a breathing space of some two months, during which the frequency and scope of PLO operations in the area declined. Meanwhile, however, the Eshkol government faced another related but different challenge—namely, PLO air piracy and spectacular feats of anti-Israeli and anti-Jewish terrorism in foreign lands. On July 22, 1968, an El Al plane was hijacked to Algiers. Israel submitted quietly to the demands of the hijackers but introduced extensive security measures in all El Al stations abroad and on the company's small fleet of Boeing 707 aircrafts. These measures notwithstanding, on December 26 another Israeli plane was attacked on the tarmac in Athens. The Eshkol government met in special session and concluded that neither purely defensive measures nor even a retaliatory act calibrated to the scope of the attack could solve the problem. What was needed was an act of massive retaliation, a spectacularly disproportionate offensive operation that would act as a deterrent against either launching or assisting in launching such attacks in the future.

Two nights later this retaliation was carried out. A party of paratroopers and special commandos descended on Beirut's international airport and destroyed on the tarmac thirteen Middle East Airlines passenger jets. There were no casualties, but the message was clear. The PLO hijackers and raiding parties had come from Beirut. If the Lebanese government continued to permit the use of their capital as a sanctuary, their business would suffer greatly. The Lebanese authorities—or at least those who were in the control of the Maronites—had no problem understanding the Israeli message. President Charles Helu (a Christian) in fact ordered the Lebanese army (through its Christian chief of staff, General Boustani) to clamp down on the PLO. But this triggered a crisis in the Lebanese government because the Moslem prime minister, Abdulla al-Yafi, opposed this compliance with Israeli demands. The latter was adamant and succeeded in forcing the government to negotiate an understanding with the PLO that purported to lay down clear rules for PLO operations in or from Lebanon.

The Lebanese–PLO understanding of January 19, 1969, survived until August 1 of that year, when the PLO attacked Kiryat Shemonah, the northernmost town in Israel, with multiple rocket launchers. There was some damage and a certain loss of life. This led to a cabinet policy reappraisal and to a decision to escalate the retributions—in particular, to employ air power. The result was a series of both air and large-scale ground attacks by the IAF and IDF during the month of August. The damage was extensive, and the Israeli raids touched off yet another cabinet crisis in the fractured Lebanese republic. Within a few weeks, sporadic fighting had broken out between Lebanese and Palestinians, and some Syrian forces masquerading as units of the PLO entered Lebanon. When matters seemed to be getting entirely out of hand, the parties to the Lebanese conflict were summoned to Cairo by President Nasser, who, acting as an intermediary, brought them to sign an accord on October 25, 1969.

The Cairo accords could not possibly work for longer than a few months. They were based on Lebanese acknowledgment of the right of the PLO to operate against Israel from a small part of south Lebanon. Although this was a concession that no other Arab state had previously made to the PLO, it also contained a devious Lebanese signal to Israel concerning the part of Lebanon in which the IDF could pursue the PLO with tacit Lebanese consent. All this was, of course, too clever by half. The PLO resumed its operations against Israel. The IDF moved a large force into an area that gave it a topographic advantage over the PLO and proceeded to blast away. The PLO in turn was impelled to seek a sanctuary in an area that extended beyond the limits of the Cairo accords. Before long the PLO and the IDF were engaged in an encounter on a wide front stretching from Naqura on the Mediterranean to Kiryat Shemonah near the Golan Heights.

By May 1970 the intensification of shooting along this line began to cause the departure from the border area of (Jewish) Israeli civilians who could no longer bear the life under constant fire. The Meir government was prompted to carry out another policy reappraisal, which led to a substantial increase in government appropriations for defense measures in the area and for financial and other inducements for people to stay there. It also led, on May 12, 1970, to a large-scale attack by a sizable armored column on the Arqoub, a narrow area north of Kiryat Shemonah that the PLO had used extensively for operations against Israeli villages.

Though involving a significant push up the escalation ladder, the operation failed to achieve its purpose. One immediate result was that the IDF turned such large-scale raids into a daily occurrence. Another result was a spectacular but nevertheless desperate Israeli raid on the PLO center in Beirut, carried out with the speed, precision, and resourcefulness of a thriller. It led to the killing in their beds of three prominent PLO personalities. It demonstrated once again, if any further proof was needed, that the Israelis had a long operational arm that could reach almost anywhere in the Arab world. It showed that Israel's military intelligence was still as good as it could be. For all this, however, the rent-a-car raid (as it was later dubbed) failed to change anything of consequence in the overall situation. Deterrence against small-scale attacks by a sizable army such as the Syrian one was within Israel's reach, but deterrence against a ragtag militia such as the PLO was almost impossible. Without bases, depots, or heavy weaponry—in fact, without anything very substantial to lose from Israeli retaliations, but with a lot to gain from constant visibility through press reports— the PLO in Lebanon succeeded in exposing one of the weakest elements in the Israeli deterrence posture. The full extent of this shortfall at the lower end of the spectrum of violence would be discovered by the Israelis only in subsequent years.[38] Meanwhile, the IDF faced another formidable challenge at the upper end of the same spectrum in the form of a bloody war of attrition along the Suez Canal.

The Suez Canal

One of Israel's greatest failures was to underestimate, almost to ignore, the importance Egypt attached to the Sinai. To Israel, the peninsula was little more than a piece of strategic real estate. Not even the most militant segments of Israeli public opinion considered the Sinai an integral part of the ancestral land; it was either a launching pad for Egyptian hostilities against Israel or the reverse. The thought that the Egyptians would find the continued occupation of the Sinai by the IDF an intolerable situation, whose termination justified almost any price, seldom occurred to the Israelis.

What Israeli policymakers apparently failed to realize was that Egypt's national pride had been unacceptably compromised by the IDF's presence along the canal; that Nasser's entire career and his place in posterity had become inseparably intertwined with his ability to retrieve the Sinai, or at least put up a good fight for it; that the Soviets' position in the Arab world in particular, and in the Third World more generally, had become critically dependent on their ability to prepare the Egyptians for a heroic attempt to recapture the lost land; that Egypt—with its self-perception as a leading power with a historical legacy of which few nations could boast—was not simply going to resign itself to the loss of these lands.

The result of this failure to develop adequate empathy for their foes' state of mind was a slow, painful process for Israelis in awakening to the facts of Middle Eastern life. The prevailing belief in Israel immediately after the war was predicated on a somewhat too simple set of assumptions. Egypt, in this view, remained hostile because as long as it continued to believe that Israel could be subdued by the force of arms, it was not adequately deterred. Having been so badly beaten, the Israelis imagined, the Egyptians would at least reappraise their strategic calculus. They would realize that vanquishing the Jewish state was a pipe dream, and they would have no alternative but to enter into meaningful negotiations. In the wistful words of Yigal Allon a year after the war, "the results of the Six-Day War led to a 'moment of truth' [in the Arab world] which may bring leaders, circles and governments to the thought or even to the conclusion that Israel is an unalterable fact in the region which cannot be undone, and that any attempt to assault it is bound to fail and to bring further calamities on the heads of the Arab states."[39]

Less than three weeks after the end of the hostilities of the Six-Day War, the Egyptians offered a kind of preview of what was in store for the IDF. On July 1, 1967, an Israeli patrol was ambushed by regular Egyptian forces near Kantara at the northern tip of the Suez Canal. The ambushed unit fought doggedly and managed to deny the Egyptians any significant gains, but its commanding officer was killed and a number of soldiers were wounded. Moreover, for the next ten days fighting in this area continued intermittently, until a precarious cease-fire was established by the UN. Meanwhile, Egypt lost seven jet fighters, and Israel had nine soldiers killed and fifty-five wounded.

For the next six weeks the canal area was quiet. Then, early in September, the Egyptians opened fire on Israeli vessels in the Gulf of Suez. The IDF returned the fire, and the fighting spread to virtually the entire front, causing the flight of thousands of Egyptians from their homes along the canal. If the Israelis thought that by escalating they would bring the Egyptians to stop out of concern for the civilian population along the Suez Canal, they were in for a rude shock. On

October 21, 1967, an Egyptian Styx missile drowned the Israeli Navy flagship *Eilat,* taking the lives of forty-seven Israeli sailors and causing injury to ninety more. Israel's reflexive choice of retaliation was to set fire to Egyptian refineries and petrochemical installations in the city of Suez. If the Israelis had more or less relied up to now on a tit-for-tat (flexible response) strategy, this particular action was already massive retaliation. It occurred four days after the sinking of the *Eilat,* but, aiming at the city of Suez in the southern end of the canal, it did not take place near the site of the Egyptian attack. Above all, although it entailed the loss of a far smaller number of Egyptian lives (eleven Egyptians were killed and ninety-two wounded, as against forty-seven Israeli dead and ninety wounded), it caused incomparably greater material damage: the fire raged for several days and destroyed equipment worth some U.S. $100 million.

The Israeli retaliation for the loss of the *Eilat* apparently convinced the Egyptians of the need to complete the absorption of new Soviet equipment and to dig in along the canal before the next major round of hostilities. Accordingly, until September 1968, the canal front was not the scene of heavy fighting. Then, on September 8, an Israeli patrol exploded an Egyptian mine and thus inadvertently gave a signal to some 1,000 Egyptian cannons across the canal to open a well-planned, expertly concerted fire along a sixty-five-mile-long front. The IDF was caught off guard and lost forty-nine men. Considerably outgunned but still determined not to escalate the fighting to the level of air strikes, the IDF concentrated for the next two months on the construction of its defenses. The purpose was to secure adequate cover for the troops on the front line, but the result was far-reaching: for the first time in its history, the IDF became confined to a system of static defenses—the Bar-Lev line.

As if to convince itself that it had not lost its flexibility and maneuverability, on the night of October 31, 1968, the IDF launched a daring raid by helicopter-borne commandos. It resulted in the destruction deep inside Egypt (300 miles south of Cairo and 150 miles north of the Aswan Dam) of two bridges on the Nile, Kena and Najh Hammadi. The blasts themselves were relatively modest, but the operation nevertheless amounted to a case of massive retaliation because of the significant measure of horizontal escalation it entailed. The message was quite clear: the IDF could reach any point inside Egypt, and would engage in such exploits in the future if Egypt would not maintain a cease-fire along the Suez Canal. The Egyptians must know that Israel would not play by their rules, which maximized their comparative advantage in staying power and minimized Israel's comparative advantage in moving power.

A hidden purpose of the raid may have been to bring the Egyptians to thin out their forces along the canal and spread them as guards of potential strategic targets throughout the country. If that was the Israeli intention, it failed to make any significant difference in the Egyptian calculus. The soldiers that the Egyptian high command sent to guard such objects were second- and third-rate; 150,000 of Egypt's best soldiers (at least ten times the size of the Israeli force across the canal) remained in the canal area. The Egyptian army was not at all deflected from its ultimate purpose—namely, to bleed Israel, weaken its resolve to stay in the Sinai, keep the Israeli occupation of the canal on the top of the international (especially superpower) agenda, and bring about the rolling back of the IDF from Egyptian territory and the recovery of Egypt's status, self-esteem, and clout in the international arena. That this was the Egyptian state of mind was evident when, on March 31, 1969, Nasser denounced the U.N.-sponsored cease-fire agreement. It was reiterated and officially declared a war of attrition for the first time in Nasser's speech of June 23. Israeli strategy, which had grown accustomed to decisive battles and clear-cut results, was in a quandary: it faced a challenge that it had utterly failed to anticipate and for which it had no simple answer.[40]

The initial response was relatively restrained. Ezer Weizman, as head of the General Staff (G3) Division of the IDF, pressed for an immediate resort to air power, but the majority of his colleagues in the IDF and the majority in the recently formed Meir cabinet demurred. The IDF's stocks of front-line planes were small and should be preserved for general war, they argued. Maximal vertical escalation at the very beginning of the confrontation, moreover, would leave Israel with no answers for a possible scenario in which Egypt would not be adequately deterred. In a word, massive, disproportionate retaliation, Israel's typical response so far, was rejected. Gradual, flexible response was (atypically) preferred.

This policy was upheld for four months, until it collapsed in the face of relentless Egyptian pressure. Israeli casualties soared, and the mood of the country was somber. The IDF had neither artillery nor manpower with which to counter the Egyptian fire. The Egyptian population, which had previously been seen as a kind of hostage against Egyptian military pressure, had fled the area. It was now a confrontation between two armies, in which Egypt had the advantage precisely because it did not attempt to recapture the Sinai in one massive strike. Egypt's comparative advantage in staying power—in its ability to absorb damages and casualties in great numbers over a long period of time—was maximized. Israel's comparative advantage in moving power— its ability to concentrate force, perform quick and imaginative maneuvers, stun its adversaries, and bring them to their knees within a matter of days—was minimized.

As this was dawning on the Meir cabinet, it began to fear a scenario in which, emboldened by their relative success, the Egyptians might attempt to conquer parts of the Sinai. The momentum that the Egyptian campaign of attrition was gaining, then, had to be checked somehow. This could be done through a mobilization and a large-scale attack on the west bank of the canal. Since such an all-out attack could be complicated from both the political and military viewpoints, without promising any major improvement, the idea was rejected out of hand.

The only other alternative was to escalate the Israeli use of force vertically. Ezer Weizman, the former commander of the IAF, advocated a coordinated operation in which pressure on the Egyptians would be increased simultaneously by both ground and air forces. The IDF may have concurred, but the cabinet was not enthusiastic. Assuming that wholesale escalation would increase the cost to Israel itself, the cabinet's instinct was to keep Israeli retaliation within bounds and to rely primarily on actions that would obtain the most powerful psychological impact for the fewest IDF casualties. Hence the IDF was instructed to intensify spectacular ground operations in the Egyptian rear and flanks (rather than in the fortified Canal Zone), whereas the IAF was ordered to provide, *in the canal area only,* a flying artillery, an airborne substitute for the IDF's inadequate firepower on the ground. This new phase began with a massive attack on July 20, 1969, on Egyptian positions and installations. It was carried on relentlessly for the next five months, and it seemed to have achieved its main purpose: Egypt suffered enormous damages, whereas IDF casualties on the Sinai front were substantially reduced.

Egypt was clearly in trouble. Having visibly lost not only the 1967 war but even the war of attrition, in which it seemingly had a fundamental advantage, the only step (other than submission) that it could still take to cut its losses was to turn to the Soviet Union for help. To the proud and sensitive Nasser, this must have been a singularly humiliating situation. Nasser, a founding father of the nonaligned bloc, the first Arab leader to have succeeded in delivering his people from foreign subjugation, was increasingly becoming the president of a virtual Soviet protectorate. Since yielding to the Israelis was even worse, Nasser apparently had no rational alternative.

The Egyptian request for assistance presented the Soviets, too, with a critical choice: Should they defend the credibility of their commitment to Egypt and thus jeopardize détente and risk a head-on confrontation with the United States? Their decision was to assist Egypt to the best of their ability in terms of hardware, training, and passive defensive measures, but to try to avoid direct involvement in actual hostilities. They would instruct the Egyptians in the use of latest-model weapons systems; they would man SAM missile sites and communication centers; they would offer advice on a routine basis to every Egyptian front-line unit down to the battalion level; they would even provide Egypt with pilots as an emergency measure designed to protect Egypt's sovereign airspace. But the Soviet pilots' presence and, more generally, the direct involvement of Soviet personnel in actual hostilities would not be officially acknowledged.

The Israelis of course, were anxious witnesses to the process whereby Soviet involvement was gaining momentum. Thus when they decided to keep up the pressure on Egypt even when Egyptian defenses seemed on the verge of collapse, the Israelis were fully aware of the possibility that escalation could lead to a head-on confrontation with the Soviets. The minister of defense, Moshe Dayan, was in fact the leading advocate of caution, precisely because of the danger of a collision with the Soviets.[41]

Yet, as on previous occasions of crucial importance (the decision to take the Golan, the decision to stay on the Suez Canal), Dayan would not fight for his views. Confronted by Yitzhak Rabin (the former chief of staff and now ambassador to the United States), Yigal Allon (as deputy premier) and Ezer Weizman (who had retired from the IDF and joined Golda Meir's National Unity government), Dayan's opposition to further escalation gradually withered away.[42] Then, on January 7, 1970, he joined the throng and embraced the idea of deep-penetration bombing—namely, of escalation from a counterforce to a countercity strategy. Tacitly, the minimum objective of the new strategy was perceived as nothing less than *decision in the war of attrition*. In other words, the Meir cabinet hoped, through a combination of massive retaliation and countercity strategy, to compel Nasser to stop shooting and start talking.

The main assumptions leading to this critical decision were as simple as their validity was difficult either to prove or to disprove. Egypt in general and Nasser in particular seemed on the verge of collapse. Hence it seemed logical that a little extra pressure would help exploit the success of previous months. Success would foster Israel's deterrence not only against Egypt but also against all other major Arab states. Indeed, a decision in the canal war would greatly augment Israel's ability to dissuade the Arabs from ever again resorting to the practice of attrition.

The Soviet Union, ever a cautious international actor, would not dare to intervene directly on the side of the Egyptians, so many thousands of miles away from home. Engaged in its own deep-penetration bombings in Vietnam, the United States would not object to Israel's doing the same thing. Indeed, Washington seemed supportive because it was glad to see a radical Soviet client restrained by the United States' own client; because it expected to benefit in southeast Asia from an Israeli policy that pinned down Soviet attention to the Middle East; and because liberal Jewish critics of the administration's Vietnam policy would be at a loss if their own most favored nation, Israel, were to indulge in deep-penetration bombings, too. Finally, having just received the first batch of twenty-five F-4 Phantom fighter-bombers from the United States, Israel at last had the means with which to perform such an operation successfully.[43]

The deep-penetration bombings continued almost without interruption until late March 1970, and in a more restrained manner until the cease-fire/ standstill agreement of August 7, 1970. They wreaked havoc in Egypt, not just in the canal area but virtually everywhere between the canal and the Egyptian capital. Also—contrary to one of the most important ground rules of Israeli national security, and for the first time since the encounter with the British pilots flying Egyptian piston-engine Spitfire fighters in the fall of 1948—they brought Israeli aviators to a dogfight with the pilots of a global power.[44] The most startling aspect of this story is that the encounter was no accident: the Soviet pilots were there in order to deter Israeli pilots. The Israeli government knew this and took a deliberate decision at the highest level to approach the very edge of the brink. In a word, this was a classical case—in a nonnuclear setting—of the rationality of the irrational, of a uniquely experienced group of decision makers thinking about the unthinkable and actually proceeding to act accordingly.

Broadly speaking, the Israeli calculus comprised the following ingredients. As long as Soviet pilots confined themselves to the defense of the Egyptian rear, Israel was quite prepared to avoid any clash with them. This implied that Israel had lost the ability to carry on the deep-penetration bombings of the previous months. But considering the dangers inherent in a fight between Israel and the Soviet Union over the freedom to fly above Cairo and the rest of the Egyptian rear, it would be utterly reckless, the Meir cabinet thought, to take on the Soviets.

Realizing that the IAF was not prepared to engage them in the skies of the Egyptian rear, the Soviets began to expand their protective umbrella over Egyptian airspace. By June 1970 Egyptian planes flown by Soviet pilots were already roaming above the canal—from which they had been barred for more than a year as a result of Israel's complete mastery of the air—and on several occasions had even fired missiles at Israeli planes. If such incidents became a daily occurrence, the Israelis calculated, the Soviets might be tempted to think that they could push the IAF farther east without as much as a dogfight. In this manner Israeli forces along the canal could easily be deprived of the air cover without which they could not possibly hold their own. It was, therefore, essential to signal to the Soviets that when it came to the canal area, not to mention the Sinai, the IAF would be both willing and able to take them on. If a Soviet pilot was shot down unannounced (because he was flying Egyptian colors), the Soviet Union would not be directly challenged. If it came to the worst and the Soviets felt that they were challenged, they would have to make a move that was almost bound to be seen as a challenge to the United States. In the event, Israel would not be facing the Soviets alone.

Such a calculus led on July 30, 1970, to the most escalatory move in the canal war—a premeditated Israeli aerial ambush of eight Egyptian MIGs flown by soviet aviators. Four of the Egyptian planes were shot down, and one barely made it to its base. Israel had a moment of satisfaction. In the final analysis, however, the incident underlined the pervasively incremental, tactical, indeed shortsighted nature of Israeli decision making. Almost every phase of the war of attrition began with a surprise to the Israelis. They managed to retain the initiative in the tactical sense, but the strategic initiative remained for most of this thousand-day period in the hands of the Egyptians.[45]

While Egypt retained the strategic initiative, Israel was constantly forced to escalate until matters reached a point at which the Israelis had more or less exhausted all their options. This was reflected by the fact that, with the Soviet deployment of SAM systems close to the canal area, Israel began to lose planes at the prohibitive rate (given the relatively small size of the IAF) of one aircraft a day. The Egyptian-operated Soviet SAMs, in Ezer Weizman's frank words, succeeded in "bending the wing" of the U.S.-made and Israeli-flown planes.[46]

At this point Egypt discovered the weapon with which to faciliate a massive crossing of the canal: Soviet SAMs could provide Egypt with a protective canopy above the canal and its vicinity on the east (Sinai) bank. All that was necessary was the deployment of these missiles close to the canal in such a form that the Israelis would not be able to knock them out. A cease-fire with Israel would thus form the first step in a larger game of deception. If diplomacy obtained a reasonable settlement from the Egyptian point of view, force would not have to be used. If, however, as seemed likely, diplomacy failed again, then the cease-fire would give Egypt an opportunity to prepare for war.

A handful of Israeli policymakers may have been vaguely aware of this as soon as Egypt deceitfully redeployed the SAMs close to the Suez Canal in violation of the standstill agreement of August 7, 1970.[47] The rest, however, were unshaken in their conviction that the massive-retaliation/countercity deep-penetration air raids during January–August 1970 had broken the resistance of the Egyptians. Seen from such a perspective, the Egyptian deceit of August 7–8, 1970, seemed more annoying than serious. It depreciated—Israeli policymakers argued—some of Israel's hard-won strategic advantages, but it did not shake a widely shared conviction that the Jewish state had won the canal war. Or had it won?

The Domestic Politics of Self-Delusion

The sequence of decisions that led Israel to the brink of a confrontation with the Soviet Union cannot be accounted for by any political struggle inside the Jewish state. The problem was approached in a purely strategic manner, from a perspective seeking to minimize the cost to Israel and to maximize the cost to Egypt. It was insulated from any party political, bureaucratic, or personal rivalry; and the commitment of the individuals who were involved in these decisions to the national interest cannot be doubted. They acted in good faith and did their utmost to obtain the best possible result for the national interest. Strictly speaking, then, this was the epitome of rational decision making.

Observed from a broader perspective, however, the process reveals many symptoms of what is sometimes referred to as *bounded rationality,* a protracted, multidimensional process of collective decision making in which every individual participant is as logical as possible but the ultimate outcome is less than optimal from the point of view of the entity on whose behalf the decision is taken.[48] What this meant in the case of Israeli strategy during the 1967–73 period was that in the background there were societal, ideological orientational, and even naked power struggles among individuals, anomic groups, institutionalized interest groups, political parties, and government bureaucracies; all these had a significant but indirect impact on the decision process.

Starting at the societal level, it is clear that during 1967–73 Israeli society was beginning to show the consequences of a long-dormant change. The European-born establishment (mainly eastern Europeans) who had built the country and were in control of all its political institutions during the first generation after independence were rapidly passing away. A new social mix, consisting of non-European Sephardic communities and of sabras (native-born Israeli Jews, primarily of European origin), was rapidly emerging.[49] The change, to be sure, was not without turbulence. Social statistics and even intuitive observation indicated a marked degree of inequality that rougly corresponded to the ethnic divisions between Sephardic and Ashkenazi Jews. Political and economic power, as well as higher education and a more elevated social status, tended to concentrate in the Ashkenazis, (less than 50 percent of the population), not in the increasingly self-aware Sephardic communities. Most government ministers, officials, bank managers, professors, senior civil servants, and army officers were of European Ashkenazi origin. Most of the population at the lowest income levels, most of the drug addicts, most of the convicted criminals, and most of the manual laborers were of Sephardic (mainly Moroccan) origin.

This had been the case ever since the mass immigrations from the Middle East and North Africa in the immediate aftermath of independence. Now, however, expectations and attitudes were changing. The official, and in many respects actual, policy since independence put nation building at the top of the national agenda. The Sephard's were seen through a melting-pot prism that tacitly assumed the complete submerging of Sephardic Jews into the ethos and cultural world of the Ashkenazis. To achieve this, the state employed a huge educational machinery, an extensive network of social welfare institutions, and even to a marked degree the IDF. In turn, the results in terms of literacy, health, employment, and housing were exceedingly impressive. The other side of the coin, however, was a revolution of rising expectations, a deepening sense of deprivation by and alienation from the Ashkenazi-controlled "system."

The intensity of such feelings could already be gauged in 1958, when riots broke out for the first time in the poor Sephardic neighborhoods of Haifa. For the next decade and a half, however, all was quiet on the Israeli ethnic front, or so it seemed. Then, in March 1971, barely six months after the conclusion of the canal war, Israel was shaken by a wave of riots in Jerusalem. These were organized by young residents of Moroccan origin from the Jerusalem slum area called Morasha (formerly Mousrara). They claimed that they were being discriminated against; they demanded better jobs, new housing, and equality of opportunity in an affirmative-action mold. Somewhat misleadingly, they called themselves Black Panthers. Prime Minister Golda Meir, who asked to meet with their leaders, proved too old, impatient, and self-righteous to deal with them. Indeed, she seems to have aggravated matters unnecessarily by telling a journalist after the meeting that Charlie Bitton and Sa'adia Marciano, the Black Panther leaders whom she met, were not "nice guys." Her colleagues and subordinates proved more adept in dealing with the issue, and the storm was weathered. The whole affair, however, alerted the Israeli political system as a whole to the existence of a grave domestic problem and generated pressures for cutbacks in the soaring defense budget. If the country was as secure as the government claimed, argued the critics, if a large-scale war in the foreseeable future had become so much less likely, then it was imperative to change the national priorities. The banner of social welfare and equality, in the language of one slogan, should be raised above the banner of national security.[50]

The trouble was that the government was not at all convinced that security against external attack had been obtained. In an attempt to keep up with the growing strength of the Arabs, Israel increased the defense budget during the 1967–73 period by 40 percent from an annual average of 12 percent of GNP to an average of close to 20 percent of GNP. According to IDF projections immediately after the Six-Day War (the so-called Goshen Plan), the available force should have been expanded in tandem with the GNP. Yet by 1972 it was clear that the GNP had not grown and was not going to grow nearly as fast as was predicted. Consequently, the chief of staff, Lieutenant-General David Elazar, ordered a thorough revision in planning. The new five-year framework (the Ofek Plan) called for a 15 percent cutback in planned growth at a time when rising oil prices and Soviet support had enabled the Arabs to step up considerably their force expansion.

Last but not least, as of April 1973 the IDF was put on alert for a general war, which was considered highly likely to break out some time in the course of the coming summer. The emergency necessitated a change in emphasis from *hitkonenut* ("preparation") to *konenut* ("alert")—that is, from investments in long-term increases in the order of battle to short-term preparation for actual fighting. One specific form that this assumed was maintaining larger quantities of reserve personnel in uniform instead of purchasing more arms and setting up new units. As a result of these anxious endeavors during the summer of 1973, the total force available to the IDF when the October war began was substantially larger than would have been the case without Elazar's revisions. But this was all achieved at a great actual cost and, according to available accounts, exerted constant pressure on the planners. The latter were thus in an unenviable situation. The press clamored daily for cutbacks and ran stories of IDF corruption, inefficiency, and wastefulness. The planners, however, were concerned that what was actually being spent fell dangerously below requirements.[51]

The rise in social discontent also had indirect influences on the social bases of the party political system. Initially, most of the new Sephardic immigrants were drafted into existing political parties in return for promises of patronage. Concretely, what most parties could offer was help in finding jobs and housing and in obtaining a number of other benefits. Opposition parties—the Communists on the left and Menachem Begin's Herut on the right—had very little to offer in this respect and therefore were quite unsuccessful in increasing their constituency as a result of the influx of hundreds of thousands of new immigrants. The main electoral benefits accrued to the center, religious, and moderate leftist parties.

This, however, was a kind of electoral taxation without political representation. Voters gave their support to a party that allowed them very little involvement in its routine business. Consequently, the bulk of the Sephardic community became increasingly aware of its status as a political periphery. This was also the prevailing feeling in Begin's Herut party. Israel thus had two discontented political peripheries, and with the rise in the Sephardis' self-awareness came the realization of a potential partnership between them and Herut.

In April 1965 the Herut party formed a parliamentary bloc with the bourgeois Liberal party under the name GAHAL (Herut–Liberal bloc). In the November 1966 elections to the Sixth Knesset, the new bloc gained twenty-six seats. In the crisis preceding the 1967 war, GAHAL was invited for the first time to join the cabinet. Menachem Begin and several of his colleagues were thus given, for the first time since independence, an opportunity to share in governing the country. They became, as a result, a legitimate political body worthy and potentially capable of running for office, even for forming a government one day. Hence if many Sephardic voters had a natural inclination to voice their protest against the left-center Ashkenazi establishment, they at last also had a major political vehicle through which to do so.[52]

All this coincided with another factor facilitating the rise and expansion of the Israeli right—namely, the reawakening of long-dormant territorial dreams. Begin's Herut had initially been insistent on Israel's right (as they saw it) to claim sovereignty, not only over every part of Palestine west of the Jordan River, but also over the territory of the Jordanian state on the east bank of the river. Between 1949 and 1967 they gradually dropped their slogan "two banks to the river." Although the West Bank remained part of their concept of the homeland, they would not go so far as to advocate a war for the purpose of obtaining it. Once the Six-Day War was over, however, and the IDF was in control of every bit of historic Palestine west of the Jordan, Herut at once revived the old territorial dream of a Greater Israel.

In advocating the annexation of the so-called liberated territories, Menachem Begin was not alone. In the hitherto moderate National Religious party (NRP) the topic became the axis of a struggle for power between a moderate pragmatic old guard and the party's younger leadership, in particular Zevulun Hammer and Yehuda Ben Meir. The latter had behind them an ever-growing camp of supporters from the party's own youth movement, Bnei Akiva. The more successful they were in recruiting support for their views, the greater the influence they exerted over the party's stance at cabinet level concerning the divisive issue of the future of the occupied territories, especially the West Bank.

A similar nationalist reawakening occurred also in the ranks of the mainly MAPAI and RAFI *moshav* movement, incorporating relatively well established owners of small private farms. These tended to lend their support mainly to Moshe Dayan, himself a well-known product of Nahalal, the first moshav in Palestine. To make the picture even more complicated, a similar and perhaps even fiercer nationalist awakening took place in Achdut Haavodah, the left-wing party of Yigal Allon and Israel Galili.

All these disparate strands of integral, territorial nationalism—a familiar phenomenon in itself but a novel experience for Jews—ultimately tended to amplify and further legitimize the role of the Israeli right while posing a real threat to the moderate Israeli left. During the Ben Gurion era, Begin and his party were virtual political outcasts; but during the tenures of Levi Eshkol and Golda Meir, Herut and its world view became acceptable, respectable, even attractive to many young Israelis, especially if they were Sephardic and/or religious. The Labor party, formed in 1969, in which the old MAPAI, Achdut Haavodah, and RAFI were integrated, thus faced a formidable domestic threat with which it could cope only by adopting an increasingly nationalist posture, too.[53]

Reinforcing this tendency was the fact that within the Labor party itself, MAPAI, Golda Meir's party and the mainstay of power in the Jewish state for decades, was faced with the powerful hawkish influence of Allon's Achdut Haavodah on the one hand, and of Dayan's RAFI on the other. Officially, all three parties had ceased to exist as of 1969, when they were united within the Labor party. In practice, however, they continued to act as intraparty factions. Meir could, of course, play Allon and Achdut Haavodah off against Dayan and RAFI, but she seldom did so. In fact, her inclination was to achieve as quickly as possible the complete integration of the party. She also had no difficulty in sharing the pragmatic-hawkish views of both Allon and Dayan. Consequently, although the prime minister herself came from the traditionally dovish-pragmatic MAPAI, she was actually instrumental in endowing the Labor party with an increasingly hawkish image.[54]

The increasingly hawkish complexion of the Labor party, however, concealed a number of internal differences of great significance from the point of view of the present discussion. Allon and Dayan, respectively, stood for two very different hawkish philosophies. Allon was a scion of an intensely ideological tradition that, though fiercely socialist in its views on socioeconomic issues, was not very different from the right-wing Herut party of Menachem Begin in its views concerning the Land of Israel—Palestine, in Jewish-Zionist lore. Dayan, by contrast, was pervasively pragmatic and worked out his opinions in the light of a semiarticulated, strategic-political world view.

In practice, the differences between them—which became the axis of a wider political division—could be discerned on one issue of great relevance to the present discussion: the question of force deployment. Allon was a territorialist and, as such, started from an irresistible fascination with the geography of politics. Consistent with this fascination, he advocated forward deployment in the Sinai and a similar posture in the Jordan valley, where, he maintained, the IDF could be greatly assisted by a north–south belt of Jewish settlements.[55] Dayan, by contrast, was exceedingly conscious of Israel's shortage of manpower. Settlements, he thought, could not solve the problem of security, but could only provide a friendly hinterland for IDF units. For that reason it was important to have them established; the question, however, was where.

Dayan's view was that the small size of the IDF's regular nucleus and its dependence on reserves made it impossible to deploy it effectively in a forward-deployment manner a short distance from the numerically far superior adversaries. A small IDF force in the Mitla and Gidi Passes in the Sinai or in three or four critical bottlenecks on the mountains of Judea and Samaria could provide an adequate instrument with which to deal with the initial wave of an Arab surprise attack until the reserves were mobilized and the war could be transferred to the adversary's territory. The same force right on the long cease-fire line, whether along the Suez Canal or along the Jordan River, would be pitifully outnumbered and outgunned.

In retrospect it appears that Dayan's views were more compatible with Israel's needs and capabilities than were Allon's. After all, if the armored division of the Sinai were deployed in the Mitla and Gidi Passes and the bulk of the Egyptian army were west of the canal, the latter would face enormous difficulty in launching a full-scale war. It would have to cross the canal and approach the Israeli positions some fifteen miles to the east. That would give the IDF both advance warning—time in which to call up reserves—and an advantageous topographic position from which effective fire would be directed against any Egyptian force moving eastward from the canal. In addition, the Egyptians would have to do battle with the Israelis while pushing their way eastward, a style of battle in which the IDF excelled but which the Egyptian army found exceedingly difficult. The October 14, 1973, attack in this style of the fourth and twenty-first armored divisions of the Egyptian army, in which they lost two hundred tanks while the IDF barely suffered a loss, provides an excellent illustration of this point. When Dayan tried in March 1971 to argue for such a strategy within the framework of his proposal for an interim agreement with Egypt, he was defeated by his colleagues. It appears that indirectly the winner in this conceptual and political contest was the territorialist/forward-deployment school, of which Allon was the chief spokesman.

Nor was Dayan successful in persuading his colleagues to apply a similar concept to the West Bank. Formally speaking, a vote was never taken. Informally, however, Dayan's views were turned into an appendage of Allon's plan. Without making a formal decision on this divisive issue, the Meir government proceeded to implement the Allon plan through settlements in the Jordan valley and the Etzion bloc south of Jerusalem. In addition, where there was no contradiction between the Allon and Dayan concepts, both would be implemented.[56]

The result was an incoherent pattern of settlement on the West Bank that suggested a barely hidden intention to annex all of this area. In this confused manner, the Meir cabinet surely projected an annexationist posture that could not but affect the Arabs' motivation.[57] The Israelis repeatedly argued throughout the 1967–73 period that "everything" (that is, all territories occupied in the Six-Day War) was negotiable and that, specifically, if only the Arabs would enter into direct negotiations, they would find Israel surprisingly pragmatic and open-minded. Yet while arguing in this vein, the Israelis were establishing settlements in northern Sinai, in the Golan, and in every plot of uninhabited land on the West Bank. Was this pattern not projecting a determined attempt to devour all the Arab territories?

The facts from the Israeli political scene do not entirely support such a suspicion. In fact, before the 1973 war, there was an abundance of evidence suggesting that in return for a peace agreement and normalization of relations, Israel would be willing to give back most of the occupied territory. But watching the Israelis from across the cease-fire lines, the Arabs could not know what exactly Israel was up to. Under these circumstances they were prone to assume, like the Israelis themselves and, in fact, like all people in a state of conflict, the very worst. The Arab motivation to challenge Israel on the battlefield was thus invigorated not only by the injury inflicted on them in 1967, or by the clear signs that Israel found the casualties of the war of attrition hard to stomach, or by the evidence of growing friction in Israeli society, or by Israel's patently slow and ambiguous response to a variety of plans for a settlement— but by the specter of the creeping annexation of Arab lands by a seemingly insatiable Israeli appetite for territories. In the language of strategy, what this may have boiled down to was an imperceptible but nevertheless real depreciation of Israeli deterrence.

The Third Strategic Package

The 1967 war and its outcome put to the test two principal Israeli theses: first, that if only Israel had a chance to deliver a decisive defeat to the Arabs, the latter would come round to the idea that peace was in their interest; and second, that Israel's main source of weakness (in addition to its small demographic size) was the lack of strategic depth. If only Israel had natural—that is, tactically defensible—boundaries, and if only it had enough strategic depth to ensure that no Arab surprise attack could ever deal it an irremediable defeat, the Arabs' incentive for starting wars would be so greatly diminished that peace would again become a realistic proposition.

The Six-Day War was by all accounts a decisive Israeli victory and an ig-nominious Arab defeat. It also gave Israel its "natural" boundaries and, with them, more strategic depth than it could swallow. Yet ultimately this did not increase the efficacy of the Israeli deterrent but, if anything, made it even more precarious than it had been during the previous decade. For one thing, the vast new expanses that the IDF had to defend, along with the gigantic boost the 1967 war had given to the regional arms race, presented the IDF with the need for an order of battle that was beyond its capacity. Instead of the small, com-pact, but easily mobilized and deployed army of the previous decade, the post-1967 IDF became big, cumbersome, prohibitively expensive, but far less capable of performing its single most important task. There were two primary reasons for this.

First, the distance of the front from the rear meant that mobilization and deployment of reserves would take far longer, especially in the Sinai, the prin-cipal front. The implication was that the regular force on duty on the cease-fire lines would have to sustain a surprise attack longer than would have been the case under the armistice regime. Second, the small distance between the IDF and its adversaries across the cease-fire lines—sometimes no more than a few hundred yards—gave the IDF totally inadequate advance warning. The bulk of the Egyptian and Syrian armies were regular soldiers. When these were permanently deployed right on the cease-fire lines, all they had to do in order to move into battle was to cross a few hundred yards. The Suez Canal and the Jordan River obviously added important obstacles. But because of the Israelis' fixation on strategic depth and their assumption that the intelligence community would be able to provide adequate early warning, many Israelis (Dayan was a notable exception) failed to realize that the advantage of formidable physical barriers could not offset the disadvantages of having to mobilize reserves in the rear and deploy them at the front, which was about a hundred miles away.

The problems of deployment resulting from this situation were never quite resolved. The IDF General Staff remained divided on this issue, not only because some of its members did not get along with one another, but also, and perhaps primarily, because it attempted to solve a problem that basically defied a satisfac-tory solution given Israel's limited resources. Under these circumstances the strategy that was officially adopted (under two code names—*Shovach Yonim* for alert and *Sela* for full-scale war), was sufficiently vague to accommodate all views. Thereafter, every OC Southern Command interpreted the spirit of the official strategy in his own way. Under Major-General Yesha'ayahou ("Shaike") Gavish, forward deployment was fully observed. Under his successor, Arik Sharon, the IDF forces on the waterfront were progressively thinned out. Then, under Sharon's successor, Gonen ("Gorodish"), the pendulum began to shift back to more substantial forward deployment.

The challenge facing the IDF was compounded by the fact that in forward deployment on boundaries publicly hailed as optimal, the IDF lost the benefit of red lines and *casi belli*. Instead of an exogenous strategic depth whose travers-ing by enemy forces would constitute an early warning, the IDF was now deployed on the outer rim of what it had previously considered to be security margins. With a few limited exceptions, it was beyond its capacity to project new red lines deeper into the adversaries' territory. There was, therefore, vir-tually nothing it could do to stop the Arabs from concentrating forces, enter-ing into alliances, deploying forces within their neighbors' territories, or—for that matter—engaging Israel in costly, protracted, and demoralizing wars of attrition. An Egyptian bombardment of Israel inside the 1967 lines amount-ing to one-tenth of what the Egyptians turned into a daily routine in the Sinai during the 1969–70 attrition period would have prompted Israel to launch a massive war effort. Similarly, attacks such as those launched by the PLO from Jordan (until 1970) and from Lebanon in the course of most of the 1967–73 period would have prompted pre-1967 Israel to carry out massive punitive strikes. Yet in the so-called defensible boundaries of the post-1967 period, Israel responded gingerly. As a result, it was dragged into drawn-out attritions that maximized its adversaries' comparative advantages and minimized its own.

A third strategic cost incurred as a result of the territorial gains of the 1967 war was the foregoing of a formal defense treaty with the United States. Hav-ing sought such an alliance ever since its inception as a state, Israel was at last presented with a clear offer. Infatuated, however, with the lure of defensible borders, pervasively cynical about the reliability of other powers, and more self-confident than ever, Israel turned down the U.S. offer without really giv-ing it serious consideration.

Subsequent events seemingly proved this decision to have been right. After all, the United States stepped up its support for the Jewish state even without a formal alliance. Yet the manner in which the Yom Kippur War broke out raises some questions. If Israel had had a formal treaty of alliance with the United States, Egypt might have been more reluctant to initiate this war for fear that a full-scale assault against an ally of the United States might be re-garded as a war against the United States. Of course, given the size of its sup-port for Israel during the 1967–73 period, the United States had become too heavily committed to the defense and well-being of the Jewish state to be able to abandon it without a damage to its credibility among other allies, especially after the departure from Vietnam. The vagueness of this form of commitment, the fact that it was neither clearly spelled out nor ever ratified in public by a legislative decision, implied that neither Egypt nor Syria—nor, above all, Israel itself—could tell in advance how far the United States would go in defense of Israel. The absence of a formal alliance, then, constituted an important win-dow of added Israeli vulnerability.

Perhaps the heaviest price Israel paid (in terms of its ability to deter) for its newly acquired strategic depth related to the topic of force employment. The IDF continued to operate on the (correct) assumption that, in the prevailing conditions of the Arab–Israeli battlefield, Israel could not afford the political luxury of a second-strike strategy. The IDF, however, was inadvertently wronged by its political chiefs, who either had not really given thought to this crucial question until the last forty-eight hours before the beginning of the October war or had changed their minds at the last minute. Consequently, the IDF had to adapt to a fundamentally different strategy within a few hours—an exercise it could not possibly have performed successfully. The adaptation to the requirements of a second-strike strategy was, in effect, carried out in the course of the actual fighting. Given this constraint, it seems that the IDF did exceptionally well. The price, however, was prohibitive in terms of human life, economic resources, morale, international status, and—as a result—deterrence.

A similar conclusion seems to be begged by the Israeli experience during this period with other dimensions of force employment—namely, retaliation and escalation. Flexible response when the opponent sought to build up pressure through attrition was a poor strategy. Under such circumstances, escalation was an inescapable imperative (that is, if a disengagement of forces was ruled out). Whereas escalation did solve the problem on the eastern border (vis-à-vis Syria and Jordan), it led to an abyss on the Egyptian front and to an inconclusive result on the northern border. But did Israel have an alternative? The answer, again, is negative. Under conditions of forward deployment along boundaries that were time and again celebrated as ideal, an escalation to general war was out of the question. The alternatives were either withdrawal or brinksmanship. The former was rejected because it would have greatly weakened the Israeli deterrent. The latter, which took the form of massive retaliation and a counter-city strategy, entailed, however, the risk of a confrontation with a superpower.

Some of the sources of this problematic strategy were psychological; some were no doubt logical. But the domestic political situation also had significant impact. With the Six-Day War, the genie of irredentism and integral nationalism was released from its nineteen years' captivity. The Meir government was incapable of stemming the tide. In fact, the government served as a mirror, if not an amplifier, of broader societal and political trends. Some members of the cabinet actually intensified the rise of nationalist aspirations, whereas others merely rode the crest, but ultimately these differences did not really matter. The territorial hawks won the day. The state's external posture became more intransigent. Internally, Israeli society became divided on foreign policy issues as deeply as it had been in the long-forgotten prestatehood days. Finally, all this took place in a situation in which Arab motivation for yet another war had been dramatically aroused by the loss of honor, the loss of territory, and the gain of an unprecedented international status. In a word, precisely when many Israelis were convinced that their nation's deterrence was at its peak, it was in fact in decline. This was demonstrated with vengeance by the thousand-day canal war and by the frequency and relative success of Palestinian terrorism. Above all, it was demonstrated by the joint Egyptian–Syrian surprise attack of October 6, 1973.

5

In Search of a New Formula: 1974–1984

I n its broad outlines the Yom Kippur War very closely resembled a war scenario with which Israeli planning had been thoroughly familiar ever since 1948: an Arab attack, a quick mobilization of reserves, and an Israeli counterattack carrying the fighting to the adversary's territory and culminating in decisive major battles. Moreover, according to Major-General Benjamin Peled, OC of the IAF during this war, the IDF's planning had anticipated intensive battles in the Golan, in the Jordan valley, and in the Sinai for about thirty days and as many as ten thousand Israeli casualties.[1] Terrible as the Yom Kippur war may have been, then, it was not nearly as bad as the IDF had anticipated and had even accepted as reasonable.

The war began with a coordinated surprise attack by the two leading Arab armies. The rest of the Arab world offered their support vicariously, in the form of military contingents in the vicinity of the main battlefields (Iraq, Jordan, and Morocco); or economic and political pressures on Israel's European and African hinterland of international support (the oil countries); or military supplies (Libya). Although the Syrians and Egyptians were successful in making significant territorial gains in the early phases of the war, the IDF regulars, whose task was to contain them, did succeed in halting their advance toward the so-called green line, Israel's border. Meanwhile, the reserves were mobilized and hurriedly dispatched to the fronts. Once the reserves arrived at the two main fronts, the IDF prepared for a counterattack. Containing the Egyptian army in the Sinai, on the one hand, and turning its main attention to the Syrians on the Golan, on the other hand, the IDF succeeded in recovering all the territory captured by the Syrians during the previous week, in reviving its own morale, in gaining bargaining chips for the postwar negotiations, in deterring other Arab armies (notably those of Jordan and Iraq) from opening a third front, and finally in generating serious strains in the Syrian–Egyptian war coalition.

Having achieved all that within less than ten days of fighting, the IDF could concentrate its attention on the Egyptian sector of the war. A decisive tank battle left in ruins the prime of Egyptian armor, the fourth and the twenty-first divisions. This was followed by a daring and imaginative crossing of the Suez Canal, which in a matter of less than a week led to the complete encirclement of the Egyptian Third Army and which would, within another day or two, have led to the encirclement of the Egyptian Second Army as well. In that event Egypt was left with only one army corps to defend its capital, Cairo.

The reason this did not happen was not the ineffectiveness of the IDF but, rather, the intervention of the United States. With the Syrians beaten and the Egyptians on the verge of a spectacular defeat, the Soviet alliance with both those countries faced its ultimate test. Eager to avoid a collision with the United States, the Soviets made threatening noises without actually involving themselves in the fighting. In turn, the United States was prompted to stand up to the Soviets, yet at the same time to press Israel to accept a cease-fire in place. Israel was thus denied a decisive victory not so much by Arab valor (although this time the Arabs fought well) or by the Arabs' strategic acumen (although they exhibited much of this as well) as by U.S. pressure.[2]

Nevertheless, the fact that the IDF was denied a decisive victory could not alter the overall military outcome of the war: a campaign begun by the Arabs in the most auspicious circumstances from their point of view had ended with the near collapse of the two largest Arab armies. The Egyptian army may have made some territorial gains on the east bank of the canal. Technically, however, the IDF, after twenty-one days of fighting, was in a position to starve two-thirds of the armed forces of the largest Arab state. Likewise, the Syrian army nearly reached the Sea of Galilee in the first forty-eight hours of the war, but by the end of the war the IDF had taken a substantial amount of additional Syrian territory and was in a position to bombard the Syrian capital with medium-range field guns.

Yet for all these remarkable achievements, and despite the fact that the October war resembled an anticipated scenario, it went down in the annals of Israeli strategy as a disastrous turning point, a near calamity, a pyrrhic victory—an "earthquake," as one widely read book described it.[3] The reasons for Israeli despondence are not difficult to guess. The war came as a rude awakening from a sweet but unreal dream. It took the lives of close to three thousand Israelis. It cost almost as much as the entire 1973 annual budget. It increased Israel's dependence on the United States. It underscored Israel's isolation in the world. Finally, accompanied by a successful Arab oil embargo and by the fourfold rise in oil prices, it illustrated the potential power of the Arabs.

All this was so depressing that it blinded many Israelis to the fact that the war had also accrued some tangible benefits. It underlined the fact that the United States had come to accept the defense of Israel as an integral part of defending the national interest of the United States. It showed that although the Israeli ability to deter the Arabs from war was not as absolute as many Israelis had led themselves to believe, Israel could still deal the Arabs devastating military blows. It confirmed Jordan in its conviction that it could not risk a war with the Jewish state. More important still, it brought Sadat's Egypt to a similar state of mind. In other words, while exposing the limits of Israeli deterrence, the 1973 war also underlined its strengths.

From this viewpoint, the sequence of Israeli–Egyptian and Israeli–Syrian disengagement and interim agreements that followed the 1973 war constituted a natural and logical offshoot of this war. President Sadat repeatedly argued that since Arab honor had been restored on the battlefields of the 1973 war, the Arabs could at last afford to embark in earnest on a search for peace. Although this must have reflected a genuine Arab feeling, it was also a more pleasing way (from the Arab point of view) of conceding that the Arab, or at least the Egyptian, strategic calculus had been altered by the war: if after the defeat of 1967 Egypt could not afford peace, then following the relative victory of 1973 it could no longer afford another war.

Shaken to the depths of their psyche by the 1973 "earthquake," most Israelis were slow to become aware of this change on the Arab side. Small wonder, then, that they were as surprised by Sadat's peace initiative of November 1977 as they had been caught unawares by his war initiative four years earlier.[4] Sadat was later called to task by his own enemies for his evident penchant for dramatic coups.[5] But the Israelis' surprise was apparently invoked by something deeper than a mere response to the Egyptian president's masterful diplomatic antics.

Sadat caught Israel in the throes of a crisis of reckoning, manifested by a collective manic-depressive state of mind. The whole nation was on edge. In October 1973 everything seemed to be on the verge of total collapse—"the pending destruction of the Third Temple." Then, in June 1976, the Jewish state experienced a rush of ecstatic pride and ebullient self-confidence when the IDF rescued the hostages from their Palestinian captors at Entebbe. The fall from this high point to the sordid resignation of Prime Minister Rabin in March 1977, when it transpired that he had kept a small but illegal bank account in the United States, was therefore particularly tormenting.

The next psychological shake-up came with the May 1977 *mahapach* (Hebrew for "abrupt turnover"), which brought to power Menachem Begin, the all-time pariah of Israeli politics. Most Israelis, including Begin's own supporters, would never have expected this development to lead to an Israeli–Arab rapprochement. At best the expectation was that, led by a defiant Begin, Israel would miraculously regain some of the self-confidence it had lost on the battlefields of October 1973. Consequently, the fact that Sadat chose to make a bid for peace so shortly after the advent of Begin only served to magnify the psychological jolt that his initative gave to the Israelis.[6]

Under Begin's government, this seesaw movement of Israeli morale and self-perception between peaks of ecstasy and depths of agony was, if anything, accelerated. Sadat's visit created unrealistic hopes for a quick peace, which were shattered prematurely at the Ismailyia summit meeting of the Israeli prime minister and the Egyptian president three months later. No sooner had the

Israelis begun to resign themselves again to an Israeli–Egyptian stalemate, when they were shocked by the PLO hijacking of a bus on the Tel Aviv–Haifa highway and by the Israeli invasion of south Lebanon (Operation Litani).

The hopes for peace with Egypt were aroused again when President Carter invited Begin and Sadat to Camp David for a marathon peace conference. Israel held its breath for two weeks and then had its spirits raised again by the signing of the Camp David peace accords. This was followed by the traumatic, acrimonious experience of withdrawing from the Sinai and, once this was over, by a new rush of national exhilaration when the IDF, in a spectacular operation, destroyed the Iraqi nuclear reactor Osiraq, near Baghdad. Yet even before the excitement about this strategic spectacle had subsided, Israeli morale had once again sunk to a new low as a result of the July 1981 mini–war of attrition with the PLO along the border with Lebanon and the resulting flight (for the first time in Israel's history) of much of the Jewish population from the area.

Shaken, perplexed, and humiliated, the Israelis watched Menachem Begin, the most pugnacious opponent of any accommodation with the Palestinians, accept a cease-fire with the PLO. This was followed by a year of virtual countdown, of which many Israelis were fully aware, toward another war, this time in Lebanon. When this war came, it began almost as a replay of the Six-Day War. The IDF made a quick advance, the PLO and the Syrians were beaten, and the IAF carried out yet another breathtaking spectacle—namely, the destruction of the Syrian missiles in the Beka'a Valley and a kill ratio of 86:1 in dogfights between IAF and Syrian pilots.

This raised Israeli morale to peaks that had not been experienced for years.[7] By the second week of the war, however, it began to dawn on the Israelis that this was not another brilliant blitzkrieg. The IDF became bogged down around Beirut; casualty figures soared; and the world press increasingly depicted Israel as an ugly Goliath out to smash the PLO, which in this script was cast in Israel's own traditional role of a gutsy little David. All this culminated in the assassination of Bashir Gemayel, the Sabra and Shatila massacre, an unprecedented domestic division in Israel, and a prolonged process of withdrawal from Lebanon during which Israel suffered casualties with seemingly nothing to show for them.

The development of a strategic concept against the unsettling and disconcerting background of such convulsive changes was predictably difficult. Indeed, in many ways this fourth phase in the evolution of the Israeli strategy deserves the title "The Era of Complexity." The weight of the decisions that had to be taken, the scope of the domestic and international political canvas that had to be surveyed when critical decisions were made, the frequency with which irreversible decisions were called for, the esoteric complexity of the technology of weapons systems, the tense and fractured domestic political background against which policy had to be promulgated—all these together rendered the making of Israeli strategy during the 1974–84 period a truly gigantic task. In a way, the agenda was almost extensive enough for a world power. The resources, however, were those of a small, psychologically exhausted country. Yet despite this overload, the strategic package that ultimately emerged, though far from perfect, was a sensible one.

The Quest for Combined Arms

After the 1973 war, as after all previous wars, the IDF embarked on a massive effort to refurbish its stocks and rethink its doctrine. The difference this time, however, was that the Israeli security establishment started off with the assumption that the 1973 war had not been as much of a success as it could have been and that Israel should never allow either political or economic constraints to influence its choices again. In terms of the strategic concept, this state of mind boiled down to an effort to find answers to all worst-case contingencies, regardless of cost.

Manpower

Such intentions notwithstanding, to find short-term—in fact, almost immediate—answers to all worst-case challenges was easier said than done. Given its size and sociopolitical structure, Israel's freedom of choice was severely restricted by major constraints. These prevented or at least limited Israel's ability to adopt a force-structure concept that would alter the basic formula on which the IDF had based itself all along. To begin with, the basic demographic constraint could not be overcome after the 1973 war any more than it could have been before. The Jewish population of the country had, of course, grown substantially since the days when the reserve system had been devised. But so had the population of the main confrontation states. Accordingly, Israel in the 1970s still had no viable alternative to the conscription/reserve formula of the 1950s.

In many ways the problem had become, if anything, more acute. For one thing, the degree of mobilization in the Arab confrontation states had been stepped up, and other Arab states such as Iraq, Libya, and even Saudi Arabia were increasingly featured as potential sources of significant expeditionary forces for the next Arab–Israeli war. Consequently, Israeli estimates of the total balance of manpower showed a decline from a 2:3 ratio in 1974 (400,000 Israeli soldiers in full mobilization versus 650,000 Arab regulars) to a 1:2 ratio in 1977 (400,000 for the IDF as against 844,000 for the Arabs) to a 1:3.5 ratio (580,000 versus 1,850,000) in 1984.[8] Second, there had been breathtaking changes in military technology. The latest vintages of planes, helicopters, tanks artillery, missiles, and engineering and communication devices required a longer period of training. Consequently, a growing family of military professionals—especially in the IAF, in the IN, and in most ground forces—called for a period of service far exceeding the long-standing three years of compulsory conscription. Of course, the problem could be solved by signing up conscripts for longer periods of service as regulars. This, however, implied a growth of the regular nucleus of the IDF beyond the prescription of the basic 1950 model. Moreover, moving to a larger regular base meant competing in a buoyant open market (whose buoyancy was, paradoxically, maintained by a huge defense budget), where manpower of the same quality could find more lucrative career opportunities.

Up to a point these new problems could be solved by an appeal to the patriotic instincts of the main reservoir of manpower from which the IDF drew service personnel. Although the shock of the Yom Kippur War had caused a certain decline in the status of the armed forces, during the first three or four years after the war there was a strong popular feeling that the country was in real danger. The decline in the status of the IDF was thus somewhat offset for a while by a rise in the prevailing perception of danger. Indeed, responding to the IDF's appeal for patriotism, successful young professions—doctors, lawyers, engineers, economists—who held positions of consequence as reserve officers and NCOs, signed up for one to five years.

Another step the IDF took in a desperate attempt to augment its inadequate manpower resources was to review the conscription registry in an attempt to identify able-bodied men who had dodged service or had simply not been called up by the IDF. This scraping of the bottom of the country's manpower reservoir took a great deal of effort and did enrich the IDF with a few thousand men who had previously not been included. The effect, however, was more psychological than real. In a society in which draft dodgers were held in contempt and in which the best and the brightest tended to volunteer for the toughest combat units, those who stayed on the sidelines and would not come forward were hardly the stuff of which good soldiers are made. The publicity attending the search for them was necessary in order to prop up demoralized reserve personnel who had to serve longer while others presumably stayed at home and attended to their careers and businesses. But the net contribution of those who were brought back into service in this way was probably negligible.[9]

Yet another method that the IDF adopted in the 1970s in order to augment its ranks, especially in combat units, was to modify the pattern of service for women. Contrary to the popular image in the world press, Israeli female conscripts had hardly ever seen real battle. For the most part they had been confined to office, paramedical, paramilitary, educational, welfare, and electronic-intelligence assignments in the rear. In the aftermath of the 1973 war, however, the IDF began to rely on women in relatively large numbers for instruction and operative positions in the army's various schools. This included instruction in combat drills involving an extensive degree of technological know-how—artillery; missile boat assignments; armor; intelligence; and of course electronic surveillance and command, control, and communication jobs.

Unlike the practice in the United States since the introduction of the all-volunteer army the IDF would not assign women to mixed units or to high-risk jobs, but female soldiers were encouraged to serve as instructors of combat units consisting exclusively of males. This began on a limited, experimental basis, but when it proved effective, the visibility of women in rear bases of combat units was substantially increased.[10]

Last but not least, the IDF simply had no alternative but to reduce numerical standards within units, on the one hand, and increase substantially the mobilization of reserves for routine, current-security assignments, on the other hand. This began in 1973, when a protracted war of attrition on both the Golan and the Sinai fronts lingered on while the parties to the conflict were engaged in negotiations. The Israelis feared that the negotiations might fail. In any event, there was a near certainty that the hostilities would be resumed. Meanwhile, both Egypt and Syria resorted to force in order to increase the pressure on Israel to make concessions at the negotiating table. Thus although a large number of Israeli reservists were sent home, several reserve divisions remained on active duty until as late as April 1974, six months after the end of the war.

This cost a lot of money, but the financial burden paled in comparison to the psychological burden. Those who were kept in uniform were mainly in combat units, which had paid a heavy toll in the course of the war—a fact that created a problematic starting point for prolonged service. In addition, many of them had businesses or farms that simply could not be run without them. The IDF devised a method whereby reasonable salaries were paid to reservists through the National Insurance Institute. This system, however, could not save the owners of small farms or legal firms, or of shops that were neglected because of the prolonged service, from virtually going into liquidation.

The lessons of this period were not forgotten, but the IDF had no alternatives. Having paid a heavy toll as a result of the decision in October 1973 not to call up the reserves until the very last minute, the IDF was determined in the course of the 1970s and early 1980s not to take any chances again. It would not allow its political superiors to restrict the growth of the order of battle for either economic or political reasons. Whenever there was even a faint sign of tension or suspicion of another Arab deception, the IDF would instantly call up some reserves. And since the choice (in terms of strategic adequacy) was between calling up many second-rate units and calling up a few first-rate ones, it was always cheaper to summon the latter. Consequently, a relatively small segment of the population found itself called to the flag with inordinate frequency.

The problem, to be sure, became far less acute after the signing of the Egyptian–Israeli interim agreements in September 1975. It became even less burdensome after the beginning of the Egyptian–Israeli peace process in the winter of 1977–78. By the spring of 1978, however, it had once again become an irritating source of domestic debate. This began with Operation Litani in

March 1978. Then, because of the escalation of the conflict with the Palestinians on the West Bank and along the border with Lebanaon, there was an ever-increasing need for larger quantities of trained military manpower than the regular kernel of the IDF and the routine volume of reserve call-up facilitated.

In the last months of 1981 the pressure to maintain growing quantities of reserve manpower in uniform reached a new peak. The passage of the Golan annexation law in December caused tensions with Syria to reach a peak as well. The IDF was ordered by Minister of Defense Ariel Sharon to mobilize substantial contingents of high-quality manpower as a means of dissuading the Syrians from making any military move. When the tensions with Syria subsided, however, most of the reserve units were not discharged. The reason, according to one well-informed source, was the decision in principle to invade Lebanon within a matter of a few months. Having resolved to carry out such a military operation, the government, or the minister of defense acting on its behalf, wished to maintain a force large enough to launch an invasion even prior to a general call-up. Whatever the reason, however, the policy of keeping a relatively large reserve force on active service generated a great deal of pent-up resentment among those civilians who were called up and kept in arms for long months.[11]

With the beginning of the war in Lebanon in June 1982, this became an important factor. Advocates of the war argued that the IDF would not have to stay in Lebanon for more than three months. Instead, the IDF became bogged down in Lebanon for two years. Initially exciting, the service there soon turned into a nightmare. As a result, the fact that there was no domestic consensus concerning the objectives and scope of the war, and the fact that there was so much resentment regarding the large number of reserve personnel who were kept there as an occupation garrison, became principal reasons for the decision to withdraw from that country without any assurance that the peace of the Galilee would be safeguarded. The limits of Israel's system of manpower allocation were thus demonstrated during the 1974–84 period in two important ways. First, it was an effective method of augmenting the size of the IDF *only* if and when reserves were called up for short periods. Second, drawing on the civilian population as it did, it could not work without a solid domestic consensus.[12]

Weapons

Difficulties of an even greater magnitude were encountered during the same period in the effort to keep abreast of the arms race. As a result of the colossal transfer of Western resources into Arab hands as a direct consequence of the quadrupling of oil prices, the Arab world enjoyed during most of the 1974–84 period a financial boom of unprecedented scale. Unable to work together as a cartel of buyers, the Western countries and Japan could only hope to offset the effects of this shift of resources through a massive export drive, in which a major item was arms for the Arab countries, some of which (such as Iraq, Kuwait, Libya, and Algeria) were also receiving weapons from the Soviets.[13]

Confronted by this race to provide arms for oil, the dormant division in the upper echelon of the Israeli military-political elite between supporters and opponents of a more explicit nuclear program resurfaced. Moshe Dayan, for one, became skeptical about Israel's demographic and economic ability to maintain a sufficiently dissuasive correlation of forces on the basis of conventional weapons alone. As he put it on one occasion:

> Israel should invest in security within the bounds of its [economic] capacity. It is not our purpose [to maintain] a conventional balance of forces with all the Arab states over whose motives and armament programs we have no control. We therefore have to put the emphasis on the IDF's quality, and not [allow ourselves] to be led into an arms race which will destroy our economy without necessarily ensuring our security. Quality and imaginative IDF solutions can preserve our edge over Arab quantity and not the current [under the Rabin–Allon–Peres team during 1974–77] attempt to compete with our adversaries quantitatively.[14]

What exactly Dayan was suggesting as an alternative to uncontrolled growth of conventional capabilities was never made entirely clear. But his cryptic comments seemed to suggest that he was advocating a return to what might be called a neo–Ben Gurionist concept. It consisted of three parts:

1. The growth of conventional capabilities should be disconnected from the growth of Arab conventional capabilities and fixed within a rigid framework determined by the growth of Israel's GNP.
2. The balance in terms of Israel's ability to deal with the threat of a combined Arab assault should be covered by a last-resort nuclear capability.
3. It was not essential that Israel should literally "go public" with the bomb, but the Jewish state should somehow bring this new national security formula to the attention of its adversaries.

Though he was speaking as a Knesset back-bencher and not as a member of the cabinet, Dayan's authority on this issue could not be questioned. Judging from a variety of unconfirmed reports, what he said was based on the knowledge that Israel had already, during the Yom Kippur War, had the capacity for the posture that he proposed in 1976, and that, at the darkest hour of the war (after the failure of the counter attack of October 8), Golda Meir had ordered a bomb to be assembled at once.[15] That such an evaluation of Israel's capacity was taken for granted by its chief adversaries cannot be doubted. In fact, leading Egyptian, Syrian, Lebanese, Jordanian, and Iraqi politicians and commentators had spoken and written freely since the immediate aftermath of

Yom Kippur War about the possibility that Israel would resort to the use of nuclear weapons in the event of an Arab conventional victory.[16]

If Israel's Arab adversaries became alarmed, so did the United States, Israel's most important friend in the world arena. This cannot be gauged by the few official U.S. statements on the topic, which mostly reject the notion that Israel has gone nuclear. Rather, *the real measure of U.S. anxieties in this regard appears to be the scope, pattern, and nature of U.S. assistance to Israel*. Since 1973 the United States has markedly stepped up its economic and military assistance to the Jewish state. The turning point was the U.S. airlift of military aid in the course of the 1973 war. Previously, the Nixon administration had often attempted to barter U.S. commitments to supply arms for Israeli counter-commitments regarding the terms of an Arab–Israeli settlement. But when the possibility of an Israeli defeat began to loom large, Washington may have become sufficiently alarmed at the possibility of a desperate Israeli move that it decided to act as swiftly and as generously as it did.

The total sum of assistance for the first year after the 1973 war, $2.2 billion, ultimately became a permanent annual allocation. Israeli analysts point out that this assistance has roughly covered the added burden resulting from the growth in Israel's conventional capabilities since 1973.[17] Therefore, it does not seem implausible to argue that the main purpose of the United States in giving this military aid has been to contain Israel's slide toward a nuclear strategy. If this has been the most important wellspring of U.S. generosity toward the Jewish state since 1973, it seems to have worked. Although Dayan's views were apparently fully shared by Shimon Peres, the minister of defense in Rabin's government, Dayan's advocacy was rejected by the Rabin–Allon–Bar-Lev team that headed the government in the mid-1970s. The thesis that appears to have won the day was that with U.S. financial backing, Israel would be able to keep abreast of the conventional arms race without introducing nuclear weapons. This view did not call for abandoning efforts to advance the nuclear program to a point at which Israel would need only several days, or even hours, to put together a bomb. It did, however, indicate a conscious wish to avoid even an implicit inclusion of nuclear weapons in the routine national security posture.[18]

The logical corollary to this view was a conventional buildup of gigantic proportions (see figures 5–1 and 5–2). Drawing on the composite experience of the Six-Day War, the canal war, the Yom Kippur War, and (since 1982) the invasion of Lebanon, the IDF General Staff started from a maximalist definition of requirements. To fulfill its chief duties, the IDF, according to Lieutenant-General Mordechai ("Mota") Gur, the chief of staff from the aftermath of the Yom Kippur War until the aftermath of Operation Litani, should be able to:

1. Ensure the widest possible latitude for political bargaining.
2. Have the ability to defend the state in both a first- and a second-strike war.

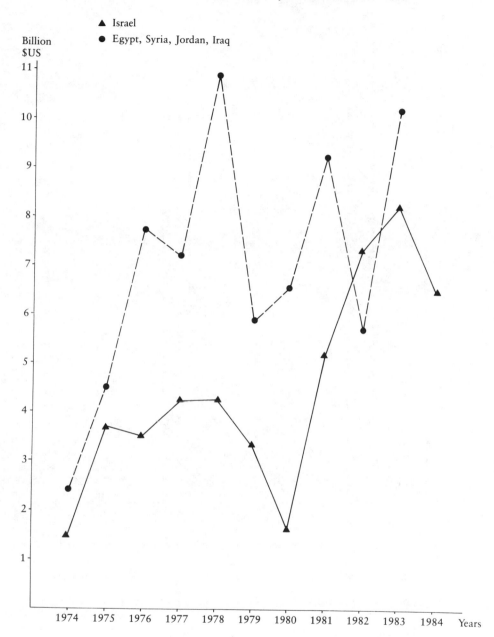

Source: Based on data in *The Military Balance* (London: International Institute for Strategic Studies, 1974–1984).

Figure 5–1. The Arab–Israeli Arms Race, 1974–1984

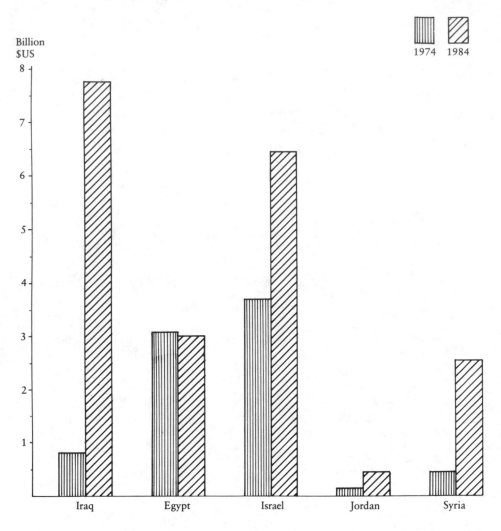

Source: Based on data in *The Military Balance* (London: International Institute for Strategic Studies, 1974–75 and 1984–85).

Note: The vast growth of Iraqi military outlays was mainly due to the Iran–Iraq war.

Figure 5–2. Selected Comparisons of Arab and Israeli Military Outlays, 1974 and 1984

3. Have sufficient power to deter any combination of adversaries from beginning a war.

4. Be capable of finishing any war with a decisive victory so that the adversary would have neither the ability to turn an unfinished encounter into a war of attrition, nor the power to start another round almost without a respite.

To achieve these ambitious goals, the General Staff determined that the IDF should grow to a size—in both manpower and equipment—that would ensure sufficient defensive power on all fronts simultaneously. In addition, it was decided to develop a central strategic reserve for ground, air, and sea operations that would be capable of critically affecting the battle on any front at any given time. A third type of force to be set up as part of this policy was a long-reach arm, based on airborne infantry, air power, and medium-range missiles, and capable of destroying any adversary expeditionary force long before the latter had the opportunity to reach the battlefield on the Israeli border. In addition, the IDF decided to develop an arm (mainly naval) capable of preventing a naval stranglehold in the Red Sea.[19]

The impact of this post-1973 program on the IDF's inventory of hardware was dramatic. In 1974 The IDF had, according to Israeli sources, 466 combat jets (mainly Mirage, Skyhawk A-4, Kfir C-2, and Phantom F-4E); by 1984 the total had grown to 580 (19 squadrons at 10 bases, consisting of 40 4-15 Eagle, 72 F-16 A/B, 140 Skyhawk A-4, 163 Kfir C-2, 132 Phantom F-4, and 40 Mirage III). In 1974 the IAF had 54 transport planes; a decade later it had 96 (C-130 Hercules, KC-130 refueling, Boeing 707, DC Dakota [C-47], Norman-Brittan Islander, Beechcraft Queen Air, Westwind 1124, and Dornier DO 1128). In 1974 the IAF had 78 helicopters (mainly French-built SA-321 Super Frelon and U.S.-built Ch-53, AB 212, and AB 206); in 1984 it had a fleet of 175 helicopters, including more than 40 AH-1G/S Cobra and MD-500 defender attack helicopters.

Nor were the changes in ground forces any less dramatic. In terms of armored divisions, the IDF grew from fewer than seven to more than twelve within less than a decade. This entailed the doubling of the number of tanks from 1,900 in 1974 (mainly M-48-A5, M-60/M-60 A1, Centurion, and remodeled, captured Soviet-built, T-55 Tiran) to 3,600 in 1984 (consisting of all these types plus a growing number of Israeli-designed Merkava). It also led to a near trebling of the number of APCs from 2,500 (mainly U.S.-built M and M-3 half track, and Soviet-built BTR-50, OT-62, and BRDM-2) to 8,000 (mainly high-quality U.S.-built M-113).

In addition, there were immense changes in personal weapons (from Israeli manufactured Uzi submachine guns and Belgian Fabrique Nationale (FN) rifles and light machine guns to U.S.-made M-16 and Israeli-designed Galil; in the numbers and quality of mortars (all Israeli-made Soltam); in the variety and quality of specialized aircraft, such as the E-2C Hawkeye AEW, OV-1E Mohawk AEW, MQM-74C Chukar IIRPV, Teledyne Ryan Model 1241 RPV, Scout (IAI) Mini-RPV; in the variety and quantity of missiles (Israeli-designed and -manufactured Shafrir and Gabriel, and U.S.-made MR-530, AIM-9 Sidewinder, AIM-7 Sparrow air-to-air missiles; AGM-65 Maverick and Walleye air-to-ground missiles; Hawk and MIM-23B improved Hawk ground-to-air missiles, and Jericho medium-range surface-to-surface missiles) and in the quantity and variety of vessels (from 16 missile boats, 2 submarines, and

48 other types in 1974 to 23 missile boats, 3 submarines, and 65 other types in 1984).[20]

The conceptual framework within which this huge order of battle was to be encapsulated was known as HaKrav HaMeshulav (the combined arms operation). In the 1973 war, the IAF, the armor, and the infantry—not to mention a variety of auxiliaries—suffered from conspicuously poor coordination. Separately, they functioned more or less coherently. But whenever the armor needed air support and whenever infantry and armor were called on to operate together, coordination was barely feasible at the macro staff level, whereas at the micro operational/tactical level, it was almost not put into practice (except through ingenious ad hoc improvisations). This was evidently the result of the incremental response in previous years to the lessons of the Six-Day War and the canal war. Having been alerted to this lack of coordination in the course of the 1973 war and, to some extent, influenced by similar notions in the U.S. armed forces, IDF planners moved in the 1970s toward an integrated concept of the combat team almost regardless of its size.

As had been the case ever since Operation Kadesh in 1956, the cornerstone of the entire edifice was a definition of the role of the IAF. The air force, it was decided, would train and equip itself for surprise attacks against enemy airfields; for overpowering enemy surface-to-air missiles; for intensive support of operations on the ground; for actual participation—based on helicopter gunships—in armored battles; for massive shuttles of troops (in both helicopters and planes); and for surveillance and long-reach operations in a huge perimeter covering the bulk of the Middle east and half the Mediterranean littoral. Such a post–Yom Kippur IAF should have been able to guarantee clear skies for every territory held by Israel. Moreover, it was perceived as a deterrent against any attempt by any force in the Arab world to launch a surprise air strike (of the kind Israel itself had carried out in June 1967) or to facilitate surprise ground attacks by disrupting the mobilization of the IDF's civilian reserves through air bombardments or deadly salvos of intermediate-range surface-to-surface missiles with conventional warheads.

But the real novelty in both the concept and its implementation was in the extensive interface that the quest for a combined arms operation decreed between the IAF and the IDF's ground capabilities. Before the 1967 war, the IAF was mainly geared for surveillance; for limited transport activities; and, of course, for a preemptive, preventive, or interceptive air strike focusing on the total disarming of enemy air forces. Before the 1973 war it added to these capabilities an extensive bombing capacity. Now, in addition to all this, it was increasingly trained and equipped for extensive tactical participation in major ground battles.

The other side of the coin was that the mainstay of the ground forces was also trained and equipped to work with the IAF. This entailed a virtual revolution in the electronics and communication systems of the armored corps and of all the various auxiliaries at its disposal. It meant that not only divisional commanders but also brigade, battalion, and even company commanders were equipped with implements that made it possible for them to call in the IAF for help; indeed, they were taught a variety of procedures for doing so. It meant an unprecedented degree of standardization in thinking, in equipment, and in training among all the field corps of the IDF. The armored corps—which before the 1973 war had dismissed the infantry as an outdated relic of a bygone style of warfare—was now called on not to devour infantry but to be integrated with it. For its part, infantry had to digest the notion of operating extensively from APCs, which in turn became part and parcel of armored fists. Both arms, moreover, had to devise together a concept of battle that would delineate optimal roles for the artillery, for the engineers, for the signals, for the medical corps, and of course for ordnance.

As a result of this simultaneous revolution in size and in operational doctrine, it did not take long for the more imaginative and more intellectually alert members of the General Staff to reach the obvious conclusion: the structure of the IDF since 1949—whereby the armored corps, the artillery corps, the engineering corps, the medical corps, the signals corps, and the ordnance corps each had its own separate staff, concept, and training structure—had become obsolete; the time had come to turn the IDF from a loose confederation of semiautonomous corps into an integrated, highly centralized command structure, a Central Field Forces Command (the Hebrew acronym is MAFCHASH, for *Mifkedet Kochot Hasadel*) that would fulfill the same comprehensive, exclusive role vis-à-vis the ground forces that the IAF and IN command structures fulfill in connection with the air and sea forces, respectively.

The organizational reshuffle that this reform entailed has lasted nearly a decade now. It called for a review of the entire command structure of the IDF. Since it could create tremendous havoc—indeed, could almost put the IDF out of commission while it was being carried out—it was implemented piecemeal over a long period of time. Meanwhile, however, the training and fighting concept that the reform proposed was gradually inculcated in the training doctrine and in operational planning for war.

Thus at the time of Operation Pinetrees (alias Peace for the Galilee, alias the 1982 invasion of Lebanon), the IDF employed an operational concept that was ahead of the organizational structure implementing it. Although the fighting in Lebanon was one of the first combined arms operations, the command structure that carried it out was in fact dual. It still retained the separate functional corps commands alongside the new integrated system. In practice, this dual structure added impetus to an already strong tendency to move with a top-heavy machinery. It led to a cumbersome General Staff operation—to the presence, to put it bluntly, of too many top brass in too many command positions, all the way from the imposing minister of defense (retired Major-General

Ariel Sharon) and his own private staff (YALAL, a Hebrew acronym for *Yechide Le-bitachon Leumi*, or National Security Unit); through the IDF General Staff under Lieutenant-General Rafael Eitan through the theater command under OC Northern Command Major-General Amir Drori; through corps commands (such as that under Major-General Avigdor Ben-Gal in the campaign against the Syrian forces in the Beka'a Valley); through no less than nine divisional commands; through numerous brigades, battalions, and other structures down the line.

More serious, perhaps, was the effect of the spectacular growth of the IDF during the 1974–84 period on the primary attributes of its modus oeprandi. The easy access to air and artillery power that the combined-arms concept gave to relatively junior ranks created an unhealthy shift of emphasis from imagination, boldness, and the indirect approach—that is, from the typical traits of a small, poor army—to a slow, and cumbersome "steamroller" style of fighting typical of large, well-endowed armies. Instead of assuming their own relative weakness and looking for ingenious and daring ways of circumventing obstacles and breaking the resistance of a sluggish but far better endowed enemy, the IDF in the Lebanon war revealed a tendency to assume that time, munitions, and weapons were not the object, and that therefore the sheer weight of superior force could achieve all its objectives.

To be sure, at the micro level many units still performed entirely up to the IDF's past (very high) standards. As a whole, however, it seems that in Lebanon the IDF acted like a rich, cautious, and relatively poorly motivated army. It seldom fought at night when night-fighting had been its forte in the past. It relied on armor, air support, and artillery where infantry in dashing and clever maneuvers could have worked wonders. In many cases it not only moved slowly but also failed to exploit its own success by keeping up the pressure on a retreating enemy force. This may, of course, be attributed to the concern with avoiding casualties and to the fact that the Begin government went to war without domestic consensus as to its objectives and scope. Nevertheless, a close look at the IDF's performance in the 1978 Operation Litani and at the credible evidence provided by a number of recently retired senior officers seems to suggest a deeper malaise that may well be, at least in part, the result of the overgrowth of the 1970s.[21]

Deployment

If the growth of the IDF in the aftermath of the Yom Kippur War entailed certain costs, it also had its very obvious benefits. In particular, what turned it into an important ingredient of deterrence was the fact that it took place against the background of a rapprochement with Egypt. Whether or not the Israeli–Egyptian peace process obtained for the Israelis the kind of "real" peace (as between Holland and Belgium or between the United States and Canada) they had dreamed of, one thing seems clear: by forcing Israel to depart from the Sinai under conditions that ensured the peninsula's continued demilitarization, the peace with Egypt made an immeasurable contribution to the efficacy of the Israeli deterrent. Indeed, the fact that this development and the greatest-ever growth of the IDF occurred simultaneously endowed Israel with the most favorable force/space ratio (from the point of view of strengthening its deterrence) in its four decades of independent statehood.

The foregoing should not lead to a confusion between foresight and after-thought. When Israel embarked on the immense expansion of the IDF's capabilities after the Yom Kippur War, it did so because of a fear that another war shortly was a foregone conclusion. The Arabs had done well in the 1973 war (compared to previous wars); they had the wherewithal, the personnel, and the international support to permit themselves yet another war; they were driven by a ceaseless rivalry among themselves over who was more militant vis-à-vis the common enemy; they tended, in this Israeli perception, to be fanatical anyway; they were supported by the Soviets, who feared that Kissinger and Nixon would really succeed in carrying out their threats to expel the Soviet Union from the region; and finally, they, the Arabs, were impressed by Israel's evident fatigue after the three-week-long, high-attrition war of October 1973. They might be tempted to act as the Israelis themselves would have preferred—namely, to exploit their success and build up further pressure on the Jewish state.

If this grim perception was on the minds of Israeli policymakers during the first two years of the Rabin cabinet, the implication was obvious: Israel faced a critical test. It could succeed in standing up to the challenge only if it quickly brought the IDF back into shape, first and foremost in terms of filling up its depleted stocks of weapons and munitions. Although the main intention of this policy was defensive—namely, to prepare for war on the assumption that the Israeli deterrent had suffered a critical eclipse—it paradoxically made war less likely. In fact, it strengthened Israel's deterence as well as its standing in the protracted negotiations following the war. Not having lost the war in military terms, and having refurbished its depots and in fact grown even stronger in terms of hardware, Israel could resist with relative equanimity Arab threats of fresh wars in the event of a failure of the negotiations. Thus Israel's added military strength offset to an extent its exhaustion in the aftermath of the war and paved the way for the disengagement agreements with Egypt and Syria and, subsequently, for the interim agreements with these countries. In both cases the Jewish state ostensibly paid a heavy price: large chunks of territory, for which many Israeli lives had been lost a year or two earlier, were ceded to Arab governments which—in the eyes of many Israelis—had failed to capture them by force and had therefore resorted to other means.

Neither Henry Kissinger, who acted as the main intermediary between Israel, Syria and Egypt, nor Golda Meir, Israeli prime minister during the first round of agreements ending in mid-April 1974, nor Yitzhak Rabin, who was Israeli prime minister during the second round of agreements, really shared this pessimistic view. They were only too aware of the possibility that the Arabs would attempt to exploit the good offices of the U.S.A., Kissinger's desire to deliver an agreement and Israel's fatigue in order to obtain more territory for fewer counter-concessions. At least Egypt seemed basically disposed to accept, for the first time in the history of Israel, an agreement that would lay the foundations for a more extensive understanding in the future.

Specifically, the Sinai II agreements with Egypt led to the creation in the Sinai of an ever-expanding no-man's land between Israel and Egypt in which U.S. rather than U.N. observers were stationed. In turn, the danger of another surprise attack declined, as did the danger of a war of attrition while the presence of an approximately eleven-hundred-strong multinational (mainly U.S.) force created a kind of U.S. tripwire. If Egypt ever attempted to force its way through the lines of the GIs in the Sinai, thin as these lines might be, Egypt would be confronting not just Israel but very likely the United States as well.

Other advantages of the interim agreements were that they placed on Egypt the onus of pressing for further talks leading ultimately to a peace agreement; they greatly improved Israel's bargaining position, and ultimately they almost removed Egypt from the Arab war coalition. Evidently aware of this, Sadat took the historic step of performing a dramatic pilgrimage to Jerusalem and thus paved the way to the Camp David accords and to the Israeli–Egyptian peace of 1979. Israel had to swallow the bitter pills of removing two major military airfields and a prosperous civilian population from the Sinai. Compared to the strategic gain, however, this was arguably a small price to pay.

Broadly speaking, two main strategic advantages accrued to Israel from the demilitarization of the Sinai. First, the Israeli evacuation of the Sinai facilitated an enormously advantageous Israeli reversion from the strategy of protracted defensive warfare on interior lines of the 1967–73 period (in which Egypt had clear advantages) to the strategy of quick-decision offensive warfare on exterior lines of the 1957–67 period (in which Israel had built-in advantages).[22] Second, the evacuation converted Egyptian space into a quality that Israel's small size renders vital—namely, extended early warning time. What this amounted to was a great decline in the Egyptian motivation to fight wars against the Jewish state; at the same time, it created something approximating an exogenous strategic depth. From the legal, ceremonial, and economic points of view, the Sinai had returned to Egypt; from the strategic point of view, however, it has remained to a certain extent under Israeli suzerainty.[23]

The combined impact of these two advantages can be portrayed through an imagined, but probably realistic, scenario. If Egypt ever wished to start another war, it would have to move its forces into the Sinai. To facilitate this, it dug tunnels under the Suez Canal. Although this has made an abrupt change in the Egyptian order of battle in the Sinai more feasible than ever before, it also introduced a crucial element of early warning from the Israeli viewpoint.

If the Egyptians were to attack, Israel could respond by calling up reserves and by rolling the IDF back into the Sinai. The result would be a race of the two armies toward a meeting point somewhere in the middle of the peninsula and, most probably, a clash between the Egyptians and the multinational force. If the Egyptian army managed that clash, it would still have to face the IDF in a head-on collision into which the parties would enter from frantic movement (a form of war in which Israel has always had a clear advantage). In short, if Egypt decides to challenge the military terms of the peace agreement, it would also have to assume the inescapability of a full-scale war with Israel in the depth of Egypt's own territory and in a method of warfare that maximizes Israel's comparative advantages. If this hypothesis is correct, it follows that whoever rules Egypt and whatever the circumstances, the likelihood of a successful Egyptian surprise attack has become very limited. The peace treaty not only reflected an Egyptian acknowledgment of Israel's ability to defend itself, but it was also in itself designed to strengthen the stability of mutual deterrence between the two countries.

As a result, by April 26, 1982, when Israel completed the withdrawal from the Sinai, it could afford to downgrade the Egyptian front, hitherto the single most dangerous front, to the lowest priority. Only under one set of circumstances would this be changed—namely, if and when Israel was bogged down in a protracted, patently unsuccessful war with, say, Syria, Iraq, and Jordan. Then, the pressure on Egypt in the Arab world and the temptation for the Egyptians themselves to reenter the war coalition would be maximized. Otherwise Israel has been virtually freed of the need to allocate any significant forces for the maintenance of the Egyptian line.

The corollary has been a dramatic change in Israel's ability to concentrate forces on other fronts. With an order of battle of unprecedented size, but without an active Egyptian front to attend to, the size of the IDF contingent that can be permanently stationed in the Golan Heights has been more than trebled. In 1973 the IDF could barely afford to deploy in the Golan one armored brigade, one battalion of infantry, and some elements of artillery. Ten years later, the size of the peacetime, regular contingent on the Golan had become more than one armored division. To be sure, the Syrian forces facing this contingent have been increased, too, to more than one army group (three to four divisions in front-line deployment). This surely has been a source of grave concern to the Israelis. Against such a background, the reduction of tensions on the Egyptian front—in fact, the elimination of Egypt as an active participant in a near-term war—saved Israel from an impossible situation in which it would have to face, in addition to the Syrians, half a million Egyptian soldiers in forward deployment.

Another critical improvement in the position of the IDF vis-à-vis its main adversaries in terms of deployment has been the shortening of the internal lines along which it would have to move in the event of war. Israeli control of the Sinai meant not only a dangerous proximity to a much larger Egyptian force but also a long distance from rear to front—in other words, long internal lines on which reserves and supplies had to move. Conversely, now that the Sinai has been returned to Egypt, the curse of long (and vulnerable) internal lines has reverted to the Egyptians again. The IDF can much more easily shift forces from front to front according to need. Thus one of the IDF's most serious concerns, the long time it takes to call up the reserves and transport them to the battlefield, has found a satisfactory solution.

During 1974–84 under Chiefs of Staff Gur, Eitan, and Levi, the IDF introduced three additional factors in an effort to improve its deployment. The first was the establishment of theater headquarters under the aegis of the three traditional main commands: the north (with responsibility for the Lebanon and Syria borders), the center (with responsibility for the West Bank and the Jordanian border), and the south (with responsibility for the Egyptian and parts of the Jordanian borders). The main function of these new command structures was operational. With the stupendous growth in the order of battle, it has become feasible, perhaps even desirable, to attach in advance specific units of division size, as well as the depots supplying them, to the theater in which they are likely to operate in the event of war. Overall coordination for battles in the area remains in the hands of the regional command. But intermediate lower echelons in charge of roughly a corps have been consolidated into permanent operational staffs as well.

A second, far more problematic novelty in the 1974–84 period has been the return to Spatial Defense. In the 1950s this was a means of creating an artificial strategic depth. Between the 1956 and 1973 wars, it had been frozen to such an extent in terms of the allocation of resources that the concept became almost totally obsolete. In the Yom Kippur War all the Golan settlements were in fact evacuated, since they had no means of defending themselves against Syrian armor. Consequently, under the hard psychological impression of this experience, the IDF—and the public—engaged in a debate over the strategic utility of these settlements.

The results of this debate were mixed. Under Chief of Staff Eitan, a vociferous proponent of Greater Israel, the IDF invested significant resources in an attempt to train and equip all border settlements for paramilitary duties in the event of another invasion of the 1973 type. This created an anomaly whreby civilians in the occupied territories, especially in the West Bank, became authorized vigilantes, capable of actually using force if and when the IDF in the area did not seem to be quick enough. Yet for all their visibility in the West Bank, these vigilantes, by almost all accounts, are not quite capable of becoming a significant obstacle to an armored thrust by the Syrians in the Golan. Their contribution to Israeli deterrence against a civilian uprising in the populated parts of the occupied territories in the course of a major war with one or another of the neighboring Arab countries is probably considerable.

Armed to the teeth as they may be, however, and in stark contrast to the settlements in the 1948 war or even to the settlements in the framework of Spatial Defense during the 1950s, the rural citadels of farmers on the Golan or in the Jordan valley cannot—in the conditions of the contemporary battlefield—be seriously regarded as an important component of general deterrence against a major war.[24]

The third and last innovation of importance in terms of Israel's deployment strategy relates to the festering wound of Lebanon. The problem from the late 1960s on was how to stem the tide of PLO attacks against the Israeli population of the Galilee in a situation in which there was no accountable Lebanese government to punish. Over the years a variety of Israeli solutions evolved, for the most part in typical trial-and-error fashion. Until the 1975–76 civil war in Lebanon, the dominant pattern of Israeli involvement was through occasional punitive strikes, followed by the immediate withdrawal of IDF forces. With the civil war, Israel adopted a new approach, which in effect incorporated small elements of Christian and Shiite forces within the territory of Lebanon into the Israeli system of defense against the PLO. Until March 1978 this remained confined to a limited framework of three noncontiguous enclaves on the Lebanese side of the border. Then, with Operation Litani, this method was expanded. The enclaves were integrated, and a narrow belt controlled by pro-Israeli forces under Major Sa'ad Haddad was established astride the entire border from Naqura on the Mediterranean to Mount Hermon on the Syrian border.

Beyond this "Haddadland" lay a parallel strip of Lebanese territory controlled by a special U.N. Interim Force in Lebanon (UNIFIL). This force, however, was not very effective in blocking the PLO, and the ensuing escalation ultimately led to an Israeli decision to invade Lebanon and eject the PLO altogether. The invasion in June 1982 backfired and led, after the death of Bashir Gemayel and the Sabra and Shatila massacres, to an Israeli reappraisal and ultimately an Israeli withdrawal in stages.

From the moment the Israelis decided to withdraw from Lebanon, the most troublesome question was whether to withdraw entirely and simply return to the status quo ante bellum or to devise a new method that would safeguard the peace of the Galilee. The argument here was, as previously on all other fronts, between two schools. One school advocated the forward deployment of the IDF within Lebanese territory until a Lebanese authority capable of policing the area had developed. The other school advocated a complete withdrawal but also some combination of mobile, active IDF presence in a security belt under the control of an Israeli-backed Lebanese force along the Israeli border.

Following a long, painful debate, the latter school won the upper hand. The IDF set up the South Lebanese Army (SLA), a regular force consisting mainly of Christian officers and a mixture of Shiite and Christian soldiers. The SLA was put under the command of General Antoine Lahad, a professional Lebanese soldier who had been among the supporters of former President Camille

Chamoun. This army, equipped and trained by the IDF, continued to operate in close cooperation with IDF units. Small contingents of IDF forces—elements of artillery, intelligence, and some armor—tend to spend long tours of duty inside the "Lahadland." Their policy, however, is to be as invisible as possible. As this book goes to press, this method of dealing with south Lebanon appears to have succeeded from the Israeli point of view inasmuch as there have been hardly any successful attacks against the Galilee. Israelis remain skeptical, however. Sooner or later the troubles in south Lebanon are expected to be resumed, and another method of deployment may have to be found.

What could that method be? Having attempted unsuccessfully to solve the problem through a comprehensive reshuffle (the 1982 invasion), and having tried a method of vicarious control through Haddad's militias and Lahad's SLA, Israel may have no alternative to forward deployment in south Lebanon. This step will not lead to a reoccupation of the area, since that would mean renewed conflict with the Shi'ites. But it could well mean the reintroduction of more force into Lahad's territory than during the first year after the withdrawal from Lebanon.[25]

The Margins of Insecurity Redefined

If the territorial acquisitions of the 1967 war rendered the casi belli of the previous decade obsolete, the post–Yom Kippur War period brought with it the revival of a vigorous reliance on casi belli for deterrence. This took two main forms. The first was the delineation and codification of what would constitute a threat, from the Israeli point of view, in the agreements between the Jewish state, Egypt, and Syria. The second was the unilateral delineation by Israeli spokespersons, with various degrees of explicitness, of casi belli and security margins.

The first instance in which a treaty contained the minimally acceptable conditions from the Israeli point of view, and thus indirectly codified and formalized a casus belli, was the disengagement agreement between Israel and Egypt. Signed on January 19, 1974, the agreement, especially its section B, dealt with the mutual thinning out of forces in the Sinai. Broadly speaking, it divided the area between the Suez Canal and the Mitla and Gidi Passes into three zones: one under Israeli control, one under Egyptian control, and one—in between—under the control of a U.N. Emergency Force (UNEF). Both Egypt and Israel accepted very strict limitations on the amount and strength of military forces in their areas of direct control. The details were spelled out in a letter from President Nixon to President Sadat and Prime Minister Meir. They set a limit of 7,000 men, 30 tanks, and 36 artillery pieces on the forces that the two belligerents could deploy in their respective zones. In addition, Egypt also agreed not to deploy surface-to-air missiles in an area encompassing its zone of control on the east bank of the canal up to 20 kilometers west of the canal.

By signing such an agreement, Israel not only undertook to refrain from certain actions itself, but also obtained, implicitly, a legitimate justification for resorting to force if and when Egypt were to fail to observe any of the specific stipulations of the agreement. In other words, the disengagement agreement was, in effect, an act of codification: it put in writing what each side would be entitled to consider sufficient cause for resorting to force.

Five months later, on May 29, 1974, Israel obtained a similar agreement with Syria. Again, the document did not speak explicitly of casi belli. Nevertheless, as in the agreement with Egypt and for similar reasons, the heart of the Syrian–Israeli disengagement agreement was a tacit recognition that certain specified changes by either side in the military status quo would constitute sufficient cause for the other side to resort to force. At Israel's insistence, both the Syrian and the Egyptian agreements included an explicit commitment to carry on the negotiations toward a full-fledged peace. In the final analysis, however, both agreements were first and foremost instances of codified, explicated casi belli.[26]

In a broad sense the same can be said of the interim (Sinai II) Israeli–Egyptian agreement of September 1, 1975, and of the Israeli–Egyptian peace agreement of March 26, 1979. In both cases the understanding went far beyond technical military arrangements. In fact, there was a coherent, logical progression from the disengagement agreements of Janaury 1974 to the peace agreements of March 1979 in terms of the scope of nonmilitary provisions. Whereas the former was almost entirely military in character, the latter was partly military and partly political. Nevertheless, the concept of casi belli remains as relevant to the limited military agreement as to the all-embracing peace agreement.

The reasons are almost self-evident. First, all three agreements included very specific military clauses that basically extended the principle of limitation of forces to larger parts of the Sinai. The first or disengagement agreement, as pointed out earlier, focuses on the thinning out of any military presence within small areas along the Suez Canal on the Egyptian side and on the rise of the Sinai massif on the Israeli side. The second or interim agreement stretched the same concept to an area that also embraced the Mitla and Gidi Passes. The IDF withdrew to the eastern approaches of the passes, whereas Egypt received back a larger part of the Sinai under the strict condition that its forces would not follow the footsteps of the retreating IDF. Finally, the Camp David accords and the peace agreement that followed led to the complete withdrawl from the Sinai of all remaining IDF forces without a corresponding redeployment of the Egyptians. The latter received sovereignty over the Sinai, but only a limited type of sovereignty, since Egypt "voluntarily" agreed not to introduce into the areas evacuated by the IDF more than a token number of civil administrators and policemen.

Each of these stipulations constituted in itself a casus belli whose transgression by one of the signatory parties could easily lead to retaliation by the other party and thus, in fact, to war. In a sense the same held true of the nonmilitary provisions of the agreements as well. The Israelis referred to most of the latter under the term *normalization* of relations. They emphasized the importance of creating channels of communication and exchange between the governments and between the societies of the two countries. Otherwise, the Israeli negotiators argued, the peace agreement would remain cold and insecure, a kind of rewritten armistice.

Conversely, if the conditions for the development of a fair degree of economic and cultural interdependence between the Egyptian and Israeli societies could be created by the instruments of peace, then the peace itself would be more real and more secure. What this meant was that any visible withdrawal of Egypt from the normalization clauses (such as a sudden imposition of limitations on tourism or a pact with another party in the Middle East that was still at war with Israel) would amount to the transgression of an invisible red line—a casus belli. It would offer Israel early warning of a pending change in the Egyptian disposition, an excuse—indeed, a justification—for retaliating in kind. Egypt, knowing that, would have to be very careful to avoid such actions. In short, the nonmilitary clauses of the peace agreement were almost as important in terms of mutual deterrence as the military and strategic stipulations. Whereas the military stipulations merely recreated the conditions of demilitarization that had existed in the Sinai during the 1957–67 period, the nonmilitary parts of the peace agreement added an intangible yet crucial safety net consisting of functional-behavioral rather than strategic-military casi belli.

During the public and parliamentary debate in Israel concerning the ratification of the peace agreement, critics of the proposed agreement dismissed this functional safety net as a poor substitute for the strategically critical real estate that Israel would return to Egyptian control. The validity of this criticism remains to be tested. Superficially, however, it seems that the agreement with Egypt had at least one crucial advantage over any other method of safeguarding Israel from the military might of its adversary: while delineating casi belli, it does so with the full consent of the Egyptians—namely, on a bilateral basis. Any other casi belli are fundamentally precarious because they entail an ineradicable element of coercion, a *Diktat* by one state to another. In 1979, when Egypt agreed not to deploy military forces in the Sinai, it did so voluntarily, not in mute acknowledgment (as before the 1967 war) that it would have liked to return its forces to the Sinai but would not for fear of a war with Israel. To say that Egypt accepted this provision enthusiastically would be to indulge in fantasy. From the Egyptian national point of view this was an unpleasant concession, a step that a proud nation like Egypt did not accept readily and could never relish. Nevertheless, it remains plausible to assume that the voluntary nature of the agreement meant a minimal Egyptian grudge and a greater degree of acceptance, resignation, and goodwill than would have been the case if Egypt had had to keep its armed forces out of its own sovereign territory in the Sinai merely because Israel had succeeded in brutally coercing it to do so.

By the same token, the Israeli experience with casi belli in Lebanon during 1976–81, though ultimately abortive, was initially a promising starting point for a new style of interaction with Syria. The background to this interesting exercise in the diplomacy of violence can be briefly summarized as follows. During the first six months of the civil war in Lebanon (April–September 1975), the fighting between the maronite Lebanese Front (LF) and its Druze, Moslem, and Palestinian opponents was primarily static. There were fierce exchanges of fire in and around Beirut, but hardly any territory changed hands. In November 1975 the LF launched a major offensive with the aim of expanding the domain under its control. The offensive, however, backfired. The LF was initially successful, but its near victory prompted the PLO, which had previously attempted to retain a semblance of neutrality, to join forces with the National Progressive Front (NPF). Consequently, by the beginning of 1976 the LF was close to collapse.[27]

The collapse of the LF would present difficulties both to Syria and to Israel. From the Syrian point of view, it could lead to the creation of a radical Lebanon, which would seek to offset Syria's influence by playing balance-of-power politics with opponents of Syria in the Arab world. From the Israeli point of view, a radical Lebanon in which the PLO was a critical factor could turn Lebanon into a confrontation state, a bastion of radicalism that could be as bad as Syria (from the Israeli point of view), if not—because of its inherent weakness—worse.

Thus both Syria and Israel were watching developments in the civil war in Lebanon with growing concern. When it became apparent that the LF was losing, both of Lebanon's neighbors became increasingly involved. Syria attempted to safeguard its interests in Lebanon by introducing, on the side of the LF, segments of the PLO that had traditionally been under Syrian influence and control. This included Zoheir Mohsein's Al Saiqa guerrillas and units of the more conventional Yarmouq Brigade of the Palestine Liberation Army.[28] Israel, for its part, was beginning to study the possibility of some support for and liaison with the Phalange. Meanwhile, Israel also moved to support Christian elements in southern Lebanon, close to the Israeli border.

This cautious posture by both Syria and Israel could not be maintained for long. When vicarious intervention failed to stabilize the situation, Syria began to move into Lebanon regular Syrian forces, which engaged the PLO and the Druze militias. In turn, Israel faced a problem of its own. According to Israel's policy since the 1950s, the Syrian Lebanese border was itself a red line. Syria was warned time and again not to interfere in either Lebanon or Jordan. When, as in September 1970, it failed to comply with this Israeli-authored rule, the Jewish state visibly braced for a large-scale intervention.

The emerging situation in Lebanon could not be solved as simply as before. In 1970 the Syrians had entered Jordan in order to save the PLO—Israel's avowed enemies—from the fury of Hussein's troops—Israel's tacit allies; in 1976 Syrian forces began to enter Lebanon in order to save the LF—Israel's tacit allies—from the PLO. If the Syrians were not allowed into Lebanon, either the LF would have to be forsaken or Israel would have to become involved on its side.

Impaled on the horns of this dilemma, the Rabin government was divided. Chief of Staff Gur advocated letting the Syrians take over Lebanon altogether. If they did, he argued, they would stabilize Lebanon, discipline the PLO, and have their own energies and attention spread very thin between Syria proper and Lebanon with all its problems. At the opposite end stood Foreign Minister Yigal Allon, a proponent of an alliance with the Christians in Lebanon and the Druzes in Syria. Such an alliance, he argued, would weaken Syria and the PLO. Rabin, the prime minister, leaned toward the advocacy of general Gur, the chief of staff, but also showed deference toward Allon, the foreign minister, who had been Rabin's superior and mentor in the 1948 war. In particular, Rabin was apprehensive about allowing Syrian armor to approach the Israeli–Lebanese border, with its vulnerable Jewish towns and villages. He therefore proposed a solution that would command a consensus—namely, allowing Syria to move forces into Lebanon within clear restrictions.

There were four such restrictions:

1. IAF planes would have complete freedom to carry out flights over Lebanese territory.

2. The Syrian army should not move farther south than an invisible line roughly stretching between Kafr Mashqi in the east and the Zaharani estuary in the west.

3. Syrian forces would not move west of the Beka'a valley east of the Metten Mountains, the main stronghold of the LF.

4. The Syrians would not deploy in Lebanon any surface-to-air missiles.

This composite (partly geographic and partly functional/behavioral) casus belli was signaled to the Syrians through the good offices of the United States. The Syrians agreed and proceeded to observe the understanding for several years thereafter. The LF was saved, and the PLO was badly beaten by the Syrian army. So were the Druze militiamen of the Shouf Mountains, whose leader, Sheikh Kamal Jumblat, was apparently assassinated by Syrian agents for refusing to accept a "pax Syriana" in Lebanon. From the point of view of the present discussion, however, the most important lesson seems to be this: though under pressure, the Rabin cabinet would not explicate the casi belli in Lebanon. Off-the-record interpretations by senior officials were offered in abundance, but a clear commitment in an "if–then" manner, threatening punishment if Israel's terms were not accepted, was scrupulously avoided. Explicating red lines and thus turning them into clear casi belli within the context of contractual agreements with Arab parties was one thing. But relying on explicit casi belli for the purpose of maximizing deterrence in a fluid context with a high risk of hostilities was something else. The age-old instincts of the Israeli leadership; their preference for ambiguity, for keeping all options open; their concern with avoiding friction with the great powers (especially the United States)—all these were clearly carried over from the pre-1967 period to the post-1973 period.[29]

This continuity was disrupted, however, when Ariel Sharon became minister of defense in Menachem Begin's second government (1981–1983). The first sign of this departure was a speech that Sharon prepared but never delivered in person for an academic conference organized by the Tel-Aviv University Center for Strategic Studies in mid-December 1981. The speech defined Israel's sphere of interests in a circle that encompassed an area stretching from the Gulf in the east to North Africa in the west and from the Black Sea in the north to black Africa in the south. It also suggested explicitly that Israel would not hesitate to resort to force if Egypt were to violate any of the terms of the peace treaty; if any Arab state were to acquire nuclear weapons; if any Arab state were to engage Israel in a war of attrition; and if guerrilla and/or terrorist activities against Israelis inside Israel, in the occupied territories, or anywhere in the world were to reach an intolerable level.

Although it is not at all clear that Sharon was expressing a fully endorsed government policy, there is little doubt that he was determined to drive the point home to all concerned. On March 18, 1982, he repeated the same thesis in a session of the Knesset Foreign Affairs and Security Committee. Then, in August 1982, while the IDF was still fighting in Lebanon, Sharon had his doctrine of "security margins" (as he referred to all these casi belli) published and widely distributed by the IDF spokesman in an English version.[30]

The announcement itself was clearly a novelty. Yigal Allon had advocated such a step for decades but had failed to obtain a cabinet endorsement of such a public statement. Moreover, Sharon's definition of the scope of Israel's security interests was unusually extensive. At the same time, however, very little in the specific content was really new. Indeed, broadly speaking Sharon merely reiterated in a characteristically bombastic form what the majority of Israel's national security planners virtually took for granted. No Israeli policymakers would resign themselves to the introduction of nuclear arsenals by any Arab state. No Israeli policymakers would accept another war of attrition of the type that had bled the IDF on the banks of the Suez Canal during 1968–70. No Israeli policymakers would advocate leniency toward the PLO, especially if and when the latter was engaged in intensive harassment of Israelis or of non-Israeli Jews—in Israel, in the occupied territories, or abroad. Finally, no Israeli policymakers would be indifferent to an adverse change in either the level of armament or the manner of deployment of any one of the main Arab armed forces facing Israel, including—even after the peace treaty—Egypt. The difference in this important regard between Sharon and most others in a similar position was mainly one of style. Sharon's style is harsh, blunt, and aggressive. The rest of the Israeli political-military elite (though in significantly variable degrees) tend to prefer greater caution in action and more ambiguity in style. In the final analysis, however, most of the changes in the status quo in Israel's strategic environment that would be deemed unacceptable by Sharon would also be deemed almost equally unacceptable by most of his peers. Differences abound, however, on the question of what should be done once an adverse change is detected.

The Management of Dependence

The Yom Kippur War had a dual effect on Israel's alliance calculus. On the one hand, it seemed to suggest that the gamble of eschewing a formal alliance but retaining the occupied territories had fully paid off. The United States had stood by the Jewish state in its hour of extreme peril even though it was not bound to do so by any formal document. The airlift of U.S. equipment, a supreme example of an alliance relationship, had arrived on time, bringing with it more equipment than the IDF needed or than Israel could afford to purchase. Later, during the critical last two days of the war, the United States had declared a worldwide alert as a means of deterring the Soviets from intervening in the war on the side of Egypt and Syria. This unusual step toward the brink of a global confrontation was taken despite the fact that it was Israeli action—the continued advance of the IDF west of the Suez Canal after the cease-fire of October 22, 1973—that actually triggered the Soviet hints of intervention.[31]

If from this point of view the gamble of self-reliance had paid off, from other perspectives it appears to have been a grave mistake. For one thing, had there been a formal U.S. security guarantee to Israel before the war, the Egyptians and the Syrians might have been even more reluctant to initiate hostilities for fear of a confrontation with the United States. Second, although it had not signed any formal commitment to consult the United States, Israel did feel obliged to consult the Americans on the eve of the October war. The upshot was the conclusion in Jerusalem that Washington would not look kindly on an Israeli preemption of the Egyptians and/or the Syrians. Consequently, the IDF's requests for permission to preempt or at least to go for an all-out mobilization were turned down by the government. The war began with a massive Egyptian–Syrian attack, and it took Israel ten days of materially and morally exhausting attrition before it succeeded in turning the tide in its favor.[32]

Heavy as the price that Israel paid in order to ensure U.S. support was, it did not give the Meir government any certainty of U.S. help. It was deemed certain that an Israeli preemption or even mobilization could foreclose the possibility of U.S. help once hostilities had begun. But the obverse—namely, that if Israel responded to the United States' call for prudence, adequate assistance would be forthcoming—could not be taken for granted. Theoretically, then, even the huge sacrifice involved in not having preempted could have been insufficient to persuade the Nixon administration that it would be beneficial from the U.S. point of view to assist the Jewish state in its hour of trial. As Kissinger admitted somewhat obliquely, "Had Israel struck [Egypt and/or Syria] first, it would have greatly complicated the prospects of American support."[33]

With such a balance sheet, it is not surprising that an Israeli disposition toward the idea of a formal alliance with the United States became increasingly conspicuous in the course of the 1970s. Gone were the brave dreams of complete self-reliance. In the aftermath of the Yom Kippur War, even Dayan, previously the most persistent supporter of defiant self-reliance, reached the conclusion that if the Untied States were to offer a "firm, binding and long-term defense treaty" (which he thought was unlikely) he for one would see it as a "cardinal achievement."[34] This clearly reflected a sober realization that the Jewish state had become so critically dependent on the United States that the question was no longer *whether* to enter into an alliance with the United States but, rather, under what terms and with what degree of formalization and institutionalization.

Israeli spokespersons, aware of how difficult it would be to bring the United States to consider a security guarantee *prior* to an Israeli commitment to withdraw from the occupied territories, tended to skirt carefully around the issue in a manner that would save them unpleasant rebuffs. According to the somewhat acid account of Zbigniew Brzezinski, President Carter's national security adviser:

> Israeli policy [was] to make the relationship an increasingly binding one, and every effort was made by Israeli supporters in the United States to elevate the status of Israel to that of U.S. "ally." Whenever possible the words "ally," "special relationship" or "strategic asset" were proposed for inclusion in Presidential statements in order to reinforce in the American public's mind the special links binding America and Israel.[35]

What Brzezinski forgot to mention in this account was the fact that time and again the Carter administration tried to lure Israel into making political and territorial concessions to the Arabs by suggesting that the United States might be willing to consider a formal security guarantee.[36]

Both sides, however, while engaging in such delicate maneuvers, remained rigidly attached to their basic positions. The United States would be willing to consider a security guarantee in return for an Israeli commitment to withdraw from virtually all the territories occupied in 1967. Faced with such a choice between territories as a component of deterrence and U.S. guarantee as an alternative, Israel, for its part, would not consider the proposition of an alliance on this basis. Indeed, as the first post-1973 decade wore on, the strength of the political forces inside Israel opposing the ceding of the territories under any conditions rapidly increased. Nonetheless, the rapid rise in the intensity and scope of Israel's relations with the United States in the course of the 1974–84 period created with increasing frequency junctures at which the matter of a contractual bond between the two countries came up for discussion and review. Such junctures mostly related either to the peace process or, alternatively, to military and strategic interdependence.

The Egyptian–Israeli peace process begot, as a by-product, a more explicit U.S. commitment to Israel than had ever been offered before. While negotiating the final details of the peace treaty, the Israeli government requested a specific U.S. commitment to act against any violation of the agreement by Egypt. The request was presented in circumstances that made it almost inconceivable that the United States would turn it down. Having led Egypt and Israel to an agreement at the Camp David conference in September 1978, President Carter, whose prestige had been so conspicuously put to the test, proceeded to carry out his own version of shuttle diplomacy with a view to bringing the parties to sign the peace agreement. The Israeli request for a formal collateral undertaking by the United States to defend the proposed peace treaty was presented to him on March 12, 1979—that is, on the last day of his trip. Thus what normally would have been a major U.S. decision was approved almost casually by a president in a hurry to save an agreement that he had been so helpful in working out.

With hindsight the undertaking by Carter does not appear to have constituted as dramatic a departure as it initially seemed. For one thing, the document, which bears the title "Memorandum of Agreement," was an executive undertaking rather than a formal treaty. Congress, therefore, did not have to approve it, which, in turn, made it a lesser commitment—and hence a lesser contribution to Israeli deterrence—than a full-fledged treaty. Second, the memorandum did not call for the establishment of a permanent organizational mechanism for strategic cooperation and military planning, not even of the limited type that existed in the early days of NATO. Third, the memorandum, because of its attachment to the Israeli–Egyptian peace treaty, was confined to Israel's relations with Egypt. It did not commit the United States to stand by Israel in the event of a threat from another Arab state or, indeed, one from any power from another part of the world (such as the Soviet Union).

Last but not least, the memorandum did not contain any unambiguous commitment on the part of the United States to intervene militarily on the side of Israel in the event of an Egyptian violation of the peace treaty. It did stipulate that

> if a violation of the Treaty of Peace is deemed to threaten the security of Israel . . . the United States will be prepared to consider, on an urgent basis,

such measures as the strengthening of the United States presence in the area, the providing of emergency supplies to Israel and the exercise of maritime rights in order to put an end to the violations.

In a sense, however, the specification of this type of assistance merely served to underline the reluctance of the United States to go further than that.[37]

Notwithstanding these very important shortfalls of the memorandum, it was a significant new departure. Added to the weighty evidence of a willingness on the part of the United States to stand by Israel in an hour of need, such a formal undertaking must have an impact on the Egyptian calculus for war and peace. It might not be enough to remove from the Egyptian mind any thought of returning to the Arab fold and rejoining the war coalition against Israel, but it must add one more important reason for not doing so. Consequently, the fact that Israel's deterrence against Egypt has been buttressed by a U.S. guarantee could have an important impact on other parts of the Arab world. If Egypt is no longer a reliable partner for a war effort against the Jewish state, the likelihood that an adequate combination of alternative forces of other Arab states would take shape has been greatly reduced. Small and limited as the literal significance of the Memorandum of Agreement may be, its overall strategic significance should not be taken lightly.

One of the most obvious traits of the birth process of the Memorandum of Agreement was that the United States was not enthusiastic about the undertaking. President Carter gave way only because the Israeli negotiators introduced the request in a context in which their bargaining power was, paradoxically, maximized. This lesson—in particular, the importance of having an adequate lever with which to extract the guarantee from the United States— was apparently not fully grasped by Begin's government when, two years later, it attempted to extract a more comprehensive U.S. guarantee. The main driving force behind this new attempt to force the United States into a more formally tightened guarantee was Ariel Sharon, minister of defense in Begin's second government. Sharon's rationale for pressing in this direction was seemingly impeccable. Over the years of intense partnership, especially since 1973, Israel had become a vital source of prime intelligence for the United States. Specifically, the data that Israel had assembled diligently and successfully about Soviet arms, doctrine, modus operandi, intentions, and constraints had a value that went beyond the Middle East theater.

In addition, Sharon argued vehemently, Israel had become the single most important military force throughout the Middle East. Iran, the other pillar of U.S. security in the region, had collapsed like a house of cards in 1978–79. Egypt, with which the United States had attempted to forge meaningful strategic relations ever since the 1973 crisis, was incapable of actually living up to U.S. expectations. Its dependence on and inclination toward the Arab world was impossible to eradicate; the assassination of Sadat proved that even its regime was unstable and, above all, that its military efficacy was in doubt. Thus Israel was, in effect, the one and only power in the region that really fit without any problem into the U.S. model of an ally.

Given these two related aspects, Sharon argued, Israel should not act on the assumption that it was receiving from the United States more than the latter was receiving from it. The contribution of Israel to U.S. security, in Sharon's view, was at least equal to the contribution of the United States to Israeli security. But this was inadequatley reflected in relations between the two countries. Henceforth, a greater symmetry and a greater equality between the two countries should be sought. The one method whereby this could be achieved, Sharon concluded, was a formal treaty of alliance.

Sharon's advocacy of a formal alliance with the United States was in a sense a Ben Gurionist thesis turned on its head. Ben Gurion had advocated an alliance, not because he thought that Israel was strong but, rather, because of his fear that without it the Jewish state could not survive for very long. Ben Gurion's successors aimed at less because they realized that the United States was not very willing to offer an alliance and because they had gradually become more confident than their teacher that Israel could look after its own interests on the basis of self-reliance. Sharon carried this retreat from the Ben Gurionist thesis to an extreme. For him, Israel was so powerful that the United States could not do without it. The United States, he concluded, should pay for that with hardware, with economic and political aid, and with a formal treaty of alliance.

Sharon's main error was not his misrepresentation of the Ben Gurionist thesis but, rather, an astonishing failure to realize how unrealistic his thesis was in terms of U.S. willingness to play its role in the Israeli defense minister's script. At Sharon's behest, Prime Minister Begin proposed the idea to President Reagan in September 1981, shortly after the president had won the battle for the AWACs deal with Saudi Arabia. Reagan's victory on Capitol Hill on this issue was not very impressive, since the ultimate approval was based on a slim majority. Thus, in a sense, the AWACs vote was an Israeli tour de force, a demonstration of how powerful the pro-Israeli element in Congress was.

If this vote affected Begin's timing (mistakenly, it seems), what brought about the very decision to start pressing for a defense treaty was the guiding philosophy of the Reagan administration in the Middle East—or, at least, what Sharon and Begin made of it. Specifically, it appears that the Israelis misinterpreted Secretary of State Alexander Haig's quest for a "strategic consensus" in the Middle East. What Haig aimed at was the harnessing of all the United States' friends in the region to a joint pro-U.S. and, by implication, anti-Soviet platform. He did not speak of a regional alliance since this would be too difficult to achieve, as earlier U.S. attempts had demonstrated. He merely spoke of a *consensus*—namely, a series of bilateral understandings between the United States and its supporters in the Middle East within the same conceptual framework.[38]

It was not long before Haig came to realize that the would-be Arab partners to this so-called consensus would have none of it. From an Israeli perspective, however, it seemed nevertheless a propitious moment in which to press
for some sort of U.S.–Israeli defense agreement. All that Israel had to do, or
so it seemed to Sharon and Begin, was to express willingness to join the consensus. If the Arabs joined, too—which no one in Israel expected—all the better. Even if they did not, however—perhaps especially if the Arabs desisted from
joining—it would be very difficult, if not utterly embarrassing, for the Reagan
administration to reject an Israeli offer to join.

The trouble with this, as with many other of Sharon's ventures, was that
its author was too clever for his own good. Without the Arabs, the Reagan
administration would not be dragged into a formal alliance with Israel. It was
an argument that even many of Israel's friends in Washington fully understood,
since the U.S. record of support for Israel had been so impressive over the
previous decade that the Israeli demand for a formal agreement appeared
somewhat self-indulgent, in fact quite unnecessary.

Secretary of Defense Weinberger, who was to be in charge of implementing
any defense treaty with Israel, was adamantly opposed. Thus when Begin's request of early September 1981 was followed by Sharon's visit to Washington late
in November, the latter found himself virtually forcing a lukewarm administration to sign an undertaking that very few people in the U.S. capital favored and
that even many Israelis opposed. The stillborn product of this affair was the
Memorandum of Strategic Understanding (MSU). The MSU was not directed
against any state in the Middle East. Rather, it entailed a U.S. commitment to
assist Israel if and when it was threatened by "the Soviet Union or Soviet-controlled
forces from outside the region introduced into the region." The agreement proposed mutual Israeli–U.S. action in the form of joint military exercises, joint
readiness activities, cooperation in research and development, and defense trade.

The MSU was signed in an embarrassing manner: Secretary of Defense
Weinberger was so strongly opposed to it that he would not even allow photog-
raphers to take pictures of the signing ceremony. A storm of criticism followed,
from two main quarters: Americans who argued that the MSU contributed
nothing to U.S. security but jeopardized U.S. relations with the Arab world, and
Israelis (represented by no fewer than 53 of the 120 members of the Knesset, who
voted against the MSU) who argued that the memorandum contributed nothing
to Israeli security while presenting the Soviets as Israel's foes for no good reason.
Then, seventeen days after the signing of the MSU, Begin introduced the Golan
Annexation Bill. When the Knesset turned this controversial bill into a law,
Washington reacted by suspending the MSU. Outraged, Begin lashed out at the
Reagan administration, accusing it of treating Israel as if it were a "banana
republic," a vassal state, or a fourteen-year-old child who deserved a slap on the
wrist for misbehaving. Thus instead of improving U.S.–Israeli relations, the ill-
conceived MSU merely led to a great deal of added friction.[39]

This incident, of course, was neither the first nor the last time that the Reagan administration and the Begin cabinet were at loggerheads. A short while earlier, Israel had bombed the Iraqi nuclear reactor. Six months after the MSU episode the IDF invaded Lebanon, thus initiating a period of ten months in which U.S.–Israeli relations were in a state of a permanent crisis. Paradoxically, however, these severe symptoms of discord actually served to underline the fundamental strength and durability of the emerging alliance. In blunt terms, only very close relations based on a persistent, resilient, and durable convergence of interests and values could withstand pressures of such magnitude. If Israel could invade Lebanon, bomb Beirut for eight weeks, move into west Beirut contrary to a U.S. pledge to the PLO that the IDF would not do so, and then disregard or treat cavalierly—or at least seem to be doing so—U.S. requests that the IDF not depart from Beirut and the Shouf Mountains—if all this could happen without a lasting rupture in relations with the United States, without a real decline in popularity with the American people, and without even losing anything in U.S. aid—then the alliance between the two countries must be as solid as a rock.[40]

This must have been the feeling not only of the Israelis and the Americans but also, above all, of the Arabs. To them, such friction as was reflected in public utterances was little more than playacting. The United States had come to support Israel almost blindly, and Israel's adversaries had no choice but to accustom themselves to this important strategic, political, economic, and psychological reality. In turn, it can be said that Israel's deterrence against an all-out Arab attack was substantially strengthened. It was still only partially effective against subwar or even limited-war threats. Together with the accumulated impact of Israeli military prowess, however, it may have already ingrained in the Arab mind an assumption that the Jewish state could not be defeated in one major military blow.

In an unexpected and paradoxical way, the development of Israel's relations with Iran and Ethiopia also made a significant contribution to Israeli deterrence. Ostensibly, the trend in Israel's relations with these countries was in the opposite direction. An unsentimental proponent of power politics, the shah of Iran, drew immediate conclusions from Israel's experience in the 1973 war. If the Jewish state's spectacular success in 1967 encouraged the shah to draw closer to it, the rise of Arab political power in the aftermath of the October war and the rise in oil prices drove the shah away from the Israelis. Nasser, the shah's great opponent, was dead and buried. Sadat was neither militant nor anti-Western. This opened the way to what the shah saw as a possible Teheran–Riyadh–Cairo axis, an alliance of major forces (as they seemed in the mid-1970s), that could check all the radicals of the region, especially Iraq, which threatened Iran's regional position. At the same time, this alliance could improve the terms of collaboration between these countries and the West. In addition, the shah forged close relations with Jordan and, although he showed very little sympathy for the PLO, began to espouse the "legitimate" rights of the Palestinians. Having thus achieved an impressive rapproachement with the Arab world, the shah moved toward a détente on his terms with Iraq. With his control of the Gulf area more or less assured, he forsook the Kurds and signed an agreement with Iraq that terminated—or so it seemed—the Iran–Iraq conflict.

The Israelis watched all this with alarm. The basis of Iranian–Israeli relations was the age-old and seemingly irreducible conflict between the Shi'ite monarchy and the Sunni movement for Arab unity. But if the shah succeeded in forging all these important ties with the leading powers in the Arab world, it could not but lead to a severe erosion of the Iranian–Israeli tacit alliance. To Israel's barely concealed relief, this did not happen. Indeed, commercial relations between the two countries peaked as a result of the oil boom, and Israeli influence over the shah's domestic policies increased as his regime faced a growing crisis. From the Israeli point of view, however, one important loss was incurred as a result of the change in the Iranian posture vis-à-vis the Arab world: when Iran decided to stop all support for the Kurdish (Iraqi) rebels of Mulla Moustapha al-Barazani, Israel lost access to this area of Iraq. The immediate collapse of the Kurdish uprising meant that an Iraqi army of some twelve armored divisions had become available for another war against Israel. In the 1948 war Iraq had taken an active part mainly in the fighting in the northwest corner of what later became the West Bank. In the 1973 war one Iraqi armored division had fought on the Golan. If Iraq no longer needed to worry about its Iranian border, it could join a Syrian-led eastern front that would include also Jordan and the PLO. Such a front could easily subject the still-fragile Israeli–Egyptian peace process to unbearable tensions.

Another alarming dimension of the Iranian–Iraqi rapprochement of August 1975 was that it had been encouraged and to an extent facilitated by U.S. diplomacy. From the U.S. point of view, it was important to stabilize the Gulf area through, on the one hand, Iranian influence in all the smaller and weaker littoral states, and, on the other hand, a détente between the two major military powers of the area—Iran and Iraq. Although Israel could understand this logic, it also could not fail to realize that the U.S. pursuit of stability ran contrary to Israel's own vested interest in a continued instability in Arab–Iranian relations. By a bizarre twist of political vicissitudes, this also happened to be the Syrian interest (though not the interest of Syria's Soviet mentors). In a word, the two elements of Israel's alliance policy—the superpower (U.S.) dimension and the regional (Iranian) dimension—were becoming somewhat incompatible.[41]

Such forebodings regarding the future of the regional dimension of this alliance edifice were only reinforced by the effects of the simultaneous changes taking place in Ethiopia. When the octogenerian emperor, Haile Selassie, was deposed in 1974, the pro-Soviet military regime that took over effected in Ethiopia a revolution that, at least in its cruel methods, resembled that of the Khmer Rouge in Cambodia. Relations with Israel were, of course, severed immediately. Consequently, the Israeli nightmare of a complete Arab or hostile control of the Red Sea seemed on the verge of becoming a reality.

Yet this grim picture of the erosion and collapse of positions that Israel had worked so hard to develop over the previous two decades did not last long. In 1978, it transpired, Israeli–Ethiopian relations had been resumed, though secretly. The Mengistu Meriam regime in Ethiopia that had replaced Selassie's imperial rule proved to be a menace to its Arab neighbors as well. In addition, its weakness encouraged the Shifta tribes of Eritrea to increase their efforts to break away from the Ethiopian state, which had imposed itself on them for centuries. Subsequently, the Mengistu regime sought Israeli military advice and assistance. As Dayan told King Hassan of Morocco in September 1977:

> Israel was not involved [as the king argued] in the war in Ethiopia but in assistance to the Ethiopians. We have a moral obligation toward them. They have in the past helped us with port services when our ships and planes were in distress. Their attitude toward us was friendly, we would not turn them down now that they are in trouble and ask for arms. The king [of Morocco] argued that we have to take note of changes. Soon Ethiopia will be without any ports and perhaps Israel should reverse its alliances and seek the friendship of the moderate element in the [Eritrean] Liberation Front along the coast [of the Red Sea]. I replied" [Dayan concludes, that] "in my view this would not succeed. The [Eritrean] Liberation Movement was already part of the Arab League and it would not come to our help if we needed it.[42]

Meanwhile, great changes had begun to take place in Iran, also. The shah's seemingly stable regime lost control. His lifelong enemy the Ayatollah Khomeini returned from exile and became the ruler of the country. This development at first shocked the Israelis, since it seemed to lead to a complete loss of relations with the Iranians. Khomeini and his lieutenants had had friendly relations with the PLO and, having expelled all the Israelis and many Pharsi Jews, hastened in fact to hand over the Israeli mission's compound in Teheran to Yasser Arafat in person.[43]

As in the case of Ethiopia, however, it did not take long for this about-face to lead to a strange new mode of tacit rapprochement with the Jewish state. Like Ethiopia, Iran was a menace to its neighbors. If anything, the Iranian brand of militant Shi'ism seemed to threaten the very foundation of the existing order throughout the Middle East. The first country to fear that was, of course, Iraq, which could also lead itself to believe that the chaos inside Iran presented an opportunity to reverse the terms of the 1975 agreement (signed at the peak of Iranian power) in Iraq's favor. This led to the fateful Iraqi decision in September 1979 to invade Iranian territory. In turn, an intermittent war between the two countries became a more or less permanent fixture of the Middle East scene. The Iraqi army was thus pinned down far from the Israeli border by Iran, not under the leadership of the seemingly benign and reasonable shah but, rather, under the reign of a religious fanatic preaching a holy war against the Jewish state. Before long, moreover, Khomeini's Iran turned back to Israel for arms and spare parts. This did not lead to the resumption of relations on the scale of the previous decade. In fact, these relations remained confined to limited dealings through third parties—all the more so since they aroused a great deal of consternation in the United States.[44] In addition, Iran continued to support the most militant wings of the Shi'ite minority in Lebanon, which ultimately succeeded in driving the IDF out of that country. Nevertheless, it is difficult to ignore the strength and fundamental durability of the Israeli connection with Iran (and Ethiopia). The root of this connection was neither history, nor ideology, nor indeed any cultural affinity. There have never been domestic constituencies in any of these countries for close relations with the other countries in the equation. Whatever the regime, however, the response of all these countries to the age-old rules of the balance-of-power game—in itself a variant of what might be called deterrence diplomacy—keeps leading them into each other's embrace. The mutual interest may be limited, but it has been real enough all along.

The Use, Misuse, and Abuse of Force

During 1974–84, as in previous periods (with the possible exception of 1949–56), Israel did not have a clearly spelled-out doctrine elaborating its preferences concerning the use of force. To a certain extent, the answer to the question of when and how the Jewish state would resort to force was implied by the lessons it learned from the October war. Because of the very high price Israel had paid for not having preempted Egypt and/or Syria, the guiding principle in its strategic posture during 1974–84 was "never again." The implications of such a disposition were starkly clear: Israel would not allow the Arabs to begin the next war; it would not desist from escalating to the very limits of its capacity if and when hostilities broke out; and if it were left with no alternative, it would not shrink from using force in both a counterforce and a countercity fashion.

This was not a doctrine but a deeply rooted disposition—an assumption on which policymakers acted. It was, above all, the overarching principle inspiring planning, training, and weapons procurement. The actual decision whether or not, how, where, and for what purpose force would be used was not taken, at least not by the cabinet. But the definition of casi belli and, in particular, the operative assumptions of the IDF left no doubts about the prevailing order of preference. The upper echelons of the IDF simply would not let the politicians present it once again with an impossible situation and then proceed to place the blame on it. The IDF now proceeded on the assumption that, given a reasonable justification, the politicians would be willing to take bold decisions; thus it prepared itself for all possible contingencies.

The initial war scenario that inspired IDF planning was a composite image of past wars. Indeed, in retrospect it appears to have been unforgivably lacking in imagination. The next war could be a worse variant of the last—namely, a combined attempt by Syria, Iraq, Jordan, Egypt, and—to a smaller degree—other Arab states to engage Israel in a war in which it would be unable to achieve a clear decision. The war would begin, if the Arabs had their way, with a simultaneous air and ground attack on all fronts and a missile attack on Israel's civilian centers with a view to disrupting the mobilization of reserves. The purpose of such a war would not be to destroy Israel in one blow but, rather, to bleed it and perhaps bog it down in an interminable war of attrition. The Israelis assumed that for fear of either an Israeli resort to nuclear weapons or, alternatively, U.S. involvement on the side of Israel, the Arabs would not actually seek to penetrate the heart of the Jewish state. Rather, they would confine their efforts to a protracted kind of attrition on all fronts—a war of the type that several Arab strategists were actually preaching in public.[45]

From the Israeli point of view, such a scenario would be the prelude to the final collapse of the Zionist edifice. Therefore, it had to be prevented by all means. The alternative that Israel preferred is not very difficult to imagine. As soon as it became clear that the balance of forces was tilting heavily in the Arabs' favor, that the Arabs had transgressed one or another of Israel's red lines, or that there were indications of an imminent Arab attack, the IDF would preempt. The IAF would strike first at the armed forces, in particular at air forces and air defense systems of the main adversary, while the ground forces would strike at a number of identified weak points in the adversary's lines and seek to effect deep penetration—vertical encirclements leading ultimately to a major battle of decision in which the main force of the leading adversary would be annihilated. All this had to take no longer than a few days since the rest of the Arab world would be watching. If this first strike fizzled out, lost momentum without a clear decision, other Arab states might be tempted to join the battle and open other fronts. To deter them from doing so, the IDF would have to maintain substantial concentrations of forces on inactive fronts as well. But if the war at the one chosen front lost momentum with a clear-cut victory, even such an intrawar exercise of deterrence might not be adequate.[46]

This, broadly speaking, was the dominant war scenario during 1974–75. Following the interim agreement with Egypt (Sinai II) the likelihood that Egypt would be the main adversary sharply declined. Attention shifted to the so-called banana front scenario—namely, to a theater of war stretching from the Mediterranean coast of Lebanon through Syria and Jordan and including Iraq and the PLO. This was, of course, a far less worrisome scenario than the previous one. However, given the rapid buildup of forces of the countries concerned and the fact that Egypt had not yet been totally removed from the war coalition, it was fearsome enough. Then came, in quick progression, the civil war in Lebanon, Sadat's peace initiative, and the Iraqi invasion of Iran. The first of these developments removed Lebanon from the danger list and seemed to have dissipated Syrian power as well. The second development removed Egypt from the Arab war coalition so completely that Egypt ceased to be a top-priority Israeli strategic concern. Finally, the third of these developments led to a near doubling of the Iraqi order of battle (to more than twenty divisions) and to its gain of immense practical experience. This concern, however, may have been substantially offset by the likelihood that the Iran–Iraq conflict ensured that, for years to come, Iraq would be too worried by the possibility of an Iranian attack to remove any significant part of its own forces from the vicinity of the Iranian border. The banana front thus shrank, and the conventional military dimension of the Arab–Israeli conflict seemed to have been suddenly reduced nearly to a bilateral affair in which Israel and Syria faced each other alone.[47]

If this were really the only important facet of the conflict, Israel's ability to maintain credible conventional deterrence would not have been in any doubt for many years. Assad's Syria, to be sure, declared openly that it was determined to achieve within a few years a "strategic equilibrium," a Syrian term for rough parity with Israel. This was logical since the obverse of parity would be Syrian inferiority and, quite possible, the need to sue for peace or at least to disembark from the Ba'ath republic's traditional commitment to fight Israel and Zionism. In the mid- and late-1970s, however, the ability of the Syrians economically and demographically to achieve such an ambitious goal seemed to be in doubt. Hence Israel could theoretically freeze its tacit slide down the slippery nuclear slope and act on the assumption that its conventional deterrence would be adequate for several years.

In practice, however, the Jewish state still faced three major—and ever-increasing—threats, both above and below (on the spectrum of violence) the threat of a general conventional war: (1) the threat of international terrorism, (2) the threat of an Arab nuclear capability, and (3) the political-military threat posed by the PLO in Lebanon. The first two of these threats found their answer in surgical, precise, and (mostly) effective uses of force. The third, however, presented Israel with grave and not entirely manageable problems.

The struggle against international terrorism had reached its peak already in the last year before the 1973 war. Broadly speaking, it entailed both offensive and defensive moves. The defensive part included the stationing of security personnel on board all El Al planes and in all Jewish and Israeli institutions throughout the West, as well as in Africa and southeast Asia. The offensive (apart from reprisal operations in Jordan and Lebanon) primarily took the form of unannounced and never fully admitted assassinations of PLO operatives abroad. Whereas the literature on this dramatic topic places the emphasis on the revenge aspect of this operation, the real purpose was far more political than emotional. Israel, in its own perceptions an island in a "boiling hot" sea of hatred,[48] cannot afford to be cut off from the West. If Israelis would not be able to travel abroad, if tourists would not be able to visit Israel, if Israeli tradespeople and diplomats would not be safe on foreign lands, then the Arabs would have won a major economic, political, and—primarily—psychological victory. It was thus essential to ensure that the risk to Israelis abroad would not be greater than the risks to any other foreigners abroad. Fearful of Arab reaction at a time when Arab power was soaring as a result of the rise in oil prices, most foreign governments tacitly collaborated with anti-Israeli terrorist activities. Terrorists who were arrested would be tried but would then have their sentences commuted and be expelled from the Western country in question, be it France, Britain, Italy, the Federal Republic of Germany, Greece, Sweden, Norway, Denmark, the Netherlands, or Spain. Israel, therefore, had no choice but to act unilaterally, even if that could lead—in the event of a failure—to some short-term friction with friendly governments on whose sovereign territory undercover Israelis would use firearms.

The ultimate purpose of these activities was to establish a rule of reciprocity: if Israelis and Jews were not safe in Europe, then Palestinians and their collaborators also would not be safe. More specifically, the Israeli rationale was not very different from the logic of Israeli reprisals closer to home: liquidating Palestinian terrorist operatives in Europe would create a situation in which these operatives would not be able to assume that they could operate safely. They would become hunted targets; they would have to preoccupy themselves with their own personal safety, which would demand so much of their attention that their efficacy would be substantially reduced.

This rationale of the Israeli letter bomb and personal liquidation campaign against Palestinian operatives in Europe during 1970–73 was the epitome of a tactically offensive but strategically defensive posture—that is, deterrence by punishment. Though involving a taxing intelligence operation while yielding only a handful of assassinations, though leading to several notable failures (such as the capture of a Mossad hit team in Lillehammer, Norway, on July 21, 1973), the ultimate cost-benefit ratio of this strategy from Israel's point of view was positive: Palestinian hijacking, bombing, and shooting operations against Israeli and Jewish targets sharply declined in frequency within several months of the initiation of this counterterrorist offensive.[49]

As with other Israeli successes, however, the result merely caused the adversaries—in this case the PLO—to search for other methods of carrying on the struggle against the Jewish state. Thus after three years of almost complete quiet (summer 1973–summer 1976) on this worldwide front, the encounter was resumed at a higher level of risk. On June 27, 1976, a party of mainly German members of the Baader Meinhof group, taking advantage of the inefficient security screening at the Athens, Greece, airport, hijacked an Air France passenger plan with 246 passengers, most of them Jews, and directed it to Libya and then to Entebbe airport in Uganda. The hijackers demanded the release of a great number of PLO and other terrorists from Israeli and German jails. They also separated Jews from non-Jews and released the latter while threatening to execute the former if their demands were not met within a few days. The event presented the Rabin cabinet with a seemingly no-win situation. If it were to resist the pressures of the hijackers (and of the families of their victims), the Jewish passengers would be liquidated. This would make the hijackers' cause look terrible—which it did, anyway—but at a prohibitive cost to Israel. On the other hand, if Israel were to meet the hijackers' demands, it would undercut entirely the hard-won credibility of its antiterrorist deterrence posture.

Initially it seemed that a military solution such as Israel had applied in the case of the hijacking of a Sabena (Belgian national airline) plane—namely, to storm the plane—was out of the question because of the distance of Uganda from Israel, the hostility of the surroundings of Entebbe, and the fact that the entire route to Uganda passed over hostile territory. A quick review suggested, however, that a military operation involving a high, but still calculated, risk was feasible after all. Thus, having misled the hijackers to believe that it was prepared to deal, the Rabin government ordered the IDF—in conjunction with the Mossad—to attempt a forcible rescue operation. This was carried out with spectacular success on July 4, 1976. It could have easily turned into a disastrous bloodbath, in which case Israel would have suffered a grave defeat. But the Israeli estimate was that ultimately even a fiasco leading to a carnage would have a more positive impact on the solvency of the Israeli deterrence than would yeilding to the hijackers and thus immediatley inviting fresh hijackings and further demands.[50]

One of the chief strategic implications of this rescue operation was that Israel's long-reach capacity had grown to an extent that made every part of the Middle East vulnerable to its punitive strikes. If Israeli soldiers, vehicles, recoilless guns, missiles, first aid and engineering teams, and fighter-bombers could fly all the way to Uganda, land there, carry out an attack, and then retreat, then surely they could cary out similar exploits in virtually every part of the Middle East. In this sense the Entebbe operation on July 4, 1976, and the bombing of Osiraq, the Iraqi nuclear site near Baghdad, on June 7, 1981, were manifestations of a related capacity. Of course, in every other sense they fell into almost opposite categories: whereas the Entebbe rescue was designed to strengthen deterrence against the smallest micro kind of blackmail, the bombing of Osiraq five years later was designed to strengthen deterrence against the largest, most ominous macro variety of blackmail.

The most important strategic assumption underscoring the Israeli decision to bomb the nearly completed, French-built, Iraqi nuclear reactor was that it was a vital Israeli interest to avoid the introduction of nuclear weapons into the Middle East. As has been pointed out in various contexts before, Israel itself has had a basic nuclear potential since the late 1960s. Whether or not this has led to the development of an actual Israeli nuclear arsenal remains a matter for ingenious speculation based on conjecture and not on any real knowledge.[51] The reason for this tight secrecy is, again, the absolute determination of all Israeli governments to date to keep the Middle East a nuclear-free zone. If Israel were to announce the introduction of nuclear weapons into its regular strategic posture, it would incur the wrath of the United States, almost certainly lead to a Soviet nuclear guarantee for their Arab clients—and do all that without being able to effect truly significant cutbacks in its own defense expenditures. A nuclear arsenal, in short, would add another formidable existential risk without reducing the burden of dealing with an already extensive inventory of more mundane threats.

The logical corollary to such a calculus was that Israel could not allow Iraq to possess a nuclear capacity, either. If Iraq were to go nuclear, with or without declaring so, Israel, too, would have no choice but to follow suit. Otherwise the Jewish state would lay itself bare to nuclear blackmail by an Arab adversary that had been notorious for its militancy, warlike record, and commitment to the most extreme version of anti-Zionism; indeed, for a variety of reasons, it had not even accepted the armistice agreements of 1949, let alone subsequent cease-fire agreements. Moreover, following Sadat's peace initiative, Iraq hosted in December 1979 an Arab summit meeting that declared a virtual boycott of Egypt unless and until it broke its peace treaty with the Jewish state.

If both Israel and Iraq were to go public with first-strike nuclear arsenals, both would find the temptation to preempt virtually irresistible. If Iraq won this deadly contest, Israel would be liquidated. If Israel won it, the damage to its international standing, to its relations with world Jewry—indeed, to its self-image—would be irreparable. Thus if an Iraqi nuclear program were allowed to progress, there was a reasonable likelihood that both Iraq and Israel would have to develop credible second-strike capabilities. Could they? Did Israel have the wherewithal and the geographic ingredients for such a program? Would it not be ultimately more costly financially than the Jewish state's burden of maintaining a conventional deterrence?

Inspired by such considerations, the Israelis watched the French, the Italians, and the Pakistanis provide Iraq with the technology and know-how necessary to build a reactor ultimately capable of producing small nuclear bombs in small quantities. The Israeli authorities pleaded with these governments, apparently also threatening to take matters into their own hands; they also employed a variety of methods in a vain attempt to dissuade professional personnel from taking part in the Tamouz I project (as the Iraqis referred to the construction of the nuclear plant). When all this did not help and it became clear that within a year or so the Iraqi reactor would become "hot," Prime Minister Begin, Ariel Sharon, then minister of agriculture, and General Eitan, the chief of staff, decided to order the IAF to carry out the mission.

One consideration that apparently added weight to the decision was that virtually every remotely relevant country in the world could be assumed to be tacitly in favor. An Iraqi nuclear arsenal, to put it bluntly, would pose a grave threat to all of Iraq's neighbors: Turkey, Syria, Iran, the Gulf states, Saudi Arabia, and even Egypt (despite the fact that it has no common border with Iraq). Such a proliferation of nuclear weapons would run contrary to the policy of both the United States and the Soviet Union, which had scrupulously struggled to prevent proliferation. Thus even though a chorus of international criticism of the attack could be taken for granted, in the final analysis Israel could assume that by attacking the Iraqi nuclear reactor, it would be making a contribution on behalf of many other countries to the cause of preventing a nuclear holocaust.

The attack was carried out on a Sunday, when most of the French personnel working on the site were enjoying their weekend rest. Its timing was also designed to stop the work before an explosion could lead to nuclear fallout in the vicinity of the reactor. Consequently, the number of casualties in this operation was negligible; the damage was material only. Following the blowing up of Osiraq, Israel, through Minister of Defense Sharon, declared any attempt by an Arab country to introduce nuclear weapons into the Middle East a casus belli from the Israeli point of view. Given the Israeli experience with other casi belli, this too will probably falter one day. Meanwhile, however, Israel's conventional deterrence has been greatly strengthened and, ipso facto, the moment in which Israel itself would have to go public with the bomb has been deferred.[52]

Contrary to the Israeli success in strengthening deterrence against worldwide terrorism, on the one hand, and against potential nuclear blackmail, on the other hand, Israel's attempts to establish a credible and successful deterrence against subwar threats of the type perpetrated by the PLO along the Lebanon border constituted a sad story of failure, for three main reasons:

1. The PLO, which should have been deterred, was split between elements that wished to respond to the Israeli threats and elements that deliberately sought to provoke Israeli retaliation.

2. The means the PLO used—light firearms, light artillery, multiple rocket launchers, RPG bazookas, and the like—constituted an elusive quality that could easily dodge most Israeli attempts to retaliate.

3. Israel had a vulnerable population along the Lebanon border, whose ability to withstand the rigors of the encounter with the PLO was far smaller than the ability of the PLO to survive the fury of Israeli retaliation.

The PLO was and still is a confederative umbrella, lumping together in uneasy coexistence a great variety of organizations and orientations. Over the years a mainstream headed by Chairman Yasser Arafat (who is also the chairman of Fateh, the main constituent organization inside the PLO) has struggled to move away from an emphasis on an armed struggle toward a more political-diplomatic posture. The use of force for this part of the organization was not a strategic but a tactical proposition, whose purpose was to strengthen recruitment as well as to enhance international recognition and thus to affix the struggle of the Palestinians on the short list of burning issues on the international agenda. Ultimately, this current in the PLO hoped, the organization would succeed in becoming a recognized party to the Middle East peace process and would thereby gain independent statehood.

This PLO mainstream has always been challenged, however, by a persistent fringe of critics who reject any idea of historic compromise with the "Zionist entity" (as they refer to Israel) and who have continued to preach the merits of a relentless armed struggle. Some proponents of this thesis, for example, George Habash of the PFLP or Naif Hawatmeh of the Popular Democratic Front for the Liberation of Palestine (PDFLP) or even Salah Halaf ("Abu Iyad"), the critical deputy of Arafat himself, were genuine in arguing for the armed struggle. Many among Arafat's critics, however, people such as Abu Moussa, Zoheir Mohsein, Ahmed Jibril, and Hasan al Bana (" Abu Nidal") have been known to act as agents for a variety of Arab governments (countries such as Syria, Iraq, Libya). These governments were eager to prevent any compromise between Israel and the Palestinians because this would be contrary either to their national interest or to the current regime's interest.

If the voluntary and loose structure of the PLO has enabled factions with such diverse interests to coexist within it, the utter dependence of the organization on the Arab world has made it very sensitive to the criticisms of the radicals and rejectionists. Yasser Arafat may have been convinced for more than a decade that if he were to announce the abandonment of the armed struggle on the one hand and his willingness to recognize Israel's right to exist (and thus to accept the legitimacy of partitioning Palestine between Jews and Arabs) on the other hand, he would immediately gain all the empathy and support he needed in the West. But the Palestinian leader has evidently acted on the assumption that previous attempts by other Palestinians (such as Said Hammami, Isam Sartawi, Aziz Shehadeh, Fahd Qawasmeh, and Za'afar al Masri, to name but a few) to preach this line have ended with their assassination. Consequently, the chairman of the PLO has had to maneuver uneasily between moderation and militancy.

When it came to Israel's Lebanon border, Arafat has had to walk a tightrope between being deterred and escalating hostilities. He evidently knew that if PLO pressure on Israel became unbearable, the IDF would enter Lebanon and eject the Palestinians. Israeli Defense Minister Moshe Dayan had made this plain as early as 1971. If Arafat were to yield to such a threat, however, he would lose his leadership, if not his life, and his critics in the PLO would then pursue the pressure against Israel. Arafat's choice, then, was between riding the crest and being swept by it. He opted, not illogically, for the former course of action, and thus ensured that escalation along the Israeli–Lebanese border would continue apace.

These political factors set a clear limit to Israel's ability to deter the PLO, whose natural choice of military means made Israel's task even more complicated. To lay ambush to a school bus, to set a rocket launcher and aim it at a city center or a village, to send a deadly salvo of rockets with an eight-mile range, to lay mines on main roads or seize schoolchildren in the school compound requires very few weapons, very few—and not necessarily very well trained—troops, virtually no command structure, and very rudimentary logistics. This is the main strength of guerrilla tactics. It is this ability to gain tremendous attention, spread fear and demoralization, preoccupy the adversary, and get away that renders such actions the most suitable strategy for a weak party facing a formidable opponent.

For years most official Israeli spokespersons continued to dismiss the PLO as an utter failure in terms of its proved ability to cause harm. The criticism was not entirely without foundation, given the failure of the PLO to establish a base on the West Bank or even to survive in Jordan. In the final analysis, however, the PLO, resorting time and again to harassment; to hit-and-run tactics; to the cold-blooded, morally despicable, but politically effective aiming of fire at civilians—in short, to precisely those methods in which it had a comparative advantage, has succeeded in sapping Israel's energies almost as much as any of the other Jewish state's key adversaries: Syria, Egypt, and Jordan.[53] As the encounter escalated, Israel's ability to exact a price from the PLO gradually increased. At first, in the late 1960s and early 1970s, Israeli retaliations in southern Lebanon tended to be a bit like hitting the head of a tiny pin with a disproportionately huge hammer. Very few PLO fighters lost their lives; most, in fact, retreated whenever an IDF party pursued them. It all appeared singularly cowardly and, in micro terms, may well have been precisely that. The aggregate impact, however, was positive from the PLO's point of view. Gradually, while resisting the Israelis, the Palestinians established for themselves an autonomous region of virtual self-rule in an area stretching from the Israeli border to Beirut along the Mediterannean coast and covering a wide patch eastward along the Israeli border.

This process was checked in 1975–76 by the Lebanon civil war, which drew most of the PLO force from the south to the center and north of Lebanon. Then the Israeli red line, setting a limit to the advance of the Syrian forces in Lebanon, created a new situation. The PLO was anxious to minimize its dependence on Syrian goodwill. Israel, by deterring the Syrian army from approaching the Israeli border, unwittingly gave the PLO a no-man's-land between Syrian and Israeli lines, in which Lebanese authority did not exist except in name; therefore, a PLO authority could be consolidated conveniently. Thus ensconced in southern Lebanon, the PLO could resume its attacks against the Israeli Galilee. IDF retaliation intensified and ultimately culminated in a mini-invasion, Operation Litani, in March 1978. During the operation, the IDF, hoping to avoid a clash with the Syrians, moved slowly and cumbersomely over a wide front from south to north. This tactical error gave the PLO every opportunity to deny the IDF any battle of decision (in which the PLO did not stand the glimmer of a chance) and simply take off. The brunt of the damage wrought in this encounter, consequently, was suffered not by the Palestinians but by the Shi'ite population of the area.

Under heavy U.S. pressure, Israel withdrew the IDF several weeks later, leaving behind a belt of mainly Christian proxies under the command of renegade Major Sa'ad Haddad and an area under the control of the U.N. Interim Force in Lebanon (UNIFIL). This double barrier forced the PLO to change its emphasis. Denied direct access to the Israeli border, it had to move from hit-and-run guerrilla tactics to an increasing use of artillery. The fire was deliberately directed against the Jewish population of the Galilee across the border, and it was shot above the heads of the U.N. and Haddad forces. This new emphasis was not to the PLO's advantage; it made it easier for the IDF to hit back with greater efficacy than previously. But the mobility of PLO gunnery, especially of the Soviet-made *katyusha* (multiple rocket launcher), was still quite high; as a result, the IDF still had to invest tremendous efforts in order to strike back effectively.

Naturally, such a continuous, protracted encounter, which gradually assumed the style of a war of attrition, defies any distinction between first and second strikes. At the same time, it does lend itself to an evaluation through the distinctions between flexible response and massive retaliation and between counterforce and countercity targeting. As a result of its failure to deter the PLO, Israel was drawn into an ever-increasing escalation, both horizontal and vertical. Flexible (tit-for-tat) response made no sense, since it was precisely the rules of the game that would be favored by the PLO. If there was any way to stop the fire, it was only through a deliberate, indeed vicious, disproportion between the level of violence used by the PLO and the level of violence in the IDF's response. This could, perhaps, create unbearable pressure on the civilian population in the area, which in turn might attempt to force the PLO to stop its fire.

Moreover, the PLO deliberately sought cover in densely populated areas. Knowing that the Israelis were, for moral and political reasons, chary of hitting civilians, the PLO deliberately turned Lebanese and Palestinian civilians into hostages. Either they would shield the PLO from IDF retaliation, or their suffering could be used against Israel in the PLO's propaganda campaign, a crucial instrument in its struggle to keep its objectives on the international agenda. The result was that Israel's massive retaliation soon turned into a countercity type of response, as it had under comparable circumstances in the Jordan valley and the Suez Canal Zone. When even this did not stop the PLO, Israel was gradually impelled to escalate horizontally—to expand the area on which IDF retaliation was inflicted from the south of Lebanon to the north and ultimately to the capital, Beirut—where the PLO concentrated all its headquarters and main depots—as well. The variety of methods used in this counteroffensive included massive aerial bombardments, shelling from the sea, deep penetration raids, and ambushes by small parties of crack IDF infantry within the areas of PLO control. All this forced the PLO to dig in deeper and to acquire more devastating weapons itself.

This gradual modification in the means used by the PLO had two cardinal results. First it forced the PLO gradually to conventionalize itself. Under the pressure of Israeli retaliation, the PLO had to acquire more and heavier weapons, which could only be absorbed effectively by a more regular organizational structure. Thus during the 1978–82 period the PLO increasingly evolved a semiconventional command and logistical structure until, shortly before the Israeli invasion in June 1982, it actually carried out a conventional exercise in which troops stormed positions under artillery cover. In turn, a more conventional PLO became an easier prey for the IDF. At last, it seemed, the IDF would ultimately be able to force the PLO to cease its operations or face annihilation by the IDF's incomparably superior conventional capabilities. From this viewpoint the escalating encounter with the PLO was a boon to Israel's deterrence in the area; from another perspective, however, it was a source of even greater danger. Desperate, convinced that a major showdown with the IDF was a foregone conclusion, the PLO developed capabilities that could wreak havoc on the Israeli side of the border. At this point it is well worth recalling the third factor accounting for the failure of Israeli deterrence against the PLO in Lebanon: the composition of the Jewish population of the Galilee.

About half the population in the vicinity of the Lebanon border on the Israeli side is Arab. For self-evident reasons, they were never subject to any PLO harassment. A second segment of this population are kibbutzim—Jewish collective farms—constituting one of the most skillful, resourceful, determined, and able segments of the Israeli population. Most of the men in the kibbutzim are veterans of the best combat units of the IDF. The women and the youth are highly motivated as well. In short, this was a population that could withstand a long period of trouble even if there were occasional casualties and even if they—including babies and the elderly—had to spend half their time underground in shelters.

The third and last component of Israel's Galilee population are mainly immigrants from Middle East and North African countries who arrived there in the course of the 1950s. Initially placed in the area more or less arbitrarily by the government, which sought to populate the border in order to consolidate it, this population was far less capable of standing up to the pressures of the PLO. The reasons are complex: these immigrants are less ideologically committed, less able to comprehend the larger meaning of the encounter with the PLO, less well educated, with lower average levels of employment and standard of living—and thus of satisfaction. The PLO planners, knowing this, deliberately—and wisely—directed their fire against locales such as Shlomi, Ma'alot, Safed, Hazor, and Kiryat Shemonah, where this type of population was concentrated. Successive Israeli governments attempted to combat demoralization there by greater public attention and a more generous allocation of public resources. But as the escalation of the encounter between the IDF and the PLO neared its peak during 1978–81, the impact on the population became increasingly devastating. At last, in the mid-July 1981, a mini–war of attrition with the PLO across the border, taking the form of vast shelling by the PLO of thirty-three Israeli communities, led to what all Israeli governments since independence had feared most: a stampede—a flight of most of the population from the town of Kiryat Shemonah. Prime Minister Begin, who visited the nearly deserted town, ordered a cease-fire, which was negotiated indirectly with the PLO. Begin knew this but had made up his mind to stop the fire and to prepare for an all-out war. The Israeli decision to invade Lebanon in June 1982 was thus rooted in an acknowledged failure to deter the PLO. Massive retaliation and countercity bombing and shelling had failed to solve the problem. Though incomparably weaker from the purely military point of view, the PLO had succeeded in turning the threat of hitting the vulnerable part of the Israeli population of the Galilee into a formidable club with which to deter Israel from punitive actions against the Palestinians. Israel's immediate response was the acceptance of a cease-fire under adverse conditions. When Menachem Begin ordered the IDF to respect this humiliating outcome, however, he was already resolved to order an initiated, first-strike invasion of Lebanon.[54]

Politics versus Strategy

One of the most striking features of the 1974–84 period was the degree to which the domestic political debate came to influence the main choices, decisions, and preferences of Israeli strategy. As the foregoing discussion has pointed out, there had always been fierce debates in Israel concerning foreign policy in general and national security in particular. The topic, after all, relates to the most urgent, burdensome, critical, and costly set of issues on the national agenda; it would be surprising, therefore, if there were no major differences of opinion. Before the 1970s, however, and to a large extent before the 1973 war, the volume and impact of large-scale public participation in the national debate concerning strategic issues were limited, almost subterranean. After the 1973 war, all hell broke loose. Since then, foreign policy in Israel has become the most salient source of division and debate in the political process. It overshadows the left-right debate concerning the distribution of resources. It is far more salient than the Sephardic-Ashkenazi friction. It even seems to be more dominant than Israel's most durable internal cleavage—that which separates the orthodox from the nonorthodox parts of the Jewish population. It is the main axis of political exchange, a daily diet for even the least politically aware segments of the population, the ultimate test by which political leadership is evaluated by the electorate.[55]

The extent to which this has impinged on Israel's ability to deter the Arabs is impossible to tell. It is possible only to point out briefly those points in the decade under review at which the domestic political debate at either the decision-making or the popular level affected the course of Israeli strategy. As a starting point it seems evident that the discussion should focus on the domestic reaction to the 1973 war. Here three distinct impacts of the domestic process can be discerned: (1) the impact of the prolonged period of national service on Israel's bargaining position in the disengagement talks; (2) the impact of the pressures of families on the government's negotiating stance during this period; and, (3) above all, the impact of the protest movement on Israel's posture during the immediate aftermath of the war and for years afterwards.

The prolonged national service of some 150,000 Israelis during the six months following the Yom Kippur War imposed a heavy direct burden on the defense budget, removed the prime segment of the labor force from any productive pursuit, and was therefore a major source of worry for the nation's economists. Beyond this, it also generated a significant degree of dissatisfaction. The slogan in the air was "equal burden-sharing." That was undoubtedly the government's purpose, too, but it was easier said than done. The IDF has never been as egalitarian as its ethos suggests. Its strategy is based on the cultivation of excellence. In many minute tactical details the fundamental guideline is an unspoken assumption that in every squad, company, battalion, battery, vessel, or group of pilots, there is a small kernel of aces, of leaders, of those who would and could do everything humanly possible to achieve the mission—and do it well.

This assumption of the existence of a leading cadre, though not entirely spelled out, operates at all levels. Consequently, it is invariably a relatively small number of individuals who are called on time and again to do more—to take greater risks and to pay more dearly in terms of their private life and economic status. This was also the case in the six months of negotiations immediately after the Yom Kippur War. The result was that those who served in front-line combat units, which suffered the greatest number of casualties, were also kept on active duty longer than most others. The result was a gradual buildup of discontent even in some of the IDF's best reserve units. Golda Meir's cabinet, fully aware of this, was consequently less prone to escalate the war of attrition that accompanied the disengagement negotiations and more eager to conclude the negotiations than was beneficial from the point of view of the national interest. In other words, although the IDF did have the power to enable to government to drive a hard bargain, the government—for fear of escalation and the need for larger mobilization—would not permit the IDF to use its firepower to the maximum extent.

An even greater impact on decision making at the highest level during these critical days was brought to bear by demonstrations of bereaved parents and families of prisoners of war and missing soldiers. The latter, a relatively small group, demonstrated noisily, literally besieged individual decision makers and thus created perpetual psychological pressure that, by Meir's and Dayan's own admission, influenced their conduct of the negotiations. Making this phenomenon even more noteworthy was the evident burden of guilt on the shoulders of the prime minister and the minister of defense, both of whom were tormented by doubts concerning their own responsibility; the abuse hurled at them constantly by this small group of citizens may have affected them even more than they would have cared to admit.

The most important development from this point of view, however, was undoubtedly the protest movement, which mushroomed after the Yom Kippur War. It began with a one-man demonstration by a reserve captain named Motti Ashkenazi. He had been the commander of "Budapest," the only Israeli *moutsav* ("stronghold") on the Suez Canal not to have been either deserted or overrun by the Egyptians. For a while this gave him something of the status of a hero and endowed him with unusual authority in the public eye. Blaming the minister of defense and the prime minister for the Yom Kippur debacle, he declared that he would not end his vigil unless and until the minister of defense accepted personal responsibility and resigned his post.

Ashkenazi's demand for a thorough review of the entire defense policy was not entirely coherent. In retrospect, his dedication was more impressive than the coherence of his arguments. But his protest took place against the background of a deep feeling of malaise and frustration. For six years the government had argued that Israel had never had it so good; how, then, could the same government explain the fact that a war had broken out in which close to three thousand Israelis had lost their lives? Consequently, Ashkenazi's lone vigil soon turned into a nationwide movement, which gave vent to a great deal of pent-up frustration without really offering any clear program except for one concrete demand: the appointment of a judicial commission of inquiry which would look into the reasons for the *mechdal* ("inaction") involved in not meeting the challenge of the war more effectively.

The pressure helped. The cabinet appointed a panel (the Agranat commission) consisting of supreme court judges and retired chiefs of staff. This turned the matter of responsibility for the war into subjudicial proceedings and thus took the wind out of the sails of the protesters. When the Agranat commission published its conclusions, it turned out that the main responsibility was hurled, not at Dayan and Meir—the main culprits, according to the protesters—but at the incumbent chief of staff, Lieutenant General David Elazar, who was asked to resign. When he did, the pressure on Dayan and Meir rose again (though not to nearly the same level as previously) and ultimately brought about their resignations as well.

It is difficult to say exactly how all this affected the government's position in its negotiations with Egypt, Syria, and the United States. It can be assumed, however, that the memory of the demonstrations, of public discontent, and of the commission of inquiry continued to lurk in the background of all major Israeli decisions on strategic matters.[56] One immediate result of the protest of 1973–74 was the advent to the premiership of Yitzhak Rabin, the chief of staff in the 1967 war. As the ambassador to Washington until shortly before the October war, he could not be directly implicated in any responsibility for either the origins or the course of the 1973 war. Rabin was also the first-ever sabra (native Israeli) to be appointed to this post. As such, he symbolized to many Israelis a long-overdue changing of the guard from the doctrinaire, overbearing, opinionated, and vindictive founders to a younger and supposedly more open-minded generation of enlightened, pragmatic, and sophisticated leaders.

Yet it was not long before Rabin's popularity began to wane. An introverted and taciturn individual, a poor speaker in an age when television image sometimes counts for more than sound decision making, Rabin generated an atmosphere of melancholy and depression. He was evidently at loggerheads with Shimon Peres, his rival for the prime ministership and the minister of defense in the government. Rabin's cabinet introduced a series of harsh economic measures designed to offset the economic impact of the 1973 war. Rabin proved unable to stem the tide of illegal settlements in the West Bank, and he had the misfortune of being a Labor prime minister at a time when a number of scandals involving top Labor leaders became known to the public. Consequently, he seemed weak and unable to give the country the buoyancy and self-confidence that had been its hallmark until the 1973 war.

In objective terms, Rabin's record in foreign affairs and national security was actually very impressive. He stood up to Henry Kissinger's pressures when the latter seemed to be more eager to obtain an Egyptian–Israeli agreement than a settlement with which Israel could live in peace. Yet he did not let this dispute with the United States turn into a real rupture; in the face of the U.S. threat of an "agonizing reappraisal," he kept his composure and ultimately brought the United States back into the negotiations. This led to the interim (Sinai II) agreement with Egypt, which removed the Egyptians from the Arab war coalition and greatly reduced the likelihood of war in the near future. He negotiated with Syria the red line understanding of April 1976 and thus seemed, at least for a while, to have contained the emerging problem of the Syrian–Palestinian–Lebanese nexus. He succeeded in obtaining from the United States not only a steady flow of economic assistance but also an impressive array of weapons systems. Above all, he was in charge when the government took the risky decision to raid Entebbe. None of these achievements, however, was enough to eradicate the melancholic and inept atmosphere that the prime minister seemed to radiate. Consequently, despite his very respectable record, Rabin's leadership accelerated the decline of the Labor party and paved the way for the advent of Menachem Begin. Significantly, one of Begin's main electoral themes was the need to recover from the state of self-doubt, melancholy, and what Begin saw as defeatism.[57]

During his first three years in office, Begin was evidently successful in improving the atmosphere in Israel. Sadat's visit to Jerusalem in November 1977 was attributed by many Israelis to Begin's success in projecting an image of strength. Moreover, the prime minister's success in bringing about peace with Israel's most important adversary and in dealing forcefully with the PLO (through Operation Litani and the subsequent military pressure on the PLO in Lebanon) as with a variety of world leaders suggested—even to Begin's domestic opponents—that Israel, at last, had a formidable leader again. This new sense of confidence and optimism began to dissipate, however, even before the end of Begin's first term. His inflexible positions with respect to the peace process with Egypt; his poor—by his own admission—management of the government (he publicly admitted *kilkulim*, or "deficiencies," in the government's performance); his increasingly frequent lapses into apathy; his tendency to appeal to the Israeli street through noisy, not particularly dignified diatribes vis-à-vis leaders of countries that were friendly to Israel; the policies of his government in the West Bank—all added up to an increasingly worrisome picture from the point of view of an important segment of Israeli public opinion.

Before long this began to show in Begin's own government. Ezer Weizman resigned his post as minister of defense because he could no longer put up with what he called Begin's "garden of statues"—ministers who would not dare challenge the prime minister on anything.[58] Moshe Dayan, another experienced national security hand in Begin's first cabinet, resigned, too, because he could not agree with the prime minister's policy concerning the West Bank.[59] Unable to find a suitable candidate for Weizman's post, Begin became his own defense minister and, to the astonishment of many Israelis, declared that he could fulfill this post well even if he devoted to it only one day's work a week. In effect, the conduct of national security affairs was increasingly divided between two mediocrites: Chief of Staff Rafael Eitan and retired Brigadier-General Mordechai Zippory, who, because of a bizarre twist of political fortunes, had become—as a civilian member of the Knesset—deputy minister of defense.

The first important decision to be taken by this new policymaking setup was the raid on Osiraq. Here, to the extent that can be judged, there was a clear link between domestic political considerations, on the one hand, and strategy on the other. Begin's critics, especially the leadership of the Labor party, charged that he took the decision on the eve of the general elections merely in order to maximize his political capital. The polls, according to this argument, showed that the Likud might lose the elections; therefore, Begin decided to launch this spectacular coup in order to reverse the trend in public opinion.[60] Others, however, argued that Begin's calculus was far more responsible. He was convinced that if the nuclear plant was not destroyed within a short while, it would become "hot." He thought that his party, the Likud, might lose the elections and he feared that Shimon Peres, the Labor candidate for prime ministership, would not dare bomb the reactor and thus let the opportunity to do so slip by.[61] Which of these theses is more reliable is difficult to say. It does seem likely, however, that while acting in pursuit of the national interest Begin did not overlook the short-term domestic political advantage that would accrue to his party. From any point of view, then, there was an inseparable link between the domestic political backdrop and a cardinal strategic decision that clearly had a far-reaching impact on Israel's deterrence.

During the same election campaign, Begin used provocative and inflammatory language against the president of Syria. He vowed to the people of Kiryat Shemonah and the rest of the Galilee that Israel would see to it that there would be no more PLO rocket attacks. The language was clearly irresponsible. By stating so unambiguously what amounted to a new Israeli definition of casi belli, Begin clearly aroused expectations. As a result, he elevated Israel's commitment to hold Syria and the PLO at bay to a new level, from which there could be no retreat without a serious loss of face. Even many Labor leaders would have admitted that if Israel was not prepared to seek a negotiated political settlement with the PLO (something that few Israelis were prepared to countenance), the Jewish state would have no alternative to another confrontation with that organization. Thus there is a strong case for the argument that a showdown between the IDF and the PLO in southern Lebanon was well-nigh inevitable. Seen in these terms, Begin's inflammatory language merely accelerated an inevitable process. At the same time, it may well be that Begin's irresponsible behavior had the effect of dragging Israel into this confrontation in the wrong way, perhaps at the wrong time, and hence in a manner that contributed greatly to the inglorious result.

The domestic political dimension of the Israeli invasion of Lebanon in June 1982, and the subsequent retreat in the course of 1983–85, is far too complex to be discussed here in detail. A few brief comments are nevertheless in order. First, to the extent that can be judged, Begin understood the objectives and outline of the war differently from his own minister of defense. Whereas the prime minister had in mind a quick move to destroy the PLO, the minister of defense and the chief of staff saw no alternative to a confrontation with Syria as well. Second, both Begin's cabinet and the leadership of the Labor opposition gave their consent to the invasion before it began, despite the fact that both the Likud ministers (in the cabinet) and the Labor leadership (in opposition) were convinced that Sharon would expand the war far beyond his brief. The motives of both groups are difficult to establish, but they were clearly either personal or political and in any event had little to do with the strategic merits of the case. The result was a decision whose sole merit was the semblance of consensus. It would have been more logical both strategically and politically either to avoid any action altogether (as was advocated by the doves) or to take a bold decision to move into Lebanon in great force and attempt to achieve a stunning and decisive victory within a few days (as was advocated by the hawks). Instead the cabinet—supported unenthusiastically by the Labor leadership— took a decision to move into Lebanon only somewhat beyond the line of advance in the 1978 Operation Litani. This was the lowest common denominator at home, but it made no sense as a guideline of how to operate abroad.

Third, because there was no clear authorization for an all-out attack against the Syrian forces, the IDF had clear orders only for the first phase of the fighting, which focused on southern Lebanon. Fourth, in the absence of clear orders, the rest of the war turned into a cumbersome, crawling operation, in which massive firepower was the chief substitute for motivation and resourcefulness. The result was a large number of Lebanese and Palestinian civilian casualties, many more IDF casualties than had been anticipated, extensive material damage, a failure to end the fighting at an optimal line of deployment, and a downhill-snowball effect on the IDF's morale. Fifth, this and the siege of Beirut generated an enormous amount of resentment in the Israeli rear and, inevitably, in the mainly reserve-based IDF itself. This became clear when the Sabra and Shatila massacres on September 14, 1982, led to the largest political rally in Israel's history, with an estimated 400,000 angry, morally anguished demonstrators demanding the dismissal of Sharon. As in the aftermath of the 1973 war, public pressure focused on the demand for a judicial commission of inquiry.

Sixth, given the degree of public discontent with the conduct of the cabinet, it is not surprising that throughout the following year (September 1982– September 1983), the IDF's presence in Lebanon was the focal point of an unprecedented public campaign to "bring the boys home." The result was a discernible weakening of Israel's already feeble bargaining posture vis-à-vis Syria. Seventh, because of the pervasively politicized atmosphere in which strategy was being made at this juncture, the IDF retreated in September 1983 to the south banks of the Awali and Bisri Rivers, despite the fact that the new line made neither strategic-military nor economic-financial sense. The bulk of Israel's casualties had been in the area south of the new line. Hence, if there was no point to holding on to the Beirut–Shouf line, in which the IDF had been deployed since the end of the war in the summer of 1982, it would have been more logical to retreat right away to a line much nearer the Israeli border. The Awali line, then, was the line of least domestic resistance, a reflection of domestic political considerations more than levelheaded strategic evaluation. The same holds true of the process of withdrawal from Lebanon, which followed. The pace and method of withdrawal—much like that of the advance into Lebanon in 1982—were dictated by the vagaries of domestic consensus building. The invasion of Lebanon, then, was the single most politicized experience in the entire history of Israeli strategy.[62]

Nevertheless, it is difficult to conclude with certainty that Israel's conventional deterrence was depreciated as a result of the war in Lebanon. The Syrians must have been duly impressed by their spectacular defeat in the encounter with the IAF. Although they fought well, they must have also taken very seriously the IDF's impressive ability to do modern, sophisticated battle on the ground. In addition, the Syrians could not ignore the unprecedented degree of leeway that the United States gave Israel. There were great tensions between Washington and Jerusalem during the first eight months of the Israeli presence in Lebanon. But as soon as Sharon was replaced by Arens in the Israeli Ministry of Defense (February 1983), relations between the two countries became closer than ever. What Syria in particular and the rest of the Arab world in general may have learned from the Israeli experience in Lebanon is not that the IDF has become a paper tiger but, rather, how short Israel's domestic political breath is. Israel fought with dogged determination in long wars in which it was attacked (1948 and 1973). It fought brilliantly in short wars it initiated itself (1956 and 1967). But its performance declined as soon as it came to a war that it initiated but that did not lead to an instantaneous, spectacular victory.

What does that imply for Israel's ability to deter the Syrians? Only one, not particularly novel thing: under the conditions of the mountainous, crowded, sophisticated, saturated Syrian–Israeli battlefield of the Golan or Lebanon, the Israelis would constitute a formidable adversary if attacked, but a far less fierce opponent in the event of a war initiated by them. Cast in the language of deterrence theory, this hypothesis implies a depreciation of Israel's ability to deter through the brandishing of a decisive first-strike capability. But it need not necessarily suggest any depreciation whatsoever in the Jewish state's ability to deter through a devastating second-strike capability.

The Fourth Strategic Package

In the same way that Israel's first (1949–56), second (1957–67), and third (1967–73) strategic packages were immensely influenced by the experience of the war that preceded them, so Israel's fourth strategic package was the direct product of the "earthquake" of October 1973. This was manifested, by the enormous emphasis on the acquisition of stupendous quantities of weapons of the latest available models and by the apparent decision to move ahead (without disclosing this news) with the development of a last-resort nuclear "insurance." Although this may seem a harsh retrospective judgment, it seems that the mainstay of the IDF's arsenal in the mid-1980s is the direct outcome of the frenzied growth that occurred in the course of the 1970s. Most of the crucial procurement and production decisions were taken in the course of the first three years after the Yom Kippur War. Money ceased to be the object. The planners were convinced that another war of similar magnitude was in the offing, and they were determined to meet the challenge with the strongest possible military force the Jewish state could produce.

The longer-term implications of this process were not fully appreciated at the time. Economically, this buildup program implied the mortgaging of growth in the defense sector in the latter part of the period. Conceptually, it may have yielded diminishing returns. An army of twelve or fourteen fully mechanized divisions cannot be run as if it were merely a larger version of an army of six or seven partly armored divisions. The growth in size can also lead at a certain invisible point to a subtle but significant mutation. Differently stated, the operational doctrine that suits a larger army may not be identical with that best suited to a small one.

The IDF tried to be attentive to this change but does not really seem to have drawn all the lessons. In the mid-1980s it is as big as it can be and as sophisticated as science and technology permit. On the whole, however, it may have become a less impressive military machine than it was in the 1960s. This is not a comment on the quality of individual officers and men. If anything, the manpower on which the IDF draws has improved in its standard of education without really suffering any major decline in dedication, motivation, and willingness to volunteer. Rather it is a comment on the organizing concept that seems to have inspired IDF planning, training, and operation. In this sense the "big" IDF of the 1974–84 model does not compare very favorably with the "small" IDF of previous periods. As Major General Abraham Rotem wrote in anguish to the minister of defense upon Rotem's retirement from the service:

> The IDF has become a train with many cars carrying heavy and expensive duty but moving slowly on a side track, headed by an ancient locomotive which has lost its power, which rather than pulling holds back; and all it can do is to honk and occasionally blow some smoke. The guards of the track are impressed from a distance by the semblence of the reality and by the expensive cargo, but they fail to notice that the train moves by the inertia invested in the cars while consuming the energy which was gained by the previous trip. . . . Hence, instead of replacing the locomotive by a new and powerful diesel, they replace some of the cars and add rusty old additional locomotives . . . soon the energy will be sepnt, the inertia will dissipate and the train will come to a halt.[63]

In terms of Israel's conventional deterrence, this relative decline is significantly offset by the great improvement in the overall deployment pattern of this large force. The withdrawal from the Sinai has created a vast DMZ that any Egyptian army seeking to attack would have to cross. This has not only reduced the Egyptians' motivation to initiate or join a war against Israel, but has also retrieved for the IDF the triple advantage of a red line away from the Israeli border, a prolonged early warning, and much shorter internal lines. Thus a bigger force than during 1967–73 is entrusted with the defense of a far smaller territory, and the once chief adversary (Egypt) is greatly constrained.

The change, however, is even more extensive than this: if Egypt is not available for a war against Israel, at least in the initial phase of such a war, the calculus of all the other Arab adversaries may have also been transformed. Since Iraq has been neutralized as a result of its own folly, Israel's main adversary remains Ba'athist Syria. Under the impact of the 1973 and 1982 wars, and conscious of the fact that it basically faces Israel alone, Syria may have increased its military capabilities to a point of near parity with the Jewish state. Nevertheless, given the greatly improved force-to-space ratio that the IDF has enjoyed in most of the 1974–84 decade, the Syrian menace is probably manageable in the short run even without relying on a first-strike posture. Israel, in a word, may have come closer than ever before to an ability to obtain an effective conventional deterrence on the basis of a defensive, denial, second-strike concept.

Few, if indeed any, knowledgeable Israelis would dispute the IDF's ability to defend the country against Syria or against any realistic combination of Arab forces. The lesson of the Yom Kippur War, however, was that eschewing a first strike may entail a prohibitive cost. The arithmetic of this calculus is deadly simple. In the 1948, 1968–70, and 1973 hostilities, which were initiated by the Arabs, Israel lost 9,395 men. In contrast, the 1956, 1967, and 1982 wars, which were initiated by Israel, took the lives of only 1,715 Israelis. The casualty ratio of first-strike to second-strike wars thus overwhelmingly favors the former.[64]

The battlefield, though, has dramatically changed over the years. The experience of the 1982 war suggests that the public at home may be easily swayed against an initiated war and thus may undermine its conduct. Furthermore, Israel can no longer count on its ability to carry out fast, effective blitzkriegs. As a former minister of defense put it:

> If peace does not bring an end to wars in the Middle East and if another war breaks out between Israel and the Arabs, we will have to conduct it in the knowledge that our ability to make great gains—territorial and political— will be very limited. Judging by past experience the superpowers would not allow the IDF to win too much, especially if we chose strategic objectives such as taking Damascus or Amman. If we try to conquer Damascus we will find ourselves on a collision course with the Soviet Union. The objectives in another war will therefore by very limited. We may succeed in destroying more weapons and troops than we will lose. But we shall not be able to make any long-term gain.[65]

Applied more specifically to Israel's leading adversary, Syria, this gloomy evaluation seems to suggest more or less the following. A realistic assessment of a war of the future would have to take into account a formidable Syrian line that is concentrated in a narrow cone-shaped area which is based on the Soviet doctrine of several parallel belts of massive defenses. Penetrating such a line without suffering prohibitive losses is virtually impossible. Circumventing it (through Lebanon or Jordan) has also become very difficult. Turning a break through it into a battle of decision (*krav hakhra'a*) under such circumstances is not a simple proposition. Finally, the economic and political costs of such an initiated war may also be prohibitive. It could cost several billions of dollars, which Israel, with an external debt the size of two-thirds of its GNP, cannot afford. Further, it could lead to unbearable tensions and discord in the strengthening, but still not formalized, alliance with the United States.

In a word, the attraction of an initiated first-strike war of the preventive type—such as the 1956 Operation Kadesh and, arguably, the 1967 war—greatly declined in the course of the 1974–84 decade, especially after the experience in Lebanon. Israel's real choice has narrowed down to one of two types of war: either an entirely defensive second-strike war or a preemptive/interceptive first-strike one. This means that only if Israel obtains incontestable evidence of an imminent Syrian attack—which cannot be counted on—will it resort to a preemptive strike. Short of that, the 1984 strategic package suggests that the Jewish state, under any government, will most probably resign itself to the proposition of a defensive–denial–second-strike posture.

So much for the question of initiation. What of the related questions of retaliation and escalation? The combined experience of the past encounters suggests, first, an unshaken Israeli faith in the absence of an alternative to massive retaliation. Israel could never tolerate wars of attrition at any level of violence. Whether it was Syria, the PLO, or—for that matter—the Shi'ites of southern Lebanon, Israel's response has been and will remain decidedly escalatory. Fatigued and exhausted as it has become as a result of the Canal war, the October war, and the Lebanon war, Israel's escalatory propensity may have become even more pronounced. Moreover, to the extent possible, the Jewish state has attempted and will continue to attempt to avoid countercity warfare. In the Canal war of 1968–70, deadly countercity practices could not be avoided because Israel had no other means of forcing Egypt to hold its fire. In Lebanon this kind of dirty fighting was impossible to avoid because the PLO deliberately chose to ensconce itself in densely populated areas. Nevertheless, in both cases, Israel's instinctive first choice was clearly to avoid countercity targeting and to confine hostilities to uniformed soldiers, delineated battlefields, and clearly recognized strategic targets. Israel's position in the future will probably be the same.

This predisposition has been strong and will remain so because of a number of persistent factors. First, Israel's cultural ethos upholds values that are incompatible with cold-blooded attacks against civilians. Second, dependent as Israel is on the United States and on the support in the United States of American Jewry, it cannot afford to be seen as perpetrating large-scale violence against civilians unless and until it is clearly evident that there is simply no alternative. In this respect the Israelis will probably long remember the dark days of the siege of Beirut (June–August 1982) as well as the reactions to the Sabra and Shatila massacres. Third, and probably of greatest importance, Israel, with its small size and high concentration of the population in a small rectangle of roughly 15 by 100 miles is more vulnerable to countercity exchanges than are most of its adversaries. Although the latter, too, are very exposed, they constitute a group of countries—whereas Israel is on its own.

6
Is the Bomb Inevitable?

Conclusions

Taken as a whole, the efficacy of Israel's conventional deterrence has been significantly increased. During the late 1940s and early 1950s it was clearly *fragile*. Less than four decades later, it can be classified as an approximation of the *stable* or even the *firm* type. A more differentiated conclusion, it seems, raises three important caveats:

1. The accumulation of dissuasive power by the Jewish state has not proceeded smoothly but, rather, in a violently fluctuating pattern.
2. Whereas deterrence against an all-out Egyptian and/or Jordanian attack seems to have become stable, deterrence against a similar threat from Syria is at best vulnerable and probably of the fragile variety. The same holds true for Israel's conventional deterrence against subwar hostilities and static wars of attrition.
3. Since 1967 Israel's deterrence has grown immensely in absolute terms. Yet in the 1980s it seems to be declining in relative terms.

To substantiate these propositions, a brief recapitulation of some of the findings of this study is in order. Israel's first strategic package during 1949–56 was deficient in almost all respects. Military capabilities were inadequate for absorbing an enemy first strike and therefore led to a strong Israeli temptation to launch a preventive war. The Jewish state evolved a clear idea of which changes in the status quo would pose an unacceptable security risk, but it would not enunciate them clearly as deterrent casi belli. An alliance with a great power was sought actively, but in vain. The disposition to rely on a first-strike, massive-retaliation posture had already taken shape by 1955. The fear of great power pressure, however, and the lack of an outright commitment to a doctrine of deterrence led to a determination to avoid pronunciation of these preferences as a means of strengthening deterrence. Thus the only area in which Israel's security was in good shape was the domestic political arena. This was underlined, paradoxically, by the turbulent situation that developed during Ben Gurion's absence from power. Apart from this fourteen-month period, Israel's security doctrine was dominated by a towering figure, a formidable political leader who exhibited a subtle understanding of the relationship of strategy to politics.

The second strategic package got off to an auspicious start but ended with the Six-Day War, an event which retrospectively appears an unmitigated disaster, a calamity of historic proportions. As far as military capabilities were concerned, the IDF moved inexorably to an exclusive emphasis on armor and (mainly tactical) air power. The purpose was to maximize deterrence by exhibiting a capacity to achieve a quick decision in any battle. The economic burden of developing such a capacity was, however, so enormous that it led to the virtual doubling of defense's share of GNP; it precluded any serious investment in defensive means; and, as a result, it led to an exclusive reliance on an implicit first-strike, massive-retaliation doctrine.

In the short run this was an effective formula for deterrence, all the more so since it went hand in hand with an increased emphasis on publicly declared casi belli. But this important instrument of deterrence did not receive adequate attention. Although some casi belli were publicly delineated, other indicators of the Jewish state's security margins remained tacit. As in the previous period, this may have been the result of Israel's inability to obtain a great power security guarantee. Indeed, although relations with the United States began to gain important momentum, and although Israel was astute in extracting U.S. military and political support in exchange for a vague commitment to slow down its nuclear program, in the final analysis Israel remained unable to obtain a firm U.S. security guarantee.

As long as Ben Gurion remained in power, the effort to obtain such a guarantee continued without respite. Ben Gurion's successors, however, did not share his sense of urgency with respect to the need for unambiguous great power patronage. Somewhat overimpressed by Israel's growing strength and enhanced international position, some of them came close to turning the lamentable necessity of self-reliance into a laudable virtue. How wrong they were—in fact, how important a firm great power guarantee might have been—became clear only with the sudden eruption of the 1967 crisis. Armed with a contractual defense understanding with a great power, Israel would have been far more capable of deterring Nasser. The visible abandonment of Israel by France, Britain, and the United States in the course of the crisis of May 1967 made the temptation for Nasser to engage in mischief too great. Since Eshkol's handling of the crisis—much like his handling of the encounter with Syria that preceded (and perhaps precipitated) the crisis—was, arguably, inept, it took only a few days for Eshkol and his government to conclude that war had become the least of all evils.

On the face of it, the 1967 war resulted in a net gain in Israel's ability to deter its adversaries. The Arabs suffered a colossal defeat, Israel had defensible boundaries at last, and the IDF had never seemed stronger. In retrospect, however, it appears that this widely held Israeli perception was based on questionable strategic premises. The Arabs' incentive for military action grew immeasurably. Israel gained strategic depth, but this forced it to abandon the posture of quick-decision offensive warfare on external lines—which suited its capabilities—and to adopt instead an incoherent mixture of this strategy with its complete opposite—a strategy of protracted defensive warfare on excessively long internal lines—which turned the Arabs' quantitative advantage into a qualitative edge.

Israel lost the advantage of red lines delineating a wide envelope of security margins beyond the formal boundaries and endowing it with an extended early warning. Israel also missed an opportunity to obtain a defense treaty with the United States. It was stripped of its political ability to launch preventive or even preemptive strikes. At the same time its defense burden more than doubled, creating in effect a creeping mortgaging of national security in the longer-term future. Last but not least, the new geographic configuration of the Jewish state also led to deepening domestic divisions. In a word, the 1967–73 strategic package demonstrated a profound confusion between strategy and geography. It disrupted the essential balance between strategic depth and other components of national power and thus caused a severe depreciation of Israel's conventional deterrence. It is not surprising, then, that the period was marked by a great intensification of violence between wars and that it ended in an all-out attack by the two largest Arab armies.

To some extent the fourth security package, which evolved in the 1970s, showed a return to strategic reason. Thus the phased demilitarization of the Sinai, leading ultimately to a complete withdrawal within the framework of a peace agreement, constituted a considerable improvement in the status of Israel's deterrence. In most other respects, however, Israel continued to follow a path of questionable strategic wisdom. The first serious mistake was to launch a rearmament program with only perfunctory regard for the economic cost. The second major mistake was to squander scarce resources on ghost settlements in the heart of the most populated parts of the West Bank. The third mistake was to launch a war against the PLO and Syria in Lebanon without sufficient domestic consensus concerning its objectives and without adequate attention to its feasibility. The cumulative result of these policies is that Israel today has a vast army but also an unmanageable external debt; it has succeeded in fulfilling the age-old dream of decoupling Egypt—traditionally the pivot of Arab politics, culture, and strategic power—from the Arab–Israeli conflict, but its deterrence against Syria is in decline; it is stronger than ever and enjoying a standard of living that two decades ago appeared unattainable, but it is internally more divided than ever before; above all, it appears to have lost the galvanizing sense of purpose, the nerve and the clarity of aim that had been its real secret weapon all along.

Against such a bleak background, the temptation to seek refuge in the deadly simplicity of a disclosed nuclear capability would appear to be enormous. After all, if despite all the casualties, the unprecedented U.S. assistance, and the peace with Egypt, Israel has been unable to obtain adequate deterrence, then an official nuclear strategy might be the panacea. Indeed, if Israel is close to exhaustion, then sooner or later it may have to go public with the bomb anyway. Why, then, not do so sooner and thus perhaps maximize the political advantage that may accrue to this declaration?[1]

The foregoing discussion suggests two principal responses to such an advocacy of an Israeli nuclear deterrent. The first is that Israel's attempt to obtain deterrence through conventional means has not been entirely a failure. The second is that although ultimately an Israeli nuclear deterrence may become inescapable, the Jewish state has every reason for making haste slowly in this regard. There are still ways of further strengthening Israeli conventional deterrence, and every effort should be undertaken to pursue them before the irreversible decision to go public with the bomb is taken.

The Lessons of the Past

The proposition that Israel's efforts to obtain deterrence through conventional means have not entirely failed rests on the principal theoretical starting point of this book—namely, that deterrence is a relative, cumulative, sequential, and pervasively political process of influence. By such a yardstick, the Israeli experience appears to have been quite successful. Israel has experienced a succession of deterrence failures both in terms of basic security and in terms of subwar (current security). Yet in the final analysis the Jewish state has forced upon its main adversaries a major revision of their order of strategic and political preferences.

A brief overview of the main trends in this respect will illustrate the validity of this contention. In 1948 Egypt decided to lead the other member states of the Arab League in an invasion of the Jewish state as soon as the latter came into existence. This decision by the most powerful Arab country made it virtually impossible for Jordan to sign a separate agreement with Israel even though one was in sight. In turn, neither Iraq nor Syria nor, indeed, Lebanon could afford not to join the invasion. The Egyptian decision was thus momentous in its overall implications. In strategic terms this is clearly a story of deterrence failure. Weak and surrounded as the Jewish Yishuv appeared, it could not deter the Arabs from launching a war whose declared purpose was politicide—the murder of a state.[2] For the next twenty-nine years Israeli deterrence remained seemingly ineffective. The Arabs, headed by Egypt, resorted to small-scale harassment as a means of keeping the pot boiling while preparing for larger wars. In 1956 Israel acknowledged the declining efficacy of its deterrence and resorted to a preventive war. This demonstration of decisive battlefield superiority bought the Jewish state a decade of tranquillity on the Egyptian border, and nine years of a similar state on the Jordanian/West Bank and Lebanese borders, but hardly any peace on the Syrian border. By 1967 Syria had succeeded in hustling Egypt back into a posture of active hostility, and Israel's management of the resulting crisis was poor. This in turn led the Israelis to launch a preemptive strike, another acknowledgment of the inadequacy of their deterrent.

In retrospect, it seems that the most important consequence of the Six-Day War was that it erased from the Arab mind the last vestiges of the pre-1948 hopes of removing Israel from the face of the earth in one major military blow. Contrary to Israeli hopes, however, this did not mean an end to war. The Arabs may have been dissuaded from attempting to destroy the Jewish state, but the Arab world as a whole and Egypt and Syria in particular were not at all deterred from continuing the fight until they retrieved the lands they had lost in the Six-Day War. In this sense Israeli deterrence remained as inadequate as it had been before June 5, 1967.

The real turning point came with the Yom Kippur War. Having stretched themselves to the very limit and having succeeded in performing at their best, the Arabs, in particular the Egyptians, came to realize that they could not vanquish Israel—that even if they succeeded in doing so, their victory might well turn out to be a Pyrrhic one. Trials, errors, and the cumulative strain of twenty-three years of protracted and ever-escalating conflict had begun to show their impact, not only on the weary Israelis but also on some of their adversaries.

Seen in these terms, the Sinai I and Sinai II agreements reflected an Egyptian acknowledgment of a change in calculus: Egypt was at last becoming, in effect, deterred. Sadat, to extend this logic *ad absurdum,* did not accept the terms of the agreements with Israel because he had come to the conclusion that Zionism was a positive contribution to the Arab cause. Rather, realizing that Egypt had been made by Israel to pay a very high price for persisting with the conflict, he was forced to rethink Egypt's priorities. The result of this reappraisal was apparently the conclusion that if Israel were to agree to return the Sinai, it would become less than worthwhile from the Egyptian point of view to carry the banner of conflict with the Jewish state. Sadat, and the Egyptian armed forces, which supported his peace program, were thus deterred.

So was King Hussein of Jordan. During the 1973 war the Israeli forces that remained in the Jordan valley to deter Hussein or defend the line if deterrence failed were negligible; the Jordanian army could have overcome them without any difficulty whatsoever. Nevertheless, Hussein chose to send an impressive expeditionary force to Syria, where it was deployed behind the Syrian army in order to ensure that it would not become involved in the fighting. The

IDF knew where this force was and was very careful to avoid any action that would draw it into the fighting. How can this Jordanian position be explained? Again, the broad concept of deterrence that has been advanced in this book is very helpful. King Hussein was deterred by his painful experience in the 1967 war. He would most probably have joined the war if and when Israel appeared to be losing. But as long as this was not an established fact, he prudently went through the motions of Arab solidarity while scrupulously avoiding any action that might conceivably give the Israelis an excuse for military action against Jordan.

The gradual withdrawal of Egypt from the Arab war coalition reached its peak in 1977, when Sadat went to Jerusalem. Having regained parts of the Sinai in the course of 1973–75, the Egyptian president in a sense foreclosed his own war option. Not to carry on the rapprochement with Israel would have amounted to an Egyptian abdication of the freedom of choice. It would have permitted the arena to be dominated by Soviet-backed Arab radicals. Egypt then would have had to toe the line in the knowledge that sooner or later this situation would lead to another war, in which what had been gained by the War of Ramadan (1973) might be lost again, possibly forever. Recalling Egypt's fate under Nasser, the consequences of the Yom Kippur War, and his own determination to wrestle Egypt from the Soviet embrace, Sadat, then, was essentially deterred from following the radicals and was induced to continue the peace process. Recognizing this, he evidently decided to make a bold move, outmaneuver Israel through adroit diplomacy, and thus maximize his bargaining position in the direct negotiations with Israel that would follow.

The Camp David peace accords resulted in a peace based on an optimal strategic arrangement. By creating a strategic reality in which a war of attrition between Israel and Egypt had become a technical impossibility, and by substantially reducing the payoffs to the parties from an attempt to carry out a surprise attack, the accords reduced the likelihood of war between them. Moreover, by ensuring that Egypt would have very limited incentives for leading an Arab war coalition, the Egyptian–Israeli peace strengthened mutual deterrence on the Jordanian–Israeli front. To be sure, Jordan could, under imaginable circumstances, decide that it would be in its interest to join an eastern front based on Syria, Iraq, and the PLO. The absence of Egypt from such a coalition, however, has made its prospects for success smaller and thus reduced considerably the incentive for Jordan to join.

In practical terms, this means that if Syria wanted to launch another war against Israel, it would have to assume that *initially* its armed forces would face the IDF virtually alone. Egypt would not join as long as a decisive Arab victory was not in sight; nor would Jordan. Lebanon and the PLO do not really belong in the big league and can be dismissed as being of no military consequence. Syria, then, would have to launch the war alone and bring it to the verge of a victory in order to obtain the active military support of other major Arab armies. For Syria, this is a tall order—all the more so since the saturated

Syrian–Israeli battlefield of the late 1980s will offer a major advantage to the party that is on the defensive. The implication, then, is clear: all these other countries have become more effectively deterred by Israel since the Egyptian defection than they had ever been before.

This picture of a substantially appreciated Israeli deterrence looks even better if the repercussions of the Iran–Iraq war are added into the equation. The war in the Gulf, of course, was not of Israel's doing, and it is also beyond the Jewish state's capacity to affect its course in any significant manner. Nonetheless, sad as it may be from a more general point of view, the war in the Gulf added critical momentum to the growing efficacy of Israel's conventional deterrence as a result of the slow rapprochement with Egypt. Specifically, if the removal of Egypt from the war coalition reduced the incentives for Jordan and Syria to engage Israel on the battlefield, the Gulf war and the commitment of Iraqi forces along the border with Iran added even more weight to the same logic.

Had it not been for such momentous changes in the Arab–Israeli balance, it is almost certain that Israel would have had to go public with the bomb by the mid-1980s. If the Jewish state had had to keep abreast of the post-1973 war regional arms race without the reassuring strategic and political arrangements resulting from the peace with Egypt, it would already have reached the point at which Arab quantity would be perceived by the Israelis themselves as an unacceptable qualitative edge. Conversely, the withdrawal of Egypt and the reduced likelihood of either Jordanian or Iraqi participation in the initial phase of a Syrian-led war has helped to contain the growing Israeli propensity to turn a nuclear device from an undisclosed weapon of last resort to a declared part of the ordinary national strategy.

The Future as an Existential Menace

All this notwithstanding, it is quite conceivable that an ultimate Israeli nuclear deterrent—indeed, the nuclearization of the Middle East—is virtually a foregone conclusion, a matter not of *if* but rather of *when*. Such forebodings are not based on any empirical evidence, but they reflect a somber appreciation that once the nuclear genie has been let loose, it becomes impossible to arrest. If the world were tightly controlled by the superpowers, the rest of the world would enjoy less freedom but would also be spared the tragic fate of living under the shadow of nuclear proliferation. Conversely, an international system dominated by an endless number of rivalries and conflicts is a scene of even greater conflict *because* of the presence of two rival giants. Rather than controlling conflicts, the latter find themselves time and again impelled to support clients and thus, against their better judgment, make matters worse.

Ever-intensifying conflicts in the Middle East and elsewhere generate insecurity and a growing demand for nuclear forms of "insurance" of national survival. On the whole, the record of the United States and the Soviet Union in this regard has been beyond reproach. Both superpowers have steadfastly refused to supply their clients with nuclear know-how. As no country knows better than Israel, however, what the primary nuclear powers have refused to supply, secondary nuclear powers like France have been willing to offer. Over the years this has led to the appearance of a kind of club of what might be called threshold or tertiary nuclear powers like India, Pakistan, Brazil, Canada, South Africa, Iraq, and—of course—Israel. How may this third group be expected to contribute to the attempt to stem the tide of proliferation? Probably only minimally. Rapid proliferation through secondary and tertiary nuclear powers can thus be more or less taken for granted, and the Middle East seems the most likely area in which the results will first be felt.

The contention that the proliferation of nuclear weapons (much like ordinary arms races) is an inexorable and perhaps even a deterministic process can also be restated in terms of the calculi of the main candidates for proliferation in the Middle East. Israel assumes that it must take for granted that the Arabs have always meant what they said about their intention to destroy the Jewish state. Faced with this prospect, Israel cannot take any chances. It simply has no rational alternative to relentless effort to acquire access to nuclear technology. The Arabs, for their part—or at least the most advanced Arab states—may have assumed that this was the Israeli calculus. Indeed, it would be only rational from the Arab viewpoint to proceed from a worst-case assumption according to which Israel, too, acts on worst-case assumptions.

Can Israel's Arab adversaries resign themselves to the thought that their foe would one day have a nuclear capability while they would remain exposed? Can they afford to act on the assumption that, in that event, they would be able to turn to Soviet and/or U.S. backing? The answer, at least theoretically, is negative. The leading Arab states cannot afford to expose themselves to the possibility of Israeli nuclear blackmail any more than Israel can afford to run the risk of an Arab nuclear blackmail. They would, therefore, tend to assume that a benign Israeli attitude toward them, if and when the Jewish state had a bomb and they did not, is unlikely. If Israel, in this worst-case perception, had a bomb, it would not hesitate to use it as a lever against the Arabs. The implication is surely that the Arabs too—or at least one or two Arab states—are logically impelled to strive for independent nuclear programs. In turn, Israeli suspicions cannot but be aroused; therefore, the incentives for Israel to accelerate its nuclear program grow further.

Such a rationale, as well as the existence of fierce Arab–Arab and, for example, Arab–Iranian conflicts, turns the Arab–Israeli race for the bomb into a rational prospect from the point of view of the leading protagonists. This does not mean that nuclear bombs are going to be exhibited in next year's Independence Day military parade, but it does seem to imply that the ultimate appearance of nuclear arsenals in the Middle East is barely avoidable. The Israeli destruction of Osiraq has postponed this awful moment; the tacit but firm collaboration of the two superpowers in restricting the possibilities for would-be nuclear powers has also been very helpful. In the long run, however, the prospects of keeping the Arab–Israeli conflict out of the nuclear ring are, to say the least, not very encouraging.

The Requisites for Conflict Reduction

Although Israeli planners probably make similar presuppositions, they have also acted on the assumption that nuclearization is not in Israel's interest and that, for this reason, the Jewish state should do everything in its power to prevent the introduction of nuclear weapons into the Middle East theater. But what could that be? What measures could Israel take in order to contain its own ever-rising temptation to go public with a nuclear weapon? In general terms the answer is that Israel should do everything in its power to prevent any decline in the efficacy of its considerable conventional deterrence. This entails a significant revision of the prevailing national security package, which can be summarized under seven headings as follows.

First, although Israel should continue to base its security on a large conventional capability, the size of this conventional effort should be rigidly delineated by the Jewish state's economic capacity. If Israel continues the policy it has adopted since 1973—and, in a sense, ever since the advent of Levi Eshkol in 1963—of building conventional forces in rigidly affixed proportion to the parallel Arab buildup (see figure 6–1) it will soon exhaust its ability to finance this effort, even with generous U.S. help. Moreover, the huge external debt that has accumulated since 1967 is already so burdensome that it has been cutting into the defense budget (as into other budgets) anyway. Therefore, rather than fighting a rearguard action against the deadweight of this burden, Israel should set a rigid limit (in terms of a percentage of GNP) on the amount of resources to be allocated for the maintenance of this conventional capability. This is not the place to specify what that limit should be. But a withdrawal from the current 20 percent of GNP back to the roughly 12 percent of the pre-1967 years seems a logical target. Indeed, if another war does not break out in the near future, the existence of a huge arsenal as a result of the pileup of capabilities in the 1970s should be able to facilitate a reduction in expenditures without a parallel decline in actual force.

Hard as such a step may be, it would ipso facto place on the Arabs the onus of the decision whether or not Israel should go nuclear. If Israel unilaterally imposes on itself restrictions and the Arabs reciprocate, a de facto form of arms control would, in fact, be created. If, on the other hand, the Arabs do not reciprocate, if the confrontation states bordering on Israel continue to amass conventional weapons as they have done since 1973, if as a result Israel

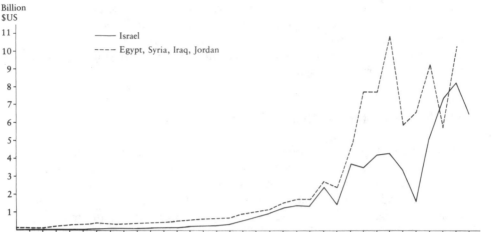

Source: Figures 2–1, 3–1, 3–2, 4–1, 4–2, 5–1, and 5–2 in this book.

Figure 6–1. Aggregate Arab–Israeli Arms Race, 1950–1984

lags behind dangerously in conventional capabilities, then its Arab adversaries should be alerted to the fact that their own policies are bringing the day nearer when Israel will have no choice but to offset Arab quantitative superiority by introducing nuclear weapons. In other words, Israel should gradually switch to an order of battle facilitating effective responses to subwar and medium-size war threats. But it should consciously withdraw from the long-standing maxim that the IDF should be prepared to defeat through conventional means a sustained Arab war effort in which all Arab armies, including substantial expeditionary forces from the Gulf and from North Africa, attack it simultaneously from all sides. This does not mean going public with the bomb. But it does mean a significant lowering of the invisible threshold for doing so.

Second, to add weight to such a policy of, in a sense, unilateral conventional arms control, Israel should reiterate time and again its intention forcibly to prevent the acquisition of nuclear weapons by any Arab state. Even before the attack on Osiraq, a threat to prevent this would have been taken quite seriously. Since this attack, however, such Israeli threats would be taken at face value—as they ought to be.

Third, to increase its ability to win small wars, to deter the Arabs from large wars, and to advance toward economic solvency, Israel should strive to surround itself with a demilitarized envelope. As the 1969–70 war of attrition and the 1973 war showed with devastating clarity, an army of the size that Israel can afford is a poor instrument for a strategy of protracted defensive warfare on interior lines. Such an army—as was demonstrated by the IDF's brilliant performance in the 1967 war—is in fact best employed within the framework of a strategy of quick-decision offensive warfare on exterior lines.

Moreover, quick-decision offensive warfare on external lines is a strategy that goes well with a policy of enunciated casi belli. As has been emphasized in this book, however, an even better formula would seek to obtain the same result on the basis of an agreement with the neighboring countries. Casi belli are annoying, unilaterally imposed restrictions on the adversary's behavior; agreements are a more promising method of obtaining a demilitarized envelope such as Israel needs.

Thus, contrary to the prevailing Israeli view, which espouses the antiquated notion of defensible borders, this book leads to the conclusion that *in order to maximize the efficacy of Israel's conventional deterrence against threats to basic security, the Jewish state should withdraw from most of the occupied territories still under its control after the implementation of the Egyptian–Israeli peace treaty.* This, of course, cannot be done on a unilateral basis. What is proposed here, rather, is that to strengthen its security, Israel should offer Syria a package deal based on the Sinai demilitarization model. Israeli forces should depart. Israeli settlements should be removed. Syrian sovereignty over the whole of the Golan should be restored. But the Syrian army should *withdraw to the outskirts of Damascus,* and an international force (consisting perhaps of NATO and Warsaw Treaty Organization troops in parallel columns) should deploy as a tripwire close to the Syrian army. In addition, this system should be buttressed by monitoring stations on the peaks of Mount Hermon of the type found in Um Hashiba (in the Sinai).[3]

Fourth, such a settlement need not be a peace treaty. Normalization of relations manifested by tourism, trade, and cultural relations, has proved a tall order in the Egyptian–Israeli context. It could prove even less feasible in the Israeli–Syrian context. But a kind of détente—a stable freezing of the Syrian–Israeli conflict according to mutually agreed rules of conduct—is so much in the interest of the Jewish state that a purely strategic standoff, based on a much improved alert time, on a great reduction in the prospects for a surpirse attack either way, and on the virtual elimination of any possibility for waging a static war of attrition, should suffice from the Israeli point of view.

Fifth, an agreement along these lines with Syria could be extended to Lebanon. Israel should recognize Syria's special interests in that country and raise no objections even if Syria proceeds to annex Lebanon. The Syrian quid pro quo should be a recognition of Israel's special security concerns in the security belt that has been established following the IDF withdrawal from Lebanon. An understanding on these issues would have two advantages. First, it would remove a festering wound, a source of endless friction between the Ba'ath republic and the Jewish state. Second, it would at last open the way to serious search for a solution to the Jordanian–Palestinian nexus. Without Syrian consent, an agreement between Israel and Jordan is very unlikely and, even if it were somehow worked out, would most probably be very frail. Conversely, an Israeli–Syrian understanding, ensuring that Syria is not left out on a limb while the rest of the Arab world follows Egypt's lead and accepts a settlement with Israel, would create favorable conditions for dealing with the Jordanian–Palestinian problem.

Sixth, the same logic that suggests that Israel has a long-term strategic interest in a withdrawal from the Golan also applies to the West Bank. Conditions in this densely populated area are, of course, radically different than on the Golan. Nonetheless, it is not inconceivable that the same type of security arrangements could be applicable there, too. The main implication of this solution is, of course, that the idea of an independent state on the West Bank, with or without the PLO, needs to be discarded. If the West Bank is ever to be returned to Arab control, it will have to be totally demilitarized insofar as Arab armed forces are concerned and will have to remain under Israeli strategic control. Such a concept is not incompatible either with Palestinian autonomy on the West Bank or with Jordanian political control there. Contrary to some widely discussed advocacies, however, it precludes the setting up of a fully sovereign Palestinian state. After all, full sovereignty implies independent armed forces, whereas the heart of this set of principles for a settlement is the idea of an envelope of demilitarized zones separating Israel from all its neighbors.[4]

What this means is that the West Bank would have to remain a province of the east bank. With such a status, its demilitarization would not be incompatible with the precedent set by the Israeli–Egyptian peace: that every bit of territory occupied in 1967 be returned to Arab sovereign control, but under conditions of strict demilitarization—that is, divided sovereignty. Indeed, in one sense the demilizarization of the West Bank should be a simpler proposition than it was with the Sinai. After all, ultimate sovereignty over the West Bank is in dispute. The Sinai, on the other hand, was acknowledged by all concerned (including Israel) to have been sovereign Egyptian territory. Syrian sovereignty in the Golan, although challenged by Israel for strategic reasons (in the Golan Annexation Law of December 1981), was never in dispute. The West Bank, on the other hand, has remained the focal point of three mutually exclusive claims, that of the Palestinians, (tacitly) that of the Hashemites, and of course that of Israel.

This state of affairs opens up the possibility of departing from the Sinai precedent in one important respect: Israel should be allowed to maintain garrisons in predetermined locations on the West Bank. They would have no extraterritorial rights and would not have the privileges of a police force. The lands on which they would be deployed could be leased. They would be concentrated in a small number of locations, as was proposed by the late Moshe Dayan in the aftermath of the 1967 war.[5] Their purpose would not be to continue the Israeli occupation under a more benign guise but, rather, to ensure that no foreign force would be able to seize control over the West Bank. If this arrangement calls for the dismantling of Israeli settlements, so be it. In any case, the majority of the settlements established since 1977 have failed to take off. Israelis are not waiting anxiously in line for their turn to obtain housing on the West Bank. Despite the enormous sums of money spent on developing most of the settlements, they remain for the most part conspicuously under-populated. Above all, while dividing Israel (and thus depreciating Israel's ability to project resolve), they arouse Arab emotions and thus strengthen Arab resolve to persist with the conflict.

Seventh, an important advantage of a national security package predicated on these principles is that it can almost certainly remove the most important stumbling bloc standing in the way of a U.S.–Israeli treaty of alliance. The long Israeli experience in dealing with successive U.S. administrations has made amply clear that if and when Israel endorses the principle of withdrawal from the occupied territories, the United States would be willing to offer a security pact. Such a pact alone would not be a sufficient deterrent; but in conjunction with a low threshold for a nuclear posture such as has been proposed above, as well as a considerable conventional strength and with the advantages of an envelope of demilitarized zones, it would make all the necessary difference. Indeed, a U.S. security guarantee, based on an open treaty signed by the heads of state and approved by a two-thirds majority in the U.S. Senate, that turns any attack against Israel into an attack against the United States would add an element that thus far has been woefully missing in Israel's deterrence.

How much of this proposed package is feasible is difficult to say. The first element—that of reducing defense expenditures and establishing a posture of conditional nuclearization—is entirely a matter for Israeli decision. The feasibility of the other elements in the package has a major Israeli domestic political dimension but is also crucially dependent on the response of others. How Syria would respond to an Israeli offer of a package such as is pro-posed here is also difficult to say. After all, Syria has gained a great deal from its encounter with Israel. From a weak and vulnerable power, torn by inter-nal divisions and seeking even Israeli support (in 1948), it has become one of the most powerful states in the Third World. Moreover, if this experience suggests that Syria has no positive incentive for seeking a settlement with Israel, the exigencies of Syria's domestic politics suggest very strong disincentives for moving in this direction. If, however, Syria does respond favorably, the whole equation of Arab–Israeli relations would be altered in one fell swoop. Jordan would have no difficulty in accepting the West Bank part of the deal if Syria were to accept its Golan part. Needless to say, for all its diplomatic visibility Arafat's PLO (as distinct from the Syrian-controlled one) would be no match to a combination of Syria, Jordan, Egypt, and Israel. It would have no choice but to jump on the bandwagon in the hope of salvaging at least some political crumbs for itself.[6]

A not dissimilar logic also suggests that if such a settlement becomes feasible, it would be supported by the majority of Israelis. Because of its internal political deadlock, Israel has been incapable of generating truly imaginative peace plans.[7] On the other hand, faced by a bold Arab offer such as Sadat's peace initiative in November 1977, Israel rose to the occasion and the vast majority of its electorate stood firmly behind the government's decision to settle with Egypt on Sadat's terms. The West Bank and the Golan are, of course, far more problematic in this regard, and negotiating their evacuation would raise immense protests inside Israel. In the final analysis, however, the constituency of those who maintain that holding on to these areas is even more important than a respectably secure Arab–Israeli settlement is far smaller than the political shadow they have cast over Israeli politics since the 1967 war.[8]

What if there is no response on the Arab side? In that event, Israel would have no choice but to adopt unilaterally as much of this package as the exigencies of domestic politics would permit. This might well be too little to have an effect. In that case, Israel's slide down the slippery nuclear slope would become virtually inescapable.

7

A Theoretical Postscript

Having examined the Israeli experience, the discussion may now move to the *problématique* of conventional deterrence in general. First, however, there is one more preliminary question that calls for a brief comment: Is Israel a typical case from which generalizations may usefully be extrapolated? Or is it, rather, a limiting case—an interesting, rich experience unto itself of a unique international actor in very special international circumstances, but with no parallels in the world today? Such a question may seem odd, considering the frequency with which students of contemporary strategy have been helping themselves to examples from Israel's rich inventory. On the other hand, it seems a valid question since many Israelis—excluding, of course, a minuscule number of social scientists—live and act on the assumption of the Zionist ethos that Israel is the unique product of an unparalleled historical and cultural experience and, therefore, is not a standard and perhaps not even a normal state among states.

That the Israelis—much like other nationalities, but perhaps more vociferously—have a need to underline the legitimacy of their state by claiming that it was born from, or at least with, a universal vocation is not altogether surprising. But is it really valid to make such assumptions in the context of a scholarly investigation? The answer seems to be both yes and no. From one point of view, every nation is entirely unique and—if one extends this observation to its logical conclusion—it may even be said that every particular moment in a nation's history is unique. Seen in these terms, there is no denying that Israel came into existence in a unique fashion; that it is an international actor in a particular international arena; that its people have their very special memories, speak a peculiar language, and have acquired a variety of habits that before World War II were referred to as "national character."

Does all this obviate the utility of generalizing from the Israeli experience? The answer seems to be emphatically negative. Israel's conflict with the Arabs may be a special encounter because of the imbalance of war potentials, because of the cultural and linguistic barrier separating the parties, and because of the coalitional structure of the Arab party to the conflict. But even if one takes into account such obvious peculiarities of this conflict, it supports the hypothesis that, rather than being sui generis, Israel merely offers a somewhat extreme example of an ordinary pattern of behavior. No matter how Israel came into existence and where it is placed, the Jewish state has ended up playing the game of nations according to the same rules, more or less, that other nations have followed since time immemorial. Where it has differed from other states has been in acting more (rather than less) strategically than have most other states. As a leading Israeli scholar put it, "Israeli foreign policy comes closer to the model of foreign and defense policy of the strategic studies school than states whose wide security margins enabled them to give a relatively lower priority to national security considerations as opposed to, say, economic, ideological or prestige considerations."[1] This, in a nutshell, is the conceptual starting point for the discussion in this concluding section.

Deterrence: General and Specific

Contemporary deterrence theory tends to be ethnocentric. Often presented as a set of universal rules, it has in fact evolved primarily as the generalized observations of Western scholars concerning East–West relations. In these relations, especially during the first two postwar decades, crises were as frequent as they were dangerous. Consequently, a great deal of theorizing on deterrence was implicitly, and often even explicitly, predicated on the assumption that *deterrence* is essentially another word for *crisis management*. Understandable as it may be, this perception of deterrence actually blurs some of the most important aspects of the problem, especially when it comes to instances of conventional deterrence.

As this study of the Israeli experience demonstrates, the issue is not merely one of preventing crises from turning into wars. It is primarily one of preventing crises altogether and thus, by implication, substantially reducing the likelihood of war as well. The real challenge facing policymakers is how to devise a long-term national policy capable of dissuading the adversary from taking steps that might render crises more likely. The emphasis on the long term is essential. If the issue were merely one of how to foster a dissuasive image in the short term, governments would face no serious problems in ordering the highest degree of mobilization. An emergency, after all, justifies a supreme effort. Such an effort, however, is a practical impossibility in the long term. A nation's ability to survive in conflict, or even to win, hinges on its military capabilities, economic potential for war, and social mobilization. Overemphasizing one of these elements of national power while disregarding the other two may be natural and quite acceptable in the course of a brief crisis, but it would be disastrous in the long term.

The cultivation of a deterrent image in the long run, then, entails a delicate balancing act. On the one hand, there are the requirements of long-term solvency. On the other hand, there is a constant need to maximize military strength on a permanent basis. An exaggerated emphasis on long-term solvency undercuts the efficacy of deterrence in the short term. The reverse, however, undercuts deterrence in the long term. Such a calculus leads to great variations in the level of required military preparedness. Deterrence in the long haul—namely, *general deterrence*, has to be sought with a far smaller military capability than the nation's overall capacity actually permits. In this regard, pluralistic democracies are particularly affected, since domestic pressures make them more prone to cut their defense budgets. Nevertheless, both pluralistic democracies and totalitarian regimes are likely to seek reassurance in a reserve system, suggesting an ability to increase their order of battle considerably as soon as an emergency looms on the horizon.

A dual organization of the manpower mobilization base provides an important, if somewhat blunt, instrument of deterrence in a crisis—namely, *specific deterrence*. It converts the seemingly technical decision of whether or not to call up reserves into an instrument of deterrence. The government of the defending nation can mobilize reserves publicly or secretly, and it can decide to mobilize only some of the available reserves or, alternatively, all of them. A total and publicly announced mobilization maximizes the defender's deterrence; at the same time, it increases the prospects for unintended escalation leading to a war that no one really wants. A secret and partial mobilization, on the other hand, minimizes both the deterrent effect and the risk of runaway escalation. In a sense this cautious move represents a border case between deterrence and defense insofar as it is primarily a precautionary defensive move rather than a deterrent signal.

A third alternative is a secret but total mobilization. This, in practice, is a nonoptimal choice, since it cannot be kept secret for very long and thus ultimately has the same effect as a public and total mobilization. Finally, there is the intriguing possibility of a publicly announced partial mobilization. Such a choice could conceivably maximize deterrence without maximizing the risk of a snowball effect leading to an unintended conflagration, but it could also prompt the adversary to preempt, in which case the defender's bluff would be exposed.

Furthermore, under routine conditions, when war appears generally possible but specifically far from imminent, the worried parties are likely to strive for a minimal military capability. As a result, they are faced with a number of critical dilemmas concerning their respective deterrents. If only a relatively small force can be afforded in the long run, the ratio of force to space will be adversely affected. Island states like Britain and mountain states like Switzerland enjoy a unique advantage in this respect because their natural physical features turn them into exceedingly well defended fortresses. Normally, however, governments are forced to make hard decisions concerning the optimal method in which to deploy their limited regular forces. If the adversary's ground forces have access only in a limited sector of the joint border and if, in addition, the line where the adversary is confronted is endowed with significant physical obstacles, then the defender's dilemma is greatly eased. If the line is long and easily penetrated by substantial forces, however, the defender's dilemmas are greatly aggravated.

In the latter case, a poor manpower-to-space ratio compels the defender to rely on a concentrated, mobile force. In other words, even if the adversary has the capacity to pursue a strategy of attrition, the defender has no alternative to a strategy of quick decision or blitzkrieg. Furthermore, the defender cannot afford forward or even checkerboard deployment. Hence it must rely on small, vulnerable contingents in forward positions as a type of tripwire. But although such forces are quite capable of showing the flag and asserting control over territory, they are so exposed to the adversary that, rather than deterring, they increase the adversary's incentives for attempting an assault, at least for limited gains. If both parties have small forces and if both are impelled to rely on a similar strategic concept, the prospects for an effective mutual deterrence are probably improved. If one party has a significant edge in force-to-space ratio, however, the other party's general deterrence may well be defective in this regard. In that event, the weaker party may seek to buttress its deterrence by relying on two principal compensating devices: *allies* and declared *casi belli.*

Alliances and Conventional Deterrence

Allies need not be attached to the defender by openly declared, signed, and ratified contractual agreements. In fact, when one speaks of alliances in the context of general deterrence, it could mean a wide range of associations, ranging from formal alliances to a tacit convergence of interests as a result of the operation of balance-of-power and/or bipolar systemic dynamics. Note, for example, Inis Claude's comparison of balance-of-power and collective-security systems:

> Both systems are based on the concept of deterrence. In their ideal operational picture they manage power and policy situations in the pluralistic world of independent states in such a fashion that potential disturbers of the peace are kept in check by the threat that their trouble-making enterprises will be defeated.

Collective security, Claude continues, "explicitly involves preponderance." Thus its relation to deterrence is clear and unambiguous. However, because of the "indelible imprint" that the idea of equilibrium—implying as it does equality among units—has left on the balance-of-power theory, it is difficult to find in it "an unambiguous strategy of deterrence." The assumption of mere equality implies, of course, that "states operating in a balance of power system" will settle willingly for "sheer equality vis-à-vis their rivals, or that the architects of an alignment designed to check a predatory power are likely to be conscientious about limiting the power of their grouping to a meticulously calculated equality." Hence a "realistic assessment of the theory of balance of power systems" *qua* deterrence relations "would suggest that states adopt the view that the 'dangerous' state or states must be held in check by the accumulation of power at least equal to and preferably greater than its own."[3]

Claude's observations are succinctly endorsed by Alexander L. George and Richard Smoke. The "core concept of the balance of power system," they wrote in their seminal study of deterrence in U.S. foreign policy, was that "the military capabilities available to any combination of powers should be sufficiently balanced so that full-scale conflict would appear profitless. In effect, 'a mutual deterrence balance' remained stable for approximately a century after the close of the Napoleonic wars."[4]

Not all alignments have the same dissuasive capacity. A formal alliance with a preponderant power that is openly ratified by the legislatures of the signatory powers and that involves a near automatic commitment to mutual military support in the event of an attack by a third party should add for the defender a crucial increment of power (and hence deterrence). By contrast, a tacit alliance with a small and distant power, whose scope is neither explicitly declared nor even fully clarified between the allies themselves, should have a far less dramatic effect on the strategic calculus of the adversary and, therefore, on the efficacy of the defender's deterrent. Needless to emphasize, these are but two ideal types, representing the extremes of the spectrum of real-life possibilities.

The dissuasive capacity of an alliance—the degree, in the words of Hedley Bull, to which a third party adds "critical weights" on the defender's side of the scale,[5] is a critical factor in nonnuclear contexts. This is not the same as saying that it plays no role in nuclear conflicts. As demonstrated by the global policy of the United States in the 1950s, and, more selectively, in the aftermath of the Vietnam War, alliances remain a crucial factor even in a nuclear balance of terror. At the same time, it does seem plausible that nuclear weapons have substantially reduced the relevance of allies to deterrence. By the same token, it may well be that in conventional conflicts alliances may sometimes prove as valuable for deterrence as the parties' own military potential. A defender enjoying the benefit of extended deterrence—that is, the automatically guaranteed military support of a powerful ally—has a dissuasive capacity above and beyond anything it can obtain through self-reliance. Indeed, in most instances of the conventional variety, powerful allies constitute one of the most important ingredients of general deterrence.

266 • *Deterrence without the Bomb*

Paradoxically, however, the weaker the defender, the smaller the likelihood that it might succeed in forging significant deterrent alliances. An alliance, after all, is seldom an act of charity, even though it may often be presented as such. If the distribution of expected utilities between prospective allies is grossly uneven, a deterrent alliance is not very likely to be formed since the party less in need of it will, in all probability, be reluctant to extend deterrence to the weaker party and thus draw upon itself the fire of the adversary without an adequate payoff.[6] It follows, then, that those powers in the greatest need of the extended deterrence of more powerful allies are the least likely to obtain them unless and until they convince their chosen partners that they are assets. To achieve this, the former are impelled to demonstrate their strength and vitality. Yet the more successful they are in proving their prowess to their friends, the greater the efficacy of their deterrent vis-à-vis their foes. Consequently, their own incentives for seeking alliances decline, whereas their bargaining power vis-à-vis prospective allies increases. In other words, deterrent alliances may be difficult to obtain when they are urgently needed and easy to come by precisely when their immediate utility appears to be waning. Given this paradox, a weak power seeking to defend itself through a posture of deterrence is impelled to look for other devices with which to reinforce its deterrence. It is in such a context that the question of deterrent threats enters the discussion.

Casi Belli, Rules of the Game, and Red Lines

Deterrent threats fall into two distinct categories: *long-standing anticipatory* threats and *ad hoc reactive* ones. The former are authoritatively enunciated casi belli designating thresholds for resorting to force. Normally these thresholds overlap with the defender's *intrinsic* interests—its boundaries and routes of communication to other parts of the world. But when a nation pursues a policy of deterrence based on an offensive military doctrine, casi belli may well apply to lower thresholds or to what have been described elsewhere as *strategic* interests.[7]

Strategic interests are more extensive in scope and less critical in nature than intrinsic interests. Like the latter, they include the nation's sovereign domain and its arteries of communication with the rest of the world. They go beyond this, however, applying, in fact, to actions that the adversary, legally speaking, is perfectly entitled to carry out. Specifically, such thresholds pertain to two kinds of modifications in the status quo that the defending nation seeks to prevent: (1) changes in the spatial array of hostile military forces, and (2) changes in the overall balance of forces, such as the adversary's acquisition of innovative weapons systems or, its gain of a significant edge in the arms race, a more menacing pattern of adversary alignment with third parties, or sometimes even a political change in the domestic politics of the adversary power.

Deterrence—especially the generic, prototypical variety as defined in this discussion—is the strategic-political posture of a nation that perceives a ubiquitous threat. It is, in a sense, a paranoid disposition, except that the defending nation normally does have real foes. Such a posture is nurtured and nourished by an overbearing fear of menacing, ubiquitous strategic inferiority. It therefore breeds hypersensitivity, even a pathological anxiety to prevent any change in the nation's political environment. A state possessed by such a disposition seeks, accordingly, to deter its adversaries from effecting any significant changes in the political and strategic status quo. It does so by unilaterally designating rules of behavior that the adversary can ignore only at its peril. As soon as the latter would attempt a change in the status quo, the defender's strategic interests are compromised, its credibility is challenged, and it may therefore be prompted to administer a punishment.

Red lines, casi belli, thresholds, and rules constitute important devices with which deterrence can be strengthened. By extending the lead time in which the defender can call up reserves and rush reinforcements to the area where an attack seems to be underway, they endow the defender with a critical multiplier of power, a compensation for its numerical inferiority. These devices are also useful, perhaps even essential, as a means of providing a defender with a badly needed envelope of security margins. They have the effect of increasing the defender's strategic depth at the expense of the adversary without, however, having to seize the latter's sovereign territory. The adversary is simply barred from the forward deployment of its forces in dangerous proximity to the defender's border, from entering into threatening alliances with hostile third parties, from allowing the stationing of foreign troops on its territory, from initiating border skirmishes, or from procuring weapons systems with the potential to alter the prevailing arms balance.

As long as the adversary acquiesces in such demands, the defender gains an important increment of security, and its power to deter is in fact reinforced. Both normatively and in terms of the adversary's status and prestige, however, the coercive imposition by the defender of such drastic limitations on the sovereign rights of the adversary, even when honestly intended to protect the status quo, is inherently provocative. Indeed, it constitutes an affront that very few nations are likely to take in stride. Herein lies another intriguing paradox. In the unlikely scenario in which the defender is the superior party (for example, the Soviet Union vis-à-vis Finland or Syria vis-à-vis Lebanon), the weaker adversary (Finland and Lebanon, respectively) has no choice but to acquiesce. If, on the other hand, there is rough parity between defender and challenger or if the defender is weaker—and these, after all, are the more common cases in which deterrence is pursued—it is almost certain that the challenger will not abide by the defender's rules for very long. Sooner or later the opponent (the *deteree*) is certain to challenge the defender's casi belli because they constitute, by their very nature, an affront that even a weak party will find extremely hard to tolerate. Casi belli, rules, and red lines, it can therefore be postulated (at least insofar as conventional deterrence is concerned), strengthen both deterrence and the likelihood of a challenge almost to the same degree.

This inherently aggravating attribute of casi belli is directly connected with another problem that such a device entails. If casi belli are to be an effective instrument of dissuasion, they ought to be both publicly enunciated and explicit. If they are clearly spelled out, however, the defender faces two possible dangers. First, the choice of if and when confrontation will take place is abdicated to the challenger. The latter merely has to break one of the defender's rules. In that event the defender is faced with a dilemma: Should it protect its credibility and risk a confrontation at a time of the adversary's choosing, or should it avoid a confrontation but sustain a serious loss of credibility that might lead soon to fresh provocations? In most instances in which this dilemma is confronted, the defender will be inclined to defend its credibility, even at the price of being dragged into confrontation when it does not wish to be. Since the challenger broke the rules, however, it is likely to be well prepared, not only to sustain the defender's riposte but, presumably, even to counter it forcefully. The government of the defending state, then, loses the critical advantage of surprise; in addition, it is also likely to be branded the aggressor by the international community and, worse still, by its domestic critics.

Explicit casi belli, furthermore, induce a would-be challenger to circumvent the obstacle through the aggregation of incremental infringements of the status quo. The challenger may move military forces in small quantities across the red lines; it may invite an ally to deploy forces on its territory in slowly growing numbers; it may attempt not to disclose the acquisition of new weapons; it may inspire proxies to engage the defender in a limited but immensely irritating and demoralizing war of attrition; or it may effect a significant domestic political reshuffle without openly presenting this move as a significant departure in terms of the relations with the defender. When the latter is faced with such small infringements, its dilemma is whether or not to invoke the rules and initiate an open crisis right at the very beginning of the process, when the first infringements are registered, or to wait until later on, when the status quo may already have been significantly altered in favor of the adversary.

An early initiation of a crisis by the defender, through, for example, a forward deployment of forces, can be construed as an irresponsible, hotheaded, even aggressive courting of a pretext for an attack. It can annoy allies and weaken their deterrence-strengthening support. Or it can lead to a divisive domestic debate that, again, depreciates the defender's dissuasive image. If the latter acts reasonably, however, its credibility could suffer; in addition, the temptation for the challenger to engage in further prods and mischief will most probably soar.

If the rules are breached gradually, almost imperceptibly, moreover, the world—and to a lesser extent the defender's domestic constituency—may resign themselves to every new increment of change in the status quo. After all, for other actors in the international arena and for some segments of the domestic constituency, a flare-up is not normally a welcome development. These spectators are worried about their own well-being and security, and they do not want the peace to be disturbed by an overanxious government rushing to defend its credibility as soon as a minor infringement is initiated by its adversary. Given this formidable constraint, the defending government faces a no-win situation. If a crisis is initiated as soon as the first infringement of the status quo is detected, it can lead to escalation, for which the defender, not the challenger, would subsequently be blamed both at home and abroad. If, on the other hand, the defender acts with restraint and does not make any consequential countermove before the accumulation of significant infringements of the rules, war may become the only way out of the impasse other than submission.[8]

Threats and the Management of Crises

Casi belli, rules, and thresholds, then, are ambiguous, inflexible, and complicated policy tools. The more a defender relies on them as instruments of deterrence, the more likely it is to see them challenged. When a challenge to the defender's rules occurs, it can do one of three things: yield and suffer a depreciation of its deterrence; administer a punishment instantly and face the possibility of a war; or, finally, issue new, ad hoc threats. When a defender chooses the third of these alternatives, it faces a crisis—a situation marked by surprise and/or short decision time and a grave threat to the national interest. A crisis is one step short of war. Managed sensibly, it can pass without hostilities. The decision about which threats to issue in the course of a crisis in progress is thus critical.

Broadly speaking, when issuing threats in the course of a crisis the defender must address itself to two interrelated questions. First, how severe should the threats be? Second, how explicit should it make the nature of the punishment that would follow a refusal by the challenger to back down? A natural inclination is to resort to the severest threat that the defender can credibly issue—for instance, "If you do not instantly stop what you are doing and revert to your previous position, I'll break your neck." Such a threat maximizes the defender's commitment and should maximize its dissuasive image, but it also has two conspicuous drawbacks. First, it is so ominous that its credibility might be questioned. Second, it might challenge the adversary's reputation and status to such an extent that the latter may feel unable to back down even if otherwise it would be prudently inclined to do so.

If either of these possibilities occurs, deterrence will fail. Indeed, if the credibility of the defender is not in doubt, its severe threats may well backfire. The challenger's reputation might stand to suffer irreparable damage, and the incentives for it to pass the ball to the defender's court might correspondingly increase. Experienced policymakers tend to be aware of these dangers and therefore to think twice—or more—before resorting to the most severe threat. The result may be a decision to articulate deterrence threats in milder terms in the hope that such a demonstration of prudence will induce the adversary to respond in kind. If such is the response of the adversary, the crisis will have been managed.

Even a mild threat carries its hazards. The challenger might interpret moderation as a sign of hesitation, trepidation, lack of resolve—in fact, weakness. In that event, the temptation for the challenger to take advantage of the defender's apparent weakness will become virtually irresistible. The latter will feel compromised and impelled to resort to a more severe threat. By then the challenger will have become irrevocably committed, and the prospects for crisis management might disappear.

If the choice of the appropriate degree of severity is complex, so is the calibration of explicitness. An explicit threat that states clearly both the nature of the opponent's provocation and the kind of punishment it should expect is seemingly the most efficient deterrence threat. It leaves no doubt in the mind of the challenger as to the earnestness of the defender. Consequently, it reduces the likelihood of an escalation owing to a misunderstanding. At the same time, however, an explicit threat can also reduce the challenger's fear. If the latter knows exactly what punishment to expect for each infringement of the rules—if, in other words, it can plan its actions in the light of a clear "price list"—the would-be challenger may be tempted to launch a series of prodding operations roughly in the style of a Greek dance—two steps forward and one back. This prodding would stop only if and when the defender reacts vigorously. Differently stated, a simple tit-for-tat, seemingly the most prudent manner in which to articulate deterrent threats, could easily play straight into the hands of the challenger.

In real life, the choice of severity and the choice of explicitness are inseparably mixed. There are four broad options: an *ultimatum*, a *request*, an *admonition*, and a *demand*. An ultimatum is an *explicit* threat to administer a severe punishment. A request is an *explicit* threat to administer a mild punishment. An admonition is an *implicit* threat to administer a mild punishment. Finally, a demand is an *implicit* threat to administer a severe punishment. Which of these four basic alternatives is most likely to defuse a crisis and avert the danger of war without a significant plummeting of the defender's shares in the relevant deterrence (alias "threat") exchange depends largely on the overall balance of forces and resolve between the parties. If the defender is superior, the ultimatum is probably the most effective form of response. The challenger will not doubt the defender's commitment; and, if the former backs down, its own loss of face can easily be explained away by its inferiority. Not so, however, when the parties are of roughly equal strength. Then the temptation for the deteree to persist is greater, and so is the cost of backing down. Hence it seems that the optimal strategy for the defender would be to articulate a demand rather than an ultimatum. Such a response maximizes uncertainty about the nature of the punishment while making clear that the defender's reputation is at stake. At the same time, a demand somewhat eases the intricate exercise of backing down without loss of face for the challenger.

The same logic applies even more clearly to a defender that perceives itself as being significantly inferior. Such a defender is likely to place a great emphasis on moving (that is striking) power, on an order of battle and on a strategy of quick-decision offensive warfare on external lines as a means of countering the deteree's edge in staying power—in other words, in protracted defensive warfare on internal lines. The defender, therefore, will strive to impress on the adversary that it (the former) prefers a showdown (in which the advantage of moving power is maximized) to a concession. Moreover, the weaker defender in an asymmetrical balance must retain the advantage of surprise if inflicting a punishment on the adversary becomes the most logical step. In seeking to emphasize severity it, therefore, should not disclose the timing, the location, and the scale of the riposte planned.

Finally, the greater the asymmetry between the defender and the challenger, the greater the dependence of the former on the support and goodwill of third parties and its consequent deference to their requests. These parties would in all probability caution the defender not to overreact. From the defender's point of view, however, the optimal policy would be to avoid a situation in which it might have to listen to such advice. One way of doing so is to desist from disclosing in advance, even to one's allies, the nature of the planned riposte. In other words, from the point of view of the defender, the logic of relying on demands (severe but inexplicit threats) rather than on ultimata (severe and explicit threats) appears more formidable.

Very little of what has been said so far about threat articulation in crisis applies exclusively to deterrence situations of the conventional variety. It is thus important to underline at this point where the conventional nature of the deterrent has an effect on the calculus of the adversaries. The answer lies, perhaps, in a greater propensity of the opponents to rely on ultimata and demands— that is, on the more severe forms of threat. If such a style leads to rapid escalation and ultimately to hostilities, the ability of the contenders to sustain the cost is, presumably, far greater than it would be in the event of a nuclear exchange, even a "small" one. Hence the parties to a conventional conflict are more prone to be reckless than the same type of players would be in a nuclear conflict, where a mistake can easily be irremediable.

This propensity should not be overstated, however. Actors in a conventional conflict do not operate in a void. They are dependent on the goodwill of allies, and they have their domestic constituencies to worry about. Both these sleeping partners in the interplay of threats and other moves are almost certain to punish a government that rushes blindly into an unwarranted military confrontation, especially if the outcome turns out to be a net loss for the defending nation. Allies may choose to deny military, economic, and diplomatic assistance in the course of the hostilities. Likewise, a critical constituency at home can create deep domestic schisms in the course of a crisis or of a war resulting from a poorly managed crisis. If such a schism occurs, the deterrence of the defending nation would be undermined, as would its ability to fight successfully the war that would follow a failure of deterrence.

Such constraints against imprudence in the articulation of ad hoc threats are reinforced by the impact of military technology. The greater the quantity, sophistication, and destructive capacity of available weapons systems, the less the temptation to go to war. Battlefields become saturated. Maneuverability is substantially reduced. Prospects for quick gains and decisive victories, especially when surprise has been lost, are greatly reduced. A highly sophisticated battlefield, even a conventional one, therefore acts as a powerful incentive for caution and prudence, all the more so since modern military machines can be sustained only by a relatively highly developed political system. In turn, the attributes of the political system themselves become crucial elements in the deterrence equation.[9]

Domestic Politics and Conventional Deterrence

Deterrence, conventional or nuclear, is in the eyes of the beholder. It entails, first and foremost, a manipulation of the adversary's images and perceptions. The defender's actual military capabilities are in this sense less important than the manner in which they are perceived by a would-be challenger. To say this is not to contend that battlefield capabilities do not count. It does imply, however, that in the final analysis, especially in the case of conventional deterrence, nonmilitary factors—more precisely, a composite image of the defender in which its objective military capabilities constitute but a part of a larger whole—have a crucial bearing on the adversary's calculus.[10]

By their very nature, many of the variables that bear heavily on a nation's deterrence are so elusive that they defy systematic analysis. Some of the more obvious among these factors, however, do call for a brief comment. The first factor that comes to mind is the perceived quality of the defender's leadership. This is crucial because decision making, especially with respect to war and peace, is an intrinsically hierarchical process containing a ubiquitous element of what the French call *personification de pouvoir*. National leaders in a war or near-war situation not only tend to concentrate in their hands the ultimate power (and responsibility) for all critical decisions, but also tend to view the conflict, at least tacitly, as a duel between themselves as individuals and the individuals who supposedly make similar decisions on the other side. Thus if the opponent is perceived as a powerful, determined, capable, crafty, and professional leader, the nation's deterrence is significantly strengthened. Conversely, if the leader is looked upon with contempt and condescension, judged to be a weakling, a nonentity, a colorless and indecisive amateur, the nation's deterrence cannot but suffer significant depreciation. Of course, in real life there is seldom such a clear-cut choice between powerful and weak leaders. Most leaders are perceived as somewhere in the middle of the scale; extremely powerful and extremely weak leaders are more the exception than the rule. Nevertheless, it is advisable to bear this factor in mind as an important determinant of deterrence efficacy, a factor that can improve or undercut a nation's deterrence even though its military capabilities may suggest the opposite.

The same holds true of a second, equally important and equally elusive factor—system traits. What this designation suggests is a political system's perceived ability to conduct effectively its business of surviving and prospering. To a certain extent this is related to leadership, since a seemingly strong leader makes a system look more effective, and vice versa, but there seems to be more to it than that. In particular, what appears relevant is the intrinsic ability of a political system to affect the level of motivation of the populace. Whatever the formal structure of a state, what ultimately counts in terms of its ability to face up to external threats is the degree to which the population feels attached to the system's values. If the people are pervasively alienated, the country may be said to be in the throes of a crisis that a foreign foe will be quick to detect and exploit to its own advantage. Conversely, if the population appears to be spirited and devoted, the temptation for a foreign opponent to produce a challenge should in most cases be reduced—even if the country in question showed no net improvement in its military capabilities in the narrow, technological, and numerical sense of the term.

These nimble, elusive, but crucial qualities are particularly important in cases of conventional deterrence. The main source of deterrent capacity in nuclear standoffs is the frightful array of nuclear weapons in the possession of the adversaries. Even if U.S. leadership seems to be declining, even if the standard of living of the American people, and with it their morale, is declining drastically, the ability of the United States to deter the Soviets would hardly decline. From the Soviet point of view, the United States will still remain capable of bombing Eurasia back to the Stone Age.

By contrast, President Nasser of Egypt—as was pointed out earlier in this book—may have been imperceptibly affected by the composite image of Israel's resolve at different points in time. Similarly, when Iraq invaded Iran in the fall of 1980, President Sadam Houssein of Iraq may have been critically affected by the perception of Iran as a country in the throes of deep domestic crisis. From the Iraqi point of view this was a unique opportunity, or so it then seemed, to obtain long-dreamed-of advantages. Previously, Iran had simply appeared far too powerful to be challenged. At the time of the Iraqi invasion, Iran's military capabilities in the formal, technical, and numerical sense were the same as they had been during the previous three to five years. In 1980, however, Iraq was no longer deterred by the Iranians because the ouster of the shah and the domestic chaos that attended the arrival of Khomeini appeared to have substantially undermined the efficacy of this deterrent. Sadam Houssein was proved fatally wrong, but this does not reduce the validity of this illustration of the impact of leadership and system traits on the calculus of a potential adversary.

Last but not least, deterrence is a policy promulgated in most cases not by rational unitary actors but by political bodies whose dynamic complexity has a critical bearing on the state's definition of goals, choice of means, actual conduct, and hence image in the eyes of the beholding adversary. This book confirms without any reservations the conclusion of George and Smoke that "judgements of interests and values" are "essentially political rather than strategic." They "are affected and shaped by political processes both operating within the governmental structure and impacting on it from the outside. The formulation of a commitment and, if deterrence fails, its implementation are subject to the play of conflicting interests, judgements and processes."[11]

Conventional Deterrence and the Use of Force

Deterrence, according to Robert Jervis, "comes from having enough weapons to destroy the other's cities. This capability is an absolute, not a relative one."[12] A closer look at the works of some of the "classical strategists" (in Michael Howard's designation) suggests, however, that (1) any type of deterrence, in particular the conventional variety, is inherently *relative*; (2) deterrence has a long-term *sequential* dimension in the sense that it can be appreciated or, alternatively, depreciated over time; and (3) from this point of view, not every resort to force is a sign of deterrence failure. Indeed, although it may sound like a contradiction in terms, to a certain extent the use of force can be regarded as an inescapable by-product of the pursuit of deterrence.

"Wars," wrote Michael Howard, "are not simply acts of violence. They are acts of persuasion as well as of dissuasion."[13] Thomas C. Schelling revealed a subtle appreciation of this as well when he contended that "war itself can have a deterrent or compellent intent, just as it can have defensive or offensive aims." The "power to hurt," he noted elsewhere, "is often communicated by some performance of it [and] it is the expectation of more violence that gets the wanted behavior, if the power to hurt can get it at all."[14]

The same general idea was also expressed by Snyder, who observed that "deterrence operates during war as prior to war." it could be defined, he continues,

> as a process of influencing the enemy's intentions whatever the circumstances, violent or non-violent. Typically the outcome of wars has not depended simply on the clash of physical capabilities. The losing side usually accepts defeat

somewhat before it has lost the physical ability to continue fighting. It is deterred from continuing the war by a realization that continued fighting can only generate additional costs without hopes of compensating gains, this expectation being largley the consequence of previous application of force by the dominant side.[15]

What the points made by Howard, Schelling, and Snyder add up to is that —unlike nuclear situations, in which deterrence either succeeds or fails—the definition of success and failure in conventional conflicts is very subtle. As Alexander L. George and Richard Smoke put it:

> Deterrence "success" or "failure" is not a one-time event. Crisis policy-making within both the defending and the potentially initiating powers is a process composed of a series of interrelated decisions, each of which must therefore be seen as imbedded in a sequential as well as a "cross-sectional" policy context. Hence, deterrence is likely to succeed or fail through time and in stages. . . . [Moreover,] deterrence does not succeed or fail in just one way. Rather, there is likely to be more than one causal pattern by which the deterrence mechanism may work or fail. And simple "success" or "failure" is frequently an inadequate typology for organizing the outcomes of deterrence attempts.[16]

It follows that the ultimate test of conventional deterrence is not so much its *absolute* success in preventing all acts of war as its *relative* success in gradually changing the strategic calculus, the order of strategic preferences, and above all the political intentions of the adversary. The short-term prevention of war is always a desirable goal. But forcing an adversary to abandon war altogether as an instrument of policy (at least toward the defender) is a superior objective, whose attainment may, paradoxically, require an occasional resort to force. This contention, however, calls for an important caveat. The utility of resorting to force as a form of investment in the future of one's deterrent declines in inverse proportion to the devastation it is expected to cause. Resorting to "small" nuclear wars for the sole purpose of "charging the batteries" of one's deterrent is clearly a council of despair, an *extensio ad absurdum* of otherwise sound logic. At the same time, resorting to small conventional wars may well be, on occasion, an unavoidable—perhaps even an imperative—instrument of deterrence. As such, however, it presents the defender with difficult decisions.

The purpose of deterrence is not to vanquish the opponent, but to teach it a lesson, to exact from it a price, and thereby to contribute to a change in its strategic and political calculus. It follows that such use of force as the defender may initiate from time to time should be at once impressive enough to have an impact but restrained enough to prevent runaway escalation, which would subvert the defender's purpose. In somewhat more specific strategic terms, the defender's main choices boil down to three basic dilemmas: initiation, retaliation, and escalation.

The dilemma of *initiation* is whether to use force in a preventive, preemptive, or interceptive manner or, alternatively, only reactively. The dilemma of *retaliation* is whether deterrent punishments should be calibrated in scale, in time, and in locus to the adversary's provocation or, alternatively, be deliberately disproportionate and lacking in clearly identified connection to the adversary's triggering action. Finally, the dilemma of *escalation* is whether punishments administered by the defender should be confined to battlefields or, alternatively, allowed to spill over to civilian centers; should the defender initiate horizontal escalation manifested by the expansion of the fire zone beyond the battlefields? The contemporary theory of nuclear deterrence labels the choice relating to initiation *first strike versus second strike*, the choice relating to retaliation *flexible response versus massive retaliation*, and the choice relating to escalation *counterforce versus countercity targeting*. There is nothing in these terms, however, suggesting that they do not apply to a conventional setting.[17]

The notion that deterrence is a sequential quality is particularly relevant in instances in which, as has been repeatedly emphasized in this discussion, the defender acts from an assumption of inferiority. After all, an imbalance in the vulnerability of the parties acts as a powerful stimulus for the deteree to initiate challenges; it suggests a built-in advantage for the latter in protracted, slow-bleeding attrition over major showdowns leading to decisive battles. For the defender, the calculus is precisely the opposite: essentially weaker; lacking in breathing capacity, so to speak; having, accordingly, a comparative advantage in the use of moving/striking power—its most pressing objective is to minimize the frequency and the intensity of hostilities by gradually impressing on the adversary that war is not in the latter's interest. This, however, can only be achieved, if indeed at all, if the defender inflicts on the deteree vicious punishments.

If this logic is extended one notch further, it suggests a crucial difference between the calculus of conventional deterrence and that of nuclear deterrence. A deliberate emphasis on a declared and demonstrated preference for, simultaneously, initiation, vigorous retaliation, and rapid escalation (IRE)—that is, first strike, massive retaliation, and countercity targeting—strengthens conventional deterrence without creating a credibility gap. It suggests resolve and determination and prevents the adversary from turning to practices of attrition—all without endowing the defender with an image of irresponsibility. Conversely, in nuclear settings, a reliance on this awesome triad of preferences is a prescription either for untold disasters or for a kind of self-deterrence. Bluntly put, a declared doctrine of nuclear first strike could well be a prelude to a global holocaust. Hence the prudent Western doctrine of no first use. A doctrine of nuclear massive retaliation can easily lead to an abyss in which the only choice is between submission and mutual annihilation. Hence this doctrine was watered down almost as soon as it was announced by the Eisenhower administration. Less clear are the pros and cons of a nuclear countercity compared to a nuclear counterforce strategy. But this does not alter the broader picture—namely, that a declared intention to initiate unlimited punishments makes ample sense in the pursuit of a conventional deterrent but appears to be a dubious, questionable proposition in the pursuit of a stable nuclear deterrent.

The advantage of a clear-cut commitment in the pursuit of conventional deterrence over a strategy of first strike, massive retaliation, and countercity targeting does not imply that, in order to strengthen deterrence, the defender should inform the adversary in advance of the specifics of the riposte in the event of the latter's failure to comply. If clarity concerning the defender's overall posture improved deterrence, so does ambiguity concerning the timing, scale, and location of the riposte. The adversary should know in advance that it will be made to pay dearly for any infringement of the status quo. If deterrence is to be increased, however, the adversary should be left entirely in the dark about what punishment will be meted out, when, and how. Indeed, in the long run the defender should strive to foster an image of being prudently and studiedly erratic. Such an image will reduce the ability of the deteree to predict the defender's response and manipulate it to its advantage by engaging in well-prepared provocations. But seemingly erratic behavior should not be confused with wavering. Ferocious unpredictability strengthens deterrence. Predictable wavering undermines it.

A perfect implementation of this recipe for conventional deterrence is, however, virtually impossible because it contains a number of incompatibilities with other components of deterrence that have been mentioned earlier. Thus ferocious reliance on the triad of first strike, massive retaliation, and countercity targeting would be clearly incompatible with the constraints imposed by a narrow mobilization base. If all the defender can afford is a small, well-trained force, then such a force is more capable of achieving clear-cut results in initiated (first-strike) wars than in defensive (second-strike) ones. It is also more suitable for dealing with an infringement of casi belli than with a surprise attack launched from positions of forward deployment by an overwhelmingly superior enemy force.

But a declared strategy of initiation, massive retaliation, and rapid escalation is difficult to uphold explicitly without damaging the defender's relations with allies abroad and causing an equally damaging breach of consensus at home. Both factors are, as has been said, essential for maximized deterrence. Yet both are far more easily cultivated when the defender appears reasonable than when it appears trigger-happy and prone to overreaction. Allies abroad that may become involved in a war that is either initiated by the defender or made more likely because of the latter's repeatedly announced intention to initiate, or that is rapidly expanding in scope because of the defender's propensity—and declared commitment—to escalate, are certain to look askance at a declared first-strike/massive retaliation/countercity posture. Public opinion at home—or at least its articulate, sensitive, and often vociferous liberal part—may well have a similar order of preferences.

For these reasons a defender's strategy in a conventional conflict is constantly plagued by the need to justify in advance any excesses, be they concerned with initiation, escalation, or retaliation. This means that a declared strategy of IRE effective as it may be in theory, may be impossible. The alternative, in the course of a long history of conflict behavior, is the accumulation over time of a *reputation* for preferring IRE. Official pronouncements hailing initiation, retaliation, and escalation as a doctrine—a preferred strategy for the future—may have to be eschewed. Emphasis in official announcements on the fact that such a strategy in the past bore significant dividends for the defender and heavy costs for the opponent may remain the only alternative. Such a policy undoubtedly muffles the defender's advance commitment to initiate, retaliate, and escalate—all three being crucial ingredients of conventional deterrence. But this may be a necessary and reasonable price to pay (in terms of increasing the efficacy of one's deterrence) for the purpose of protecting the defender's alliances and domestic cohesion.

Notes

Preface

1. Avner Yaniv, "Deterrence and Crisis in a Protracted Conflict: The Case of Israel," paper presented at the twelfth IPSA International Conference, Rio de Janeiro, August 9–14, 1982.

2. Alexander L. George and Richard Smoke, *Deterrence in American Foreign Policy* (New York: Columbia University Press, 1974).

3. Patrick Morgan, *Deterrence: A Conceptual Analysis*, 1st ed. (Beverly Hills, Calif.: Sage Publications, 1977).

4. See Michael Brecher, *Decisions in Israel's Foreign Policy* (New Haven: Yale University Press, 1974); Michael Brecher (with Benjamin Geist), *Decisions in Crisis: Israel 1967, 1973* (Berkeley: University of California Press, 1980).

5. Avner Yaniv, "Deterrence and Defense in Israeli Strategy," *State, Government and International Relations* 24 (1985):27–62.

6. Avner Yaniv, "Israel and Syria: The Politics of Escalation," in Moshe Ma'oz and Avner Yaniv, eds., *Syria under Assad* (London: Croom Helm and New York: St. Martin's, 1986), pp. 157–178. Avner Yaniv, "Israel's Conventional Deterrent: A Reappraisal," in Rene Louis Beres, ed., *Security or Armageddon* (Lexington, Mass.: Lexington Books, 1986), pp. 45–60; Ze'ev Ma'oz and Avner Yaniv, "Game, Supergame and Compound Escalation: Israel and Syria, 1948–1984," *International Interaction* (in press).

7. Avner Yaniv, *Dilemmas of Security: Politics, Strategy and the Israeli Experience in Lebanon* (New York: Oxford University Press, 1987).

Chapter 1
Deterrence Theory and Israeli Strategy

1. Dan Horowitz, "The Israeli Concept of National Security and the Prospects of Peace in the Middle East," in G. Sheffer, ed., *Dynamics of a Conflict* (Atlantic Highlands, N.J.: Humanities Press, 1975), p. 244. For mention of deterrence as the pinnacle of Israeli policy, see David Ben Gurion, *Distinction and Destiny* (Tel Aviv: Am Oved, 1971), pp. 338–340; Yigal Allon, *The Making of Israel's Army* (London: George Weidenfeld &

Nicholson Ltd., 1970), p. 72; Shimon Peres, *David's Sling* (London: Weidenfeld and Nicholson, 1970), p. 18; Michael Brecher, *The Foreign Policy System of Israel* (London: Oxford University Press, 1972), p. 268; Michael Handel, *Israel's Political-Military Doctrine* (Cambridge, Mass.: Harvard Center for International Affairs, 1973), pp. 37, 76; Nadav Safran, *Israel: The Embattled Ally* (Cambridge, Mass.: Belknap Press, Harvard University Press, 1978), pp. 271–272; Edward Luttwak and Dan Horowitz, *The Israeli Army* (London: Allen Lane, 1975), pp. 341, 359, 361; Yair Evron, "The Role of Arms Control in the Middle East," *Adelphi Papers*, no. 138 (London: International Institute of Strategic Studies, 1977), p. 11; Janice Gross Stein and Raymond Tanter, *Rational Decision Making: Israel's Security Choices, 1967* (Columbus: Ohio State University Press, 1980), passim; Yo'av Ben-Horin and Barry Posen, *Israel's Strategic Doctrine* (Santa Monica, Calif.: Rand Corporation, 1981); Major-General Israel Tal, "Israel's Security in the Eighties," *Jerusalem Quarterly* 17 (1980):14–15.

2. For example, George H. Quester, *Deterrence before Hiroshima: The Airpower Background of Modern Strategy* (New York: Wiley, 1966). Richard N. Rosecrance, "Deterrence and Vulnerability in the Pre-Nuclear Era," *The Future of Strategic Deterrence*, part 1, *Adelphi Papers*, no. 160 (London: International Institute of Strategic Studies, 1980): James W. Morley, trans., *Deterrent Diplomacy: Japan, Germany and the USSR, 1935–40* (New York: Columbia University Press, 1976); John J. Mearsheimer, *Conventional Deterrence* (Ithaca, N.Y.: Cornell University Press, 1983); Samuel Huntington, "Conventional Deterrence and Conventional Retaliation in Europe," *International Security 8* (1984):32–56; Richard Betts, "Conventional Deterrence: Predictive Uncertainty and Policy Confidence," *World Politics 37* (1985):153–179.

3. Raymond Aron, *Peace and War* (New York: Doubleday, 1966), p. 404. The same point was made by Bernard Brodie in *Strategy in the Missile Age* (Princeton, N.J.: Princeton University Press, 1971), pp. 271–273, and by Thomas C. Schelling in *Arms and Influence* (New Haven: Yale University Press, 1966), p. 18.

4. Reprinted by permission of Westview Press from Alexander L. George, *Presidential Decisionmaking in Foreign Policy: The Effective Use of Information and Advice*, pp. 248–250. Copyright © 1980 by Westview Press, Boulder, Colo.

5. Quoted in Patrick Morgan, *Deterrence: A Conceptual Analysis*, 2nd ed. (Beverly Hills, Calif.: Sage Publications, 1983), pp. 19–26.

6. Mearsheimer, *Conventional Deterrence*, pp. 23–66.

7. Quoted from Glenn H. Snyder, "Deterrence and Defense," in Robert J. Art and Kenneth N. Waltz, eds., *The Use of Force* (New York and London: Lanham, 1983), p. 129.

8. See Basil H. Liddell Hart, *Strategy* (London: Faber and Faber, 1967), pp. 353–360.

9. On both the pro- and anti–status quo postures, see Hans J. Morgenthau, *Politics among Nations* (New York: Knopf, 1963), pp. 36–68.

10. Ibid.

11. Snyder, "Deterrence and Defense," pp. 133–134.

12. Morgan, *Deterrence*, p. 32.

13. A similar point is made by Huntington in "Conventional Deterrence and Conventional Retaliation."

14. Robert Jervis, *The Illogic of American Strategy* (Ithaca, N.Y.: Cornell University Press, 1985), p. 164.

15. See Brodie, *Strategy in the Missile Age*, p. 275; Andre Beaufre, *Stratégie pour demain* (Tel Aviv: Ma'arachot, 1977). (I have used the Hebrew version.) See also, on the French theory of limited deterrence, Pierre Galois, *Balance of Terror: A Strategy for the Nuclear Age* (Boston: Houghton Mifflin, 1961).

16. For a discussion of open and closed socieites, see Norton E. Long, "Open and Closed Systems," in R. Barry Farrell, ed., *Approaches to Comparative and International Politics* (Evanston, Ill.: Northwestern University Press, 1966), pp. 155–166.

17. On this, see the classic treatise by Carl J. Friedrich and Zbigniew Brzezinski, *Totalitarian Dictatorship and Autocracy* (New York: Praeger, 1956). For more recent attempts to illuminate aspects of this complexity, see Juan Linz, "Totalitarian and Authoritarian Regimes," in Fred Greenstein and Nelson Polsby, eds., *Handbook of Political Science*, vol. 2 (Reading, Mass.: Addison-Wesley, 1972), pp. 175–211.

18. This section, as well as the bulk of the attempt to define deterrence in comparison to defense and offense, draws on Yaniv, "Israel's Conventional Deterrent: A Reappraisal," in Beres, *Security or Armaggeddon*, pp. 45–60.

19. David Ben Gurion, *The Restored State of Israel*, vol. 1 (Tel Aviv: Am Oved, 1975), pp. 469, 509.

20. Allon, *The Making of Israel's Army*, p. 72.

21. Moshe Dayan, *Story of My Life* (Tel Aviv: Idanim, 1976), p. 601.

22. Ezer Weizman, *Lecha Shamayim Lecha Aretz* (Tel Aviv: Ma'ariv, 1975), p. 172. (The English translation of this title is *Thine the Skies, Thine the Land*).

23. *Interview with Ha'aretz*, June 5, 1984.

24. For a historical overview, see Howard M. Sachar, *A History of Israel* (New York: Knopf, 1979). A detailed statistical analysis of the views of all Knesset members between 1967 and 1977 revealed conclusively that for the overwhelming majority of them, the future of the occupied territories would be affected by Arab conduct. If the Arabs appeared bellicose, Israel should hold onto most of the territories occupied in the Six-Day War. If not, a great deal could be returned. See Avner Yaniv and Fabian Pascal, "Doves, Hawks and Other Birds of a Feather," *British Journal of Political Science* 10 (1980):260–267. For a contrary view by an Arab apologist, see David Hirst, *The Gun and the Olvie Branch*, 2nd ed. (London: Faber and Faber, 1984). Hirst's tortuous interpretation of the origins of the Six-Day War is refuted in a well-informed analysis by a retired Israeli general. See Haim Benyamini, "The Six-Day War, Israel 1967: Decisions, Coalitions, Consequences: A Sociological View," in Moshe Lissak, ed., *Israeli Society and Its Defence Establishment* (London: Frank Cass, 1984), pp. 64–82.

25. On this, see Rael Jean Isaac, *Israel Divided* (Baltimore: Johns Hopkins University Press, 1976), as well as Amnon Sella and Yael Yishai, *Israel: The Peaceful Belligerent, 1967–1979* (London: Macmillan, 1986).

26. This point has never been stated clearly by Israeli policymakers. It can, however, be surmised. See p. 17.

27. Ben Gurion, *The Restored State of Israel*, p. 399.

28. Allon, *The Making of Israel's Army*, 63–64.

29. Me'ir Pa'il, "The Security Concept: Doctrine and the Human Factor," lecture delivered at a *Ma'arachot* (IDF monthly) symposium on "Dilemmas of Quality versus Quantity and the Construction of Military Force," Beit Sokolov, Tel Aviv, February 9, 1984. For a published version of the lecture, see Me'ir Pa'il "Takhbula, Ruakh Lekhima VeTechnologia" ["Tactics, Fighting Spirit and Technology"], in Zvi

Offer and Avi Kober, eds., *Quality and Quantity in Military Buildup* (Tel Aviv: Ma'arachot, 1985), pp. 361–372.

30. For a useful comparative survey of national security policy statements, see J.B. Poole and J.K.A. Brown, "Survey of National Defense Statements," *Survival 24* (1982), pp. 220–228.

31. Allon, *A Curtain of Sand* (Tel Aviv: Hakibbutz HaMeuchad, 1981), p. 433. This theme is stated in detail in Yaniv, "Israel's Conventional Deterrent: A Reappraisal."

32. As my colleague Ze'ev Ma'oz pointed out to me, this hypothesis is in itself logical and consistent enough to be encapsulated in a mathematical formula as follows:

$$\frac{\Delta X(V)}{\Delta T} = D$$

$$\frac{\Delta (D + N)}{\Delta T} = P$$

33. For a similar use of the concept of strategic package, see Shai Feldman, "Peacemaking in the Middle East: The Next Step," *Foreign Affairs 59* (1981):756–780. Other Israeli scholars suggest the same periodization. See Yair Evron, "Two Periods in Arab–Israeli Strategic Relations: 1957–67, 1967–73," in Itamar Rabinovitch and Haim Shaked, eds., *From June to October* (New Brunswick, N.J.: Transactions Books, 1978), pp. 93–126.

34. This is the main thesis in Yoram Peri, *Between Battles and Ballots* (Cambridge: Cambridge University Press, 1983), pp. 1–3.

35. Gabriel Ben Dor, "Milchemet Yom Hakipurim: Hahafta'a Hagdola" ["The Yom Kippur War: The Great Surprise"], *State, Government and International Relations 6* (1974):156–166.

36. "Dayan: Atoms, Not Tanks Should Defend Israel," *Jerusalem Post*, November 30, 1976.

37. Steven J. Rosen, "A Stable System of Mutual Nuclear Deterrence in the Middle East," *The American Political Science Review 71* (1977): 1367–1383; Shlomo Aronson, *Israel's Nuclear Options*, ACIS Working Paper no. 17 (Los Angeles, Center for Arms Control and International Security, University of California, November 1977); Aronson, "Nuclearization of the Middle East: A Dovish View," *Jerusalem Quarterly 2* (1977):27–44; Robert Tucker, "Israel and the United States: From Dependence to Nuclear Weapons?" *Commentary 60* (1975):29–43.

38. Shai Feldman, *Israeli Nuclear Deterrence: A Strategy for the 1980s* (New York: Columbia University Press, 1982).

Chapter 2
The Formative Years: 1949–1956

1. For the background, see Trevor N. Dupuy, *Elusive Victory: The Arab–Israeli Wars 1947–74* (New York: Harper and Row, 1978), vol. 1, esp. pp. 112–117; Chaim Herzog, *The Arab–Israeli Wars* (New York: Random House, 1982), vol. 1; Safran, *Israel: The Embattled Ally*, pp. 43–64.

2. On this, see Shlomo Aronson, *Conflict and Bargaining in the Middle East* (Baltimore: Johns Hopkins University Press, 1978), p. 8.

3. For an old but still very succinct case history of this chapter in Arab–Israeli relations, see Roney E. Gabbay, *A Political Study of the Jewish–Arab Conflict* (Geneva: Librairi Droz, 1959), pp. 313–340. See also Earl Berger, *The Covenant and the Sword: Arab–Israeli Relations, 1948–56* (London: Routledge & Kegan Paul, 1965), pp. 14–20.

4. For a comprehensive history of this process, see Howard M. Sachar, *Europe Leaves the Middle East* (London: Allen Lane, 1972).

5. For a statistical analysis of this wave of immigration, see Moshe Sicron, *Immigration to Israel 1948–53* (Jerusalem: Jerusalem Post Press, for the Falk Project for Economic Research in Israel, 1957).

6. A vivid and lucid description of this situation was offered recently by an Israeli journalist. See Tom Segev, *1949—The First Israelis* (Jerusalem: Domino Press, 1984), part 2.

7. Gershon Rivlin and Elhanan Orren, eds., *The War of Independence: Ben Gurion's Diary* (Tel Aviv: Misrad HaBitachon–HaHotsa'a La'Or, 1982), vol. 3, p. 774.

8. For details about Arab order of battle during various stages of the 1948 war, see Colonel (Ret.) Me'ir Pa'il, "From Hagana through War of Independence to the IDF," in Ya'akov Erez and Ilan Kphir, eds., *Tsahal Bekheilo—Encyclopaedia LeTsava Uvitachon* [*The IDF as an Army: Encyclolpaedia of Military Affairs and Security*] (Tel Aviv: Revivim, 1982), pp. 29–59.

9. For details, see Yoav Gelber, *Garin LeTsava Ivri Sadir* [*A Nucleus of a Hebrew Army*] (Jerusalem: Yad Ben Tsvi, 1986), ch. 40; Luttwak and Horowitz, *The Israeli Army* pp. 71–104. For an interesting if patchy firsthand account of the genesis of this system by one of its architects see retired Colonel (subsequently world-renowned astrophysicist and then a right-wing member of the Knesset) Yuval Ne'eman, "The Planning of a National Security System for a Nation in the Making," in Zvi Lanir, ed., *Israeli Security Planning in the 1980s* (Tel Aviv: Misrad HaBitachon, 1985), pp. 153–161. Ben Gurion's war diaries bear witness to his detailed interest in the Swiss experience with a reserve system. See Rivlin and Orren, *Ben Gurion's Diary*, vol. 2, p. 708.

10. See Pa'il, "From Hagana."

11. On the Arab–Israeli arms race during this period, see Paul Jabber, *Not by War Alone* (Berkeley: University of California Press, 1981), pp. 96–106.

12. Luttwak and Horowitz, *The Israeli Army*, 119–133.

13. These estimates are quoted in the account of the then chief of staff. See Moshe Dayan, *Story of My Life*, p. 176.

14. Ibid., pp. 183–184.

15. Segev, in *The First Israelis*, pp. 48–52, documents in detail the confident mood of Israeli leaders during the first two post–1948 war years.

16. For a detailed statement of the strategic rationale of Spatial Defense, see Allon, *A Curtain of Sand*, pp. 239–264. Allon saw Spatial Defense as nothing less than a fourth arm, along with the traditional air, sea, and (mobile) ground forces.

17. On the NAHAL program, see Irving Haymont, "The Israeli Nahal Program," *Middle East Journal* 21 (1967):314–324. A popular and folksy account of the Nahal story is offered in Erez and Kphir, *Tsahal*, vol. 5.

18. For a Socratic dialogue between Ben Gurion and Dayan on this issue, see Dayan, *Story of My Life*, pp. 171–172.

19. This is my own expanded interpretation of a cryptic statement of the case for an offensive emphasis in Dayan, *Story of My Life*, p. 178.

20. Gabbay, *A Political Study*, pp. 227–267; Berger, *The Covenant and the Sword*, pp. 41–59.

21. See Bowyer J. Bell, *The Long War* (Englewood Cliffs, N.J.: Prentice-Hall, 1969), pp. 227–245; Berger, *The Covenant and the Sword*, pp. 154–161.

22. See Dayan, *Story of My Life*, pp. 135, 140, and Moshe Sharett, *Yoman Ishi* (Tel Aviv: Am Oved, 1978), pp. 422–423, 434–435, 577.

23. Shrett, *Yoman Ishi*, p. 266.

24. Ibid., p. 947.

25. Bell, *The Long War*, pp. 253–254.

26. For a singularly lucid statement of this official Israeli perception, see Moshe Dayan, "Why Israel Strikes Back," in Donald Robinson, ed., *Under Fire: Israel's Twenty Years' Struggle for Survival* (New York: W.W. Norton, 1968). Allon advanced a similar view in *A Curtain of Sand*, p. 427.

27. For the classical statement of the concept of coercive diplomacy, see Alexander L. George, David Hall, and William Simons, *The Limits of Coercive Diplomacy* (Boston: Little, Brown, 1971).

28. See the personal account of the British commanding officer of Jordan's Arab Legion, Lieutenant-General Sir John Baggot Glubb, *A Soldier with the Arabs* (London: Hodder and Stoughton, 1957), pp. 331–343.

29. For Ben Gurion's public position on these issues, see his own account in *The Restored State of Israel*, pp. 466 ff.

30. See Howard M. Sachar, *Egypt and Israel* (New York: Richard Marek Publishers, 1981), pp. 78–79.

31. More details about these negotiations are offered in Shabtai Teveth, *Moshe Dayan* (Jerusalem: Schocken, 1971), pp. 336–338.

32. This period in Fertile Crescent politics has yet to be discovered by scholars of the Middle East. Meanwhile, some background material can be gleaned from Ann Sinai and Allen Pollack, eds., *The Hashemite Kingdom of Jordan and the West Bank* (New York: Association of American Academics for Peace in the Middle East [AAAPME], 1977), pp. 28–31; Clinton Baily, *Jordan's Palestinian Challenge 1948–83* Boulder, Colo.: Westview Press, 1984), pp. 1–26.

33. See Patrick Seale, *The Struggle for Syria: A Study of Postwar Arab Politics* (London: Oxford University Press, 1965), esp. chap. 20, "Syria's Road to Suez II."

34. See Sharett, *Yoman Ishi*, pp. 332, 374, 712, 868, 948–949, 989, 996, 1248, 2284, 2309–2310; see also Abba Eban's biography, *Pirkei Chaim* [*Chapters of Life*] (Tel Aviv: Ma'ariv, 1978), vol. 1, p. 197.

35. For such a scenario, see Yigal Allon, *The Making of Israel's Army*, pp. 50–54.

36. The distinction between these two types of deterrence is drawn in Schelling, *Arms and Influence*, pp. 69 ff., 79 ff., 174 ff.

37. The outline of this escalation process draws on Dayan, *Story of My Life*, pp. 216–270; Sachar, *Egypt and Israel*, pp. 62–105; Lieutenant-General E. L.M. Burns, *Between Arab and Israeli* (Toronto: Clarke, Irwin, 1962), passim.

38. See Sachar, *A History of Israel*, pp. 41–64, 89–115, 195–314, and Michael Bar-Zohar, *Ben Gurion: A Political Biography*, (Tel Aviv: Am Oved, 1975), vol. 1, pp. 233–566.

39. See Ben Gurion, *The Restored State of Israel*, vol. 1, pp. 52–88; Bar-Zohar, *Ben Gurion*, vol. 1, pp. 567–576.

40. For a recent and comprehensive account, see Steven L. Spiegel, *The Other Arab–Israeli Conflict* (Chicago: University of Chicago Press, 1985), pp. 16–49.

41. See, for example, Sachar, *Europe Leaves the Middle East*, pp. 580–618.

42. Bar-Zohar, *Ben Gurion*, vol. 2, pp. 820–821.

43. For an excellent account, see Arnold Krammer, *The Forgotten Friendship: Israel and the Soviet Bloc, 1947–1953* (Chicago: University of Illinois Press, 1974).

44. Jabber, *Not by War Alone*, pp. 63–95.

45. These negotiations are described in Bar-Zohar, *Ben Gurion*, vol. 2, pp. 902–917; see also Sharett, *Yoman Ishi*, pp. 265, 434, 473, 517, 561, 563, and Dayan *Story of My Life*, pp. 122–123.

46. For details, see the account of Meir Avidan, *Hebetim Iqryim BeYachasei Israel Artsot HaBrit [Principal Aspects of Israeli–U.S. Relations]* (Jerusalem: Leonard Davis Institute, 1982), pp. 8–27.

47. Spiegel, *The Other Arab–Israeli Conflict*, pp. 50–71; Eban, *Pirkei*, pp. 162–192; Sharett, *Yoman Ishi*, passim; Bar-Zohar, *Ben Gurion*, pp. 1029–1033, 1152–1170.

48. Bar-Zohar, *Ben Gurion*, pp. 1171–1184.

49. See Sylvia Kowitt-Crosbie, *The Tacit Alliance* (Princeton, N.J.: Princeton University Press, 1974), pp. 29–76.

50. On the evolution of the Hagana doctrine, see Meir Pa'il, *The Emergence of ZAHAL (IDF)* (Tel Aviv: Zmora-Bitan-Modan, 1979). On the political dispute concerning retaliation versus restraint, see Ya'akov Shavit, *Havlaga oh Tguva [Restraint or Retaliation]* (Ramat Gan: Bar Ilan University, 1983).

51. For a statement of the IZL/Stern Group position concerning the use of force, see Eli Tavin and Yonah Alexander, eds., *Psychological Warfare and Propaganda: Irgun Documentation* (Wilmington, Del: Scholarly Resources, 1982), pp. xxxviii–xliv.

52. Rivlin and Orren, *Ben Gurion's Diary*, vol. 2, pp. 475, 478, 504, 593, 598, 601.

53. For a meticulous analysis of Israeli self-image during the early years of independence, see Brecher, *The Foreign Policy System of Israel*, esp. part 2, "Psyhological Environment."

54. The figures are quoted in an article by Moshe Dayan, "Peulot HaTagmoul" ["The Reprisals"], in Erez and Kphir, *Tsahal*, vol. 1, p. 98.

55. One example attesting to the crucial importance that the Israeli government attached to this was Ben Gurion's comment a day after an attack on the new immigrants' village of Patish that "there was no escape from seizing the Gaza Strip whence the attack had come." Meanwhile, the prime minister ordered the infusion of capital to such villages and called on the younger generation from well-established villages to volunteer to help infirm new immigrants' villages of the Patish type. See Dayan, *Story of My Life*, pp. 122, 143.

56. According to one account, the IDF carried out fifty-one operations of this type from 1949 to 1953. See Erez and Kphir, *Tsahal*, vol. 1, pp. 70, 84. It seems plausible to assume, however, that this was only the general headquarters count and that smaller operations were carried out unannounced at the initiative of lower echelons.

57. See Colonel (Ret.) Yehuda Wallach, "Rav Aluph Makleph—Adifut LaDereg HaLochem" ["Lieutenant-General Makleph—Priority for the Combat Echelon"], in Erez and Kphir, *Tsahal*, vol. 1, p. 80. Also Dayan, *Story of My Life,* pp. 113–114.

58. On the Qibyeh raid, see Uzi Benziman, *Sharon: An Israeli Caeser* (New York: Adama Publications, 1985), chap. 3.

59. Dayan, *Story of My Life*, pp. 115–116; Teveth, *Moshe Dayan*, pp. 389–396.

60. For a good example of a well-argued and richly documented critique, see Barry M. Blechman, "The Consequences of Israeli Reprisals: An Assessment," Ph.D. thesis, Georgetown University, 1971.

61. Moshe Dayan, "Peacetime Military Operations," in *Ma'arachot 118–119* (1959):54–61. The point that punishment or pure revenge was not the objective was reiterated many years later by Major-General Israel Tal in "Israel's Security in the Eighties," pp. 14–15.

62. For details, see Burns, 136–148, and Dayan, *Story of My Life*, p. 152.

63. Saadia Touval, *The Peace Brokers: Mediators in the Arab–Israeli Conflict, 1948–79* (Princeton, N.J.: Princeton University Press, 1982), pp. 106–134; see also Elmore Jackson, *Middle East Mission* (New York: W.W. Norton, 1983).

64. Allon, *The Making of Israel's Army*, pp. 64–65.

65. See Robert Jervis, "Cooperation under the Security Dilemma," *World Politics* 30 (1978):167–214. For a detailed statement of this thesis with reference to Israel, see Yaniv, *Dilemmas of Security*, chapter 1, "The Sources of Israeli Conduct."

66. The main sources for understanding Dayan are his own writings. See, in this connection, *Story of My Life*, pp. 116–263; see also Teveth, *Moshe Dayan*, chap. 15, and Brecher, *The Foreign Policy System of Israel*, pp. 335–339, 353–358.

67. This brief profile of Sharett's outlook and policy draws first and foremost on his own eight-volume personal diary, *Yoman Ishi*. For other discussions of Sharett, see Brecher, *The Foreign Policy System of Israel*, chap. 12; Dayan, *Story of My Life*, pp. 137–139; Golda Meir, *My Life* (London: Futura, 1975), pp. 234–239; Gabriel Sheffer, *Resolution versus Management of the Middle East Conflict*, Jerusalem Papers on Peace Problems, no. 32 (Jerusalem: Leonard Davis Institute, 1980); Uri Bialer, "Ben Gurion veSharett: Shnei Dimuyim Shel Hasichsuch HaIsraeli Arvi" ["Ben Gurion and Sharett: Two Images of the Arab–Israeli Conflict"], in *State and Government 1* (1971):71–84; Kenneth Love, *Suez: The Twice-Fought War* (New York: McGraw-Hill, 1969), pp. 47–54; Avi Shlaim, "Contending Approaches to Israel's Relations with the Arabs: Ben Gurion and Sharett, 1953–1956," *Middle East Journal 37* (1984):180–201.

68. This profile of Ben Gurion is based on Bar-Zohar, *Ben Gurion*, esp. vol. 2; Dayan, *Story of My Life*, esp. pp. 116–271; Sharett, *Yoman Ishi*, passim; Brecher, *The Foreign Policy System of Israel*, chap. 12; and Aronson, *Conflict and Bargaining in the Middle East*, chap. 1.

Chapter 3
Deterrence Comes of Age: 1957–1967

1. For detailed analyses of the military campaign, see Dupuy, *Elusive Victory*, pp. 129–220; Moshe Dayan, *Yoman Ma'arechet Sinai* [*Diary of the Sinai Campaign*] (Tel Aviv: Am Hasepher, 1965); Herzog, *The Arab–Israeli Wars*, pp. 109–142.

2. Ben Gurion, *The Restored State of Israel*, pp. 518 ff.; Bar-Zohar, *Ben Gurion*, pp. 1207–1315; Eban, *Pirkei*, pp. 193–246; Meir, *My Life*, pp. 245–255; Sachar, *Egypt and Israel*, pp. 96–119.

3. For a concise overview, see Sachar, *A History of Israel*, pp. 515–614.

4. On this period in the Arab world, see the succinct account of the late Malcolm H. Kerr, *The Arab Cold War*, 3rd ed. (New York: Oxford University Press, 1971). For an attempt to explain these developments as a reflection of the inter-Arab balance of power mechanism, see Alan R. Taylor, *The Arab Balance of Power* (Syracuse, N.Y.: Syracuse University Press, 1982), pp. 36–48.

5. See Luttwak and Horowitz, *The Israeli Army*, pp. 165–209.

6. Ibid.

7. See the contributions by Generals Meir Zorea, Chaim Laskov, Tsvi Tsur, and Itzhak Rabin, in Erez and Kphir, *Tsahal* vol. 1, pp. 143–166, 183–208.

8. The IAF entered the Sinai campaign with 24 Mystère jet fighters, 21 Ouragan jet fighters, 15 Meteor jet fighter-interceptors, 28 Mustang piston-engine fighters, 13 Mosquito piston-engine reconnaissance bombers, 2 B-17 Flying Fortress piston-engine bombers, 16 Harvard two-seat piston-engine trainers, 15 Dakota DC-3 and Nord 2501 transporters, 17 Piper Cubs, and 24 Steerman trainers. The grand total was 175 planes, for which the IAF had 210 pilots, but only 47 pilots for its fleet of 60 jets. At the same time Egypt had 210 jets and 150 pilots, which meant that the nominal ratio was 1:1.6 in favor of Egypt. See Erez and Kphir, *Tsahal*, vol. 3, p. 70.

9. Allon, *A Curtain of Sand*, p. 177.

10. Erez and Kphir, *Tsahal*, vol. 1, p. 98.

11. See Dupuy, *Elusive Victory*, p. 337, and Erez and Kphir, *Tsahal*, vol. 10, pp. 78–81.

12. See Pinhas Zusman (a former director-general of the Israeli Ministry of Defense), "Why Is the Burden of Security So Heavy in Israel?," in Zvi Offer and Major Avi Kober, eds., *The Price of Power* [*Mechir Haotzma*] (Tel Aviv: Ma'arachot, 1984), pp. 17–27.

13. See Amos Perlmutter, Michael Handel, and Uri Bar-Joseph, *Two Minutes over Baghdad* (London: Corgi, 1982), pp. 21–28; Alan Dowty, "Nuclear Proliferation: The Israeli Case," *International Studies Quarterly* 22 (1978):79–120; and Uri Bar-Joseph, "The Hidden Debate: The Formulation of Nuclear Doctrines in the Middle East," *Journal of Strategic Studies* 5 (1982):205–227.

14. See Spiegel, *The Other Arab–Israeli Conflict*, pp. 79–81; Meir, *My Life*, pp. 254–256; Eban, *Pirkei*, pp. 222–246.

15. Allon, *A Curtain of Sand*, pp. 343–348.

16. For more details, see Yehezkel HaMeiri, "Demilitarization and Conflict Reduction: The DMZs on the Israeli–Syrian Border," M.A. thesis, University of Haifa, 1979.

17. See Sharett, *Yoman Ishi*, esp. vols. 2–4, passim, for rich material on this problem. For a comprehensive, well-documented discussion of the decision-making process, see Brecher, *Decisions in Israel's Foreign Policy* pp. 173–225.

18. See the memoirs of Itzhak Rabin, then IDF chief of the General Staff under the Hebrew title *Pinkas Sherut* (Tel Aviv: Ma'ariv, 1979), pp. 106–108.

19. See Avraham Sella, *Ahdut BeToch Perud: Veidot HaPisga HaArviot* [*Unity in Disunity: Arab Summit Meetings*] (Jerusalem: Magnes Press, 1984), p. 27.

20. Shimon Peres, "Meimad HaZman" ("The Time Dimension"), *Ma'arachot 146* (1962):3–5.

21. Quoted in Brecher, *The Foreign Policy System of Israel*, p. 67.

22. Yigal Allon, "Hagana Pe'ila: Aruva LeKiyumenu" ("Active Defense: A Guarantee of Our Existence"), *Molad 1* (1967):137–163. This interpretation, which emphasizes the persistent reluctance of the Israeli military-political elite to enunciate clear casi belli, is endorsed by Yair Evron in "Two Periods in Arab–Israeli Strategic Relations," pp. 102–104. It is somewhat at variance, however, with the excellent study of the same problem by Gross Stein and Tanter, *Rational Decision Making*, and with Michael I. Handel's *Israel's Political-Military Doctrine*. Neither study seems to distinguish between tacitly assumed *precipitants* of military action and publicly enunciated casi belli.

23. See Kowitt-Crosbie, *The Tacit Alliance*, pp. 98 ff.; see also Samy Cohen, *De Gaulle, les Gaullistes et Israel* (Paris: Alain Moreau, 1974), pp. 75–118, and Edward A. Kolodziej, *French Foreign Policy under De Gaulle and Pompidou: The Politics of Grandeur* (Ithaca, N.Y.: Cornell University Press, 1974), part 3.

24. Dayan, *Story of My Life*, p. 356; Perlmutter et al., *Two Minutes over Baghdad*, pp. 23–24.

25. Allon, *A Curtain of Sand*, p. 158; Perlmutter et al., *Two Minutes over Baghdad*, pp. 27–28.

26. Allon, *A Curtain of Sand*, pp. 141–162.

27. Eban, *Pirkei*, pp. 247–252; see also Sharett, *Yoman Ishi*, passim, for details about Eban's earlier views on this topic.

28. See Peres, *David's Sling*, pp. 137–162; see also Matti Golan, *Peres* (Jerusalem: Schocken, 1982), pp. 51–53, 71–74, 75–83; Lilly Gardner Feldman, *The Special Relationship between West Germany and Israel* (Boston: George Allen and Unwin, 1984), pp. 126–136; Perlmutter et al., *Two Minutes over Baghdad*, pp. 27–28.

29. Meir, *My Life*, pp. 263–290.

30. The concept of *terms of collaboration*—a political equivalent of the economic concept of *terms of trade*—was introduced by Robert E. Osgood in *NATO: The Entangling Alliance* (Chicago: University of Chicago Press, 1962), pp. 42–43.

31. For details, see Yaniv, *Dilemmas of Security*, chapter 2.

32. The regional background for this period can be traced from diverse sources, such as Kerr, *The Arab Cold War*, chap. 1; Sachar, *Egypt and Israel*, chaps. 10–11; Brecher, *Decisions in Israel's Foreign Policy*, chaps. 6, 7; George and Smoke, *Deterrence in American Foreign Policy*, pp. 309–362.

33. For traces of the main components of this scheme, see Peres, *David's Sling*, pp. 137–162, 281–291; Rabin, *Pinkas*, vol. 1, pp. 102–104; Bar-Zohar, *Ben Gurion*, pp. 1316–1322.

34. David Ben Gurion, "Isreal's Security and Her International Position before and after the Sinai Campaign," in State of Israel, *Government Yearbook 1959/60* (Jerusalem: HaMadpis HaMemshalti, 1960), p. 86.

35. This overview draws on Nelson Frye, *The United States, Turkey and Iran* (Cambridge, Mass.: Harvard University Press, 1952), pp. 130–132; George S. Harris, *Troubled Alliance* (Washington, D.C.: American Enterprise Institute/Hoover Policy Studies, 1972), pp. 49–85; Sharett, *Yoman Ishi*, passim; George E. Gruen, "Turkey, Israel and the Palestine Question, 1948–60," Ph.D. thesis, Columbia University, New York, 1972.

36. The main source on these relations is a book in Hebrew by Shmuel Seguev entitled *The Iranian Triangle* (Tel Aviv: Ma'ariv, 1981), pp. 87–115. For an interesting account of Israel's early contacts with Iran, see Uri Bialer, "The Iranian Connection in Israel's Foreign Policy, 1948–1951." *Middle East Journal 39*, no. 2 (spring 1985): 292–315.

37. See an article by "Correspondent" in *New Outlook 6* (1963):32–35; see also Bar-Zohar, *Ben Gurion*, pp. 1331–1332.

38. During a meeting at Palm Beach between President John F. Kennedy and the Israeli foreign minister, Golda Meir, the president told Meir that "the United States has a special relationship with Israel in the Middle East really comparable only to that which it has with Britain over a wide range of world affairs" and that "it is quite clear that in the case of an invasion of Israel the United States would come to the support of Israel." This, according to a former Israeli diplomat, was as close to a security guarantee as Israel had ever come before. See Mordechai Gazit, *President Kennedy's Policy toward the Arab States and Israel,* Studies Series (Tel Aviv: Shiloah Center for Middle Eastern and African Studies, 1983), pp. 46–48. On Israel's trading of a partial suspension of the Dimona nuclear program for U.S. commitments to step up support and supply sophisticated arms, which until then had been persistently denied, see Perlmutter et al., *Two Minutes over Baghdad*, pp. 26–28; Aronson, *Conflict and Bargaining in the Middle East*, pp. 50–51.

39. The title of this section is, of course, adopted from the title of the first chapter of Thomas C. Schelling's classic *Arms and Influence.*

40. This is quoted from *HaYom* of May 1, 1968, in Dan Horowitz, *Israel's Concept of Defensible Borders*, Jerusalem Papers on Peace Problems, no. 16 (Jerusalem: Leonard Davis Institute, 1975), pp. 4–5.

41. Quoted in Yehezkel HaMeiri, *Mishnei Evrei HaRama* (Tel Aviv: Levin-Epstein, 1970), p. 38.

42. Allon, *A Curtain of Sand*, p. 344.

43. Weizman, *Thine the Skies*, p. 177.

44. The importance that the Kennedy administration attached to changing Israel's visible (but undeclared) predisposition to prefer a first-strike posture and Israel's dogged determination not to yield on this point can be seen from an encounter between presidential envoy Averill Harriman and Lieutenant-General Yitzhak Rabin, then chief of the IDF General Staff. The U.S. diplomat said that the United States would consider large-scale supply of weapons if Israel undertook to avoid a preemptive strike, come what may. Rabin's reply was typically blunt: "We are not prepared," he told Harriman, "to eschew preventive war. We'll do everything to settle conflict peacefully; but to tie our hands in advance to a commitment to avoid a preemptive war come what may means only one thing: to deny ourselves the right of self-defense." Rabin, *Pinkas*, pp. 128–129.

45. Weizman, *Thine the Skies*, pp. 226–227.

46. See Gazit, *President Kennedy's Policy*, p. 121.

47. Weizman, *Thine the Skies*, p. 173. This pre-1967 Israeli image of the next war is culled from Weizman's account as well as from the accounts of three Israeli chiefs of staff during this period (Laskov, Tsur, and Rabin) in Erez and Kphir, *Tsahal*, vol. 1.

48. In the summer of 1958 Lebanon was stabilized with the help of a U.S. landing of a contingent of marines on the shores of Beirut, and the hashemite monarchy in Jordan was saved from collapse by a British airlift of troops. Both operations were indirectly assisted by Israeli threats, moves, signals, and more direct forms of assistance to elements in Lebanon, to the Hashemites, and to both the United States and the United Kingdom. See George and Smoke, *Deterrence in American Foreign Policy*, pp. 309–362, and Alan Dowty, *Middle East Crisis: U.S. Decision-Making 1958, 1970 and 1973* (Berkeley: University of California Press, 1984), pp. 23–110.

49. The literature on this topic is vast. For a bibliographic survey, see Moshe Ma'oz and Avner Yaniv, "The Study of Syria," in Ma'oz and Yaniv, *Syria under Assad*, pp. 1–8.

50. See Brecher, *Decisions in Israel's Foreign Policy*, pp. 173–224.

51. Rabin, *Pinkas*, pp. 121–122; see also Lieutenant-Colonel Shimon Golan, "The Struggle for the Jordan Waters," in Avshalom Shmueli, Arnon Sofer, and Nurit Kleot, eds., *The Lands of Galilee*, vol. 2 (Haifa: University of Haifa Press, 1982), pp. 856–857.

52. For profiles of Eshkol, see Terrence Prittie, *Eshkol: The Man and the Nation* (London: Pitman, 1969); Brecher, *The Foreign Policy System of Israel*, pp. 291–301; Weizman, *Thine the Skies*, pp. 237–247.

53. For a more detailed discussion of the same theme, see Yaniv, "Syria and Israel: The Politics of Escalation," in Ma'oz and Yaniv, *Syria under Assad*, pp. 160–166.

54. On the Syrian calculus in allowing the formation of Fateh, see Moshe Ma'oz and Avner Yaniv, "On a Short Leash: Syria and the PLO," in Ma'oz and Yaniv, *Syria under Assad*, pp. 189–193; see also Helena Cobban, *The Palestine Liberation Organization* (Cambridge: Cambridge University Press, 1984), pp. 195–200; Alan Hart, *Arafat* (London: Sidgwick and Jackson, 1984), chaps. 9–10.

55. See the detailed and authoritative biography of General Elazar by Hanoch Bar-Tov, entitled *Daddo: 48 Years and 20 More Days* (Tel Aviv: Ma'ariv, 1978), vol. 1, pp. 106–120; also Robert Slater, *Rabin of Israel: A Biography* (Jerusalem: Idan, 1977), pp. 68–71.

56. Weizman, *Thine the Skies*, pp. 253–254.

57. On the Assad–Jedid rivalry, see Nicolas Van Dam, *The Struggle for Power in Syria* (London: Croom Helm, 1979), pp. 83–97, and Moshe Ma'oz, "The Emergence of Modern Syria," in Ma'oz and Yaniv, *Syria under Assad*, pp. 21–25.

58. Eshkol's personal responsibility for the escalation with Syria caused Ben Gurion to lose his temper. Eshkol, Ben Gurion wrote in his diary, "turned a reprisal against Syria into a quasi war (80 planes, 130 sorties) flies over Damascus, called up reserves prematurely. As a prime minister he [Eshkol] is a liar and a coward." Quoted in Bar-Zohar, *Ben Gurion*, p. 1588; on Eshkol's (clearly unintended) contribution to the escalation, see also Erez and Kphir, *Tsahal*, vol. 1, p. 179, and Yaniv, "Syria and Israel: The Politics of Escalation," pp. 164–165.

59. Prittie, *Eshkol*, p. 244.

60. See Brecher (with Geist), *Decisions in Crisis*, p. 43.

61. Sachar, *Egypt and Israel*, p. 139.

62. Hirst, *The Gun and the Olive Branch*, p. 206.

63. For specific attempts to trace the putative link between the turbulent exigencies of Syria's domestic situation and its external conduct, see Robert Burrows and Bertram Spector, "The Strength and Direction of Relationship between Domestic Conflict

and External Conflict and Cooperation: Syria, 1961–7," in James N. Rosenau and Jonathan Wilkenfield, eds., *Conflict Behavior and Linkage Politics* (New York: McKay, 1973), pp. 294–324; Yaakov Bar-Siman-Tov, *Linkage Politics in the Middle East: Syria between Domestic and External Conflict, 1961–70* (Boulder, Colo.: Westview Press, 1983).

64. Dan Horowitz, a leading Israeli national security intellectual, presents the principle of "autonomy" of strategic-military decision making as a distinct feature of the pre-1967 Israeli situation. See Horowitz, "The Israeli Concept of National Security." The validity of Horowitz's assertion seems, however, to be questioned by a number of more recent studies. See, for example, Aronson, *Conflict and Bargaining in the Middle East*, and Peri, *Between Battles and Ballots*. In very different ways and from very different perspectives, both studies emphasize the pervasively politicized nature of Israeli national security policymaking.

65. Bar-Zohar, *Ben Gurion*, pp. 1437–1470; Yossi Beilin, *Banim BeTsel Avotam* (Tel Aviv: Revivim, 1984), pp. 16–85.

66. Sharett, *Yoman Ishi*, vol. 3, chaps 1–3.

67. See Bar-Zohar, *Ben Gurion*, pp. 1471–1518, and Nathan Yanai, *Political Crises in Israel* (Jerusalem: Keter Publishing, 1982), pp. 110–140.

68. See Rael Jean Isaac, *Party and Politics in Israel* (New York and London: Longman, 1981), pp. 118–121.

69. See Aronson, *Conflict and Bargaining in the Middle East*, pp. 51–54; Perlmutter et al., *Two Minutes over Baghdad*, pp. 27–28; and Bar-Joseph, "The Hidden Debate. The Formation of Nuclear Doctrines in the Middle East."

70. Bar-Zohar, *Ben Gurion*, pp. 1573–1586.

71. Weizman, *Thine the Skies*, p. 240.

72. Teveth, *Moshe Dayan*, p. 427.

73. Ben Gurion's handling of the 1960 crisis, stressing the secrecy in which the Israeli response was deliberately shrouded, is described in Bar-Zohar, *Ben Gurion*, p. 1587. This account is confirmed by the recollections of the then chief of staff, Lieutenant-General Laskov, who also adds the important fact that the Egyptian force was withdrawn within thirty-two hours. See Erez and Kphir, *Tsahal*, vol. 1, p. 149. This interpretation is also generally confirmed in Evron, "Two Periods in Arab–Israeli Strategic Relations," pp. 102–104.

74. This brief review of the 1967 crisis draws primarily on Brigadier-General Israel Lior, "Levi Eshkol: Breaking into New Frontiers," in Erez and Kphir, *Tsahal*, vol. 1, pp. 175–178; Teveth, *Moshe Dayan*, pp. 556–575; Dayan, *Story of My Life*, pp. 398–432; Brecher, *Decisions in Crisis*, passim; and Gross Stein and Tanter, *Rational Decision Making*, passim.

Chapter 4
The Perils of Victory: 1967–1973

1. This is an important theme in Fouad Ajami, *The Arab Predicament* (Cambridge: Cambridge University Press, 1981).

2. See, for example, a collection of essays by Arab writers in the aftermath of the 1967 defeat, which Major-General (Ret.) Professor Yehoshafat Harkabi introduced to the Hebrew reader under the title *Lekach Ha'arvim MiTvusatam (The Arabs' Lesson from Their Defeat)* (Tel Aviv: Am Oved, 1969).

3. Gad Ya'akobi, *Otsmata Shell Eichut* (*The Power of Quality*) (Haifa: Shikmona Press, 1972).

4. Erez and Kphir, *Tsahal*, vol. 1, pp. 186, 206, vol. 2, pp. 56–57.

5. Ibid.

6. Quoted in Bar-Tov, *Daddo*, p. 99.

7. For an outstanding example, see Shabtai Teveth, *Hasufim BaTsariach* (*Exposed in the Turret* (Jerusalem: Schocken, 1968).

8. Dayan, *Story of My Life*, pp. 427–432, 471.

9. Teveth, *Hasufim*, esp. pp. 252–273.

10. The most typical and simpleminded statement of this view is Golda Meir's in *My Life*, pp. 318–352.

11. See Avraham Adan, *On Both Banks of the Suez* (Jerusalem: Idanim, 1979), pp. 49–52. The author, a now retired major-general, was in charge of the Sinai defense plan.

12. Dayan, *Story of My Life*, pp. 527–528; Teveth, *Moshe Dayan*, pp. 575–576; Eban, *Pirkei*, pp. 466–477; William B. Quandt, *Decade of Decisions* (Berkeley: University of California Press, 1977), chaps. 3, 5; Lawrence L. Whetten, *The Canal War* (Cambridge, Mass.: MIT Press, 1974), chap. 7.

13. Adan, *On Both Banks of the Suez*, pp. 25–26, 43–55; Bar-Tov, *Daddo*, pp. 198–201.

14. For a detailed strategic evaluation of the geography of this area and of the Jordanian–Israeli balance of forces, see Brigadier-General (Ret.) Aryeh Shalev, *The West Bank: Line of Defense* (Tel Aviv: HaKibbutz HaMeuchad for the Center for Strategic Studies at Tel Aviv University, 1982), pp. 23–38.

15. On Israeli policies in the West Bank during this period, see Dayan, *Story of My Life*, chap. 38; Shabtai Teveth, *Kilelat HaBeracha* (*The Cursed Blessing*) (Tel Aviv: Schocken, 1969); Moshe Ma'oz, *Palestinian Leadership on the West Bank* (London: Frank Cass, 1985); Major-General (Ret.) Shlomo Gazit, *The Stick and the Carrot* (Tel Aviv: Zmora-Bitan, 1985). Dayan masterminded this policy, and Gazit was his right-hand man during the early, formative years. Ma'oz, a professor at the Hebrew University of Jerusalem, was adviser on Arab affairs to the military governor of the West Bank.

16. For details, see Benziman, *Sharon*, pp. 113–117.

17. See Ma'oz and Yaniv, "On A Short Leash," in Ma'oz and Yaniv, *Syria under Assad*, pp. 189–206.

18. For a detailed analysis of the military activity across the Jordan River ceasefire line, see Hanan Allon, *Countering Palestinian Terrorism: Toward a Policy Analysis of Countermeasures, no. N-1567-FF* (Santa Monica, Calif.: Rand Corporation, 1980), pp. 68–88.

19. For detailed and extensively documented discussion of the Israeli problem with the PLO during 1967–73, see Yaniv, *Dilemmas of Security*, chapter 2.

20. On the Syrian side of the front during the Six-Day War, see HaMeiri, *Mishnei Evrei HaRama*, passim.

21. See his account in Erez and Kphir, *Tsahal*, vol. 1, pp. 230–233.

22. See *A Curtain of Sand*, p. 382. For biographical details about Allon, see a handbook by Ze'ev Schiff and Eitan Haber, *Israel: Army and Defense* (Tel Aviv: Zmora-Bitan-Modan, 1976), pp. 43–45. See also Allon's own account, *My Father's House* (New York: W.W. Norton, 1976).

23. Brecher, *Decisions in Crisis*, pp. 275–276, 228–229. General Elazar, according to a Voice of Israel correspondent in the area during the Six-Day War, did not try to conceal the weight of personal motives in his agitated pressure on Rabin, the chief of staff, to obtain a permission to attack the Syrian positions on the Golan (Yehezkel HaMeiri, interview). See also Teveth, *Moshe Dayan*, pp. 578–582.

24. For the background on the U.S. position, see Spiegel, *The Other Arab–Israeli Conflict*, pp. 153–218. An approximation of the State Department's Near East Bureau (NEB) view is offered by Quandt in *Decade of Decision*, whereas the White House National Security Council view is vividly depicted in the first volume of Henry Kissinger's memoirs, *White House Years* (Boston: Little, Brown, 1979), pp. 341–380, 558–631, 1276–1300.

25. See Gerald M. Steinberg, "Deliberate Ambiguity: Evolution and Evaluation," in Beres, *Security or Armaggeddon*, pp. 32–33.

26. For an excellent analysis of these issues, see Dowty's award-winning study, *Middle East Crisis*, part 2, as well as Touval, *The Peace Brokers*, pp. 165–202.

27. This analysis of the Israeli disposition regarding the question of a formal treaty of alliance with the United States relies substantially on a discussion with the former Israeli ambassador to Washington, Efraim Evron.

28. See Seguez, *The Iranian Triangle*, pp. 111–130. A vivid personal account of a mission on behalf of the IDF with the Kurdish rebels in northern Iraq is available in Rafael Eitan, *Raful: A Soldier's Story* (Tel Aviv: Ma'ariv, 1985), pp. 117–124. See also R.K. Rumazani, "Iran and the Arab-Israeli Conflict." *Middle East Journal 32* (1978):413–428.

29. The most articulate apostle of this concept was the late Yigal Allon. See *A Curtain of Sand*, pp. 402–415. For a comprehensive analysis of the mainstream view, see Dan Horowitz, *Israel's Concept of Defensible Borders*.

30. On this Israeli trait, see Ira Sharkanski, *What Makes Israel Tick?* (Chicago: Nelson-Hall, 1985), pp. 7–15; also see the Foreword by Bertram Gross to Benjamin Akzin and Yehezkel Dror, *Israel: High Pressure Planning* (Syracuse, N.Y.: Syracuse University Press, 1966), pp. xiii–xviii, and Gerald Caiden, *Israel's Administrative Culture* (Berkeley, Calif.: Institute of Government Studies, 1970), pp. 51–52. The same thesis is also implicit in an excellent recent study of Israeli politics by Daniel Shimshoni, entitled *Israeli Democracy* (New York: Free Press, 1982).

31. See Michael I. Handel, *Perception, Deception and Surprise: The Case of the Yom Kippur War* Papers on Peace Problems, no. 19 (Jerusalem: Leonard Davis Institute, 1976), pp. 51–52.

32. As in Avi Shlaim, "Failure in National Intelligence Estimates: The Case of the Yom Kippur War." *World Politics 28* (1976):348–380.

33. Bar-Tov, *Daddo*, vol. 2, pp. 1–26, provides conclusive evidence to support this thesis.

34. See Major-General Rehavam Ze'evi, "The War against Arab Terror," in Erez and Kphir, *Tsahal*, vol. 2, pp. 45–51. As OC Central Command, Ze'evi was Dayan's main adviser on the military aspects of dealing with Palestinian guerrilla warfare from across the river. See also Alon, *Countering Palestinian Terrorism*, pp. 68–82; Herzog, *The Arab–Israeli Wars*, pp. 202–207; and Luttwak and Horowitz, *The Israeli Army*, pp. 303–314.

35. On this, see Ma'oz and Yaniv, "On a Short Leash."

36. Van Dam, *The Struggle for Power in Syria,* pp. 86–94.

37. Dowty, *Middle East Crisis,* pp. 138–144, 162–174, 179–181.

38. This is a brief summary of parts of the discussion in Yaniv, *Dilemmas of Security,* chapter 2.

39. Allon, *A Curtain of Sand,* p. 391.

40. See Herzog, *The Arab–Israeli Wars,* pp. 197–200.

41. Weizman, *Thine the Skies,* pp. 309–323; Ya'akov Bar-Siman-Tov, *The Israeli–Egyptian War of Attrition, 1969–70* (New York: Columbia University Press, 1980), pp. 118–120.

42. On Rabin's persistent support for massive retaliation, see his own *Pinkas,* pp. 273–291, as well as Eban, *Pirkei,* pp. 459–460.

43. The decision-making process that led to this policy is analyzed in detail in Avi Shlaim and Raymond Tanter, "Decision Process, Choice and Consequence: Israel's Deep Penetration Bombing in Egypt, 1970," *World Politics 30* (1977):483–516. Other important sources on the same topic include Bar-Siman-Tov, *The Israeli–Egyptian War of Attrition,* pp. 117–145; Lieutenant-General (Ret.) Chaim Bar-Lev, "The Thousand Day War," and Bar-Lev, "The History of the War of Attrition," in Erez and Kphir, *Tsahal,* vol. 2, pp. 21–37; Whetten, *The Canal War,* chap. 5.

44. This is, of course, a reminder of Ben Gurion's classic maximum that Israel should never engage a great power on the battlefield. See Bar-Zohar, *Ben Gurion,* p. 873.

45. For a detailed description of the planning of the encounter with the Soviet pilots, see Erez and Kphir, *Tsahal,* vol. 3, pp. 140–143.

46. Weizman, *Thine the Skies,* part 7.

47. Sachar, *Egypt and Israel,* pp. 173–174.

48. On the bounded-rationality theory of decision making, see Glenn H. Snyder and Paul Diesing, *Conflict among Nations* (Princeton, N.J.: Princeton University Press, 1977), pp. 345–348, 363–366, 369–371.

49. For a powerful and moving tapestry of impressions on this transition, see Amos Elon, *The Israelis: Founders and Sons,* 2nd ed. (Jerusalem: Adam Publishers, 1981).

50. This societal inequality is richly documented in Sammy Smooha, *Israel—Pluralism and Conflict* (Berkeley: University of California Press, 1978), pp. 151–183. This book is based on Smooha's doctoral dissertation, completed in 1973—at the end of the period discussed in this section.

51. See Lieutenant-General (Ret.) Chaim Bar-Lev, "Lieutenant-General David Elazar: A Storm Looms on the Horizon," in Erez and Kphir, *Tsahal,* vol. 2, pp. 53–66. All this is also corroborated by Elazar's biographer. See Bar-Tov, *Daddo,* vol. 1, pp. 181–213.

52. This is one of the main points in this author's "National Security and Nation-Building: The Case of Israel," in *International Interactions 11* (1983):193–217.

53. On this see Gershon R. Kieval, *Party Politics in Israel and the Occupied Territories* (Westport, Conn.: Greenwood Press, 1983), pp. 3–94.

54. This has been richly documented by Yossi Beilin in *Mechiro Shell Ichud* [The Price of Union] (Tel Aviv: Revivim, 1985).

55. See Yerucham Cohen, *Tochnit Allon* [*The Allon Plan*] (Tel Aviv: HaKibbutz HaMeuchad, 1973).

56. Dayan's memoirs are strewn with numerous comments, which add up to such a concept. This is confirmed by Major-General (Ret.) Shlomo Gazit, who was Dayan's principal aide during the immediate aftermath of the 1967 war. See Gazit, *The Stick and the Carrot,* pp. 137–139, 173–174.

57. This general point—namely, that Israel's settlement policy until the advent of Menachem Begin's Likud in 1977 was largely the result of domestic bargaining and chaotic decision making—was made by this author (in collaboration with Yael Yishai) in "Israel's West Bank Settlement Policy: The Politics of Intransigence," *Journal of Politics* 43 (1981):1105–1128.

Chapter 5
In Search of a New Formula: 1974–1984

1. Major-General (Ret.) Benjamin Peled, "Security without a Limit," in Offer and Kober, eds., *The Price of Power,* p. 79.

2. The literature on this war is voluminous. See, for example, Chaim Herzog, *The War of Atonement* (Jerusalem: Steimatzki, 1975); Dupuy, *Elusive Victory,* pp. 398–605; Peter Allen, *The Yom Kippur War* (New York: Scribner, 1982); Bar-Tov, *Daddo,* vol. 2; Dayan, *Story of My Life,* pp. 569–601; Brecher, *Decisions in Crisis,* passim; Henry A. Kissinger, *Years of Upheaval* (Boston: Little, Brown, 1982), pp. 450–613.

3. Ze'ev Schiff, *October Earthquake: Yom Kippur 1973* (Tel Aviv: University Publishing Project, 1974).

4. This point is elegantly made by Michael I. Handel, *The Diplomacy of Surprise: Hitler, Nixon and Sadat,* Harvard Papers on International Affairs, no. 44 (Cambridge, Mass.: Harvard University Press, 1981).

5. See, for example, Mohammed Heikal, *Autumn of Fury: The Assassination of Sadat* (London: Corgi Books, 1983).

6. These ups and downs in Israeli mood against the backgorund of a steadily low morale are analyzed by Israel's leading public opinion analyst, Louis Guttman, and his associate Shlomit Levi, in "Dynamics of Three Varieties of Morale: The Case of Israel," in Shlomo Breznitz, ed., *Stress in Israel* (New York: Van Nostrand, 1983), pp. 102–113.

7. See Shai Feldman and Heda Rechnitz-Kijner, *Deception, Consensus and War: Israel in Lebanon,* Paper no. 27 (Tel Aviv: Jafee Center for Strategic Studies, 1984), pp. 61–62.

8. The data have been compiled from the following sources: Erez and Kphir, *Tsahal,* vol. 2, pp. 144, 155, and Reuven Pdahtsur, "The Threat of the Eastern Front," *Ha'-aretz,* November 25, 1984. Pdahtsur's estimates are also quoted in Yaniv, "Israel's Conventional Deterrent," in Beres, *Security or Armaggeddon,* p. 201, n. 32. The Israeli estimates of the specifics for each Arab adversary (in 1985) were as follows: Syria—500,000 soldiers in nine divisional formations; Iraq—800,000 soldiers in thirty-seven divisional formations or seven to eight army groups; Egypt—453,000 regular soldiers and 600,000 reserve soldiers in twelve divisional formations. These Israeli worst-case estimates are reported by Oded Zarai in *Ha'aretz* of December 18, 1985, and by Reuven Pdahtsur in *Ha'aretz* of November 12, 1985.

9. On this policy see Shimon Peres "A New Generation of Commanders." In Erez and Kphir *Tsahal* vol. 2, p. 134.

10. For a comprehensive, up-to-date survey, see Tsvia Cohen, "Chel Nashim" ("Women's Corps") in Erez and Kphir, *Tsahal,* vol. 15, pp. 13–86.

11. Ze'ev Schiff and Ehud Ya'ari, *Israel's Lebanon War* (New York: Simon and Schuster, 1984), p. 47.

12. This is discussed in great detail in Yaniv, *Dilemmas of Security,* esp. chapters 4 and 5.

13. For analyses of the political background, see Robert J. Lieber, *The Oil Decade* (New York: Praeger, 1983), and Steven L. Spiegel, ed., *The Middle East and the Western Alliance* (London: Allen and Unwin, 1982). for an anlaysis of the arms flow to the region, see Andrew J. Pierre, *The Global Politics of Arms Sales* (Princeton, N.J.: Princeton University Press, 1982), pp. 136–209.

14. Dayan's words are quoted in Aryeh Avneri, *HaMahalumah* [*The Strike*] (Tel Aviv: Revivim, 1983), p. 40.

15. See Peter Pry's complete collection of speculations about Israel's nuclear policy under the "hot" title *Israel's Nuclear Arsenal* (Boulder, Colo.: Westview Press, 1984), pp. 19–22.

16. For a rich assortment of such Arab reactions, see Feldman, *Israeli Nuclear Deterrence,* pp. 87–90.

17. See, for instance, Asaf Razin, "On the Honey and the Sting: The Impact of American Assistance," In Offer and Kober, *The Price of Power,* pp. 47–59.

18. For more details on Israel's lingering (nuclear) great debate, see Steinberg, "Deliberate Ambiguity," in Beres, *Security or Armaggeddon,* pp. 34–35.

19. See Lieutenant-General Mordechai Gur, "The Restoration and Building of the Army," in Erez and Kphir, *Tsahal,* vol. 2, pp. 143–161.

20. The main sources for this overview were Erez and Kphir, *Tsahal,* vol. 2, p. 144 (for details about the 1974 picture); Pdahtsur's data in Yaniv, "Israel's Conventional Deterrent," p. 201; Mark Heller et al., *The Middle East Military Balance, 1983* (Tel Aviv: Jaffee Center for Strategic Studies, 1983), pp. 112–120; Meir Bleich, reporting in *Ma'ariv,* November 29, 1985.

21. For a somewhat rosy evaluation, see Richard A. Gabriel, *Operation Peace for the Galilee* (New York: Hill and Wang, 1984). For a more critical analysis, see Yaniv, *Dilemmas of Security,* chapter 3. See also Tsvi Lanir, "Political Goals and Military Objectives in Israel's Wars," in Lanir, *War by Choice* (Tel Aviv: Jaffee Center for Strategic Studies, 1985), p. 151.

22. The terms are borrowed from Mao Tse Tung. See his *Selected Military Writings* (Peking: Foreign Languages Press, 1966), pp. 229–235. The great Chinese leader thought that even in the struggle between China and Japan the quick-decision battle on external lines would be optimal. All the more so, then, in the case of an uneven struggle like that between Israel and the Arabs.

23. These advantages of demilitarization were advocated by Yair Evron shortly after the Yom Kippur War. See Yair Evron, *The demilitarization of the Sinai,* Jerusalem Papers on Peace Problems, no. 11 (Jerusalem: Leonard Davis Institute, 1975). Within the Israeli military-political decision-making elite, the most powerful and consistent advocate of such views was Major-General Avraham Tamir. During the 1973–77 period Tamir was head of the Planning Division of the IDF General Staff and, in this capacity,

turned himself into an indispensable adviser to the minister of defense on all matters relating to the peace process. For glimpses into Tamir's thinking, see his articles, "Bitachon Be'et Shalom," in Erez and Kphir, *Tsahal,* vol. 2, pp. 179–189, and "BeTichnun Tsorchei HaBitachon HaLeumi," in Zvi Offer and Avi Kober, eds., *Quantity and Quality in Military Buildup* (Tel Aviv: Ma'arachot, 1985), pp. 341–348. For evaluations of Tamir's role as a tireless advocate of dovish solutions to military-strategic problems, see Ezer Weizman, *The Battle for Peace* (Jerusalem: Idanim, 1982), pp. 127–128; see also Uzi Benziman, *Prime Minister under Siege* (Jerusalem: Adam Publishers, 1981), pp. 69–73.

24. For Eitan's views on Spatial Defense, see Ze'ev Schiff, "The Military Potential of the [West Bank] Settlers," *Ha'aretz,* November 15, 1985, and Eitan, *Raful,* p. 181; for brief updates on the status of Spatial Defense after the 1973 war, see Schiff and Haber, *Israel: Army and Defense,* p. 158. For a post-1973 advocacy of the return to Spatial Defense by the main proponent of this idea, see Yigal Allon, "Settlements in the National Struggle," in Allon, *Communicating Vessels* (Tel Aviv: HaKibbutz HaMeuchad, 1980), pp. 169–175. Neither Dayan nor Weizman was really persuaded by these arguments concerning the putative strategic value of the settlements. See Weizman, *The Battle for Peace,* pp. 213–216.

25. The *problématique* of Lebanon in Israeli strategy is discussed at great length in Yaniv, *Dilemmas of Security,* chapters 2, 4, 5.

26. On the Sinai I and II and the Syrian–Israeli agreements, see Touval, *The Peace Brokers,* chap. 9; Weizman, *The Battle for Peace,* pp. 136, 154, 279–280; Rabin, *Pinkas,* pp. 417–501.

27. See P. Edward Haley and Lewis W. Snider, eds., *Lebanon in Crisis* (Syracuse, N.Y.: Syracuse University Press, 1979), esp. the contribution of John K. Cooley; Walid Khalidi, *Conflict and Violence in Lebanon* Harvard Studies in International Affairs, (Cambridge, Mass.: Harvard University Press, 1979), pp. 47–66; and Itamar Rabinovich, *The War for Lebanon* (Ithaca, N.Y.: Cornell Univesity Press, 1984), pp. 34–60.

28. On the Syrian intervention in Lebanon, see Adeed I. Dawisha, *Syria and the Lebanese Crisis* (New York: St. Martin's Press, 1980).

29. The genesis of this episode in Lebanon is discussed in detail in Yaniv, *Dilemmas of Security,* chapter 2.

30. State of Israel, Ministry of Defense, "National Security Issues" (Tel Aviv: August 1982, mimeo). According to some of Sharon's advisers, the document was apparently never endorsed by the government in any official manner.

31. See Dowty, *Middle East Crisis,* part 3.

32. Brecher, *Decisions in Crisis,* pp. 69–77, and Bar-Tov, *Daddo,* pp. 13–15.

33. Kissinger, *Years of Upheaval,* p. 477.

34. Moshe Dayan, *Breakthrough* (Jerusalem: Adam Publishers, 1981), p. 24.

35. Zbigniew Brzezinski, *Power and Principle* (New York: Farrar-Strauss-Giroux, 1983), p. 236.

36. Dayan, *Breakthrough,* pp. 24, 69; Benziman, *Prime Minister under Siege,* p. 157.

37. Yair Evron, *An American–Israeli Defense Treaty,* Paper no. 14 (Tel Aviv: Jaffee Center for Strategic Studies, 1981), pp. 13–14, 63–64. For a vivid personal account of the negotiations that led to this paper, see Cyrus Vance, *Hard Choices* (New

York: Simon and Schuster, 1983), pp. 245–252; Brzezinski, *Power and Principle,* pp. 281–288; and Dayan, *Breakthrough,* chap. 15.

38. For the general background, see Barry Rubin, "The Reagan Administration and the Middle East," in Kenneth Oye, Robert J. Lieber, and Donald Rothchild, eds., *Eagle Defiant* (Boston: Little, Brown, 1983), pp. 367–390. For Haig's own explanation of his views regarding the Middle East, see Alexander Haig, *Caveat* (London: Weidenfeld and Nicolson, 1984), chap. 9.

39. Spiegel, *The Other Arab–Israeli Conflict,* pp. 399–418, and Bernard Reich, *The United States and Israel* (New York: Praeger, 1984), pp. 108–110.

40. U.S.–Israeli relations at this juncture are discussed in detail in Yaniv, *Dilemmas of Security,* chapters 3–5.

41. Seguev, *The Iranian Triangle,* pp. 131–158. For the U.S. view, see Kissinger, *Years of Upheaval,* pp. 678–699, 883–890.

42. Quoted in Dayan, *Breakthrough,* p. 48. The existence of an Israeli assistance program for Ethiopia after the advent of Mengistu Meriam was disclosed by Dayan in February 1978. See *Ha'aretz,* December 17, 1982.

43. Seguev, *The Iranian Triangle,* 16–81.

44. For an unconfirmed cloak-and-dagger story about Israeli arms supplies to the Khomeini regime, see *The Observer,* September 29, 1985.

45. A widely quoted Arab war scenario was described in an article by Hytham al Ayubi, a retired Syrian army officer of Palestinian descent, under the title "Future Arab Strategy in the Light of the Fourth [Arab–Israeli] War." The article, which advocates a strategy of phased, graded, and multidimensional attrition was published in Hebrew by the former Israeli director of military intelligence (later a professor of strategy and international relations), Yehoshafat Harkabi, in *The Arabs and Israel,* no. 5 (Tel Aviv: Am Oved, 1975), pp. 9–22.

46. Such a war scenario seems to be suggested by several authors. See, for example, Steven J. Rosen, *What a Fifth Arab–Israeli War Might Look Like: An Exercise in Crisis Forecasting,* ACIS Working paper no. 8 (Los Angeles: Center for Arms Control and International Security, University of California, 1977); implicitly, this is also the message in Ben-Horin and Posen, *Israel's Strategic Doctrine,* pp. 29–47.

47. This point is also made in Yaniv, "Syria and Israel."

48. For a typical use of this metaphor, see David Vital, "The Definition of Goals in Foreign Policy," in Ahser Arian, ed., *Israel: The Formative Generation* (Tel Aviv: Zmora-Bitan-Modan, 1979), pp. 13–26.

49. See Richard Beacon, *The Israeli Secret Service* (New York: Taplinger, 1980), pp. 222–256; Stewart Steven, *The Spymasters of Israel* (New York: Ballantine Books, 1980), pp. 283–334.

50. For firsthand reports by the principal Israeli decision makers, see Gad Ya'akobi (minister of transport at the time of this event), *The Government* (Tel Aviv: Am Oved, 1983), pp. 227–232; Rabin (then prime minister), *Pinkas,* pp. 523–533; Gur (then IDF chief of staff), "The Restoration of the Army," pp. 156–157; see also Deacon, *The Israeli Secret Service,* pp. 271–285.

51. This point is made very persuasively by Alan Dowty in "Going Public with the Bomb : The Israeli Calculus," in Beres, *Security or Armaggeddon,* pp. 15–28.

52. For a well-informed account of the decision to raid Osiraq, see Perlmutter et al., *Two Minutes over Baghdad,* pp. 67–141. See also Shai Feldman, "The Bombing of

Osiraq Revisited," *International Security* 7 (1983):114–142; Amos Perlmutter, "The Israeli Raid on Iraq," *Strategic Review* 10 (1982):34–43; and Avneri, *HaMahalumah,* pp. 38–48.

53. This is the main message of an Israeli expert. See Alon, *Countering Palestinian Terrorism.*

54. The discussion in this section offers a summary of the main argument in Yaniv, *Dilemmas of Security,* chapter 2.

55. For an up-to-date analysis of cleavages in the Israeli polity, see Yitzhak Galnoor, *Steering the Polity* (Beverly Hills, Calif.: Sage Publications, 1982), pp. 48–64. For an even more comprehensive presentation of this Israeli problem, see Asher Arian, *Politics in Israel: The Second Generation* (Chatham, N.J.: Chatham House Books, 1985).

56. See Meir, *My Life,* pp. 337–381, and Dayan, *Story of My Life,* pp. 687–688, 724–728.

57. For a lively and rich, if journalistic, portrait of this period in Israeli domestic politics, see Aryeh Avneri, *HaMapolet* [*The Collapse*] (Tel Aviv: Revivim, 1977).

58. Weizman, *The Battle for Peace,* chap. 9.

59. Dayan, *Breakthrough,* pp. 243–249.

60. Golan, *Peres,* pp. 266–267.

61. Avneri, *HaMahalumah,* pp. 40–43; Perlmutter et al. *Two Minutes over Baghdad,* pp. 53–86; Eitan, *Raful,* pp. 185–190.

62. This is the gist of an elaborate case history in Yaniv, *Dilemmas of Security,* chapters 3–5.

63. This is a small part from a long letter which Rotem submitted to Minister of Defense Sharon in 1981 and which was published in *Yediot Ahronot* of April 13, 1984.

64. For the details, see Baruch Kimmerling, "Making Conflict a Routine: Cumulative Effects of the Arab–Jewish Conflict upon Israeli Society," in Moshe Lissak, ed., *Israeli Society and Its Defense Establishment* (London: Frank Cass, 1984), p. 17.

65. Weizman, *The Battle for peace,* p. 280.

Chapter 6
Is the Bomb Inevitable?

1. This is the main thesis of Feldman, *Israeli Nuclear Deterrence.* For similar advocacies, see chapter 1, note 35.

2. For Arab war aims in the 1940s and 1950s, see Yehoshafat Harkabi, *Arab Strategies and Israel's Response* (New York: Free Press, 1977), chap. 1, as well as Gabbay, *A Political Study of the Jewish–Arab Conflict,* pp. 35–38, 87–88.

3. Not dissimilar views seem to be suggested by Major-General Avraham Tamir in "BeTichnun Tsorchei HaBitachon HaLeumi" ["In Planning the Needs of National Security"], in Offer and Kober, *Quality and Quantity in Military Buildup,* pp. 341–348.

4. For advocacies of a Palestinian state, see Walid Khalidi, "Thinking the Unthinkable: A Sovereign Palestinian State," *Foreign Affairs* 56 (1978):695–713, and Mark A. Heller, *A Palestinian State: Implications for Israel* (Cambridge, Mass.: Harvard

University Press, 1983). The former dismisses the argument that a PLO State could pose a menace to Israel. The latter argues that a totally demilitarized Palestinian state is something the Palestinians would accept. Both arguments seem somewhat wistful.

5. Gazit, *The Stick and the Carrot*, p. 138.

6. For an earlier statement of the same thesis, see Avner Yaniv and Robert J. Lieber, "Reagan and the Middle East," *Washington Quarterly* 6 (1983):125–137.

7. The domestic political sources of Israel's apparently inherent inability to initiate a serious dialogue are discussed by me, together with Avi Shlaim, in an article published half a decade ago. See Avi Shlaim and Avner Yaniv, "Domestic Politics and Foreign Policy in Israel," *International Affairs* 56 (1980):242–262.

8. For compelling evidence supporting this view, see Yadin Kaufmann, "Israel's Flexible Voters," *Foreign Policy* 61 (1985):109–124.

Chapter 7
A Theoretical Postscript

1. Dan Horowitz, "The Israeli Concept of National Security (1948–1972)," in Benjamin Neuberger, ed., *Diplomacy and Confrontation* (Tel Aviv: Everyman University, 1984), p. 107.

2. The author of this useful distinction between general and specific deterrence is Morgan. See his *Deterrence*, pp. 27–49.

3. Inis L. Claude, *Power and International Relations* (New York: Random House, 1962), pp. 124–128.

4. George and Smoke, *Deterrence in American Foreign Policy*, p. 14.

5. Hedley Bull, "The Balance of Power," in Milton Rakove, ed., *Arms and Foreign Policy in the Nuclear Age* (New York: Oxford University Press, 1962), p. 262.

6. For a similarly utilitarian view of the calculus of international alignment, see Steven J. Rosen, "A Model of War and Alliance," in Julian R. Friedman, Christopher Bladen, and Steven J. Rosen, eds., *Alliances in International Politics* (Boston: Allyn and Bacon, 1970), pp. 233–234. On the concept of extended deterrence and its inherent weakness, see Paul Huth and Bruce Russett, "What Makes Deterrence Work: Cases from 1900 to 1980," *World Politics* 36 (1984):496–526.

7. For a discussion of intrinsic and strategic interests see Robert Jervis, "Deterrence Theory Revisited," *World Politics* 31 (1979):289–324.

8. This discussion of threats is inspired by Schelling, *Arms and Influence*, chap. 2, "The Art of Commitment," esp. pp. 66–69.

9. The same theme is discussed in two previous works by this author. See Avner Yaniv and Eliyahu Katz, "MAD, Détente and Peace: A Hypothesis on the Evolution of International Conflicts and Its Mathematico-Deductive Extension," *International Interactions* 7 (1980):223–239, and Ze'ev Ma'oz and Avner Yaniv, "Game, Supergame and Compound Escalation: Israel and Syria 1948–84," *International Interactions,* in press.

10. Kissinger makes a similar point in *White House Years,* p. 67. See also Robert Jervis, "Deterrence and Perception," *International Security* 7 (1982–83):3–30, as well as George and Smoke, *Deterrence in American Foreign Policy*, pp. 530–531.

11. George and Smoke, *Deterrence in American Foreign Policy,* p. 557.

12. Robert Jervis, "Why Nuclear Superiority Does Not Matter," *Political Science Quarterly* 94 (1980):618.

13. Michael Howard, "The Classical Strategists" and "Strategy and Policy in Twentieth Century Warfare," in Howard, *Studies in War and Peace* (London: Temple Smith, 1970), pp. 154–183, 193.

14. Schelling, *Arms and Influence,* pp. 3, 80.

15. Glenn H. Snyder, *Deterrence and Defense* (Princeton, N.J.: Princeton University Press, 1961), p. 11.

16. George and Smoke, *Deterrence in American Foreign Policy,* p. 93.

17. See Yehoshafat Harkabi, *Nuclear War and Nuclear Peace* (Jerusalem: Magnes Press, 1967), chaps. 4–5.

Bibliography

Books and Monographs

English and French

Ajami, Fouad. 1981. *The Arab Predicament*. Cambridge: Cambridge University Press.

Akzin, Benjamin, and Dror, Yehezkel. 1966. *Israel: High Pressure Planning*. Syracuse: Syracuse University Press.

Allen, Peter. 1982. *The Yom Kippur War*. New York: Scribner.

Allon, Yigal. 1970. *The Making of Israel's Army*. London: George Weidenfeld & Nicholson Ltd.

———. 1976. *My Father's House*. New York: W.W. Norton.

Alon, Hanan. 1980. *Countering Palestinian Terrorism: Towards a Policy Analysis of Countermeasures*. Paper no. N-1567-FF. Santa Monica, Calif.: Rand Corporation.

Arian, Asher. 1985. *Politics in Israel: The Second Generation*. Chatham, N.J.: Chatham House.

Aron, Raymond. 1966. *Peace and War*. New York: Doubleday.

Aronson, Shlomo. 1977. *Israel's Nuclear Options*. ACIS Working Paper no. 17. Los Angeles: Center for Arms Control and International Security, University of California.

———. 1978. *Conflict and Bargaining in the Middle East*. Baltimore, Md.: Johns Hopkins University Press.

Baily, Clinton. 1984. *Jordan's Palestinian Challenge, 1948–1983*. Boulder, Colo.: Westview Press.

Bar-Siman-Tov, Ya'akov. 1980. *The Israeli–Egyptian War of Attrition, 1969–70*. New York: Columbia University Press.

———. 1983. *Linkage Politics in the Middle East: Syria between Domestic and External Conflict, 1961–70*. Boulder, Colo.: Westview Press.

Bell, Bowyer J. 1969. *The Long War*. Englewood Cliffs, N.J.: Prentice-Hall.

Ben-Horin, Yo'av, and Posen, Barry. 1981. *Israel's Strategic Doctrine*. Paper no. R-2845-NA. Santa Monica, Calif.: Rand Corporation.

Benziman, Uzi. 1985. *Sharon: An Israeli Caeser*. New York: Adama Publications.

Berger, Earl. 1965. *The Covenant and the Sword: Arab–Israeli Relations, 1948–56*. London: Routledge & Kegan Paul.

Blechman, Barry M. 1971. "The Consequences of Israeli Reprisals: An Assessment." Ph.D. thesis, Georgetown University, Washington, D.C.

Brecher, Michael. 1972. *The Foreign Policy System of Israel: Setting, Images, Processes*. London: Oxford University Press.

——. 1974. *Decisions in Israel's Foreign Policy*. New Haven: Yale University Press.

Brecher, Michael (with Benjamin Geist). 1980. *Decisions in Crisis: Israel 1967–1973*. Berkeley: University of California Press.

Brodie, Bernard. 1971. *Strategy in the Missile Age*. Princeton, N.J.: Princeton University Press.

Brzezinski, Zbigniew. 1983. *Power and Principle*. New York: Farrar-Straus-Giroux.

Burns, Lieutenant-General E.L.M. 1962. *Between Arab and Israel*. Toronto: Clarke, Irwin.

Caiden, Gerald. 1970. *Israel's Administrative Culture*. Berkeley, Calif.: Institute of Government Studies.

Claude, Inis L. 1962. *Power and International Relations*. New York, Random House.

Cobban, Helena. 1984. *The Palestine Liberation Organization*. Cambridge: Cambridge University Press.

Cohen, Samy. 1974. *De Gaulle, les Gaullistes et Israel*. Paris: Alain Moreau.

Dawisha, Adeed I. 1980. *Syria and the Lebanese Crisis*. New York: St. Martin's Press.

Deacon, Richard. 1980. *The Israeli Secret Service*. New York: Taplinger.

Dowty, Alan. 1984. *Middle East Crisis: U.S. Decisionmaking in 1958, 1970 and 1973*. Berkeley: University of California Press.

Dupuy, Trevor N. 1978. *Elusive Victory: The Arab–Israeli Wars, 1947–1974*. New York, Harper and Row.

Elon, Amos. 1981. *The Israelis: Founders and Sons*, 2nd ed. Jerusalem: Adam Publishers.

Evron, Yair. 1975. "Arms Races in the Middle East and Some Arms Control Measures Related to Them." In Gabriel Sheffer, ed., *Dynamics of a Conflict*. New York: Humanities Press.

——. 1975. *The Demilitarization of the Sinai*. Jerusalem Papers on Peace Problems, no. 11. Jerusalem: Leonard Davis Institute.

——. 1978. "Two Periods in Arab–Israeli Strategic Relations: 1957–1967; 1967–1973." In Itamar Rabinovich and Haim Shaked, eds., *From June to October: The Middle East between 1967 and 1973*, pp. 93–126. New Brunswick, N.J.: Transaction Books.

——. 1981. *An American–Israeli Defense Treaty*. Paper no. 14. Tel Aviv: Jaffee Center for Strategic Studies.

Evron, Yair. 1977. *The Role of Arms Control in the Middle East*. Adelphi Papers, No. 138. London: International Institute of Strategic Studies.

Feldman Gardner, Lilly. 1984. *The Special Relationship between West Germany and Israel*. Boston: George Allen and Unwin.

Feldman, Shai. 1982. *Israeli Nuclear Deterrence: A Strategy for the 1980s*. New York: Columbia University Press.

Feldman, Shai, and Rechnitz-Kijner, Heda. 1984. *Deception, Consensus and War: Israel in Lebanon*. Paper no. 27. Tel Aviv: Jaffee Center for Strategic Studies.

Friedrich, Carl J., and Brzezinski, Zbigniew. 1956. *Totalitarian Dictatorship and Autocracy*. New York: Praeger.

Frye, Richard N. 1951. *The United States, Turkey and Iran*. Cambridge, Mass.: Harvard University Press.

Gabbay, Roney, E. 1959. *A Political Study of the Jewish–Arab Conflict*. Geneva: Librairie Droz.

Gabriel, Richard A. 1984. *Operation Peace for the Galilee*. New York: Hill and Wang.

Galnoor, Itzhak. 1982. *Steering the Polity*. Beverly Hills, Calif.: Sage Publications.

Galois, Pierre, 1961. *Balance of Terror: A Strategy for the Nuclear Age*. Boston: Houghton Mifflin.

Gazit, Mordechai. 1983. *President Kennedy's Policy toward the Arab States and Israel*. Studies Series. Tel Aviv: Shiloah Center for Middle Eastern and African Studies.

George, Alexander. 1980. *Presidential Decisionmaking in Foreign Policy: The Effective Use of Information and Advice*. Boulder, Colo.: Westview Press.

George, Alexander; Hall, David; and Simons, William. 1971. *The Limits of Coercive Diplomacy*. Boston, Little, Brown.

George, Alexander L., and Smoke, Richard. 1974. *Deterrence in American Foreign Policy*. New York: Columbia University Press.

Glubb, Sir John Baggot. 1957. *A Soldier with the Arabs*. London: Hodder and Stoughton, 1957.

Gross Stein, Janice, and Tanter, Raymond. 1980. *Rational Decision Making: Israel's Security Choices, 1967*. Columbus: Ohio State University Press.

Gruen, George E. 1972. "Turkey, Israel and the Palestine Question, 1948–60." Ph.D. thesis, Columbia University, New York.

Haig, Alexander. 1984. *Caveat*. London: Weidenfeld and Nicholson.

Haley, P. Edward, and Snider, Lewis W., eds., 1979. *Lebanon in Crisis*. Syracuse, N.Y.: Syracuse University Press.

Handel, Michael I. 1973. *Israel's Political-Military Doctrine*. Harvard Studies in International Affairs. Cambridge, Mass.: Harvard University Press.

——. 1976. *Perception, Deception and Surprise: The Case of the Yom Kippur War*. Jerusalem Papers on Peace Problems, no. 19. Jerusalem: Leonard Davis Institute.

——. 1981. *The Diplomacy of Surprise: Hitler, Nixon and Sadat*. Harvard Studies in International Affairs. Cambridge, Mass.: Harvard University Press.

Harkabi, Yehoshafat. 1967. *Nuclear War and Nuclear Peace*. Jerusalem: Magnes Press.

——. 1977. *Arab Strategies and Israel's Response*. New York: Free Press.

Harris, George S. 1972. *Troubled Alliance*. Washington, D.C.: American Enterprise Institute/Hoover Policy Studies.

Hart, Alan. 1984. *Arafat*. London: Sidgwick and Jackson.

Heikal, Mohamed. 1983. *Autumn of Fury: The Assassination of Sadat*. London: Corgi.

Heller, Mark A. 1983. *The Middle East Military Balance*. Tel Aviv: Jaffee Center for Strategic Studies.

——. 1983. *A Palestinian State: Implications for Israel*. Cambridge, Mass.: Harvard University Press.

Herzog, Chaim. 1975. *The War of Atonement*. Jerusalem: Steimatzki.

———. 1982 *The Arab–Israeli Wars*. New York: Random House.
Hirst, David. 1984. *The Gun and the Olive Branch*, 2nd ed. London: Faber and Faber.
Horowitz, Dan. 1975. *Israel's Concept of Defensible Borders*. Jerusalem Papers on Peace Problems, no. 16. Jerusalem: Leonard Davis Institute.
Howard, Michael. 1970. *Studies in War and Peace*. London: Temple Smith.
Isaac, Rael J. 1976, *Israel Divided*. Baltimore: Johns Hopkins University Press.
———. 1981. *Party and Politics in Israel*. New York: Longman.
Jabber, Paul. 1981. *Not by War Alone*. Berkeley: University of California Press.
Jackson, Elmore. 1983. *Middle East Mission*. New York: W.W. Norton.
Jervis, Robert. 1985. *The Illogic of American Strategy*. Ithaca, N.Y.: Cornell University Press.
Kerr, Malcolm. 1971. *The Arab Cold War*, 3rd ed. New York: Oxford University Press.
Khalidi, Walid. 1979. *Conflict and Violence in Lebanon*. Harvard Studies in International Affairs. Cambridge, Mass.: Harvard University Press.
Kieval, Gershon R. 1983. *Party Politics in Israel and the Occupied Territories*. Westport, Conn.: Greenwood Press.
Kissinger, Henry A. 1979. *White House Years*. Boston, Little, Brown.
———. 1982. *Years of Upheaval*. Boston: Little, Brown.
Kolodziej, Edward A. 1974. *French Foreign Policy under De Gaulle and Pompidou: The Politics of Grandeur*. Ithaca, N.Y.: Cornell University Press.
Kowitt-Crosbie, Sylvia. 1974. *The Tacit Alliance*. Princeton, N.J.: Princeton University Press.
Krammer, Arnold. 1974. *The Forgotten Friendship: Israel and the Soviet Bloc, 1947–53*. Chicago: University of Illinois Press.
Liddell Hart, Basil H. 1967. *Strategy*. London: Faber and Faber.
Lieber, Robert J. 1983. *The Oil Decade*. New York: Praeger.
Love, Kenneth. 1969. *Suez: The Twice-Fought War*. New York: MacGraw-Hill.
Luttwak, Edward, and Horowitz, Dan. 1975. *The Israeli Army*. London: Allen Lane.
Mao Tse, Tung, 1966. *Selected Military Writings*. Peking: Foreign Languages Press.
Ma'oz, Moshe. 1985. *Palestinian Leadership on the West Bank*. London: Frank Cass.
Ma'oz, Moshe, and Yaniv, Avner. 1986. *Syria under Assad*. London: Croom Helm and New York: St. Martin's.
Mearsheimer, John J. 1983. *Conventional Deterrence*. Ithaca, N.Y.: Cornell University Press.
Meir, Golda. 1975. *My Life*. London: Futura.
Morely, James W. 1976. *Deterrent Diplomacy: Japan, Germany and the USSR, 1935–40*. New York: Columbia University Press.
Morgan, Patrick. 1983. *Deterrence: A Conceptual Analysis*, 2nd ed. Beverly Hills, Calif.: Sage Publications.
Morgenthau, Hans J. 1963. *Politics among Nations*. New York: Knopf.
Osgood, Robert E. 1962. *NATO: The Entangling Alliance*. Chicago: University of Chicago Press.
Peres, Shimon. 1970. *David's Sling*. London, Weidenfeld and Nicolson.
Peri, Yoram. 1983. *Between Battles and Ballots*. Cambridge: Cambridge University Press.

Perlmutter, Amos; Handel, Michael I.; and Bar-Joseph, Uri. 1982. *Two Minutes over Baghdad.* London: Corgi.

Pierre, Andrew J. 1982. *The Global Politics of Arms Sales.* Princeton, N.J.: Princeton University Press.

Prittie, Terrence. 1969. *Eshkol: The Man and the Nation.* London: Pitman.

Pry, Peter. 1984. *Israel's Nuclear Arsenal.* Boulder, Colo.: Westview Press.

Quandt, William. B. 1977. *Decade of Decisions.* Berkeley: University of California Press.

Quester, George C. 1966. *Deterrence before Hiroshima.* New York: Wiley.

Rabinovich, Itamar. 1984. *The War for Lebanon.* Ithaca, N.Y.: Cornell University Press.

Reich, Bernard. 1984. *The United States and Israel.* New York: Praeger.

Rosen, Steven J. 1977. *What a Fifth Arab–Israeli War Might Look Like: An Exercise in Crisis Forecasting.* ACIS Working Paper no. 8. Los Angeles: Center for Arms Control and International Security, University of California.

Sachar, Howard M. 1972. *Europe Leaves the Middle East.* London: Allen Lane.

———. 1979. *A History of Israel.* New York: Knopf.

———. 1981. *Egypt and Israel.* New York: Richard Marek Publishers.

Safran, Nadav. 1978. *Israel: The Embattled Ally.* Cambridge, Mass.: Belknap Press, Harvard University Press.

Schelling, Thomas C. 1966. *Arms and Influence.* New Haven: Yale University Press.

Schiff, Ze'ev. 1974. *October Earthquake: Yom Kippur 1973.* Tel Aviv: University Publishing Project.

Schiff, Ze'ev, and Yaari, Ehud. 1984. *Israel's Lebanon War.* New York: Simon and Schuster.

Seale, Patrick. 1965. *The Struggle for Syria: A Study of Postwar Arab Politics.* London: Oxford University Press.

Sella, Amnon, and Yishai, Yael. 1986. *Israel: The Peaceful Belligerent, 1967–1979.* London: Macmillan.

Sharkansky, Ira. 1985. *What Makes Israel Tick?* Chicago: Nelson-Hall.

Sheffer, Gabriel. 1980. *Resolution vs. Management of the Middle East Conflict.* Jerusalem Papers on Peace Problems, no. 32. Jerusalem: Leonard Davis Institute.

Sicron, Moshe. 1957. *Immigration to Israel 1948–53.* Jerusalem: Jerusalem Post Press for the Falk Project for Economic Research in Israel, no. 60.

Sinai, Ann, and Pollack, Allen, eds. 1977. *The Hashemite Kingdom of Jordan and the West Bank.* New York: Association of American Academics for Peace in the Middle East.

Smooha, Sammy. 1978. *Israel: Pluralism and Conflict.* Berkeley: University of California Press.

Snyder, Glenn H. 1961. *Deterrence and Defense.* Princeton, N.J.: Princeton University Press.

Snyder, Glenn H., and Diesing, Paul. 1977. *Conflict among Nations.* Princeton, N.J.: Princeton University Press.

Spiegel, Steven L., ed. 1982. *The Middle East and the Western Alliance.* London: Allen and Unwin.

———. 1985. *The Other Arab–Israeli Conflict.* Chicago: University of Chicago Press.

Steven, Stewart. 1980. *The Spymasters of Israel.* New York: Ballantine Books.

Taylor, Alan R. 1982. *The Arab Balance of Power.* Syracuse, N.Y.: Syracuse University Press.

Tavin, Eli, and Alexander, Yonah, eds. 1982. *Psychological Warfare and Propaganda: Irgun Documentation.* Wilmington, Del.: Scholarly Resources.

Touval, Sa'adia. 1982. *The Peace Brokers: Mediators in the Arab–Israeli Conflict 1948–1979.* Princeton, N.J.: Princeton University Press.

Vance, Cyrus. 1983. *Hard Choices.* New York: Simon and Schuster.

Van Dam, Nicolaos. 1979. *The Struggle for Power in Syria.* London: Croom Helm.

Whetten, Lawrence L. 1974. *The Canal War.* Cambridge, Mass.: MIT Press.

Yaniv, Avner. 1987. *Dilemmas of Security.* New York: Oxford University Press.

Hebrew

Adan, Avraham. 1979. *On Both Banks of the Suez.* Jerusalem: Idanim.

Allon, Yigal. 1980. *Communicating Vessels.* Tel Aviv: HaKibbutz HaMeuchad.

———. 1981. *A Curtain of Sand.* Tel Aviv: HaKibbutz HaMeuchad.

Avidan, Me'ir. 1982. *Hebetim Iqryim BeYachasei Israel-Artsot HaBrit.* Jersualem: Leonard David Institute.

Avneri, Aryeh. 1977. *HaMapolet.* Tel Aviv: Revivim.

———. 1983. *HaMahaluma.* Tel Aviv: Revivim.

Bar-Tov, Hannoch. 1978. *Daddo: 48 Years and 20 More Days.* Tel Aviv: Ma'ariv.

Bar-Zohar, Michael. 1975. *Ben Gurion: A Political Biography.* Tel Aviv: Am Oved.

Beaufre, Andre. 1977. *Strategie pour demain.* Tel Aviv: Ma'arachot.

Beilin, Yossi. 1984. *Banim BeTsel Avotam.* Tel Aviv: Revivim.

———. 1985. *Mechiro Shel Ichud.* Tel Aviv: Revivim.

Ben Gurion, David. 1971. *Distinction and Destiny.* Tel Aviv: Am Oved.

———. 1975. *The Restored State of Israel.* Tel Aviv: Am Oved.

Benziman, Uzi. 1981. *Prime Minister under Siege.* Jerusalem: Adam Publishers.

Cohen, Yerucham. 1973. *Tochnit Allon.* Tel Aviv: HaKibbutz HaMeuchad.

Dayan, Moshe. 1965. *Diary of the Sinai Campaign.* Tel Aviv: Am Hasepher.

———. 1976. *Story of My Life.* Tel Aviv: Idanim.

———. 1981. *Breakthrough.* Jerusalem: Adam Publishers.

Eban, Abba. 1978. *Pirkei Chaim.* Tel Aviv: Ma'ariv.

Eitan, Rafael (with Dov Goldstein). 1985. *Raful: A Soldier's Story.* Tel Aviv: Ma'ariv.

Gazit, Shlomo. 1985. *The Stick and the Carrot.* Tel Aviv: Zmora-Bitan.

Gelber, Yo'av. 1986. *Garin LeTsava Ivri Sadir.* Jersualem: Yad Ben Tsvi.

Golan, Mati. 1982. *Peres.* Jersualem: Schocken.

HaMeiri, Yehezkel. 1970. *Mishnei Evrei HaRama.* Tel Aviv: Levi-Epstein.

———. 1979. "Demilitarization and Conflict Reduction: The DMZs on the Israeli–Syrian Border." M.A. thesis, University of Haifa.

Harkabi, Yehoshafat. 1969. *Lekach HaArvim Mitvusatam.* Tel Aviv: Am Oved.

Pa'il, Meir. 1979. *The Emergence of ZAHAL (IDF).* Tel Aviv: Zmora-Bitan-Modan.

Rabin, Itzhak (with Dov Goldstein). 1979. *Pinkas Sherut.* Tel Aviv: Ma'ariv.

Rivlin, Gershon, and Orren, Elhanan, eds., 1982. *The War of Independence: Ben Burion's Diaries.* Tel Aviv: Misrad HaBitachon–HaHotsa'a LaOr.

Schiff, Ze'ev, and Haber, Eitan. 1976. *Israel: Army and Defense.* Tel Aviv: Zmora-Bitan-Modan.

Segev, Tom. 1984. *1949—The First Israelis.* Jerusalem: Domino Press.

Seguev, Shmuel. 1981. *The Iranian Triangle.* Tel Aviv: Ma'ariv.

Sella, Avraham. 1984. *Achdut BeToch Perud: Veidot HaPisga HaArviot. Jerusalem:* Magnes Press.

Shalev, Aryeh. 1982. *The West Bank: Line of Defense.* Tel Aviv: HaKibbutz HaMeuchad for the Center for Strategic Studies at Tel Aviv University.

Sharett, Moshe. 1978. *Yoman Ishi.* Tel Aviv: Am Oved.

Shavit, Ya'akov. 1983. *Havlaga oh Tguva.* Ramat Gan: Bar Ilan University.

Slater, Robert. 1977. *Rabin of Israel: A Biography.* Jerusalem: Idan.

State of Israel. 1982. "National Security Issues." Tel Aviv, mimeo.

Teveth, Shabtai. 1968. *Hasufim BaTsariach.* Tel Aviv: Schocken.

——— . 1971. *Kilelat HaBracha.* Jerusalem: Schocken. (a)

——— . *Moshe Dayan.* Jerusalem: Schocken. (b)

Weizman, Ezer. 1975. *Lecha Shamayim Lecha Aretz.* Tel Aviv: Ma'ariv.

——— . 1982. *The Battle for Peace.* Jerusalem: Idanim.

Ya'akobi, Gad. 1972. *Ozmata Shel Eichut.* Haifa: Shikmona Press.

——— . 1983. *The Government.* Tel Aviv: Am Oved.

Yanai, Nathan. 1982. *Political Crisis in Israel.* Jerusalem: Keter Publishing.

Articles

English

Aronson, Shlomo. 1977. "Nuclearization of the Middle East: A Dovish View." *The Jerusalem Quarterly* 2:27–44.

Bar-Joseph, Uri. 1982. "The Hidden Debate: The Formation of Nuclear Doctrines in the Middle East." *Journal of Strategic Studies* 5:205–227.

Benyamini, Haim. 1984. "The Six Day War, Israel 1967: Decisions, Coalitions, Consequences: A Sociological View." In Moshe Lissak, ed., *Israeli Society and Its Defense Establishment,* pp. 64–82. London: Frank Cass.

Betts, Richard. 1985. "Conventional Deterrence: Predictive Uncertainty and Political Confidence." *World Politics* 37:153–179.

Bialer, Uri. 1985. "The Iranian Connection in Israeli Foreign Policy, 1948–1951." *Middle East Journal* 39 (2):292–315.

Bull, Hedley. 1962. "The Balance of Power." In Milton Rakove, ed., *Arms and Foreign Policy in the Nuclear Age,* pp. 259–271. New York: Oxford University Press.

Burrows, Robert, and Spector, Bertram. 1973. "The Strength and Direction of Relationship between Domestic Conflict and External Conflict and Cooperation: Syria, 1961–7." In James N. Rosenau and Jonathan Wilkenfeld, eds., *Conflict Behavior and Linkage Politics,* pp. 294–324. New York: Mackay.

"Correspondent." 1963. In *New Outlook* 6:32–35.

Dayan, Moshe. 1968. "Why Israel Strikes Back." In Donald Robinson, ed., *Under Fire: Israel's Twenty Years' Struggle for Survival,* pp. 120–123 New York: W.W. Norton.

Dowty, Alan. 1978. "Nuclear Proliferation: The Israeli Case." *International Studies Quarterly* 22:79–120.

Dowty, Alan. 1986. "Going Public with the Bomb." In Louis R. Beres, ed., *Security or Armaggeddon,* pp. 15–28. Lexington, Mass.: Lexington Books.

Evron, Yair. 1975. "Arms Races in the Middle East and Some Arms Control Measures Related to Them." In Gabriel Sheffer, ed., *Dynamics of A Conflict,* pp. 95–136. Atlantic Highlands, N.J.: Humanities Press.

———. 1978. "Two Periods in Arab–Israeli Strategic Relations: 1957–67, 1967–73." In Itamar Rabinovich and Haim Shaked, eds., *From June to October,* pp. 93–126. New Brunswick, N.J.: Transaction Books.

Feldman, Shai. 1981. "Peacemaking in the Middle East: The Next Step." *Foreign Affairs* 59:756–780.

———. 1983. "The Bombing of Osiraq Revisited." *International Security* 7:114–142.

Haymont, Irving. 1967. "The Israeli NAHAL Program." *Middle East Journal* 21:314–324.

Horowitz, Dan. 1975. "The Israeli Concept of National Security and the Prospects of Peace in the Middle East." In Gabriel Sheffer, ed., *Dynamics of a Conflict,* pp. 235–276. Altantic Highlands, N.J.: Humanities Press.

Huntington, Samuel. 1984. "Conventional Deterrence and Conventional Retaliation in Europe." *International Security* 8:32–56.

Huth, Paul, and Russett, Bruce. 1984. "What Makes Deterrence Work? Cases from 1900 to 1980." *World Politics* 36:496–526.

Jervis, Robert. 1978. "Cooperation under the Security Dilemma." *World Politics* 30:167–214.

———. 1979. "Deterrence Theory Revisited." *World Politics* 31:289–324.

———. 1980. "Why Nuclear Superiority Does Not Matter." *Political Science Quarterly* 94:617–633.

———. 1982–83. "Deterrence and Perception." *International Security* 7:3–30.

Kaufman, Yadin. 1985. "Israel's Flexible Voters." *Foreign Policy* 61:109–124.

Khalidi, Walid. 1978. "Thinking the Unthinkable: A Sovereign Palestinian State." *Foreign Affairs* 56:695–713.

Kimmerling, Baruch. 1984. "Making Conflict a Routine: Cumulative Effects of the Arab–Jewish Conflict on Israeli Society." In Lissak, *Israeli Society and its Defense Establishment,* pp. 13–45.

Levi, Shlomit, and Guttman, Louis. "Dynamics of Three Varieties of Morale: The Case of Israel." In Shlomo Breznitz, ed., *Stress in Israel,* pp. 102–113. New York: Van Nostrand.

Linz, Juan. 1972. "Totalitarian and Authoritarian Regimes." In Fred Greenstein and Nelson Polsby, eds., *Handbook of Political Science,* vol. 2, pp. 175–211. (Reading, Mass.: Addison-Wesley.

Long, Norton E. 1966. "Open and Closed Systems." In R. Barry Farrell, ed., *Approaches to Comparative and International Politics,* pp. 155–166. Evanston, Ill.: Northwestern University Press.

Ma'oz, Moshe. 1986. "The Emergency of Modern Syria." In Moshe Ma'oz and Avner Yaniv, eds., *Syria under Assad,* pp. 9–35. London: Croom Helm and New York: St. Martin's.

Ma'oz, Ze'ev, and Yaniv, Avner. 1986. "Game, Supergame and Compound Escalation: Israel and Syria, 1948–1984." In *International Interactions.* (forthcoming). (a)

———. 1986. "On a Short Leash: Syria and the PLO." In Ma'oz and Yaniv, *Syria under Assad,* pp. 191–208. (b)

———. 1986. "The Study of Syria." In Ma'oz and Yaniv, *Syria under Assad,* pp. 1–8. (c)

———. 1986. "The Syrian Paradox." In Ma'oz and Yaniv, *Syria under Assad,* pp. 249–261. (d)

Perlmutter, Amos. 1983. "The Israeli Raid on Iraq." *Strategic Review* 10:34–43.

Poole, J.B., and Brown, J.K.A. 1982. "Survey of National Defence Statements." *Survival* 24:220–228.

Ramazani, R.K. 1978. "Iran and the Arab–Israeli Conflict." *Middle East Journal* 32 (3):413–428.

Rosecrance, Richard N. 1980. "Deterrence and Vulnerability in the Pre-Nuclear Era." In *The Future of Strategic Deterrence,* part 1. Adelphi Papers, no. 160. London: International Institute of Strategic Studies.

Rosen, Steven J. 1970. "A Model of War and Alliance." In *Julian R. Friedman,* Christopher Bladen, and Steven J. Rosen, eds., *Alliances in International Politics,* pp. 215–237. Boston: Allyn and Bacon.

———. 1977. "A Stable System of Mutual Nuclear Deterrence in the Middle East." *American Political Science Review* 71:1367–1383.

Rubin, Barry. 1983. "The Reagan Administration and the Middle East." In Kenneth Oye, Robert J. Lieber, and Donald Rothchild, eds., *Eagle Defiant,* pp. 367–390. Boston: Little, Brown.

Shlaim, Avi. 1976. "Failure in National Intelligence Estimates: The Case of the Yom Kippur War." *World Politics* 28:348–380.

———. 1984. "Contending Approaches to Israel's Relations with the Arabs: Ben Gurion and Sharett, 1953–1956." *Middle East Journal* 37:180–201.

Shlaim, Avi, and Tanter, Raymond. 1977. "Decision Process, Choice and Consequence: Israel's Deep Penetration Bombing in Egypt, 1970." *World Politics* 30:483–516.

Shlaim, Avi, and Yaniv, Avner. 1980. "Domestic Politics and Foreign Policy In Israel." *International Affairs* 56:242–262.

Snyder, Glenn H. 1983. "Deterrence and Defense." In Robert J. Art and Kenneth N. Waltz, eds., *The Use of Force,* pp. 123–141. New York: Lanham.

Steinberg, Gerald M. 1986. "Deliberate Ambiguity: Evolution and Evaluation." In Beres, *Security or Armaggeddon,* pp. 29–44.

Tal, Israel. 1980. "Israeli Security in the Eighties." *Jerusalem Quarterly* 17:13–18.

Tucker, Robert. 1975. "Israel and the United States: From Dependence to Nuclear Weapons?" *Commentary* 60:29–43.

Yaniv, Avner, and Katz, Eliyahu. 1980. "MAD, Détente and Peace: A Hypothesis on the Evolution of International Conflicts and its Mathematico-Deductive Extension." In *International Interactions* 7:223–239.

Yaniv, Avner, and Pascal, Fabian. 1980. "Doves, Hawks and Other Birds of a Feather." *British Journal of Political Science* 10:260–267.

Yaniv, Avner, and Yishai, Yael. 1981. "Israel's West Bank Settlement Policy: The Politics of Intransigence." *Journal of Politics* 43:1105–1128.

Yaniv, Avner. 1983. "National Security and Nation-Building." *International Interactions* 11:193–217.

Yaniv, Avner. 1986. "Israel's Conventional Deterrent: A Reappraisal." In Beres, Security or Armaggeddon, pp. 45–60. (a)

Yaniv, Avner. 1986. "Syria and Israel: The Politics of Escalation." In Ma'oz and Yaniv, *Syria under Assad,* pp. 157–176. (b)

Yaniv, Avner, and Lieber, Robert J. 1983. "Reagan and the Middle East." *Washington Quarterly* 6:125–137.

Hebrew

al-Ayubi, Hytham. 1975. "Future Arab Strategy in the Light of the Fourth [Arab–Israeli] War." In Yehoshafat Harkabi, ed., *The Arabs and Israel,* no. 5, pp. 9–22. Tel Aviv: Am Oved.

Allon, Yigal. 1976. "Hagana Peila Aruva LeKiyumenu." *Molad* 1:137–163.

Bar-Lev, Chaim. 1984. "A History of the War of Attrition." In Erez and Kphir, *Tsahal,* vol. 2, pp. 33–37. (a)

———. 1984. "Lieutenant-General David Elazar: A Chief of Staff in War." In Ya'akov Erez and Ilan Kphir, eds., *Tsahal BeCheilo: Encyclopaedia LeTsava UVitachon,* vol 2, pp. 67–76. Tel Aviv: Revivim. (b)

———. 1984. "The Thousand Day War." In Erez and Kphir, *Tsahal,* vol. 2, pp. 21–32. (c)

Ben Dor, Gabriel. 1974. "The Yom Kippur War: The Great Surprise." *State Government and International Relations* 6:156–166.

Ben Gurion, David. 1960. "Israel's Security and Her International Position before and after the Sinai Campaign." In State of Israel, *Government Yearbook 1959/60.* Jerusalem, HaMadpis HaMemshalti.

Bilaler, Uri. 1971. "Ben Gurion and Sharett: Two Images of the Arab–Israeli Conflict." *State and Government* 1:71–84.

Cohen, Tsvia. 1984. "Chel Nashim." In Erez and Kphir, *Tsahal,* vol. 15, pp. 13–86.

Dayan, Moshe. 1959. "Peacetime Military Operations." *Ma'arachot* 119:54–61.

———. 1984. "Peulot HaTagmoul." In Erez and Kphir, *Tsahal,* vol. 15, pp. 97–112.

Golan, Shimon. 1982. "The Struggle for the Jordan Waters." In Elhanan Shmueli, Arnon Sofer, and Nurit Kleot, eds., *The Lands of Galilee,* vol. 2, pp. 853–862. Haifa: University of Haifa Press.

Gur, Mordechai. 1984. "The Restoration and Building of the Army." In Erez and Kphir, *Tsahal,* vol. 2, pp. 143–161.

Lanir, Tsvi. 1985. "Political Goals and Military Objectives in Israel's Wars." In Tsvi Lanir, ed., *War by Choice,* pp. 117–156. Tel Aviv: Jaffee Center for Strategic Studies.

Ne'eman, Youval. 1985. "The Planning of a National Security System for a Nation in the Making." In Tsvi Lanir, ed., *Israeli Security Planning in the 1980s,* pp. 153–161. Tel Aviv: Misrad HaBitachon.

Pa'il, Me'ir. 1984. "From Hagana through War of Independence to the IDF." In Erez and Kphir, *Tsahal,* vol. 1, pp. 29–58.

———. 1985. "Tachbula, Rouach Lechima veTechnologia." In Tsvi Offer and Avi Kober, eds., *Quantity and Quality in Military Buildup,* pp. 361–372. Tel Aviv: Ma'arachot.

Pdahtsur, Reuven. 1984. "The Threat of the Eastern Front." *Ha'aretz,* November 25.

Peled, Bejamin. 1984. "Security without a Limit." In Tsvi Offer and Avi Kober, eds.,
The Price of Power, pp. 75–80. Tel Aviv: Ma'arachot.

Peres, Shimon. 1962. "Meimad HaZman." *Ma'arachot* 146:3–5.

———. 1984. "A New Generation of Commanders." In Erez and Kphir, *Tsahal,* vol.
2, pp. 133–142.

Razin, Asaf. 1984. "On the Honey and the Sting: The Impact of American Assistance."
In Offer and Kober, *The Price of Power,* pp. 47–59.

Schiff, Ze'ev. 1985. "The Military Potential of the [West Bank] Settlers." *Ha'aretz,*
November 15.

Tal, Israel. 1984. "Lieutenant-General David Elazar: A Storm Looms over the Horizon."
In Erez and Kphir, *Tsahal,* vol. 2, pp. 53–66.

Tamir, Avraham. 1984. "Betichnun Tsorchei HaBitachon HaLeumi." In Offer and
Kober, *Quantity and Quality in Military Buildup,* pp. 341–348. (a)

———. 1984. "Bitachon BeEt Shalom." In Erez and Kphir, *Tsahal,* vol. 2, pp.
179–189. (b)

Vital, David. 1979. "The Definition of Goals in Foreign Policy." In Asher Arian, ed.,
Israel: The Formative Generation, pp. 13–26. Tel Aviv: Zmora-Bitan-Modan.

Wallach, Yehuda. "Rav Aluf Maklef: Adifut LaDereg HaLochem." In Erez and Kphir,
Tsahal, vol. 1, pp. 79–86.

Yaniv, Avner. 1985. "Deterrence and Defense in Israeli Strategy." *State, Government
and International Relations* 24:27–62.

Ze'evi, Rehchavam. 1984. "The War against Arab Terror." In Erez and Kphir, *Tsahal,*
vol. 2, pp. 45–51.

Zusman, Pinchas. 1984. "Why Is the Burden of Security So Heavy in Isreal?" In Offer
and Kober, *The Price of Power,* pp. 17–26.

Index

About the Author

Avner Yaniv teaches political science and international relations at the University of Haifa. Born and bred in Israel, Yaniv received his doctorate at Oxford University (1973). He has been a Visiting Fellow at the Institute of Peace Research and Security Policy, at the University of Hamburgh (1978–79); Director of the Institute of Middle Eastern Studies at the University of Haifa (1980–82); and a Visiting Professor at the Government Department, Georgetown University (1982–83, 1986–87), and at the Department of Government and Politics, University of Maryland, College Park (1985). His most recent writings include *Dilemmas of Security: Politics, Strategy, and the Israeli Experience in Lebanon* (Oxford University Press, New York, 1987) and (as coeditor with Moshe Maoz) *Syria Under Assad* (Croom-Helm, London, and St. Martin's, New York, 1986).